Introducing Apologetics

Cultivating Christian Commitment

James E. Taylor

Baker Academic
a division of Baker Publishing Group
Grand Rapids, Michigan

© 2006 by James E. Taylor

Published by Baker Academic
a division of Baker Publishing Group
P.O. Box 6287, Grand Rapids, MI 49516-6287
www.bakeracademic.com

Paperback edition published 2013
ISBN 978-0-8010-4890-6

Printed in the United States of America

The Library of Congress has cataloged the hardcover edition as follows:
Taylor, James E., 1956–
    Introducing apologetics : cultivating Christian commitment / James E. Taylor.
      p. cm.
    Includes bibliographical references (p.   ) and index.
    ISBN 0-8010-2786-1 (cloth)
    1. Apologetics. I. Title.
BT1103.T39 2006
239—dc22   2005021025

Contents

Acknowledgments   4

Introduction: I Believe, but Help My Unbelief!   5

Part 1 Apologetics and Commitment

1   A Reason for the Hope Within: The Nature of Apologetics   17

2   Faith and Human Wisdom: Evidentialist Apologetics   29

3   Jerusalem and Athens: More Objections to Apologetics   39

4   A God-Shaped Vacuum: The Relevance of Apologetics   51

5   Ears to Hear and Eyes to See: Apologetics and the Heart   63

6   Critics, Seekers, and Doubters: Audiences for Apologetics   75

Part 2 Commitment to God

7   The Global Village: Worldview Options   87

8   The Lord Our God Is One: Monotheism   99

9   In the Beginning: Cosmological Explanations   113

10 What the Heavens Declare: Teleological Explanations   127

11 Why Do the Righteous Suffer? The Problem of Evil   141

12 A God Who Hides Himself: The Problem of Evidence   155

Part 3 Commitment to God in Christ

13 Who Do You Say I Am? The Person of Jesus   171

14 Lazarus, Come Forth: The Miracles of Jesus   185

15 He Is Risen Indeed! The Resurrection of Jesus   199

16 The Word Became Flesh: The Trinity and the Incarnation   213

17 The Sheep and the Goats: Salvation and Damnation   227

18 No Other Name: The Problem of Religious Pluralism I   241

19 East Meets West: The Problem of Religious Pluralism II   255

Part 4 Contemporary Challenges to Christian Commitment

20 The Spirit of Truth: Commitment, Canon, and Community   269

21 The Spirit of the Age: Critiques from the Social Sciences   283

22 The Origin of Species: Christianity and Natural Selection   299

23 The Dust of the Earth: Resurrection, Minds, and Bodies   317

24 The Death of God: Postmodern Challenges to Christianity   331

25 It's All Relative: Cultural Differences and Moral Universalism   347

Conclusion: Cultivating Christian Commitment   361

Other Books on Christian Apologetics   363

Index   364

Acknowledgments

I am grateful to Stanley Obitts for introducing me to Christian apologetics when I was a college student and to Robert Hosack of Baker Academic for inviting me to write this book. I also wish to thank the following colleagues at Westmont and elsewhere who read parts of the manuscript and gave me helpful comments: Robert Gundry, Robert Wennberg, David Vander Laan, Tremper Longman, Charles Farhadian, Jeffrey Schloss, Stephen Davis, Michael Murray, Daniel Howard-Snyder, Frances Howard-Snyder, and Jonathan Wilson (whose Christian apologetics class at Acadia Divinity College read an early draft of the book). Conversations with colleagues Telford Work, Bruce Fisk, Karen Jobes, William Nelson, Jon Lemmond, Greg Spencer, Richard Pointer, Warren Rogers, Nivaldo Tro, Paul Willis, and Thomas Senor were also beneficial. I used earlier drafts of this book in a number of my Christian apologetics courses in the past few years, and I received valuable feedback from many of my students. I also gave talks based on selected chapters at various events in which members of the audience asked good questions and offered interesting ideas. These occasions included an adult Sunday school class at Montecito Covenant Church; the ninth annual "Reasons to Believe" apologetics conference at South Valley Community Church, Gilroy, California; the Westmont College Paul C. Wilt Phi Kappa Phi Faculty Lecture of fall 2004; and the spring 2005 meeting of the San Diego Philosophical Society. The Westmont College professional development committee provided a grant in the summer of 2004 that assisted me in making substantial progress on the book. Most recently, the book has been improved by the editorial work of Melinda Timmer and Wells Turner at Baker. I thank them for their assistance and flexibility. I also wish to thank Paula Gibson, who is responsible for the cover, for her creativity and openness to new ideas. Finally, I owe my wife, Jennifer, and my children—Sarah, Ben, and Nathaniel—a huge debt of gratitude for their constant loving encouragement, support, and patience. It is to them, and to the glory of God, that I dedicate this book.

Introduction

I Believe, but Help My Unbelief!

» **Outline**

- **Christian Belief and Believability**
  - *What Christians Believe*
  - *Concerns about Christian Beliefs*
  - *The Need for Christian Apologetics*
- **My Story of Doubt and Faith**
  - *My College Experience of Doubt and Renewed Faith*
  - *My Story and Christian Apologetics*
    - Experience of God and Reasonable Christian Belief
    - My Denial of Evidentialism
    - My Affirmation of the Value of Apologetics
- **Faith, Reason, and Christian Commitment**
  - *Faith and Reason*
    - Augustinian Fideism
    - Balancing Faith and Reason
  - *Christian Apologetics and Christian Commitment*
    - The Need for Confident Christian Conviction
    - Cultivating Christian Commitment

» **Summary**

Christians believe a number of things that are difficult to believe. Nontheists and non-Christian theists reject all or part of core Christian convictions. Even Christians can have concerns about central Christian claims. In college, I struggled with doubts about whether God exists. My doubts were alleviated by an experi-ence of God on a mission trip. Now I believe that faith rooted in experience of God's grace is prior to philosophical arguments and historical evidences for Christianity and that objective reasons are not required for faith. However, Christian apologetics is necessary for some people at some times and beneficial for everyone all the time.

» **Basic Terms, Concepts, and Names**

agnostics
Anselm
Apostles' Creed
atheists
Augustine
creeds
evidentialism
fideism
heresy
Lewis, C. S.
mere Christianity
nontheists
orthodoxy
Plantinga, Alvin
rationalism
theists

» **Reflection and Discussion**

» **Further Reading**

> I believe in God, the Father almighty, creator of heaven and earth. I believe in Jesus Christ, his only Son, our Lord, who was conceived by the Holy Spirit, born of the Virgin Mary, suffered under Pontius Pilate, was crucified, died, and was buried; he descended to the dead. On the third day he rose again; he ascended into heaven, he is seated at the right hand of the Father, and he will come to judge the living and the dead. I believe in the Holy Spirit, the holy catholic Church, the communion of saints, the forgiveness of sins, the resurrection of the body, and the life everlasting. Amen.
>
> The Apostles' Creed

Christian Belief and Believability

This is a book about Christian apologetics. Christian apologists defend the truth of Christian claims. In doing so, they try to show that it is reasonable to believe what Christians believe. What do Christians believe? They believe that Jesus of Nazareth, a human being who lived in Palestine during the first century AD, not only claimed to be God but also is God. Christians believe that this God-man Jesus preached about God's kingdom, taught people how to be fit to live in it, and showed people what this kingdom would be like by forgiving their sins, miraculously healing their diseases, and delivering them from evil. Christians believe that Jesus chose and equipped twelve disciples to carry on this preaching, teaching, forgiving, healing, and delivering work of the kingdom. Christians believe that Jesus was betrayed by one of these disciples and then died on a cross—really died. But Christians believe that this dead man Jesus came back to life—real life—and appeared to his disciples for a period of time. They believe that Jesus then ascended to heaven while his disciples watched, created the Christian church by sending them the Holy Spirit, and through this Spirit emboldened and empowered these disciples to preach to the whole world the good news of salvation through faith in Jesus. Christians believe that Jesus died on the cross to take on himself the punishment for people's sins so that the sins of those who believe in him would be forgiven. They believe he was then resurrected from the dead to show God's acceptance of his sacrificial death and to make it possible for believers to have eternal life. Christians believe that this God is a Trinity of persons: Father, Son, and Holy Spirit. Christians also believe that the Bible is God's authoritative Word to human beings that reveals how he plans to save them through Jesus, who is God the Son, the Second Person of the Trinity. They believe that when Jesus returns to judge the human race, those who do not accept God's offer of salvation through Jesus will suffer eternal damnation, but those who do will be resurrected to eternal life in heaven to be with God and other believers forever.

Do Christians really believe *all* these things? The answer to this question is a qualified yes. Many people who have identified themselves as Christians since the time of Jesus would disagree with at least one of the things just said. Christians have always been aware of these disagreements, and they have always been concerned about them because of the divisions to which they naturally tend to lead. For the sake of unity in the church, therefore, Christians have repeatedly tried to come up with a list of statements that all Christians can agree are true. This is how the great Christian creeds and confessions of faith came about. Examples of these are the Apostles' Creed and the Nicene Creed. The adoption of these creeds did not stop the disagreements, but they did make official a distinction between orthodoxy (right belief) and heresy (wrong belief) in the Christian church. Are *all* the things stated above orthodox Christian beliefs? Probably. Are these the *only* orthodox Christian beliefs? Probably not. The statements above are not one of the creeds accepted by the Christian church, so there may be errors, and there are most likely important omissions. Since a book about Christian apologetics is a book about giving reasons for thinking that the essential or core claims of Christianity are true,

however, it is important to start with at least a rough outline of what these claims are.

Do Christians believe *only* these things? The answer to this question is an unqualified no. Anyone with even a superficial knowledge of the history of the Christian church is well aware of the divisions that have arisen within it in spite of the efforts of Christians to prevent them. The most obvious divisions include the split between the Eastern Orthodox Church and the Roman Catholic Church around AD 800 and the one between the Roman Catholic Church and the Protestants in the 1500s. The splintering of Protestants into various denominations after that time multiplied these divisions significantly. These divisions were the result of various disagreements, many of which were differences of opinion about Christian doctrines. So Christians believe a lot of things in addition to those listed above, but if I were to add all of them to the list, it would be full of contradictions. That is why, for the purposes of this book, I will stick to what C. S. Lewis called "mere Christianity": those things about which there has been historic consensus, for the most part, in spite of differences about more peripheral matters.[1] In this spirit, Lewis puts the task of Christian apologetics as follows: "We are to defend Christianity itself—the faith preached by the Apostles, attested by the Martyrs, embodied in the Creeds, expounded by the Fathers."[2] I hope the things listed above

1. C. S. Lewis, *Mere Christianity* (New York: Macmillan, 1952), vii.
2. C. S. Lewis, "Christian Apologetics," in *God in the Dock: Essays on Theology and Ethics*, ed. Walter Hooper (Grand Rapids: Eerdmans, 1970), 90.

fall into this category. You will need to decide for yourself whether they do.

Assuming they do, are these things believable? Try to think about this question from the standpoint of someone who is not a Christian. Such a person may or may not believe in God. People who believe that God exists are called theists, and people who do not believe that God exists are called nontheists. Nontheists who believe that there is no God are called atheists, and nontheists who withhold belief about whether there is a God are called agnostics. Many theists are not Christians. These include many Jews and Muslims, some Hindus, as well as theists in other religious traditions that are not as generally well known. But there are also a number of people who would say they believe there is a God but do not associate themselves with a particular religion.

All these non-Christian theists may have a number of reactions to core Christian beliefs. But it is likely that their disbelief will be directed primarily to the claims made about Jesus, in particular, that he is God the Son, the Second Person of the Trinity, who became incarnate as Jesus of Nazareth and who died and was resurrected for our salvation. These are the claims that distinguish Christianity from other theistic religions. Can you see how, for various reasons, it would be difficult for non-Christians to accept these claims about Jesus, even if they already believe in God? For one thing, how could the one God also be three persons? And how could one of these persons be both completely divine and completely human at the same time? Moreover, why would God forgive sins just because Jesus died on a cross? And how could a human being who had been dead for three days come back to life? Furthermore, even if Jesus could and did come back to life from the grave, how could those who were not there at the time have good reasons for believing that this resurrection occurred? These are only a few of the most central concerns non-Christian theists are likely to have.

Now consider these claims from the point of view of a person who does not even believe that God exists—either an atheist or an agnostic. These people will join the theistic non-Christians in their denial of the main doctrines about Jesus. They will also reject other things about which Christians and many non-Christian theists agree. These include various claims about things God has done or will do, such as that he (1) created the universe, (2) communicated with humans by means of divine revelations of various kinds, (3) performed miracles, and (4) will enable some humans to enjoy an afterlife. Just as non-Christian theists deny Christian claims about Jesus, nontheists deny any affirmation, Christian or otherwise, of supernatural reality or activity.

Non-Christians do not find all the core Christian claims believable. At least they do not believe them all to be true. Since you are reading this book, you are probably among those who believe these Christian claims about God and Jesus. If so, you must find them believable. But have you ever wondered—do you wonder now at times—whether they are *really* believable? Have you ever had—do you sometimes now have—questions or even doubts about the truth of any of these claims? If you have or do, then you are like many other reflective Christians. You are definitely not alone. It is natural to have questions and even doubts about central Christian claims. Think about it. A lot of people do not accept them. When you reflect on them, especially from their perspective, perhaps you can see why. These claims can be hard to believe. That is why as long as there has been Christianity, there has been such a thing as Christian apologetics (i.e., an effort to make the Christian message and what it implies believable on the basis of human reason).

That is why I have written this book about Christian apologetics. As long as there are people who find Christianity unbelievable—or hard to believe, at least sometimes—there will be a need for books like this. Of course, Christian faith is more than just belief. It also involves trust and obedience. But it is really difficult to trust and obey Jesus if you have a hard time believing that he is God or that there is a God at all. I know this to be true from painful firsthand experience.

My Story of Doubt and Faith

During the summer between my junior and senior years at a Christian liberal arts college, I suddenly began to experience serious and intense doubts about the existence of God. I remember waking up periodically during this time with a sick feeling in the pit of my stomach. Having been a committed Christian most of my life up to that point, this experience of doubt hit me like a ton of bricks. To shift the metaphor, I felt like the rug had been pulled out from under me. I wanted very much to believe in God, but during that time I could not. I was a philosophy major, and during my junior year I had taken courses covering the entire history of Western philosophy. One thing that struck me as a result of taking these courses was that if the great

It is really difficult to trust and obey Jesus if you have a hard time believing that he is God or that there is a God at all.

philosophical minds of history could not agree with one another about whether we could *know* that God exists (or even whether God *does* exist), then who was I to think I could figure it out?

At the same time, I was assuming, without realizing it, the philosophical view that what it would take for a belief in God to be reasonable was sufficient evidence in the form of an adequate philosophical argument for God's existence. Given this evidentialist assumption, it is not surprising that I concluded that it was unreasonable for me to believe in God when it seemed that all the arguments for God's existence were inadequate in some respect. Since it never occurred to me at that time to question this evidentialism, I spent much of my senior year trying to find arguments for God's existence that seemed adequate to me. But my philosophical training had enabled me always to find a flaw in any theistic argument I considered. Now, it is true that many nontheists find problems with theistic arguments because they do not really *want* to believe that God exists. But I really *did* want to believe that he exists. I was desperate to find a solid rational foundation for my faith.

My experience of intellectual doubt about something so fundamental to Christian belief as God's existence left me unable to trust and obey him completely and confidently. How could I, when I was not at all sure that he was real, when a lot of the time I did not even believe that he existed? This quandary made it difficult for me to carry out my duties as director of on-campus ministries. I went through the motions nonetheless. But something happened in the spring semester of my senior year that eventually led to the dissolution of my doubts and the corresponding strengthening of my Christian conviction and commitment. Surprisingly, what happened was not my discovery of philosophical arguments for God's existence so strong as to withstand my critical scrutiny. Instead, it was a spring break trip to Mexico with a few hundred fellow students to lead vacation Bible school programs and evangelistic meetings in various neighborhoods around Ensenada. What I found during that trip was that the experience of Christian service, evangelism, worship, and fellowship revived my faith in God. This revival happened because through these experiences I had a strong sense of God's presence and activity. It is true that when I returned I could not resist entertaining the suspicion that it only *seemed* as though God were there because I was with so many people who believed that he was. At the same time, however, the experiences I had in Mexico had so effectively renewed my Christian conviction and eroded my doubts that I never found this purely sociological explanation convincing.

A few years later while I was in graduate school getting my Ph.D. in philosophy, I encountered a number of philosophical essays written by various Christian philosophers about the relationship between Christian faith and philosophical reason. Reading these helped me to think philosophically about the experiences of intellectual doubt and experiential faith I had encountered in college. I found the essays written by Alvin Plantinga especially helpful.[3] It was from reading his work that I found out about theistic evidentialism—the thesis that belief in God can be rational, reasonable, or justified only if it is based on adequate propositional evidence (philosophical arguments). I found Plantinga's objections to evidentialism convincing (see chap. 2 for an explanation of them). As a result, I came to believe that belief in God can be reasonable apart from adequate theistic arguments—as long as it is grounded in the right kinds of experiences. I also came to believe that the experiences I had undergone in Mexico during my senior year are among the sorts of experiences that can ground reasonable belief in God.

That is my story, and it has shaped the way I think about Christian apologetics. My denial of evidentialism means that I do not think the use of human reason in the form of philosophical arguments or historical evidences is always *necessary* for theistic or Christian belief to be reasonable, rational, or justified. This denial may sound surprising. If I do not think arguments and evidences are required for warranted Christian conviction, then why am I bothering to write a book about Christian apologetics? And how could anything I write about Christian apologetics from this standpoint support apologetic goals? My answer to these important questions is that, though I do not think arguments and evidences are

3. See especially Alvin Plantinga, "Reason and Belief in God," in *Faith and Rationality: Reason and Belief in God*, ed. Alvin Plantinga and Nicholas Wolterstorff, 16–93 (Notre Dame: University of Notre Dame Press, 1983).

required for reasonable Christian belief for *everyone at all times,* I do believe there are *some people,* whether all the time or just some of the time, for whom it is at least useful and perhaps even necessary to have their faith supplemented by reason. These people may at least sometimes find it helpful or even necessary to consider philosophical arguments and historical evidences either so that their Christian beliefs become sufficiently *reasonable* or so that they come to hold these beliefs with a sufficient degree of confidence. When might a person be in such a position? People may find themselves in a position to benefit from Christian apologetics when they have sincere intellectual questions about core Christian claims that prevent them from confidently endorsing them, even when they are engaging in practices of the sort likely to bring about faith-generating Christian experiences. In other words, Christian apologetics is helpful or needed whenever people either open to Christ or acquainted with Christ begin genuinely to wonder whether central Christian tenets are believable—that is, whether it is reasonable to believe that they are true. I say more about this in chapter 2.

My ongoing experience as a reflective Christian provides an example of the beneficial role apologetics can play on occasion in a believer's life. Though I have not been troubled again by prolonged and debilitating doubt, I have considered many questions over the years that have challenged my faith and led to moments of doubt. I have experienced these moments in spite of my steadily growing and increasingly rich experience of God's gracious love through regular Christian worship, fellowship, and private devotion. As I have faced these questions and experienced these doubts, I have found it helpful to draw on the wealth of apologetic resources available to Christians today. I have not discovered in these materials any proofs or demonstrations that would compel all rational people to believe that God exists or that Christianity is true. Instead, I have encountered arguments and evidences that have reassured me that it is at least not irrational to be a Christian and, even more, that the Christian worldview is more reasonable than its competitors.

Faith, Reason, and Christian Commitment

My Christian faith is grounded primarily in my experience of God in Christ through the ministry in my life of the Holy Spirit. My faith is a response to God's offer of love, forgiveness, and new life. Since he has initiated a relationship with me by means of making this offer and has enabled me to respond to him by accepting the offer, there is an important sense in which my faith is a gift from God. At the same time, as I reflect on all that is implied by the gospel of Christ, I have questions about the extent to which it is reasonable to believe these things. This questioning is intensified by the startling nature of the claims themselves (look again at the first paragraph of this introduction) and the fact that so many people—even people who believe in God—reject these claims as false (or at least not sufficiently evident to be believable). So I reflect on these questions, and when I do, I make use of another of God's wonderful gifts to me: my mind. I find that when I use my mind to reason about the answers to these questions, my faith can be strengthened as a result.

The great Christian philosopher and theologian Augustine (354–430) took the following approach to the relationship between faith and reason. He said, "I believe in order to understand."[4] Another important Christian thinker who followed in his footsteps, Anselm of Canterbury (1033–1109), expressed the same idea in terms of "faith seeking understanding."[5] Their view of faith and reason is called fideism (from the Latin word for faith, *fide*) as opposed to rationalism, since it gives faith priority over reason. Since I agree with Augustine and Anselm on this issue, I classify myself as a sort of fideist. But since many think of fideists as people who say that reason should play no role at all in Christian belief, it is important to point out here that I am not an adherent of nonrational (or even irrational) fideism but of what can be called responsible fideism.[6]

As a responsible fideist, I will attempt in this book to steer a middle course between an overemphasis on reason and an overemphasis on faith. Too much confidence in reason may lead to doubt or unbelief because no combination of arguments and evidences can prove conclusively that God exists or that Christianity is true. If a Christian apologist should nevertheless claim to have demonstrated that either of these claims is true, as many have claimed to do, his or her readers or audience may well develop a false sense of security in human reason, which can lead to disillu-

sionment later when reason's limitations become apparent. This danger is especially severe when such overconfident claims are accompanied by the evidentialist assumption that such proofs are required for reasonable Christian belief. At the same time, however, too much emphasis on faith to the exclusion of reason may also lead to doubt or unbelief because there are legitimate questions of an intellectual sort about Christianity, such as the problem of evil or the problem of religious pluralism, that trouble sincere believers and seekers. If people who are challenged by such questions are told to "just have faith," then they may persist in needless doubt and perhaps even reject their faith, when there are excellent intellectual resources available that address these concerns. So it is for the sake of cultivating confident Christian conviction and commitment that I will attempt to find a good balance between faith and reason.

There are many practical reasons for seeking to strengthen the degree of confidence with which Christians maintain their beliefs (without, of course, sacrificing their intellectual integrity in the process). During the worship service at our church last Sunday morning, I was struck by the extent to which heartfelt devotion to Jesus Christ of the sort expressed by my fellow congregants in song and prayer is possible only for those who are deeply convinced that Jesus is really the risen Lord of the universe. Moreover, as I pray for the missionaries sent out by my denomination, I am aware of how much they are in need of a steady conviction that the gospel is true as they seek to share it in various places around the world—often in the face of opposition and discouragement. Indeed, confident conviction is needed by every

---

4. Augustine, *De Trinitate*, 1.1.1.

5. Anselm, *Proslogium*, preface.

6. See C. Stephen Evans, *Faith beyond Reason: A Kierkegaardian Account* (Grand Rapids: Eerdmans, 1998), 52.

Christian, every day and in every place, who strives to live a life governed by the reality of Jesus' resurrection in the midst of a society that is, to a large extent, secular, materialistic, immoral, relativistic, and even nihilistic. The challenge is that it is often difficult to believe Christian claims with full confidence (as Paul says to the Corinthians, his preaching of Christ crucified is "a stumbling block to Jews and foolishness to Gentiles" [1 Cor. 1:23]), and yet it is also important to believe confidently. The sincerity of Christian worship and prayer and the effectiveness of Christian service and evangelism depend on it.

It is for this reason that I conceive of Christian apologetics as *ultimately* a contribution to the cultivation of Christian commitment, though it is *primarily* an effort to defend the reasonableness of believing that Christian claims are true. Whether the efforts of the apologist are directed mostly to seekers who are considering a commitment to Christ or largely to Christians who are struggling with intellectual challenges to their faith, the goal ought to be to cultivate Christian commitment (belief, trust, and obedience). The word *cultivate* is important for my purposes in this book. Following Jesus' parable of the sower and the soils (Matt. 13:3–23), I like to think of the gospel as a seed that falls on the soil of people's lives. Whether the seed grows into a flourishing plant or not depends on many factors. In the end, some of these factors are under human control, and others are up to God. Every gardener knows that there is only so much one can do to make a plant grow. One can put it in good soil in a place likely to receive adequate sunlight, give it ample water and fertilizer, and keep the weeds and insects at bay. After doing all this,

however, one needs to let these things do the work they were designed by God to do. Gardening is an art, but it is a *cooperative* art—an art involving the cooperation of the gardener with nature. In the same way, apologetics and evangelism are cooperative arts. The evangelist preaches the gospel, and the apologist defends it, but it is God who enables it to take root in a human soul and to yield the fruit of confident Christian commitment.

The first part of this book discusses apologetics—a component of the means to the end of Christian commitment—and Christian commitment itself, the end to which apologetics contributes. In discussing apologetics, part 1 says more about what it is, what it is for, and what it cannot do (chap. 1); why, though useful, it is not always needed (chap. 2); why it is possible and not harmful (chap. 3); and why it is relevant to human needs and concerns (chap. 4). Chapter 5 discusses the role of the heart in Christian commitment, and chapter 6 focuses on how different conditions of the heart can affect the way in which people ask questions about Christianity. Chapter 1 also provides an overview of the strategies used in the rest of the book as it considers questions about

> **The evangelist preaches the gospel, and the apologist defends it, but it is God who enables it to take root in a human soul and to yield the fruit of confident Christian commitment.**

Christianity one by one. In general, these strategies involve both watering and weeding. In other words, they focus on both (1) providing arguments and evidences *for* Christian truth claims (watering) to help the seed of the gospel grow in the human soul into full commitment and (2) constructing a rational case *against* objections to the Christian faith (weeding) to prevent these criticisms from undermining full commitment. The last three parts of the book encourage this sort of watering and weeding with respect to commitment to God (part 2), commitment to God in Christ (part 3), and contemporary challenges to Christian commitment (part 4). This last part provides opportunities for apologetic weeding relative to two general areas of contemporary concern: challenges to Christian commitment based on science and challenges to Christian commitment based on postmodernism.

Reflection and Discussion

1. What Christian claims do you have the hardest time believing? Why do you think this is?
2. Has your Christian faith ever been threatened by serious and painful doubts? If so, what did you do about it? If not, how would you help someone who struggles with doubt?
3. What do you think is the proper relationship between faith and reason? Are you a fideist or a rationalist? Why?

Further Reading

Clark, Kelly James. *When Faith Is Not Enough.* Grand Rapids: Eerdmans, 1997.

Lewis, C. S. *Mere Christianity.* Temecula, CA: Textbook Publishers, 2003.

Swinburne, Richard. *Faith and Reason.* New York: Oxford University Press, 1984.

Part 1

Apologetics and Commitment

1

A Reason for the Hope Within

The Nature of Apologetics

» **Outline**

- **The Nature of Christian Apologetics**
  - *Two Consequences of Faith-based Apologetics*
    - The Rejection of Neutrality
    - The Consistency of Faith and Rationality
  - *Specific Apologetical Tasks*
    - Four Forms of Rational and Critical Thinking about Christianity
    - Four Metaphors for Positive and Negative Apologetics
- **The Purpose of Christian Apologetics**
  - *The Cultivation of Christian Commitment*
  - *Issues Addressed by Christian Apologists*
  - *Noncomparative and Comparative Rationality*
  - *Modest Apologetics versus Ambitious Apologetics*
- **The Limits of Christian Apologetics**
  - *The Practical Limits of Christian Apologetics*
    - A Heart of Humility
    - An Irenic Approach
  - *The Theoretical Limits of Christian Apologetics*
    - The Limits of Arguments and Evidences
    - How Apologetical Theory and Practice Work Together

Apologists draw on objective reasons, arguments, and evidences for this purpose. Apologists employ these rational resources both to help faith grow by offering a positive case for Christian claims (watering) and to prevent faith from dying by arguing against objections to Christian claims (weeding). The goal is to try to show that Christianity is at least as reasonable as its most reasonable competitor or, if possible, that it is more reasonable than any worldview with which it competes. But there are both theoretical and practical limits to apologetics. Apologists need to be humble, irenic, and aware that all their arguments are rationally resistible.

» **Basic Terms, Concepts, and Names**

ambitious apologetics
apologetics
apology
circular arguments
comparative rationality
modest apologetics
negative apologetics
noncomparative rationality
polemics
positive apologetics
rational resistibility
worldviews

» **Summary**

Christian apologetics is a defense of the reasonableness of believing that the Christian worldview is universally and objectively true.

» **Reflection and Discussion**

» **Further Reading**

> Do not fear . . . and do not be intimidated, but in your hearts set apart Christ as Lord. Always be ready to make your defense [*apologia*] to anyone who demands from you a reason for the hope that is in you; yet do it with gentleness and reverence.
>
> 1 Peter 3:14–15, author's translation

Nowadays, an apology is an expression of regret for a wrong done. When you apologize to someone for something you did to that person, you are (ideally) not trying to prove something or to defend your actions but instead to admit that you were wrong about something you both can agree you did. In contrast, an apology in ancient Greece (Greek: *apologia*) was a legal defense against an official charge. If you have taken a philosophy class, you may be familiar with Plato's *Apology,* in which he describes Socrates' defense at his trial in response to the charges brought against him by some of his fellow citizens. In this dialogue, Plato records the arguments Socrates employed for the purpose of convincing the jury not to convict him of these charges. Socrates gives reasons in support of the claim that he is innocent so that his fellow Athenians might see the accusations leveled at him as unreasonable. In ancient Greece, therefore, an apology involved formulating arguments and giving reasons in one's defense.

In the New Testament, the author of the Epistle of 1 Peter exhorts his persecuted Christian readers to be prepared to provide an *apologia* for their Christian hope when their opponents challenge them (3:15). In light of the legal context in which this Greek word was typically used, it seems clear that the recipients of this epistle were being urged to defend themselves against criticism by giving reasons for the truth of the beliefs on which their hope was based. When we look at 1 Peter as a whole, it becomes apparent that the aim of this letter was to encourage Christians in Asia Minor to cultivate faith, hope, and love so that they might obtain the salvation of their souls (1:9) and cause nonbelievers to glorify God by their good example (2:12). This is the context in which we must understand the passage quoted above, a passage often cited as a scriptural mandate for Christian apologetics—the defense of the Christian faith. If this mandate applies to Christians today, and I believe it does, then all followers of Jesus are called to be apologists. This passage teaches three things about the nature, purpose, and limits of Christian apologetics.

The Nature of Christian Apologetics

The first thing the 1 Peter passage teaches is that Christian apologetics is a reasoned defense of Christian belief that starts with a *foundation of faith* in Jesus Christ as Lord ("set apart Christ as Lord"). Christian apologetics is not a neutral study of religion in general or of Christianity in particular (like religious studies or philosophy of religion) but a defense of the truth of Christian convictions from the standpoint of Christian commitment. At least two important consequences follow from this starting point.

First, apologists are not people who suspend all their fundamental beliefs and values in order to investigate how reasonable it is to have them. Such a completely neutral stance is neither possible nor desirable. It is not possible, since we do not have direct voluntary control over our fundamental beliefs and values. We cannot simply decide to get rid of our convictions and ideals at the drop of a hat. Moreover, a change in people's fundamental beliefs and values always results in the adoption of alternative beliefs and values. Complete neutrality about fundamental beliefs and values just is not possible. Furthermore, a complete suspension of fundamental beliefs and values would not be desirable even if it were possible. For one thing, healthy living requires some basic convictions and commitments. Moreover, even if people have not examined their beliefs and values carefully, it is usually more reasonable for them to continue affirming them than to withhold them. Therefore,

> **Christian apologetics is a reasoned defense of Christian belief that starts with a *foundation of faith* in Jesus Christ as Lord.**

a complete suspension of conviction and commitment would be unreasonable. It is often reasonable to maintain the same perspectives and principles even in the face of apparently good arguments against them, because further investigation may well show that these opposing arguments are not so good after all. This sort of thing happens in the sciences frequently when scientists initially encounter evidence that seems to falsify their theories. If these theories have explanatory value and have survived prior tests, it is reasonable to keep them until the evidence against them is overwhelming. If this practice is reasonable for scientists, then it is also rational for Christians and Christian apologists.

Second, Christian faith is consistent with rational and critical thinking about Christian claims. This is further support for the position about the relationship between faith and reason given in the introduction. Both faith and reason are valuable Christian resources. Christians are called to engage in rational and critical thinking about their faith, as long as this thinking is *Christian*. Christian thinking involves reflecting on life and the world from a Christian perspective—that is, from the standpoint of Christian beliefs of the sort listed in the introduction. There is a sense in which Christian theology is thinking about everything—God, the world, and human life—from the standpoint of the basic Christian convictions that are derivable from the Bible. The end result of such contemplation is not only a Christian theology but also a Christian *worldview*, a big, unified way of seeing everything from a Christian perspective. There are, of course, non-Christian worldviews as well, and we will look at some of these in chapters 7, 8, 18, and 19. Chapter 24 also considers the postmodern idea that the idea of a worldview as traditionally conceived is wrongheaded. But for now we will concentrate primarily on the rational and critical evaluation of the Christian worldview.

To say that Christian apologetics involves rational and critical thinking about the Christian worldview from the standpoint of Christian commitment is *not* to say that the arguments and evidences employed by a Christian apologist will presuppose the truth of Christian claims. If they did, they would be circular arguments, and circular arguments cannot provide rational support for their conclusions. Instead, a Christian apologist is a committed Christian who is motivated by this commitment to engage in rational and critical thinking about the Christian worldview in order to show that it is reasonable to adopt it. On the other hand, once an argument has been offered for a claim, it is legitimate to use this claim as a premise in an argument for another conclusion. For instance, once an apologist has given adequate reasons for believing that God exists, it is appropriate to assume God's existence in an argument for the possibility of miracles. If it were not for this possibility of employing the conclusions of some arguments as premises in other arguments, it would not be possible to construct the kind of cumulative case

for the Christian worldview illustrated in this book.[1] Such a cumulative case for Christianity is based on the accumulation of a range of philosophical arguments, historical evidences, scientific observations, and personal experiences.

This kind of defense employs the following four forms of rational and critical thinking about the Christian worldview:

1. giving reasons for thinking that the core claims of the Christian worldview are true
2. arguing that objections against the Christian worldview do not succeed in showing that it is unreasonable or false
3. giving reasons for thinking that the claims of worldviews that are logically inconsistent with the Christian worldview (such as naturalism and many but not all the claims of Islam, Judaism, Hinduism, and Buddhism) are unreasonable or false
4. arguing that the arguments given for the claims of alternative worldviews that are inconsistent with Christianity do not succeed in showing that those alternative worldviews are true

Historically, the word *apologetics* has often applied narrowly only to tasks 1 and 2. Tasks 3 and 4 have traditionally been labeled "polemics," since they not only have to do with defending the rationality of the Christian worldview but also involve

1. Contemporary philosophers who have attempted to construct a cumulative case for a theistic worldview include Basil Mitchell, *The Justification of Religious Belief* (New York: Oxford University Press, 1981); and Richard Swinburne, *The Existence of God* (Oxford: Clarendon, 1979).

arguing against other worldviews. This book uses the word *apologetics* broadly to include tasks 1 through 4 (both apologetics and polemics in the narrow sense of these terms).

Apologetic tasks 1 through 4 can be classified in terms of the two apologetic strategies mentioned at the end of the introduction: watering and weeding. Task 1 is a watering task, and tasks 2 through 4 are weeding tasks. Recall that apologetic watering involves preparing for the cultivation of Christian commitment by giving reasons that contribute to the case for the rationality of belief in the Christian worldview. Other metaphors may be helpful in expressing the main idea here. With a theater metaphor, we could talk about setting the stage. A play cannot occur until the appropriate scenery and props are provided. A metaphor from competitive sports would characterize this apologetic task in terms of a positive, offensive strategy that would make it more likely that your team would score a goal. In regard to construction, we could think in terms of laying the groundwork for a building. What all these metaphors are intended to convey is the idea of giving reasons for thinking that Christianity is true. Apologetic weeding involves removing reasons for thinking that Christianity is false. We can express the same idea by talking about clearing the stage or removing obstacles (theater), a defensive strategy aimed at preventing the other team from scoring points (sports), and retrofitting a building to protect it from earthquakes (construction).

I have chosen the gardening metaphor because, as explained above, it reminds us that there is a role for both humans and God in the cultivation of Christian commitment. All these metaphors can be misleading, because they may seem to imply that apologetic arguments and evidences are always necessary for reasonable faith, a view I rejected above and will argue against in the next chapter. To avoid misunderstanding along these lines, we should remember that, though watering is always required for a garden to grow, this water can be and often is supplied by rain, something over which humans have no control. It is only in special conditions—drought, for instance—that humans need to intervene with additional water.

The Purpose of Christian Apologetics

The second lesson we can learn from 1 Peter 3:14–15 is that the aim of Christian apologetics is to cultivate Christian commitment among both believers and unbelievers by means of a relevant *reservoir of reasons* ("always be ready to make your defense to anyone who demands from you a reason for the hope that is in you"). These are reasons in support of Christian faith that can be given at different times ("always") and to different people ("to anyone"). The history of Christian apologetics is a history of defenses of the eternal gospel of Jesus Christ that address the concerns of the apologists' times in the language of those times.[2]

Some of the concerns addressed by Christian apologists are perennial—they are the same from one generation to the next. The questions raised in the introduction about Jesus' divinity and resurrec-

2. See C. S. Lewis, "Christian Apologetics," in *God in the Dock: Essays on Theology and Ethics*, ed. Walter Hooper (Grand Rapids: Eerdmans, 1970), 96–99, for some wise words about the use of language in apologetics.

tion from the dead are among these (see chaps. 13–16). Another is the problem of evil, the problem of trying to understand why God allows the kinds and quantities of sin, pain, and suffering that exist in the world (see chaps. 11–12). However, there are other issues that are not on the apologist's front burner as they used to be. An example is polytheism, the belief in and worship of many gods. Though this was a topic of Paul's address to the Athenians at the Areopagus (see Acts 17:16–34), it is no longer a major competitor with the Christian faith, at least in our society and culture.[3] Idolatry, however, is a concern closely related to polytheism that survives in altered form to this day. Though we are not tempted in our culture to bow down physically to idols like statuettes, the attitudes and behaviors we manifest toward rock musicians, movie stars, and famous athletes are similar to the thoughts and actions of worshipers. We also tend to treat money as an idol. Jesus' warning that it is not possible to serve both God and money (Matt. 6:24) is just one of many New Testament admonitions against this form of idolatry. Our culture's materialism and consumerism are signs that the almighty dollar has not stopped competing with God.

The focus of this book, however, is on more intellectual threats to the Christian worldview, theoretical alternatives that vie for belief rather than practical alternatives that compete for behavior. Among the more intellectual challenges to contemporary Christian belief (that have not always faced Christians so urgently as they do today) are skepticism about the existence of God (chaps. 11–12), the problem of religious pluralism (chaps.

18–19), the higher critical approach to the Bible (chaps. 13–15, 21), various scientific challenges (such as Darwinian evolutionary theory; chaps. 10, 22), and postmodern relativism and nihilism (chaps. 24–25).

The purpose of apologetics, therefore, is to provide a rational defense of Christianity that addresses concerns like these in language hearers can understand. But what would count as a successful apology, an apology that has fulfilled its purpose? And how can an apologist know when his or her apology has succeeded? There are at least two general questions about apologetics that bear on the question of success. First, how reasonable is it to accept Christian doctrines from the standpoint of an absolute standard of rationality? Second, how reasonable is it to believe the claims of Christianity rather than those of other competing major worldviews (such as naturalism, versions of pantheism, and other forms of theism [see chaps. 7–8])? Both of these questions are important, since it is theoretically possible that Christianity is more reasonable than any competing worldview and yet not very reasonable in itself (this would be the case if Christianity were the least implausible among a group of relatively implausible worldviews).

There are three possible general answers to the first question. Christianity could be:

1. unreasonable (there is more reason to reject it than to accept it)
2. maximally reasonable (capable of being shown conclusively or decisively to be true)
3. reasonable to some non-maximal degree

---

3. Nonetheless, chap. 8 discusses polytheism.

Outcome 1 is clearly inadequate from the standpoint of traditional apologetics. Traditional apologists agree that Christian faith, though it may in some respects be *above* reason, is not *against* reason. Though outcome 2 would seem to be ideal, the history of Christian apologetics shows that it is simply not possible. In addition, if there were a *conclusive* rational proof of the truth of the Christian faith, it would not be clear why submission to Christ requires a supernatural work of the Holy Spirit. Moreover, as we will see in chapter 5, there are good reasons for thinking that God set things up in such a way as to preclude the possibility of such conclusive rational proofs of Christianity. So the desired outcome of Christian apologetics, from the standpoint of a noncomparative standard of rationality (a standard that shows how rational Christianity is on its own rather than in comparison with competing worldviews), is to show that Christian belief is rational to some less than maximal degree (option 3). But again, even if this could be shown, there is still the question concerning how Christian faith fares rationally relative to the alternative worldviews with which it competes.

There are four possible general answers to the second question. Christianity could be:

1. less reasonable than the most reasonable worldview with which it competes
2. at least as reasonable as (but not more reasonable than) the most reasonable worldview with which it competes
3. more reasonable than all the worldviews with which it competes

4. the only genuinely reasonable alternative

Perhaps outcome 4 would seem to be the best. However, it is implausible. Most if not all major alternatives to Christianity are reasonable *to some extent.* Moreover, all Christian claims are "rationally resistible."[4] That is, it is always possible to give a reason (though perhaps not a very good one) to resist accepting a Christian claim, even if a good argument has been offered on behalf of it (we will see how this works in chap. 9). One need only have a reason to reject a premise of the argument.

If 4 is not an acceptable goal, then from the standpoint of the nature and purpose of traditional apologetics, outcome 3 is clearly the most desirable one, and outcome 1 is clearly the least desirable. Traditional Christian apologetics would fail to accomplish its goal of defending the reasonableness of Christian belief if it should turn out that Christianity is less reasonable than the most reasonable worldview with which it competes, because it would be unreasonable to believe it rather than to endorse a more reasonable alternative. What about outcome 2? If an apology for the Christian faith could make a good case for the claim that Christianity is just as reasonable as its most reasonable competitor, then it would have accomplished a worthy goal. We could say that by meeting this goal, an apology has shown that Christianity is cosmically competitive.[5] However, it would clearly be better to

4. See Michael J. Murray, "Reason for Hope (in a Postmodern World)," in *Reason for the Hope Within,* ed. Michael J. Murray (Grand Rapids: Eerdmans, 1999), 10–14, for a helpful discussion of the rational resistibility of arguments for and against theism.

5. My colleague Bob Wennberg came up with this label.

show that Christianity is more reasonable than its most reasonable competitor. This latter result would be to show the cosmic superiority of Christianity. Let us call an apologetic strategy that shows Christianity to be only cosmically competitive a strategy of modest apologetics, and an apologetic strategy that shows Christianity to be cosmically superior to all its competitors a strategy of ambitious apologetics. It would seem that the best tack to take as a Christian apologist is to pursue the outcome of ambitious apologetics and to settle for the outcome of modest apologetics if it turns out to be the best one can do.

Some would say that a successful ambitious apologetic strategy must *prove* or *demonstrate* that Christianity is true or at least that God exists. This conception of apologetics, however, borders on defining apologetic success in terms of outcome 4 above (according to which the Christian worldview is the only reasonable alternative). Let me reiterate here that I do not believe such a conclusive case for Christianity is either possible or even desirable. This would be a case of "overwatering." This much water is not available, it would be detrimental to the "plants," and it is not really necessary for their growth. Faith based on the experience of God's gracious love is, as I claimed above and will argue below (in chap. 2), all a garden really needs, except in certain special circumstances. So the watering task will not involve demonstrative and conclusive proofs but instead plausible arguments and rational evidences. But though the watering will not involve *showing* that Christianity is true, the weeding will have the goal of making it reasonable to think that Christianity has not

been shown false. The goal of weeding, then, is to give good reasons for thinking that it *is not irrational* to hold Christian beliefs. The goal of watering is to show that it *is rational* to adopt the Christian worldview.

The Limits of Christian Apologetics

The third and final conclusion we can draw about Christian apologetics from 1 Peter 3:14–15 is that this activity requires having a *heart of humility* toward those who criticize, object to, and doubt Christianity ("yet do it [make your defense] with gentleness and reverence"). Though it is well and good for Christian apologists to be confident, arrogance is out. Unfortunately, defenders of Christianity throughout history have not always restricted themselves to a humble approach. Manifestations of such humility include the following. Apologists should (1) listen to and try to understand those with concerns about Christianity, (2) seek common ground with those with whom they disagree, (3) be open to the possibility that the reasons they give for their faith are in need of improvement, and (4) put alternative positions against which they argue in the best possible light.

Another way to put this point is that Christian apologetics ought to be *irenic* (conducive to peace and harmony). Though the purpose of Christian apologetics is to defend the Christian faith, it does not have to be *defensive*. Many apologetic works throughout history have been written in such a way as to alienate the very audience to which they were directed. These books were written in highly adversarial ways that tended to polarize Christianity and its competitors needlessly. There are various ways in which this has been done. One way is by using language that characterizes the adherents of alternative faiths or points of view as either intellectually or morally deficient without an admission of similar deficiencies on the part of Christians. Instead, this book is written in the spirit of the familiar idea that Christians who share or defend their faith should be like beggars helping other beggars find bread.[6]

Another way to put people off unnecessarily is to say or imply that no worldview other than the Christian worldview has any truth or value in it whatsoever. Clearly, if Christianity is true, then any claim made by an alternative worldview that is logically incompatible with the central claims of the Christian faith must be false. But this leaves open the possibility of common ground between Christianity and other traditions. An irenic approach looks for and affirms whatever Christianity shares with competing points of view. It is also open to the possibility that Christians can learn something important from alternative visions of reality.

A third source of antagonism in some apologetic efforts stems from an overconfidence in the efficacy of human reason in demonstrating the truths of the Christian faith and a corresponding failure to appreciate the relative ambiguity and inconclusiveness of much evidence for Christianity and the relative uncertainty that this engenders. There is a skeptical

An irenic approach looks for and affirms whatever Christianity shares with competing points of view.

streak in these postmodern times that leads many people to reject overly optimistic and rationalistic approaches as intellectually naive or dishonest. Though I believe much postmodern skepticism is overblown (see chap. 24), I do think there is good reason not to expect too much out of human reason. This book affirms the relative inconclusiveness and lack of absolute objective certainty of the rational case for Christianity without diminishing the relatively high degree of rationality it is possible to achieve through a combination of arguments, evidences, and the corresponding relatively high degree of Christian commitment that this makes possible.

This book is irenic, therefore, in that it does not vilify opponents, seeks common ground, and admits some uncertainty. This is in line with the admonition in 1 Peter always to be ready to defend one's faith "with gentleness." After all, though the gospel can be offensive in some respects (because, for one thing, it assumes that all human beings are sinners), those who preach and defend the gospel ought not to be offensive.

In addition to these practical, moral limits, Christian apologetics also faces theoretical limits. As already pointed out, the history of Christian apologetics shows that no case for the Christian faith is conclusive or decisive in such a way as to show that all competing alternatives are clearly false. Moreover, adherents of

---

6. According to James B. Simpson, comp., *Simpson's Contemporary Quotations* (Boston: Houghton Mifflin, 1988), the Sri Lankan theologian D. T. Niles was quoted by the *New York Times* on May 11, 1986, as saying that "Christianity is one beggar telling another beggar where he found bread."

some alternatives often have good reasons for their views and often have plausible reasons, given their other beliefs and experiences, to reject Christian views—at least temporarily. These theoretical limits provide a good reason for the practical, moral limits already discussed. Humility requires acknowledging these historically demonstrated facts about the theoretical limits of Christian apologetics. The task of the Christian apologist, then, is not to prove conclusively that Christianity is true and that all competitors are false (or even that only Christianity is rational) but rather to provide reasons for thinking that it is more reasonable to believe Christianity than to accept any alternative worldview.

Another important point about the theoretical limits of Christian apologetics is that it is not possible for rational argumentation alone to make a person into (or sustain a person as) a follower of Jesus Christ. Jesus told Nicodemus, "No one can see the kingdom of God unless he is born again" (John 3:3). He also told some Jewish critics, "No one can come to me unless the Father who sent me draws him" (John 6:44). One very important reason for this is that the cultivation of Christian commitment is not merely an intellectual matter but also, and perhaps mostly, a matter of the heart and the will. Sinful human beings are incapable of a conversion of their wills to Christ apart from the supernatural grace of God. This does not mean that an appeal to the mind by means of rational argumentation and broader kinds of evidences is of no value in bringing someone to Christ (and keeping him or her committed to Christ). Though the work of the Holy Spirit is required for submission to the lordship of Christ, the Spirit can make use of human reasoning in the process of bringing a person to faith (and restoring faith in the case of Christians who have doubts).

Apologists are best seen as partners of the Holy Spirit in the process of cultivating Christian commitment. Here the metaphor of cultivating a garden is especially helpful. As said above, just as plants cannot grow solely as a result of the efforts of a gardener but also need various natural contributions beyond his or her control, so an apologist and/or evangelist cannot make a person a follower of Jesus apart from the work of the Holy Spirit. A gardener supplies water, soil, and a place in the sun, but the plant will not grow apart from the natural powers intrinsic to these things, which the gardener does not create. In the same way, an evangelist can preach the gospel eloquently, and an apologist can defend it rationally, but only the Holy Spirit can enable the listeners to respond with faith to what they hear.

There is another interesting connection between these practical and theoretical limits that is worth mentioning here. To the extent that rational arguments and evidences of a philosophical or historical sort do not suffice by themselves to establish the truth of Christian belief, other kinds of considerations become important. Among these alternative considerations are those that have to do with the practical consequences of Christian commitment.

One of the things that Christians claim to be true is that people who live lives of faith in Jesus Christ can be radically transformed for the better. Paul states that the fruit of the Spirit—that is, the attitudinal and behavioral result of the work of the Holy Spirit in one's life—is "love, joy, peace, patience, kindness, goodness, faithfulness, gentleness and self-control" (Gal. 5:22–23). The Greek word for gentleness here (*prautes*), which can also be translated "humility," is a form of the same word used in 1 Peter 3:16 ("yet do it with gentleness [*prautetos*]"). If we put these passages together, we can see that Christians who manifest the fruit of the Spirit can be Christian apologists who are always ready to defend the hope within them in the way they are admonished to do so in 1 Peter. Christian apologists, therefore, can supplement their theoretical arguments with practical evidence. If Christianity is true, then there really is a Holy Spirit who can make people humble and gentle. Consequently, humble apologists can contribute to the confirmation of the Christian worldview by how they live in general and how they defend their faith in particular. But they can also contribute to the disconfirmation of Christianity if their lives and apologetic methods are characterized by arrogance and manipulation. Accordingly, the existence of the theoretical limits to apologetics makes it very important for apologists to remember the practical limits.[7]

7. See John G. Stackhouse Jr., *Humble Apologetics* (New York: Oxford University Press, 2002), especially 227–32, for more along these lines.

Reflection and Discussion

1. Is your foundation of faith in Jesus strong enough at this point in your life for you to engage in a defense of your faith? If not, what do you need to do to strengthen it?
2. Are you more in favor of "modest" apologetics or "ambitious" apologetics? Why?
3. Do you know people who have not shown enough humility in their defense of the Christian faith? What have been the consequences of their arrogance?

Further Reading

Mitchell, Basil. *The Justification of Religious Belief.* New York: Oxford University Press, 1981.

Murray, Michael J. "Reason for Hope (in the Postmodern World)." In *Reason for the Hope Within,* edited by Michael J. Murray, 1–19. Grand Rapids: Eerdmans, 1999.

Stackhouse, John G., Jr. *Humble Apologetics.* New York: Oxford University Press, 2002.

2

Faith and Human Wisdom

Evidentialist Apologetics

» **Outline**

- **Objection 1: Christian Apologetics Is Unnecessary**
  - *Argument: Faith Is Always Sufficient without Arguments*
  - *Definitions of Faith and Reason*
  - *Paul's Approach with the Corinthians*
- **The Need for Christian Apologetics**
  - *Faith, Reason, and Free Will*
  - *Paul's Approach in Athens*
  - *The Need for Apologetic Arguments for Some People Sometimes*
  - *The Benefits of Apologetic Arguments for All People Always*
- **An Argument against Evidentialism**
  - *Proportionalist Evidentialism*
  - *Evident Beliefs That Are Not Based on Evidence*
    - Self-evident Beliefs
    - Beliefs Evident to the Senses
  - *How Belief in God Can Be Evident but Not Based on Evidence*
  - *Evidentialism as Self-defeating*

» **Summary**

Some people argue that apologetics is unnecessary because faith is always sufficient apart from objective evidences and arguments. Paul's initial approach to the church at Corinth seems to support this view. However, apologetics is sometimes needed by some people at some times. Paul's strategy in Athens is an indication that this conclusion is true. Apologetics is not, however, *always* necessary. Apologetics would always be required only if evidentialism were true, but evidentialism is false because it is too stringent and self-defeating.

» **Basic Terms, Concepts, and Names**

Anselm
Augustine
evidentialism
evident to the senses
faith
fideism
Hume, David
Locke, John
Paul, St.
Plantinga, Alvin
proportionalism
rationalism
reason
self-defeating thesis
self-evident claims

» **Reflection and Discussion**

» **Further Reading**

> When I came to you, brothers, I did not come with eloquence or superior wisdom as I proclaimed to you the testimony about God. For I resolved to know nothing while I was with you except Jesus Christ and him crucified. I came to you in weakness and fear, and with much trembling. My message and my preaching were not with wise and persuasive words, but with a demonstration of the Spirit's power, so that your faith might not rest on men's wisdom, but on God's power.
>
> 1 Corinthians 2:1–5

First Peter 3:14–15 seems to make preparedness to defend one's Christian convictions mandatory. Many Christians throughout history have heeded this admonishment. However, Christian apologetics has always had critics too. These detractors have included Christians and non-Christians. It is easy to see why many non-Christians would dismiss Christian apologetics. But why have some *Christians* objected to it? Christian anti-apologists have considered it unnecessary, impossible, or harmful. None of these charges is completely true, but each contains a grain of truth. This chapter discusses the first objection, and the next chapter considers the latter two.

One way to respond to the first objection, that Christian apologetics is *never* necessary for Christian faith, is to insist that it is *always* necessary. However, this is a mistake, as already mentioned in the introduction. Consequently, after respond-

ing to this objection, I will argue against the evidentialist thesis that reasonable or rational Christian belief always requires the sorts of philosophical and historical evidences that make up the apologist's tool kit. I will instead maintain that apologetics is only sometimes necessary for some people.

Objection 1: Christian Apologetics Is Unnecessary

Here is one way to argue that apologetics is unnecessary: "Isn't religion in general and Christianity in particular just a matter of *faith*? If so, then Christian belief should not require knowledge based on reason, argumentation, and evidences. If you have to engage in reasoning for Christian belief, then it is not faith but rational knowledge that is required, and rational knowledge precludes faith. If you know on the basis of reason that something is true, then you do not have to have faith that it is. Conversely, if you have to have faith about something, then you do not really know it rationally. Since Christian apologetics involves the use of reason, and reason leads to rational knowledge, then Christian apologetics leaves faith out of the picture. But being a Christian is all about having faith! So Christians do not need to and even should not engage in Christian apologetics."

This objection raises the age-old philosophical question about the relationship between faith and reason. Christians have answered this question in a number of ways. The objection above seems to presuppose a version of fideism as opposed to rationalism, the competing viewpoints about the relationship between faith and reason mentioned in the introduction. Roughly speaking, fideism about religious belief puts a priority on faith over reason, whereas rationalism about religious belief emphasizes reason over faith. There are many versions of each of these two approaches to the faith/reason question, and the issue is complicated. A full-fledged discussion of this issue would examine all the meanings of the ambiguous words *faith* and *reason*. Without engaging in this definitional work, it would not be possible to know exactly what the different viewpoints about the relationships between faith and reason amount to. People who seem to agree with one another might really disagree, and people who seem to disagree with one another might really agree given their definitions of *faith* and *reason*. Though we do not need to canvas all the meanings of these words, it will be helpful to say just a few things about faith and reason by way of definition be-

fore considering the objection above that makes use of these words.

The author of Hebrews defines faith as "being sure of what we hope for and certain of what we do not see" (11:1). Though, as mentioned earlier, the biblical concept of faith is surely more than sure conviction or certain belief (it also involves trust and obedience), it seems clearly to include belief (to trust God is at least to believe that God exists, that what God has revealed is true, and that what God has promised will happen). It is this component of biblical faith that is most relevant when it comes to discussions of faith and reason that bear on Christian apologetics because, as we have seen, the primary goal of Christian apologetics is to defend the rationality of Christian *belief* (though the ultimate goal of apologetics is to cultivate Christian *commitment*, a psychological state that involves both the mind and the heart, like biblical faith). The concept of reason relevant for our purposes here is the one that involves giving reasons for belief. Reasons for belief can take the form of evidences or arguments. Given these definitions, Christian apologetics can be characterized as the use of reason in support of faith, that is, the offering of reasons in the form of evidences and arguments to try to show that Christian belief (the intellectual aspect of Christian faith) is reasonable. The objection we are considering is that Christian faith does not ever need to be supported by reason in this sense.

The objector could strengthen his or her argument here by referring to 1 Corinthians 2:1–5, quoted at the beginning of this chapter, in which Paul reminds his Corinthian readers how he preached the gospel to them initially. What Paul says here implies that Christian faith does not require the support of either philosophy ("superior wisdom," "men's wisdom") or rhetoric ("eloquence," "persuasive words"). It is hard to get around the implication that Paul's view is that Christian faith does not require support from reason. I think this is Paul's view, and I agree with him. However, it is important to clarify that what Paul tells the Corinthians does not imply that reason is *never* required for faith. What he says implies only that reason is *not always* needed for faith. This is the aspect of truth in the objector's position. But this leaves at least two important questions unanswered. First, what is the value of Christian apologetics, if any, if Christian faith does not always need support from human reason in the form of evidences and arguments? Second, are there any reasons, beyond Paul's apparent endorsement of it, to accept this fideist position?

The Need for Christian Apologetics

Chapter 1 argued that rational argumentation can never be sufficient in and of itself to bring a person to Christ. The question at this point is whether it is ever necessary or at least helpful (as affirmed in the introduction that it sometimes is). If the work of the Holy Spirit is always necessary for the cultivation of Christian commitment, then might it always be sufficient? After all, if God is all-powerful, then surely God could bring a person to faith (or sustain a person's faith) without the need for rational arguments and evidences. And if God *could* do this, then perhaps God *always does* do this. However, though God could always do this, and often does do this (as illustrated by the

case of the Corinthians), there are good reasons for thinking that God does not always choose to do this. Before we look at these reasons, let's consider a general point about God's role in the cultivation of Christian commitment, whether or not it involves rational argumentation and evidences.

Human nature includes intellectual, volitional, and affective elements. That is, we have minds, wills, and hearts. Moreover, we are capable of exercising our minds rationally and our wills freely. It is plausible that these capacities are at least a part of what it means for us to be created in the image of God (Gen. 1:26–27). It would be odd if God created us with these capacities and then overrode them in the process of bringing us to faith in Christ (or restoring or sustaining our faith in him). It is true that as fallen human beings our minds and hearts have been affected by sin (we will discuss this at more length in chaps. 3, 5). Because of this, we require supernatural assistance to turn from our sin and to submit ourselves to God. However, the Bible shows that God always accomplishes his purposes through human agency—not by treating people as mere tools but by respecting human autonomy. So we should expect that in bringing people to faith or helping them to persevere in faith, God would work with and through their rational minds and their free wills (there will be various other points at which an appeal to human freedom will be important in this book). In other words, God would not just cause, force, or coerce people to believe. Instead, he would woo, coax, and persuade them. The way to do this is to appeal to a person's mind and heart in such a way as to give him or her room for reflection and autonomy.

But this does not yet show that the philosophical arguments and historical evidences employed by a Christian apologist would ever be needed for the cultivation of Christian commitment. Perhaps the work of an evangelist in preaching the gospel would always be adequate. A person who hears the message of God's salvation in Christ could freely choose to accept Christ on the basis of Spirit-prompted recognition of and sorrow for his or her sin together with a strong sense of God's reality and God's gracious offer of forgiveness and new life. In such a case, there would be clear thinking, free willing, and genuine feeling but not abstract philosophical reasoning, careful historical investigation, and inference to the best explanation of the psychology of religious experiences. In short, there would be evangelism but not apologetics.

Evangelism is often—perhaps usually—enough without apologetics. However, nothing that has been said up to this point indicates that apologetics is *never* needed; we have only seen good reason to think that apologetics is *not always* needed (and we will consider further arguments for this position in section three of this chapter). In the case of the Corinthians' initially coming to faith, Spirit-empowered evangelism was enough. In contrast, Paul's approach to the people he met when he visited Athens involved both preaching and *reasoning*. Luke reports in Acts 17:16–34 that, as a result of being distressed at seeing the city full of idols, Paul "reasoned in the synagogue with the Jews and the God-fearing Greeks, as well as in the marketplace day by day with those who happened to be there" (v. 17). A group of Epicurean and Stoic philosophers began to dispute with him and eventually took

him to the Areopagus, where they asked Paul to tell them about his "new teaching." Paul then made a speech to them that contained not only the gospel message but also arguments for the general Christian conception of God as opposed to the pagan polytheistic idolatry of Greek religion. In the process of presenting these arguments, Paul sought to establish common ground with his hearers by appealing to elements of their religious tradition and reinterpreting them in Christian terms. Paul's strategy with the Athenians seems clearly to contain apologetic elements. The general principle we should glean from this is that apologetics is needed for *some people at certain times.*

People clearly differ from one another in their degree of education, intelligence, and concern for intellectual problems and puzzles. Some people are content to have a "simple faith," whereas others find faith and belief anything but simple. Moreover, some people may experience seasons of their lives that are relatively free of troubling questions or doubts about God and Christianity and yet go through other times when such questions or doubts are very real to them. In some cases, these challenging questions may come primarily from other people. In other cases, the questions may be their own. Christian apologetics is needed for people who are asking difficult questions or enduring uncomfortable doubts, whether they are Christians or non-Christians, whether their perplexity

> **The general principle we should glean from this is that apologetics is needed for *some people at certain times.***

is due to personality or time of life, and whether the questions are their own or those of other people. Therefore, though apologetics is not needed for all people at all times, it is needed for some people at some times.

The long history of active and fruitful apologetic activity from the earliest Christian times to the present bears witness to the ongoing need for apologetics to supplement evangelism in many cases. As long as there are people with questions and doubts about the faith, there will be a need for apologetics. Whether it is needed in a specific case is a rhetorical question (rhetoric is the art and science of persuasive communication) that requires sensitivity to the needs of one's audience. But even when it is needed, the work of the Holy Spirit to convict, convince, comfort, and encourage is always required as well. Sometimes the Holy Spirit works apart from apologetic arguments, and sometimes he works with and through them.

One final important thought about this issue is that even people who do not *need* apologetic arguments to cultivate Christian commitment may find apologetic arguments and evidences *helpful.* Though these people's faith may be based ultimately only on their experience of God, they may still experience a substantial *strengthening* of their faith by thinking carefully about a rational case for the Christian faith. In other words, though people can have justified Christian beliefs apart from the use of reason in apologetics, the latter can enhance and deepen their faith. As pointed out in the introduction, this approach is very much in line with Augustine's motto "I believe in order to understand" and Anselm's similar "faith seeking understanding." Whether apolo-

getics is needed or merely helpful, however, there is an important sense in which it is temporary. This is because, as Paul so eloquently expresses it in 1 Corinthians 13, even though we now "see but a poor reflection as in a mirror; then we will see face to face" and "know fully" (v. 12). When we are with the Lord in heaven, we will not need arguments and other evidences to assure us of his presence with us and of his love for us.

An Argument against Evidentialism

Let's now consider reasons to affirm the fideist view that acceptable Christian belief does not always require evidence or argument. As stated in the introduction, the rationalist view to the contrary (that Christian faith is acceptable only if it is based on adequate arguments or evidences) is often called evidentialism (about Christian belief). A prominent variant of evidentialism is proportionalism. This is the thesis that people ought to hold their beliefs in proportion to the evidence they have for them. That is, they are justified in holding a belief only if there is adequate evidence for it, *and* they are justified in holding the belief only as firmly as the strength of the evidence warrants. Both the Christian John Locke (1632–1704) and the agnostic David Hume (1710–76) were philosophers who advocated this proportionalist version of evidentialism. What explains their different religious convictions is that Locke believed there is adequate evidence for Christian belief and Hume was convinced there is not. Since fideism and rationalist evidentialism are contradictories (if one is true, the other must be false), one good way to defend the brand of fideism under consideration is to argue that, though faith and reason are not opposed, evidentialism is false, unfounded, or both. Alvin Plantinga has shown that a good case can be made for both of these claims.[1]

There are good reasons for thinking that evidentialism is not generally true, since there are clear cases of justified beliefs that are not based on evidence. Examples of these include the belief that 2 + 2 = 4 and the belief you have right now that you are reading some words printed on a page in a book on Christian apologetics. These two claims are both evident. The first, arithmetic claim is *self*-evident. A claim is self-evident when just by thinking about what it means you can see that it has to be true. The second, perceptual claim is evident to the senses. A claim is evident to the senses when you believe it on the basis of one or more of your senses without having any reason to think it is false or unjustified. Both of these claims are evident, but they are not based on evidence (something else you believe to be true). To say that 2 + 2 = 4 is self-evident is not to say that it rests on itself as evidence, since no claim can make itself evident. It just *is* evident. Normally, what makes a perceptual claim evident is your simply believing it to be true on the basis of a characteristic kind of experience (e.g., believing that something red is in front of you on the basis of having the visual experience of there seeming to be something red in front of you).

1. Alvin Plantinga, "Reason and Belief in God," in *Faith and Rationality: Reason and Belief in God,* ed. Alvin Plantinga and Nicholas Wolterstorff, 16–93 (Notre Dame: University of Notre Dame Press, 1983).

Quite a few common justified beliefs are not based on evidence.

One need not, and normally does not, treat a perceptual experience as evidence on the basis of which one infers that a particular perceptual claim is true. For instance, I do not usually reason in such a way as to believe first of all that I am having a certain kind of visual experience and then reason on the basis of that belief to the belief that I am seeing something red in front of me. The experience is a *ground* for my belief that *causes* my belief without being a *reason* or *evidence* for my belief. Quite a few common justified beliefs, therefore, are not based on evidence. But evidentialism says that a belief can be justified only if it is based on evidence, so evidentialism is not generally true. Moreover, it is not the case that all beliefs ought to be proportional to the evidence that exists for them. When we believe something that is either self-evident or evident to the senses, we do not believe it on the basis of any evidence at all. There is no evidence for these beliefs to which we need to proportion them.

There are other examples of beliefs that are evident—and so justified, reasonable, and rational—but not based on evidence (in the form of additional beliefs). For instance, I believe that I had a bowl of oatmeal for breakfast this morning. I do not now *perceive* this oatmeal with any of my five senses, of course, so this is not a *perceptual* belief. However, it is *like* a perceptual belief in that it is not a conclusion I have reached on the basis of other beliefs. Rather, it is grounded in a characteristic kind of subjective *experience*. This experience is not sensory but *memorial*. It is simply the experience of it seeming to me—with that characteristic "past" quality that only memorial experiences possess—as though I had oatmeal for breakfast this morning. Because of this similarity between normal justified perceptual beliefs and normal justified memory beliefs, we can broaden the use of the phrase "evident to the senses" to include the latter as well as the former.

Other examples of evident beliefs not based on evidence include some beliefs about the mental states of other people (for instance, when I believe that my wife is curious about something on the basis of my experience of seeing a particular look on her face) and some beliefs of experts in certain areas about the objects of their expertise (for instance, the belief of a chef that the soup needs more seasoning of a particular kind). We can include these two kinds of examples in the category of beliefs that are evident to the senses as well. Notice that I am not saying there is no evidence *available* for any of these beliefs; I am only suggesting that it is possible (and even normal) to be justified in holding these beliefs without basing them on propositional evidence when they are based on the appropriate kind of experiential ground.

Many evidentialists accept this conclusion and yet deny that religious beliefs are either self-evident or evident to the senses. For instance, they say that the claim that God exists is neither self-evident nor evident to the senses and so must be based on adequate evidence to be justified. But why should we think this is true? The passage from 1 Corinthians quoted above gives Christians a good reason to deny this.

If the Corinthians' faith was based on a demonstration of the Holy Spirit's power rather than on human wisdom, then it would seem that it was justified for them to hold their Christian beliefs on the basis of the former rather than the latter. The reality of God could have been made evident to them on the basis of their experience of the Holy Spirit's power rather than on the basis of evidence of a propositional sort (the sort of evidence the evidentialist says is required for justified belief in God). Many Christian testimonies over the centuries would seem to support this. And *non-Christians* who have not experienced God's power in this way would seem not to have a good reason for denying the potential role of such an experience in justifying Christian belief. After all, a number of other common beliefs are evident, justified, or rational without being based on evidence, as we have seen. Why couldn't this also be the case with the Christian conviction that God exists? Evidentialists do not seem to have a good reason to deny that it could be rational or reasonable for people to believe that God exists even if their belief is not based on evidence in the form of a philosophical or historical argument. It seems arbitrary to allow many nonreligious beliefs (such as the ones discussed above) to be justified or rational apart from evidence and yet to say that no religious beliefs can have this status.

A number of examples of religious beliefs arguably do possess this feature.[2] For instance, when I feel guilty about something I have done, I find myself believing that God is displeased with my behavior. Upon seeing an especially breathtaking

2. These are the sorts of examples Plantinga uses in ibid., 80–81.

sunset, I discover myself thanking God for his handiwork. Moreover, when I read Psalm 103, I spontaneously have the renewed conviction that God loves me and forgives me. All these psychological responses to the experiences mentioned involve a belief about God, and each of these beliefs presupposes that God exists. They are examples of beliefs about God that are based on experiences rather than on propositional evidence (e.g., philosophical argument). Arguably, they are also rational, reasonable, and justified, just as the examples of nonreligious beliefs mentioned above are. What good reason is there for thinking they are not?

The second nail in evidentialism's coffin is that evidentialism does not pass its own test.[3] According to the version of evidentialism under consideration, for it to be rational to believe a given claim, that claim has to be self-evident, evident to the senses, or based on evidence in the form of reasoning or argument that consists of premises that are either self-evident or evident to the senses. But the thesis of evidentialism is none of these. It is not self-evident, since it is not a claim that

one can see has to be true just by thinking about what it means (if you are not sure about this, just think about what it means, and then ask yourself whether your understanding its meaning suffices for you to see that it has to be true). It is not evident to the senses. There is no sensory experience of any sort that would cause a normal person to believe it in such a way as to be justified in believing it. Evidentialism is an abstract *philosophical* thesis—and a controversial one at that—so it seems clear that it would be rational to believe it only if we could show it to be true by means of a philosophical argument. But no one has been able to construct such an argument. Therefore, evidentialism does not pass its own test. The upshot is that if evidentialism is true then no one would ever be justified or rational in believing it to be true! Evidentialism is, in this sense, self-defeating. If evidentialism is self-defeating, then there is no good reason to believe it to be true and to implement it in an evaluation and criticism of religious faith and belief (indeed, there is good reason to think that it is false). If evidentialism is unacceptable, then there is no good reason to think that Christian faith is illegitimate apart from reason in the form of evidence and argument. And then there is no good reason to reject the fideist view that Christian belief (and therefore faith) is justifiable apart from rational evidence and argumentation.

3. Though Plantinga (in ibid., 59–63) applies this argument to the thesis of classical foundationalism, on which he believes the thesis of evidentialism is based, the same sort of argument applies to evidentialism itself. The case against evidentialism can be simplified by setting aside a discussion of classical foundationalism.

Reflection and Discussion

1. Do you agree that reason in the form of apologetical evidences and arguments is not always needed for confident and reasonable Christian faith? Why or why not?
2. Do you sometimes feel a need for what Christian apologetics has to offer? Do you know of others who sometimes do? If so, when does this need usually arise?
3. Are you convinced by the arguments against evidentialism? Why or why not?

Further Reading

Clark, Kelly James. *Return to Reason.* Grand Rapids: Eerdmans, 1990.

Kenny, Anthony. *What Is Faith? Essays in the Philosophy of Religion.* New York: Oxford University Press, 1992.

Plantinga, Alvin. "Reason and Belief in God." In *Faith and Rationality: Reason and Belief in God,* edited by Alvin Plantinga and Nicholas Wolterstorff, 16–93. Notre Dame: University of Notre Dame Press, 1983.

3

Jerusalem and Athens

More Objections to Apologetics

» Outline

- Objection 2: Christian Apologetics
  Is Impossible
  - *Mystery*
    - God Is Too Mysterious for Reason
    - Reply: Reason Can Employ General
      Revelation
  - *Depravity*
    - Sin Makes Reason Powerless
      for Unbelievers
    - Reply: Sin Darkens but Does Not
      Blind the Mind
  - *Relativity*
    - Christian Truths Are Subjective
      and Relative
    - Reply: Christian Claims Are Objective
      and Universal
- Objection 3: Christian Apologetics
  Is Harmful
  - *The Approximation Argument*
    - Contingent Historical Claims Do Not
      Support Total Commitment
    - Reply: Commitment Need Not
      Be Proportional to Evidence
  - *The Postponement Argument*
    - Commitment Should Not Be
      Postponed Due to Ongoing Debates
    - Reply: Commitment Need Not Be
      Based on Arguments Alone
  - *The Passion Argument*
    - Passionate Faith Requires Objective
      Uncertainty
    - Reply: Faith Requires Only
      a *Willingness* to Risk

» Summary

An objection to apologetics is that God is too
mysterious for human reason. But this ignores
general revelation and the partial success of
some arguments for God's existence. Also,
sin does not entirely blind nonbelievers, and
Christian truths are objective and universal if
true rather than subjective and relative. Finally,
Kierkegaard's concerns about Christian apologetics are ultimately unfounded (and rely on
evidentialism to some extent). The probabilistic
and inconclusive nature of apologetic arguments
is consistent with total commitment to Christ,
and passionate faith does not require actual
objective uncertainty as much as a willingness
to trust when objective grounds are lacking.

» Basic Terms, Concepts, and Names

Adams, Robert

Aquinas, Thomas

common grace

contingent truths

Evans, C. Stephen

free will

general revelation

Kierkegaard, Søren

necessary truths

objective reasoning

objective truth

objective uncertainty

proportionalist evidentialism

relative truth

special revelation

subjective truth

universal truth

» Reflection and Discussion

» Further Reading

> What indeed has Athens to do with Jerusalem? What concord is there between the Academy and the Church? What between heretics and Christians? Our instruction comes from "the porch of Solomon," who had himself taught that "the Lord should be sought in simplicity of heart."
>
> Tertullian, *Prescription against Heretics*, 7

In response to the objection that Christian apologetics is unnecessary, the previous chapter argued that, though it is not *always* necessary to provide arguments and evidences for Christian belief, it is *sometimes* necessary to do so for some people and often useful, even if not needed, for other people. This chapter considers and replies to two additional objections against apologetics. The first is that Christian apologetics is impossible, and the second is that it is harmful. As before, I will both reject these claims and yet also affirm whatever grains of truth can be found in them.

Objection 2: Christian Apologetics Is Impossible

A common complaint of opponents of apologetics is that it is not possible for apologetics to achieve its goals. Their claim is that the use of reason in the form of arguments and evidences cannot provide knowledge or even justified belief about God and Christianity. What reasons have they given for this? Three fall under

the categories of mystery, depravity, and relativity.

Mystery

Many say Christian truths are too mysterious to be knowable by reason. It is a common assumption that one cannot prove the existence of God. Why not? The reason given is that God is too exalted to be reached by the human mind. Humans may know a lot about the universe, at least those parts of it we can observe, but God, as creator and sustainer of the universe, exists outside it. God may reveal himself through the Bible or to select individuals, but knowing him or knowing about him in either of these two ways is not to know anything about him by unaided human reason. God may be knowable by faith through such a revelation or encounter, but God is too mysterious to be knowable by means of reasoning—even reasoning guided by the Holy Spirit.

From a Christian standpoint, a serious problem with this position is that it ignores or denies the theological doctrines of common grace and general revelation.

The doctrine of common grace is that God gives a certain kind of grace to all human beings in common. According to this doctrine, in addition to the special saving grace God gives to those who submit themselves to Christ in faith, God also graciously provides for all human beings in various ways so that sin and its consequences are prevented from being as serious as they could be. An important aspect of common grace is general revelation. Just as God revealed himself in special ways to the people of Israel, as recorded in the Old Testament, and then through Jesus and the New Testament, he has also revealed himself generally to all human beings externally through nature and internally through our consciences. The psalmist says that "the heavens declare the glory of God" and "the skies proclaim the work of his hands" (Ps. 19:1). Paul tells his Roman readers that "since the creation of the world God's invisible qualities—his eternal power and divine nature—have been clearly seen, being understood from what has been made" (Rom. 1:20). This last verse seems to be an especially clear statement of the doctrine of general revelation. God has "put his stamp" on the universe in such a way that anyone who observes creation can come to know about its Creator.

The medieval Christian theologian and philosopher Thomas Aquinas (1225–74) constructed five arguments (the "five ways") for God's existence that illustrate Paul's point. Each of these arguments starts with an observation of something that is true about the universe (that things move, that some things cause other things to happen or to exist, etc.) and then claims that these observable created phenomena must have a cause. The arguments conclude that the only ultimate cause they could have is God. Aquinas thinks humans can prove, by means of these philosophical arguments, that God exists. He also believes that we can prove some things about God's nature and about the human soul by means of reason as well. He agrees, however, that we cannot know *everything* about God and God's relation to us by reason alone. For instance, he says that only faith in God's special revelation in the Bible can enable us to know that God is Triune, that Jesus is God incarnate, and that our salvation was accomplished for us by means of his death and resurrection.

The Bible seems clearly to teach that God can be known by means of observing creation, and the prominent Christian philosopher Aquinas developed five philosophical arguments that purport to show specifically how this can be the case. Isn't this enough to show that the objection under consideration fails? Unfortunately, in the history of philosophical thought since Aquinas, a large number of objections have been raised against his theistic proofs (and others like them). Though there is not a consensus among contemporary philosophers that these objections have undermined these arguments or the many later ones like them, the fact that these objections have not been decisively refuted to everyone's satisfaction serves to cast a shadow on arguments for God's existence. Consequently, it is more difficult today to be confident that the arguments establish their conclusions than it was in the time of Aquinas. Because of this, many Christians today—even many Christian apologists—shy away from saying that there are any philosophical arguments that *prove* or *demonstrate* that God exists.

However, though this may be the case, it may still be possible for theistic arguments to serve an evidential role in Christian belief. Such arguments may help to make it more reasonable than not that God exists. They may function at least as clues, cues, signposts, pointers, or indications that there is a God. Together with other evidences of the sort considered in this book, they may well contribute to a good cumulative case for the existence of God and the truth of Christianity. The Christian worldview may well be the best explanation for all the evidences available, including those on which the traditional arguments for God's existence are based.

But doesn't the idea of this more limited role of reason in leading to knowledge of God conflict with the passage from Romans quoted above? We can see that this is not the case by looking at the wider context within which these verses appear. In the preceding two verses, Paul says the following: "The wrath of God is being revealed from heaven against all the godlessness and wickedness of human beings who suppress the truth by their wickedness, since what may be known about God is plain to them, because God has made it plain to them" (Rom. 1:18–19 TNIV). Given this, we should expect that the arguments for God's existence and for various claims about God's nature would not be universally accepted as establishing these things. This is because of the effect of sin on the human intellect, what Paul calls "suppressing the truth by wickedness." Therefore, though we have biblical and philosophical grounds for being confident about the use of human reason to secure evidence of God's existence, the complication of human sin or depravity prevents us from being as confident as we might like to be. The existence of human depravity has also been given as a reason for thinking that it is impossible to meet the goals of Christian apologetics.

Depravity

Paul tells the Corinthians that "the person without the Spirit does not accept the things that come from the Spirit of God but considers them foolishness, and cannot understand them because they are discerned only through the Spirit" (1 Cor. 2:14 TNIV). Some Christians take this verse and others like it to indicate that non-Christians are simply unable to understand or to know any truths about God or Christianity. The reason they give is that such people are slaves to sin and are completely blinded by sin. The theological ideas here are that God originally created human beings with minds capable of knowing the truth about God and about what God wants for people but that humans fell into sin. This depravity affected the human mind so thoroughly as to blind people to important truths about God. Therefore, the only way the human intellect can be restored to its original state of being capable of grasping such truths is by means of God's supernatural work of salvation from the power of sin by means of the Holy Spirit. As with the mystery-based objection, it follows again that human reason is completely powerless to enable people to have knowledge or justified beliefs about God. According to this view, the truth about God is accessible to humans only by means of a supernatural saving act of God apart from the operations of human reason. The idea is that one cannot know any important truths about God or Christianity unless one becomes a Christian first. If this were correct, then clearly it would be impossible for Christian apologetics to meet its goals, at least with non-Christians. But there are good reasons for thinking this is not correct.

First of all, there is an important sense in which some knowledge and understanding is required for any belief or article of faith. One cannot believe something to be true or take on faith that it is true unless one first knows what it means. In other words, understanding the meaning of a claim is required in order to believe that it is true. So belief, faith, or acceptance requires some minimal understanding. How does this fact apply to the objection being considered? According to this objection, human reason is useless as a means of understanding, knowing, or even justifiedly believing Christian claims as long as a person is blinded by sin. And people are blinded by sin until they are freed from sin. Now, to release people from their sin in such a way as to respect their autonomy (and not merely force them to turn from their sin against their will), God must take some action to which sinners can freely respond. For sinners to respond freely to God's overture, they must be capable of recognizing it as an offer on God's part. For this to be possible, God must reveal to them, in a way they can understand, that he is offering them salvation from their sin. But then sinners must be capable of understanding the meaning of God's revelation *before* they believe it or take it on faith. They must be capable of understanding the claim that God is offering them forgiveness for their sins before they accept God's offer and appropriate this forgiveness and the freedom from sin that it makes possible.

Therefore, the kind of rational reflection involved in understanding and accepting revelation must be possible in order for belief or faith in the truth of that revelation to be possible.

Moreover, the Bible gives a number of examples of people *reasoning* with sinful non-Christians in the midst of preaching the gospel to them (as pointed out in chap. 2), and this mix of evangelism and argument is often effective in convincing people to come to Christ. The Holy Spirit is no doubt involved in this process, but it is arguable that the Spirit can and does work with and through natural rational reflection in these cases. This makes sense in light of the point made in the previous paragraph about God's respect for human freedom. A free response to God's offer of salvation requires not only the use of reason to understand what God is offering but also enough rational thought to be justified in believing that God is the one who is making the offer and that what God communicates in revealing the offer is true.

It is true that the kind of rational thought required for this purpose may not involve the kinds of philosophical arguments and historical evidences that are the Christian apologists' tools. However, if even a minimal amount of natural human understanding and knowing is required (and therefore possible) in coming to faith, then it is hard to see why an extension of these capacities involving arguments and evidences would not be possible. If the human mind is not completely blinded by sin, then the door is open for it to be employed effectively, to some extent at least, in Christian apologetics (the "to some extent" is an important qualification explained more fully in chap. 5, which discusses the role of sin in distorting access to the truth).

Relativity

It is true that the Christian faith contains mysteries and that the human mind has been affected by sin, but it does not follow from either of these facts that Christian apologetics is impossible. The third and final argument for the impossibility of Christian apologetics is based on the claim that Christian truth is subjective and relative rather than objective and universal. Though there are some important kinds of relativity that Christian apologists must grant (such as the relativity of a person's experiences and beliefs to his or her circumstances and personal history), it is not the case that Christian *truths* are relative. This objection, therefore, also fails to show that Christian apologetics is impossible.

What does it mean to say that Christian truth is subjective and relative? To say that a truth is subjective is to say that what makes it true is a mental state of a subject of consciousness, such as a human being. Examples of such subjective states are opinions and preferences. A familiar assessment of religious beliefs is that they are just matters of opinion. This implies

> **Though there are some important kinds of relativity that Christian apologists must grant, it is not the case that Christian *truths* are relative.**

that, if they are true at all, what makes them true is a subjective state of a person rather than the way the "objective" world is. Moreover, since different subjects (different people) have different religious opinions, it follows from this subjectivist thesis about religious truths that such truths are *relative* as well. They are relative to the people whose opinions make them true. This sort of relativism about truth may be expressed by the common claim that "what is true for you may not be true for me."

It is easy to see that if religious truths in general and Christian truths in particular are both subjective and relative, then it would be impossible for Christian apologetics to satisfy its goal, which is to show that it is reasonable to believe that the Christian worldview is universally and objectively true. If something is universally true, then it is not relatively true. To say that the Christian faith is universally true is to say that there is *one* truth that is the same for all people in all times and in all places. If this is the case, then the Christian worldview cannot be true for some people and false for others. To say that the truths of the Christian faith are objective is to say that what makes them true is not anyone's subjective mental state but rather how the world really is (what the objects that exist in the world really are and how they are related to one another). It may be that when people say, "Christianity may be true for you, but it is not true for me," they do not mean to imply that the truth about Christianity is subjective and relative and therefore not objective and universal. They may instead mean either that you believe that Christianity is (objectively) true and they do not or that you may have good reason for thinking that Christianity is true but they do not. Nonetheless, the view that truth is relative is held by many people (it is included in a view called religious pluralism, which we will examine in chaps. 18–19).

Are Christian truths subjective and relative, or are they (assuming Christianity is true) objective and nonrelative? The best way to answer this is to ask what it is that Christians are *claiming* when they claim that God exists and that the Christian worldview is true. It is clear that, whether they are right or not, Christians who make these claims are claiming that the real, objective world is one way rather than another way. So when Christians say that God exists, they are claiming that reality contains not merely a physical universe but also a personal being who created and sustains the universe and who exists, in some sense, above and beyond the universe. If this is what Christians are claiming, then they are making a claim that is objectively and universally (rather than subjectively and relatively) true if it is true at all (and it need not be assumed for the purposes of this argument that it is). Since this is the kind of claim they are making (a claim about the objective world), then if they are wrong about it, if it is false, then it is universally and objectively false. Compare the claim that there is intelligent extraterrestrial life. Some people think there is, and some people think there is not. But what they both agree about is that it is either objectively false or objectively true that there is intelligent life on other planets.

Compare these claims (about God's existence and about the existence of in-telligent extraterrestrials) with the claim that anchovies taste good on pizza. This claim, unlike the former two, is clearly a claim that is, if it is true, subjectively and relatively true. It is easy to see that this is the case. Both people who say that anchovies taste good on pizza and people who say that anchovies do not taste good on pizza can be saying something true. This is because what they are really saying is that anchovies do (do not) taste good on pizza *to them*. This qualification implied by anyone who makes such a claim clearly shows that the claim is *relative*. The reason it is relative is that taste is subjective. In other words, whether it is true that something tastes good to a person or not is entirely (or at least partly) a matter of what is true of that person's subjective preferences or opinions. So when people say that anchovies taste good, they are implicitly making a claim about themselves. But when people claim that God or intelligent extraterrestrials exist, they are not making claims about themselves. Therefore, there is good reason to think that Christian claims are universally and objectively true if they are true. This undermines the claim that Christian apologetics is impossible on the basis of the alleged relativity of Christian truth claims.

Objection 3: Christian Apologetics Is Harmful

There are good reasons for thinking that, although Christian apologetics is never sufficient for cultivating Christian commitment, it is possible, often needed, and always useful. But the last objection concludes that Christian apologetics is not merely useless but downright harmful. What reasons could possibly be given for this charge?

This discussion focuses on three objections to the Christian use of objective reasoning raised by the nineteenth-century Danish Christian philosopher Søren Kierkegaard (1813–55). His objections do not succeed in showing that Christian apologetics is always a bad thing, but his concerns are based on some valuable insights. The contemporary American Christian philosopher Robert Adams has discussed these objections and has given them the following labels: (1) the approximation argument, (2) the postponement argument, and (3) the passion argument.[1] These three arguments are directed primarily against the efforts of scientific historians to establish on the basis of objective reasoning the historical truths on which the overall truth of the Christian faith depends (such as the truth that Jesus was raised from the dead). Objective reasoning is reasoning that is as free as possible from bias, prejudice, and personal interest in the outcome of the investigation. A perfectly objective approach to such historical questions would not proceed from a particular point of

view but would instead adopt a view from nowhere (or a view from everywhere—something like a God's-eye point of view). To some extent, the objections could also be applied to philosophical arguments for God's existence and to other related claims as well, since these arguments are a form of objective reasoning and, like historical arguments, are not absolutely conclusive.

The Approximation Argument

Kierkegaard's approximation argument points out, first, that the evidence for the historical claims of Christianity can never rule out the possibility of error, since this evidence only approximates the claims for which it is evidence. Relevant examples of such claims include the various things that Jesus is reported to have said and done by the four writers of the New Testament Gospels (Matthew, Mark, Luke, and John). By its very nature, the study of human history is not an exact science that can lead to absolutely certain conclusions. Mathematics is an example of such an exact science. The reason that mathematical theorems can be proven and therefore known with absolute certainty is that they are necessary truths, and it is possible, at least in the case of many relatively simple mathematical theorems, to see or demonstrate their necessity. A necessary truth is a truth that does not just merely *happen* to be true but *must* be true. For instance, it is not possible for the arithmetic proposition $2 + 2 = 4$ to be false.

Historical truths, however, are not necessary but *contingent*. Though they are true, they do not *have* to be true. It is possible for them to be false. For example,

1. Robert M. Adams, "Kierkegaard's Arguments against Objective Reasoning in Religion," in *The Virtue of Faith and Other Essays in Philosophical Theology*, 25–41 (Oxford: Oxford University Press, 1987) (originally published in the *Monist* 60 [1976]). See also C. Stephen Evans, *Faith beyond Reason: A Kierkegaardian Account* (Grand Rapids: Eerdmans, 1998), 106–10. Evans thinks it is not clear that Kierkegaard's arguments are intended to oppose the use of objective reasoning. My discussion adopts Adams's interpretation. The source for Kierkegaard's arguments is *Concluding Unscientific Postscript*, trans. Howard V. and Edna H. Hong (Princeton: Princeton University Press, 1992); and *Philosophical Fragments*, trans. Howard V. and Edna H. Hong (Princeton: Princeton University Press, 1992).

though it is true that Washington, D.C., is the capital of the United States, the founding fathers could have decided to keep the capital in Philadelphia, in which case it would now be false that Washington, D.C., is the capital of the United States. Historical truths are actually doubly contingent.[2] This is because it is a contingent truth that the universe exists at all and that the events that transpire in the universe conform to the natural laws that happen to govern the universe (call this natural contingency), and it is also a contingent truth that human beings have made all the free choices they have actually made (call this the contingency of human freedom). Since neither natural history nor human history had to happen the way it has, there is no way to know in advance of looking at the past itself what actually happened in history. Moreover, access to these contingent truths about the past is always mediated by evidences that we must interpret. No historical evidence wears its correct interpretation on its sleeve. The upshot is that we can never be absolutely, 100 percent certain that a particular historical claim is true.

But according to Kierkegaard, Christian faith, on which our eternal happiness depends, must disregard even the smallest possibility of error. We must either commit ourselves to Christ completely or not; there is no such thing as partial commitment. Since there is so much at stake (whether or not we will be eternally happy), and we must commit ourselves completely or not at all, then even the smallest chance of error becomes of great concern. If we

2. See Evans, *Faith beyond Reason*, 87, where he makes this point in the midst of exposing Kierkegaard's discussion of contingency in *Philosophical Fragments*, 75–78.

are evidentialists of the proportionalist variety (see chap. 2), we will proportion our beliefs to the evidence we have for them and therefore believe a historical claim no more firmly than is warranted by the evidence at our disposal. But if we do this, our ideally total commitment to Christ will not be commensurate with our less than total degree of belief in the claims on which this commitment is based. The gap between what the objective historical reasoning warrants us to believe and the total commitment we need for our eternal happiness will need to be traversed, Kierkegaard thinks, by means of a leap of faith. But if we base our belief exclusively on objective historical evidence as mandated by proportionalist evidentialism, such a leap of faith is illegitimate. This objection to apologetics concludes that, from the standpoint of faith, reason in the form of objective historical reasoning is a bad thing. To follow reason in this case would be harmful to faith (because it would make faith unreasonable).

Notice that this objection to reason from the standpoint of faith presupposes a form of evidentialism, which we have already given reasons for rejecting in chapter 2. Given this, the main lesson of Kierkegaard's approximation argument is not that objective historical reasoning is always harmful to Christian faith but that Christians should not base their faith on objective historical reasoning alone, understood from an evidentialist perspective. Rather, historical evidences and philosophical arguments have value for Christians only if such things depend on faith and are consequently supplementary to faith. After all, there is no such thing as an absolutely objective point of view (a view from nowhere or from everywhere) for individual humans, each of whom has a particular point of view colored by his or her subjective assumptions and interests. How we interpret and respond to evidences and arguments—especially those with moral and religious implications—is in part a function of what we already believe to be true and what we want to be true (chap. 5 says more about this).

The Postponement Argument

Kierkegaard's postponement argument can be generalized as follows. The scholarly debates about the philosophical arguments for God's existence and the historical reliability of the New Testament (among other relevant philosophical, theological, and historical issues) are ongoing and never finally resolved. Anyone familiar with the continuing conversations about these things will know that any argument that tends to favor the reasonableness of Christian belief will soon be challenged by an argument that leans in the opposite direction and vice versa. If one based one's faith on these arguments alone, then one would forever need to postpone absolute commitment to Christ. In such circumstances, one's faith experience would be like a perpetual roller-coaster ride. When the arguments that tend to support Christianity seem to come out ahead, one is on the uphill climb. When

> **If one based one's faith on these arguments alone, then one would forever need to postpone absolute commitment to Christ.**

the counterarguments appear to be winning, then one makes a rapid descent. The resulting experience is anything but stable, secure, and peaceful. It is not the sort of faith foundation from which bold and radical Christian discipleship and service can easily develop.

From a psychological point of view, in such circumstances, there is likely to be more questioning, doubting, and uncertainty than a normal human being can satisfactorily handle over a relatively long period of time. This is clearly incompatible with the kind of faith the author of Hebrews has in mind ("being *sure* of what we hope for and *certain* of what we do not see" [11:1, emphasis added]). It also seems to be a case of what Paul chose *not* to allow to happen to the Corinthians ("so that your faith might not rest on men's wisdom, but on God's power" [1 Cor. 2:5]). So Kierkegaard has good reason to be concerned about the potentially harmful consequences of basing faith on philosophical arguments and historical evidences alone. But again, this seems to show only that Christians should not base their faith *entirely* and *solely* on such arguments and evidences. This leaves open the possibility, as before, that faith can be grounded in an experience of God's transforming grace and yet supplemented and strengthened in various ways by reasons and evidences that are interpreted and appropriated in the light of faith.

The Passion Argument

Kierkegaard's passion argument starts with the surprising claim that genuine religious faith is a passion that requires objective *uncertainty*. As mentioned above, though faith has an intellectual element (belief), it is more than that as well. Kierkegaard thinks of it as involving an intense and prolonged concern about or interest in the object of faith. Certainly, faith in God is ideally not merely a belief that God exists but also a deep trust in God and an established readiness to obey God motivated by a passionate love for God. Kierkegaard thinks that people who look for arguments and evidences to make their faith more objectively certain are actually demonstrating a *lack* of love (and trust and readiness to obey). Lovers do not keep looking for objective reasons to trust their beloved. Instead, they look for opportunities to show how real their love is by taking a risk on the beloved even when there is objective uncertainty about whether the beloved really loves them. Indeed, according to this view, it would seem that the more objective uncertainty there is, the more commendable would be the lover's persistent faith in the beloved in the face of it. Consequently, the search for objective reasons for faith that characterizes Christian apologetics would seem to be not useful, helpful, and supportive of faith but rather detrimental to faith and indicative of a lack of faith.

Adams replies to this argument by pointing out that, though genuine faith may require the *disposition* to take a risk by continuing to have faith in spite of objective uncertainty, faith does not require always *actually* risking in this way.[3] For instance, though my faith in my wife requires that I continue to trust that she loves me and is faithful to me even if someone

were to present me with strong evidence that she was having an affair (evidence that I would immediately discount as false or misleading), my faith in her does *not* require that I ignore or refrain from seeking reasonable assurances of her loyalty to me. It is true that a demand for *excessive* demonstrations of her commitment to me would betray a lack of trust on my part, but it seems reasonable to desire at least a moderate amount of ongoing evidence of her love (and at least adequate reasons to believe that she is not being unfaithful). Therefore, the passion of faith is compatible with the use of reason to strive toward the attainment of objective certainty (or at least a reasonable degree of objective assurance).

Though C. Stephen Evans agrees with Adams about this, he points out that faith and love can grow and develop in circumstances of objective uncertainty in ways that they do not or cannot when such objective uncertainty is absent.[4] This would seem to be the sort of faith testing the author of 1 Peter has in mind when he says of the trials in which his readers have had to suffer grief, "These have come so that your faith—of greater worth than gold, which perishes even though refined by fire—may be proved genuine and may result in praise, glory and honor when Jesus Christ is revealed" (1:7). Evans's point is well taken, but it does not undermine Adams's reply to Kierkegaard's passion argument against Christian apologetics. It merely qualifies it.

3. Adams, "Kierkegaard's Arguments against Objective Reasoning in Religion," 35.

4. Evans, *Faith beyond Reason*, 110.

Reflection and Discussion

1. To what extent do you think the limits of the human mind and heart in the form of ignorance and sin prevent us from knowing things about God?
2. How would you respond to someone who told you that "it may be true for you that God exists, but it is not true for me"?
3. Does it bother you that the arguments for God's existence and the historical evidences for the truth of Christianity provide at best only probable and controversial reasons to believe? Do you think it makes sense to be totally committed to Christ in spite of these evidential limitations? Why or why not?

Further Reading

Adams, Robert M. "Kierkegaard's Arguments against Objective Reasoning in Religion." In *The Virtue of Faith and Other Essays in Philosophical Theology*, 25–41. Oxford: Oxford University Press, 1987.

Evans, C. Stephen. *Faith beyond Reason: A Kierkegaardian Account*. Grand Rapids: Eerdmans, 1998.

Murray, Michael J. "Reason for Hope (in the Postmodern World)." In *Reason for the Hope Within*, edited by Michael J. Murray, 1–19. Grand Rapids: Eerdmans, 1999.

4

A God-Shaped Vacuum

The Relevance of Apologetics

» **Outline**

- **The Need for Meaning**
  - *Sartre on Objective Meaninglessness without God*
  - *The Relevance of Christian Apologetics to the Need for Meaning*
  - *The Explanation of the Need for Meaning by Appeal to God*
- **The Need for Transcendence**
  - *The Inadequacy of Human Love Alone*
  - *The Need for Loving Union with a Transcendent God*
  - *Guilt Feelings and Three Human Needs*
    - The Need for Forgiveness
    - The Need for Reconciliation
    - The Need for Moral Transformation
  - *How the Satisfaction of These Three Needs Requires God in Christ*
  - *How These Needs Are Related to the Needs for Meaning and Love*
  - *How Complete and Permanent Happiness Requires Immortality*
- **The Need for Understanding**
  - *Examples of the Desire (and Need) to Understand*
  - *How Satisfaction of the Other Needs Requires Understanding*
  - *How Genuine Understanding Requires God's Existence*

» **Summary**

Humans need to lead meaningful lives and to love and be loved completely and eternally. These needs can be fulfilled only if God exists, and the Bible claims that they can be fulfilled in a relationship with Christ. Therefore, people who acknowledge these needs and the need for God to meet them have practical reasons to care about what Christian apologetics offers. Moreover, feelings of guilt indicate the human needs for forgiveness, reconciliation, and moral transformation. These needs must be satisfied before the needs for meaning and love can be satisfied. Since Christianity claims to meet these needs, people who acknowledge them should find Christian apologetics relevant. Finally, humans need to understand themselves and the world in which they live in order to meet these needs.

» **Basic Terms, Concepts, and Names**

Aristotle
Augustine
existentialism
Heidegger, Martin
Nietzsche, Freidrich
objective meaning
Pascal, Blaise
Sartre, Jean-Paul
subjective meaning

» **Reflection and Discussion**

» **Further Reading**

> O Lord, . . . you stir man to take pleasure in praising you, because you have made us for yourself, and our heart is restless until it rests in you.
>
> Augustine, *Confessions*, book 1, chap. 1, par. 1

One feature of postmodern culture is that many people care as much about relevance as they do about truth (some may even care *more* about relevance than they do about truth). Why should one care whether Christian beliefs are true? What is the relevance of Christian apologetics to human needs, desires, interests, and concerns? The purpose of this chapter is to answer this question. It argues that all humans have at least three basic needs that can be satisfied only if God exists: (1) the need for meaning, (2) the need for transcendence, and (3) the need for understanding. Moreover, the Bible claims (or implies) that each of these needs can be fulfilled in a relationship with Jesus Christ. If these things are true, then anyone who acknowledges them and recognizes himself or herself as having these needs will have a good reason to care about whether it is true that God exists and also whether the claims of the Christian faith are true. Consequently, Christian apologetics is relevant to some deep human needs. It involves the heart as well as the mind.[1]

The Need for Meaning

The existentialist philosophers of the last two centuries were eloquent in their articulation of the human need for a sense of meaning, purpose, and value in life and existence. Human beings have a built-in desire for their lives to count, to make a significant contribution to something or someone beyond themselves. People want to feel and be useful—to matter. Those

1. Though Kierkegaard rejected traditional apologetic methods (as shown in the previous chapter), he employed narratives portraying different modes of human existence (viewpoints and lifestyles) in an attempt to enable his readers to come to the conclusion that only the Christian way of life can satisfy human needs. See his *Either/Or,* 2 vols., trans. D. F. and L. M. Swenson and W. Lowrie (Princeton: Princeton University Press, 1962); and idem, *Fear and Trembling,* trans. H. V. and E. H. Hong (Princeton: Princeton University Press, 1983).

with a long-range perspective will say that they want to leave a legacy. This need is evident in both the satisfaction people experience through such things as work, family, social and political causes, and artistic creations and the dissatisfaction they have when their lives are devoid of such things. People without a sense of purpose in life are prone to depression, despair, and even suicide. A common reason for suicide is a feeling of being worthless.

The twentieth-century French atheistic existentialist philosopher Jean-Paul Sartre (1905–80) has actually done us a service by offering a plausible argument for the claim that if God does not exist, then human existence is objectively meaningless. His argument is that, for human existence to have a point (to be meaningful and valuable) outside whatever purposes humans create for themselves, there has to be a human nature or essence that precedes human existence and defines the objective value and purpose of human existence. But an essence of something is like a blueprint or plan for it, and there can be such a plan in advance of something existing only if there is a planner who can have this plan in mind. Therefore, if God does not exist, there is no superhuman, transcendent planner to determine a plan for the purpose of human existence. If God does not exist, then human existence is objectively meaningless.

Since Sartre denies the existence of God but not the human need for meaning, he concludes that human beings must create meaning and purpose for themselves by means of the choices they make. Here he is much like other atheistic or agnostic existentialist philosophers such as Friedrich Nietzsche (1844–1900) and Martin Heidegger (1889–1976). But is it really possible for human beings to create their own meaning, purpose, or value? And if this is possible to some extent, would such self-made meaning satisfy the fundamental and universal human need for meaning? Though these nontheistic philosophers believe that meaning can be constructed, their evaluation of the human condition shows that they are aware that such subjectively based meaning is ultimately unfulfilling. Sartre, Heidegger, and others use the words *anguish, forlornness,* and *despair* to describe the condition of human existence in a godless world. Surely they are right about this.

It follows that if God does not exist, then the fundamental and universal human need for objective meaning is unsatisfiable. Consequently, people who hope to satisfy this need have a good reason to hope that God does exist and to engage in an active investigation of whether he does. Furthermore, living in such a way as to seek meaning outside ourselves for the purpose of meeting this need makes sense only if there is a God who is the source of such objective meaning. Living in this way would give people at least a good reason to *believe* that there is a God (even if it does not necessarily give them a straightforward indication of the *truth* of this claim). This would put them in a position to search for reasons that might *justify* this belief. Along these lines, the great seventeenth-century French mathematician, scientist, and Christian apologist Blaise Pascal (1623–62) wrote in his *Pensées,* "Only two kinds of people are reasonable: those who, knowing God, serve Him with their whole heart; and those who, not knowing Him, seek Him with

> **People who recognize their need for meaning have excellent reasons to seek God and then to serve him once they have found him.**

their whole heart."[2] People who recognize their need for meaning and the dependence of meaning on God's existence have excellent reasons to seek God and then to serve him once they have found him.

Moreover, the Bible clearly claims that the human need for meaning and purpose can be satisfied in Christ. The teaching of Scripture about this matter is that God created human beings for the sake of fellowship with God (Acts 17:27) and with their fellow human beings (Gen. 2:18–24). He also created them to be stewards of the earth (Gen. 1:26–28). Though human sin constitutes an obstacle to the fulfillment of these purposes, the New Testament teaches that sinful people can be reconciled with God (Rom. 5:1–11), one another (Eph. 2:11–21), and creation (Rom. 8:18–22) through Jesus Christ. This reconciliation makes possible an eternal life of loving fellowship and service. Jesus says that this meaningful life he makes possible is a life that those who follow him may "have . . . to the full" (John 10:10). The life of Jesus himself is a model for this kind of life. It involves finding meaning and purpose through self-sacrificial and loving service to others. The best evidence that this claim is true can be found in the testimonies of Christians throughout the history of the church who have committed

2. Blaise Pascal, *Pensées*, trans. A. J. Krailsheimer (London: Penguin, 1966), #427 (p. 160).

themselves to Christ and to a Christlike way of life.

This biblical claim and corresponding testimonial evidence of its truth give people who recognize their need for meaning and the dependence of meaning on God's existence a good reason not only to hope that God exists and to make it a priority to find out whether he does but also to consider the case for the Christian faith as well. While other religious traditions may make similar claims backed up by similar testimonies, a reasonable person will put Christianity on the list of alternative worldviews to investigate. A comparison of the claims of alternative faiths can be accomplished only if each tradition is studied.

As argued, the human need for meaning provides excellent practical reasons to take steps to consider the case for both God's existence and the truth of Christianity. The existence of a fundamental and universal human need for objective meaning can also contribute to some theoretical reasons for thinking that God exists and that Christianity is true. These reasons by themselves do not amount to proofs or demonstrations. They are instead pointers, indications, suggestions, or hints of the reality of God and the truth of Christianity. First, the hypothesis that God exists and created human beings for the purpose of loving relationships with him and one another could *explain* the existence of this need (though of course much more would have to be said to make a case for the claim that this is the *best* explanation). Moreover, to the extent that this is the case, there is also good reason for believing that the *Christian* God created us. This is because, as explained above, Christianity takes this need into account and claims that it can be satisfied in Christ (though a thorough case of this sort would have to take other religious traditions into account as well). If God created humans to need meaning, then it makes sense that God would provide us with a means to satisfy this need. This is what Christ claims to do.

The Need for Transcendence

In addition to having a need for meaning, human beings also have a deep need for union with a reality that transcends them. In his *Confessions*, Augustine expresses this need in his opening prayer to God: "You stir man to take pleasure in praising you, because you have made us for yourself, and our heart is restless until it rests in you."[3] Blaise Pascal is reported to have made a similar claim by saying that every human being is made with a "God-shaped vacuum."[4]

It may be clear that human beings need to experience loving union with persons other than themselves. Many philosophers, both Christian and non-Christian, have observed the human need for personal relationships. Aristotle said that human beings are "political animals."[5] But it should also be clear to the sensitive participant in and observer of human interactions that these "horizontal" relationships alone do not ultimately fulfill the deep human longing for perfect and lasting intimacy, to love and to be loved with complete constancy and unconditional acceptance. Human

relationships are inevitably irregular and conditional. What humans need is to experience a "vertical" relationship with a person capable of loving them faithfully and completely. It seems clear that this need is capable of satisfaction only if God exists, since only God would have the loving nature that would make such love and acceptance of human beings possible. Given this, anyone who recognizes in himself or herself a need for a higher kind of love that transcends imperfect human love will have a good practical reason to explore the possibility that God exists. Whether God exists would then be relevant to such a person's felt needs.

Moreover, people who discern in themselves a need for union with a transcendent God have good reason to investigate the Christian faith. Both the Old and the New Testament portray God as a personal being who offers humans union with God in a loving relationship. In the Old Testament, God is portrayed in many ways that manifest his loving concern for humans and his desire to be united with them in fellowship. He is creator, redeemer, king, and provider. Even as disciplinarian and judge, God's intention is to prepare people, if possible, for renewed covenantal relationship with him. In the New Testament, Jesus portrays himself, or is portrayed, as creator (Col. 1:15), redeemer ("The Son of Man came to seek and to save what was lost" [Luke 19:10]), and so on. Especially in the Gospel of John, Jesus makes it clear that God wants to be united with human beings (3:16; 17:3) and that a relationship with Jesus is the means by which such a union can occur (14:6). It is also clear that union with Jesus is claimed to satisfy deep human needs. He is the source of living water (4:10–14), the bread of life

---

3. St. Augustine, *Confessions*, 1.1.1.

4. This appears to be a paraphrase of *Pensées*, #148 (p. 75): "This infinite abyss can be filled only with an infinite and immutable object; in other words by God himself."

5. Aristotle, *The Politics* (1253a1), trans. T. A. Sinclair, rev. ed. (New York: Penguin, 1981), 59.

(6:35), the good shepherd (10:11), and so on. The life Jesus offers his followers is both abundant and eternal. Therefore, people who recognize their need for loving union with a transcendent being capable of loving them as they need to be loved have a good reason to examine carefully the claims of the Christian faith.

As mentioned, people often discover their need for meaning both through the satisfaction they experience from meaningful activities and through the discouragement and even despair they undergo when they see themselves as not living worthwhile lives. Similarly, people find out they need to love and be loved through both rewarding human relationships and the absence of such ties and the loneliness this can engender. Moreover, people often become aware of their need for union with a transcendent, personal, loving being through the feelings of dissatisfaction they experience in merely human relationships, regardless of how relatively fulfilling these human encounters are. Human needs, therefore, are often manifested through emotional experiences. This general principle suggests that we may discover additional universal and fundamental human needs by surveying the range of universal and fundamental human emotional experiences.

In addition to the feelings of worthlessness, loneliness, and dissatisfaction already discussed, there is also the feeling of guilt. There was a period of time recently when certain schools in clinical psychology advocated the therapeutic eradication of guilt feelings on the ground that they are a form of neurosis brought about by unhealthy or dysfunctional childhood experiences and relationships. According to this view, guilt feelings are unhealthy

and should be permanently removed for the purpose of personal psychological health. However, any morally sensitive person knows that many feelings of guilt are legitimate, since they are the product of a person's awareness of having intentionally wronged another person. If I have purposely wronged someone, then I am (objectively) guilty of wrongdoing. If I am guilty, then it is perfectly appropriate for me to *feel* guilty. This feeling of guilt is useful, since it is an indication that I may well have done something wrong, and it is an uncomfortable feeling I will want to eliminate if possible. This feeling will motivate me to acknowledge any wrongdoing I have done and to take steps to undo, as much as possible, the effects of my wrongdoing. The feeling of guilt, therefore, is often a legitimate and useful feeling. Is this feeling an indication of a human need?

Notice that in each of the cases considered there is an uncomfortable emotion or feeling that can be characterized in terms of the absence of something we need. This is certainly the case when it comes to hunger and thirst, which are unpleasant sensations indicating the need for food and drink. Similarly, when we feel worthless or aimless, we are experiencing the need for meaning and purpose. When we feel lonely or unloved, we are experiencing the need for loving union with another person. When we feel dissatisfied with human relationships, we are experiencing the need for a loving relationship with a transcendent personal being capable of loving us as we need to be loved. What lack do we experience when we feel guilty?

The answer to this question is somewhat complicated. Part of what the guilt feelings express is a need not to have engaged in the wrongdoing in the first place. But once we have done it, it is impossible for us to undo it. What's done is done. We cannot change the past. However, though it is not possible to alter what has happened in the past, it is possible for the person wronged to alter his or her *attitude* about what has occurred in the past. People we have wronged can either carry a grudge or forgive us for what we have done to them. To the extent that our guilt feelings are accompanied by regret for what we have done, they reflect our need for forgiveness. This need has to do with our past. Guilt feelings are also indicative of two additional needs, the first a present need and the second an ongoing need for the future: the need for reconciliation with the person we have wronged and the need not to continue to be the kind of person who does wrong things (that is, our need for personal moral transformation). If we did not need these things, then why would we feel bad about the wrong thing we did?

These needs for forgiveness, personal reconciliation, and moral transformation are, like the needs for meaning and love, needs that cannot be met by human efforts alone. We can often successfully procure forgiveness and mend broken relationships to some extent on our own by means of apology and renewed commitment. We can also often make some gains in personal character development through a sincere desire for change and diligent effort. However, we learn eventually that we are incapable, through mere human means, of restoring relationships as thoroughly as they need to be and of making ourselves as good as we want and need to be. We are also sometimes aware of feelings of guilt for wrongs that were not done to a human being but that nonetheless require our being forgiven. Alternatively, many wrongs done to other humans may seem to involve more than just human relationships. All of this suggests three things. First, we need superhuman help if we are to stop doing wrong to others and damaging relationships with others. Second, our acknowledgment of failing to meet a standard that we tacitly allow to govern our actions and relationships reveals our (perhaps unwitting) submission to a higher, nonhuman moral authority (I will have more to say about such an objective moral standard in chap. 25). Finally, our sense of having done wrong that does not involve a human being (or that involves more than a human being) makes sense only if there is a personal reality beyond human persons that our behavior affects.

For these reasons, it is reasonable to think that the human needs for forgiveness, reconciliation, and moral improvement can be satisfied both completely and permanently only if God exists. Accordingly, people who find in themselves a need for these things and believe that these needs can be met only if God exists have a good practical reason to hope that God exists and to make an effort to find out whether there are good theoretical reasons for thinking he does. Moreover, there is a wealth of material in the Bible that demonstrates that Christianity is a religious tradition that claims to provide its adherents with an opportunity to satisfy once and for all their deep needs for forgiveness (1 John 1:9), reconciliation (2 Cor. 5:19, 21), and moral perfection (Rom. 8:1–4). Therefore, people who see themselves as having these needs have good reasons to look into the case for the Christian faith.

We are now in a position to see how a number of the things discussed in this chapter are tied together. The human need for meaning is a need for one to see his or her life as having a purpose, as making a contribution. This need is connected to the need for loving union with other persons. We cannot make a significant contribution unless we are engaged in loving relationships with other people. A contribution requires a recipient, a person who receives the contribution. For a contribution to be genuinely worthwhile, it must be a contribution motivated by love for the recipients. The contrary is true as well. For genuine loving relationships with other people to exist, meaningful interpersonal giving must take place. The needs for meaning and loving union can only be satisfied together.

But remember that the need for union is ultimately unsatisfiable apart from loving union with a transcendent loving person. This need can be satisfied only when we have a relationship with a divine person characterized by meaningful giving and receiving. This is where guilt comes in. Feelings of guilt are often an indication of real objective guilt, of wrongdoing. If there is a God who has a standard of moral perfection to which he holds us accountable, then our feelings of guilt are indications of our sin (wronging God). But if we are sinners and if a holy and righteous God exists, then our relationship with God is severed. We need to have our sins forgiven by God, we need to be reconciled to God,

and we need to be empowered to become the kind of morally perfect people we need to be to have fully loving relationships with God and other human beings. That is, our needs for forgiveness, reconciliation, and moral transformation need to be satisfied before our needs for meaningful and loving relationships with God and others can be satisfied. As before, all these observations give us excellent reasons to strive to determine whether a God capable of meeting these needs exists and whether Christianity is true.

It may have occurred to you that people whose needs for these things were met would be very happy people. This suggests that happiness is a matter, at least in part, of need satisfaction and that these needs in particular are among the needs that must be fulfilled for a person to be happy. But though the satisfaction of these needs is arguably individually necessary for true happiness, they do not seem to be jointly sufficient. Thomas Aquinas can help us here. In the first place, he distinguishes between natural happiness and supernatural bliss. The first is attainable by natural human means alone but is temporary and not completely fulfilling. The second requires a relationship with a wholly good and loving God. It requires supernatural assistance, and it is ultimately eternal and completely fulfilling. Aquinas characterizes it as "total immersion in absolute goodness *forever*."[6] If Aquinas is right, then the ideal form of happiness requires eternal life, and eternal life requires some form of personal immortality (or permanent re-

> ## The needs for meaning and loving union can only be satisfied together.

6. This is Norman Melchert's wording, emphasis added. See his *Great Conversation: A Historical Introduction to Philosophy*, 4th ed. (Boston: McGraw-Hill, 2002), 293, for a discussion of Aquinas on the topic of eternal bliss.

creation of the person in case of temporary annihilation [more on this in chap. 23]). Isn't it true that what we really desire is not merely meaningful and loving relationships made possible by forgiveness, reconciliation, and moral transformation but an *eternal enjoyment* of these things? This eternal enjoyment of these important goods is possible only if personal immortality is possible. All the needs discussed to this point, therefore, entail the additional need for the eternal ongoing existence of persons after their deaths. Again, eternal life is possible only if there is a God, and the New Testament clearly claims that life after death is possible through Jesus Christ (see, for instance, John 11:25–26; 14:1–4; 1 Cor. 15). There are additional reasons, therefore, to consider the question of God's existence and the truth of Christianity.

The Need for Understanding

The ancient philosopher Aristotle (384–322 BC) said that "all men by nature desire to know."[7] This desire is manifested in many ways. Aristotle mentions the enjoyment people receive simply from using their senses to discover things about the world around them. Moreover, to some extent, most if not all people like to be "in the know." They like to know what is going on at least in their family and their friendship group. Many are also curious about what is happening in the wider world. The proliferation of newspapers, magazines, and news sources on the Internet is evidence of this widespread human desire to know and understand human events. Furthermore, the presence in every culture of some kind of system of

7. Aristotle, *Metaphysics*, 1.1.

education, whether formal or informal, is evidence of the human recognition of the importance of learning and knowledge. In addition, our culture places a high value on the empirical sciences—important means of knowing more about the natural and the social world and thus understanding them better. Whether or not people are scientists, they generally have a great respect for science as a means of coming to know the truth about things both natural and social (though there is a postmodern suspicion in some quarters about any claim to know the truth about reality, as we will see in chap. 24).

In addition to all these exhibitions of the human desire for knowledge and understanding, the human needs already discussed also reveal the need for understanding ourselves, the world, and our place in the world. As shown, there is good reason to think that the needs for meaning, transcendence, forgiveness, reconciliation, transformation, fulfillment, and immortality can be met only if there is a God and that Christianity claims to offer the means by which all these needs can be satisfied. People who recognize these things have a good reason to engage in a process of intellectual exploration into the questions of God's existence and Christianity's truth. Let us take this one step further. If humans have fundamental needs that can be fulfilled only if a God exists who is able and willing to meet these needs, then it seems reasonable to assert that we thereby have a deep need (and not merely a good reason) to search for the truth about God with all the effort and intelligence we can muster. Such a search involves understanding the world, ourselves, and our place in the world (Is there a God in this world? If so, did God create me? If so, did God create me for a certain purpose? etc.). Consequently, if we have a need to know whether there is a God and to understand ourselves in relation to God, then we have a need for understanding. This kind of understanding has traditionally been the goal of philosophy, the sciences, and theology.

Just as the other human needs are arguably satisfiable only if God exists, there are at least two reasons for thinking that the need for understanding also seems to require the reality of God. In the first place, if there is no God, many things about ourselves and the world would remain inexplicable (and so not understandable). The next three parts of this book talk about a number of these sorts of things. Second, there is good reason to think that human beings could be capable of genuine understanding of reality and knowledge of the truth only if God is ultimately responsible for the existence and nature of human beings; if God exists, we can explain the possibility of genuine human knowledge and understanding in terms of God's pre-establishing a harmony between the human mind and the world. If knowledge involves an agreement between the mind and the world, then what explains the possibility of such an agreement? The hypothesis that God exists can explain this possibility. It is not clear that a purely naturalistic hypothesis can. If someone believes that nature is the only reality and that there is thus no designer of the world and of our minds, what reason would that person have for thinking that our minds can ever agree with the world in the way required for genuine knowledge of the world? Therefore, the general need for understanding itself generates a particular need to understand whether God exists.

The burden of this chapter has been to show that Christian apologetics is relevant to human needs. It has argued that important human needs can be met only if we can discover that there is a God and that Christianity is true. This is an investigation to which Christian apologetics can make an important contribution. Therefore, Christian apologetics is relevant to important human needs, and thus, there are good practical reasons to engage in the activity of Christian apologetics. The existence of these human needs can also provide us with good theoretical reasons as well. That is, just as reflection on these needs provides us with good reasons to *practice* apologetics, such reflection can also lead to good apologetical *theory* as well. The theory I have in mind is simply the claim that God exists and that Christianity is true. This theory can go a long way in explaining why human beings have the needs we have been discussing. Thus, we can look at the thesis of Christian theism as an explanation of the data of these human needs. Even more, we can hope to reason from our observation of these data to what could be argued is the *best* explanation of them: that God made human beings to need meaning, transcendence, understanding, and immortality and that because of human sin we need forgiveness, reconciliation, and transformation for these needs to be satisfied. The existence of these needs can be explained by the Christian doctrines of creation and sin just as their fulfillment can be explained by the Christian doctrines of the Trinity, the incarnation, the atonement, salvation, and resurrection. This foray into human psychology, therefore, has given us both motivation and materials with which to engage in Christian apologetics.

Reflection and Discussion

1. Have you ever felt that life is meaningless or that your life does not matter, or do you know people who have felt this way? Does it seem to you that this feeling is an indication that humans need a sense of objective purpose? Why or why not?

2. How would you try to persuade a nontheist that he or she has a need for loving union with a transcendent personal being?

3. Why would God have created us with a need for understanding that cannot be completely fulfilled because of all the things about the world, life, and God that we cannot fully explain?

Further Reading

Adler, Mortimer J. *Aristotle for Everybody.* New York: Touchstone, 1997.

Kreeft, Peter. *Heaven: The Heart's Deepest Longing.* San Francisco: Harper & Row, 1980.

Sartre, Jean-Paul. "Existentialism Is a Humanism." In *Existentialism: From Dostoyevsky to Sartre,* edited by Walter Kaufman, 345–68. New York: Penguin, 1975.

5

Ears to Hear and Eyes to See

Apologetics and the Heart

» **Outline**

- Foolish Hearts: Paul and Christian Apologetics
  - *Paul's Message in Romans 1:18–23*
    - The Relationship between Belief and Desire
    - How a Desire to Sin Can Lead to Unbelief
  - *Paul's Message in Romans 1:24–32*
    - How God Allows Humans to Experience the Consequences of Sin
    - The Role of Human Freedom and the Grace of God
- Restless Hearts: Augustine and Christian Apologetics
  - *God, Sin, Misery, and the Desire for Happiness*
  - *The Primacy of the Will over the Intellect*
  - *Practical Reasoning before Theoretical Reasoning*
- The Heart's Reasons: Pascal and Christian Apologetics
  - *Pascal on the Clarity and the Obscurity of Evidence for God*
    - The Role of Humility and Arrogance in God's Revealing
    - Enough Obscurity for Misery and Enough Clarity for Hope
  - *Pascal's Wager as Pre-apologetics*
    - The Wager Explained
    - How the Wager Can Prime the Heart for Apologetics

» **Summary**

What people believe can be influenced by what they want. People who want to keep sinning can be motivated to downplay or disregard evidence for God's existence and end up denying God's existence. God lets people experience the negative consequences of their sin both to respect their freedom and to motivate them to stop sinning and return to him. Since happiness requires communion with God, and sin separates people from God, sin leads to misery. Misery can lead people to search for happiness and to be open to the possibility that God exists and that Christianity is true. People with humble hearts are more open to evidence for God's existence and the truth of Christianity than are arrogant people. Pascal's wager can be used as a pre-apological tool to open minds and hearts to what Christian apologists have to offer.

» **Basic Terms, Concepts, and Names**

Augustine
John, St.
Pascal, Blaise
Pascal's wager
Paul, St.
practical reasoning
primacy of will over intellect
theoretical reasoning

» **Reflection and Discussion**

» **Further Reading**

> Even after Jesus had done all these miraculous signs in their presence, they still would not believe in him. This was to fulfill the word of Isaiah the prophet: "Lord, who has believed our message and to whom has the arm of the Lord been revealed?" For this reason they could not believe, because, as Isaiah says elsewhere: "He has blinded their eyes and deadened their hearts, so they can neither see with their eyes, nor understand with their hearts, nor turn—and I would heal them." Isaiah said this because he saw Jesus' glory and spoke about him.
>
> John 12:37–41; quoting Isaiah 53:1; 6:10

In this passage, John explains the reason some did not believe in Jesus even though he had performed miracles in front of them. These verses illustrate the fact that the same evidence is accepted by some and rejected by others as grounds for commitment to Christ. Even evidence provided by the Lord himself in the form of miracles fails to convince everyone. John's explanation for the unbelief of those who witnessed Jesus' miracles suggests that their lack of faith is a result of God's plan. John says that their unbelief occurred to fulfill Isaiah's prophecies. But one of the prophecies concerns God's blinding people's eyes and deadening their hearts. Why would God deliberately prevent people from seeing, hearing, and understanding the evidences, signs, hints, and pointers that would lead them to saving and healing conviction and commitment? Another passage of Scripture, found in the Epistle to the Romans, may shed light on this question.

Foolish Hearts: Paul and Christian Apologetics

After greeting the Roman church, expressing his longing to visit them for the first time, and affirming his desire to preach the gospel to them there, Paul launches into an affirmation of God's wrath against humankind:

> The wrath of God is being revealed from heaven against all the godlessness and wickedness of human beings who suppress the truth by their wickedness, since what may be known about God is plain to them, because God has made it plain to them. For since the creation of the world God's invisible qualities—his eternal power and divine nature—have

been clearly seen, being understood from what has been made, so that people are without excuse. For although they knew God, they neither glorified him as God nor gave thanks to him, but their thinking became futile and their foolish hearts were darkened. Although they claimed to be wise, they became fools and exchanged the glory of the immortal God for images made to look like mortal human beings and birds and animals and reptiles.

Romans 1:18–23 TNIV

Here Paul makes the following claims: (1) God has *revealed himself* in the created order in such a way that it contains evidence adequate to enable everyone to come to know God's nature (and, by implication, God's existence and will for their lives), but (2) sinful people have *suppressed this truth* by means of their sin. Consequently, what otherwise would have been evident to their minds, by virtue of God's making it sufficiently clear for them to see, hear, and understand, has been rendered ineffective as evidence because of their willful rebellion against God's will for them. What we will is what we desire, what we desire is what we love, and what we love is a result of the condition of our hearts. What this passage indicates about human beings is that our hearts affect our minds. What we believe and know is often a result of what we desire and love.

How does this work? A person who not only is a sinner but also *enjoys* being a sinner (this is not necessarily the way such people would describe their situation, of course) will be disinclined to want to have reasons for thinking he or she ought to stop sinning. Such a person, rather, will be intent on downplaying, discounting, and even denying such reasons. But whoever has a reason to believe that a God exists

What we believe and know is often a result of what we desire and love.

who disapproves of sin and holds sinners accountable for their sinful behavior has a good reason to think he or she ought to stop sinning. Therefore, people who enjoy sin will reject reasons to believe in God (or at least reasons to believe that a God exists who places moral demands on people) if they can. But how can people do this when, as Paul says, God has made *plain* to them what can be known about him? Humans can do this because we have the capacity to distort and then deny evidence that is clear to a more objective observer when our interpretation of the evidence is influenced by what we *want* to be true.

We see this (and experience it) all the time in life. A wife whose husband comes home late with lipstick on his collar and smelling of perfume believes his fabricated excuse because she does not want to believe he is having an affair—she has too much at stake. Of course, she may have other reasons to think he is faithful that make this belief reasonable and rational, but she has been interpreting the evidence in his favor for some time now. At a certain point, the evidence that he is having an affair becomes too overwhelming to be reasonably understood in another way. But by then, she has made such a large number of judgments to the contrary that what would be clear to an impartial observer is not clear to her at all. Here is a case in which evidence that is clear to one person is unclear to another. What makes the difference is that the latter has constructed a theory motivated more by a desire to preserve her marriage than to know the truth. The same is true of sinful humans who care more about continuing to sin than about knowing the truth about God and themselves.

How does this truth about human psychology help us understand why God would deliberately prevent people from seeing, hearing, and understanding evidence they need to be saved, as suggested by the passage from the Gospel of John quoted above? The rest of the first chapter of Romans will help us discern the answer:

> Therefore God gave them over in the sinful desires of their hearts to sexual impurity for the degrading of their bodies with one another. They exchanged the truth of God for a lie, and worshiped and served created things rather than the Creator—who is forever praised. Amen. Because of this, God gave them over to shameful lusts. . . . Furthermore, since they did not think it worthwhile to retain the knowledge of God, he gave them over to a depraved mind, to do what ought not to be done. They have become filled with every kind of wickedness, evil, greed and depravity. . . . Although they know God's righteous decree that those who do such things deserve death, they not only continue to do these very things but also approve of those who practice them.
>
> verses 24–26, 28–29, 32

Paul's point in a nutshell is that, as a result of humans' sinful suppression of the truth about God, God "gave them over" to "sexual impurity" (v. 24), "shameful lusts" (v. 26), and "a depraved mind" (v. 28). To say that God gave them over to sinful hearts and minds is to say that God allowed them to experience unhindered the full extent of the consequences

of their sinful choices—consequences of their thinking, willing, and behaving. It is reasonable to interpret the passage from John (and Isaiah) discussed above in light of this Pauline passage. God's act of blinding eyes and deadening hearts is simply God's means of sustaining and preserving the consequences people face who have devoted themselves to sin instead of to him.

Why does God uphold these negative consequences? Why doesn't he graciously intervene to save sinners from them? One important point to make here (as Paul himself goes on to make to the Romans) is that God *has* graciously intervened to save sinners by becoming incarnate in Jesus of Nazareth and dying on their behalf on the cross. But this saving work by itself does not mean that those whom God has given over to depraved minds will automatically have the futility of their minds and the darkness of their hearts reversed. God's work in Christ does not in itself guarantee this psychological transformation because sinful people must *freely choose* to accept God's offer of salvation in Christ before they can be free of the sin that prevents them from seeing the truth. Here is an affirmation that is fundamental in many ways to the whole enterprise of Christian apologetics: God has made us genuinely free, and his love for us prevents him from overriding that freedom, even to rescue us from sin, death, and eternal damnation. Whatever God does to persuade us to accept his offer of salvation, his efforts to bring about this goal stop short of coercion.

But then how can the efforts of Christian apologists to persuade unbelieving sinners to accept the truth of the Christian faith and submit their lives to Christ be effective if these people have been given over by God to the consequences of their suppression of the truth? What makes this especially problematic is that, as Paul explains to the Romans later in his letter to them, not only have all sinned (3:23), but all are *slaves* to sin apart from God's grace (6:6–19). To be a slave to sin is to be unable not to sin. If one cannot avoid sin, then one is also stuck with the consequences of sin. We have seen that one of the consequences of sin is the suppression of truth about God. So a slave to sin is incapable of seeing the truth about God. Anyone who is not free to stop sinning is also not free to see the truth about God. In the end, it is a mystery how God in his grace reverses this situation without overriding human freedom, but it seems clear that he makes use of the efforts of evangelists, apologists, and the Holy Spirit in the process. Let us turn now to Augustine for help in seeing how the light of God's grace and the natural light of human reason can overturn the sinful heart's darkening of the mind.

Restless Hearts: Augustine and Christian Apologetics

The sinner blinded by sin to the truths about God needed for salvation might be forever stuck in this condition were it not for another important consequence of sin and life apart from God: misery. As shown in chapter 4, in the first paragraph of his *Confessions*, Augustine affirms in prayer to God that "you stir man to take pleasure in praising you, because you have made us for yourself, and our heart is restless until it rests in you."[1] Augustine then goes on to document his own restlessness and

misery apart from God as an illustration of the plight of humankind in general. Augustine's remarks highlight three important truths: (1) God made humans to be capable of lasting happiness only by being united with him; (2) this explains why sin, which is a way of being and living in separation from loving communion with God, is the cause of human unhappiness; and (3) God is actively involved in an attempt to "stir man to take pleasure in praising" him. Augustine makes it clear that one important way in which God does this is by allowing sinful human beings to experience the full extent of their unhappiness apart from him.[2] As a result, humans are motivated to search for happiness, and their desire to alleviate their suffering leads them to look for wisdom, which is simply what one needs to know in order to be happy. History shows that this search for happiness and wisdom takes people in many directions. Nonetheless, God the Holy Spirit is continually at work drawing people to him and away from other things.

This Augustinian account of the human search for happiness and wisdom can be explained in terms of his thesis of the primacy of the will over the intellect. His view is that people use their intellects in the pursuit of wisdom only because they want to be happy, that is, only because it is their *will* to find a lasting good. People are moved to use their intellects to find the truth about what is good because they want to be happy, and they think they can

1. Augustine, *Confessions*, 1.1.1.

2. There is support for Augustine's idea in the Bible. In Hosea, after God denounces the Israelites for their sin, he says, "Then I will go back to my place until they admit their guilt. And they will seek my face; in their misery they will earnestly seek me" (5:15).

be happy only by discovering what is truly good. Augustine uses the word *love* to talk about the pursuit and enjoyment of things people consider good. Loving what someone takes to be good is a function of what Augustine calls the heart. A person with a restless heart is a person who loves something good other than God, the ultimate and eternal Good. What such people need is for their hearts to be turned away from lesser goods and toward God. Such people (sinners) need to experience a *conversion* of their hearts. In sum, restlessness, unhappiness, and misery lead to a desire for happiness. This desire in turn brings about a will to find what is truly good (something that will truly satisfy). This willing to find something good (which involves the heart's loving goodness) engages the intellect in a search for the truth about what is really good. There is an important sense, therefore, in which, in the search for truth, the will precedes the intellect.

Augustine's view about the relationship between the intellect and the will should be distinguished from that of many philosophers who think that the intellect has primacy over the will. According to this view, one first relies on intellect or reason alone to discover the truth about what is really good, what will make one truly happy. Only when one discovers this truth does one will to live on the basis of it. The problem with this approach, as far as Augustine is concerned (and here he agrees with Paul), is that the proper use of intellect and reason depends on the proper orientation of the will (or condition of the heart). Again, people who love to sin (though not necessarily the way they would put it) will employ their intellectual resources to construct a rationale to justify the godless way of life to which they have

become accustomed. Such a rationale will surely be inconsistent with belief in the Christian God. The use of reason in the search for wisdom about how to be happy requires an openness of the heart to the possibility of the truth of the Christian worldview.

At this point, it is important to point out that in following Augustine by saying that the proper use of the intellect requires a prior act of will or condition of heart, I am not suggesting that there will be no *reasons* for which this act of will is made (or condition of heart adopted). My point is only that the use of reason or intellect cannot be fully adequate without some prior change of heart on the part of the sinner. An opening of heart of the sort required will surely be the result of a process involving some thinking and reasoning. An example of the sort of reasoning that might have this result is the following: "It's clear that the way I've chosen to live my life has made me unhappy. I want to be happy. Therefore, I should investigate some alternative ways of living." This kind of reasoning is more *practical* than *theoretical*, since its immediate goal is a course of action (a practice) rather than a change of belief (a theory). Another Christian thinker who saw the value of practical thinking for Christian apologetics and who also has something to say about the relationship between the mind and the heart is Blaise Pascal.

The Heart's Reasons: Pascal and Christian Apologetics

Pascal was a brilliant scientist and mathematician who also aspired to write a book on Christian apologetics. Though he died before he could write it, many of the thoughts he jotted down on small pieces of paper in preparation for writing it have been preserved and collected in what has become known as Pascal's *Pensées* (*pensées* is the French word for thoughts). One of these *pensées* picks up the theme, developed above, of the influence of the sinful desires of the heart on the operations of the mind in regard to evidence for the truth of Christianity. It also touches on the need for God to graciously intervene to reverse this dynamic:

> The prophecies, even the miracles and proofs of our religion, are not of such a kind that they can be said to be absolutely convincing, but they are at the same time such that it cannot be said to be unreasonable to believe in them. There is thus evidence and obscurity, to enlighten some and obfuscate others. But the evidence is such as to exceed, or at least equal, the evidence to the contrary, so that it cannot be reason that decides us against following it, and can therefore only be concupiscence and wickedness of heart. Thus, there is enough evidence to condemn and not enough to convince, so that it should be apparent that those who follow it are prompted to do so by grace and not by reason, and those who evade it are prompted by concupiscence and not only by reason.[3]

For Pascal, as for John, Paul, and Augustine, reason alone is never *sufficient* to convince unbelievers of the truth of the Christian faith. What is needed for reason to be effective is a change of heart prompted by God. At bottom, this change of heart must involve a recognition of dis-

satisfaction with the way of life they have chosen and, what is more, doubt that they are sufficient by themselves to live a fulfilling life. People are capable of experiencing such changes in attitude only if they are humble. Pascal thinks that a certain degree of humility is required not only for a person to come to faith in Christ but also for at least some people (those with a need for convincing philosophical arguments) to be able to exercise their reason in such a way as to become convinced on the basis of it that Christianity is true. Pascal would say that the "blinding of sinners" by God can be explained in terms of God's allowing prideful people to experience the consequences of their arrogance in the form of a diminished ability to see the truth about God and what he expects of them. Pascal thinks God has a reason for this. Two *pensées* express these ideas:

> We can understand nothing of God's works unless we accept the principle that he wished to blind some and enlighten others.[4]

> God wishes to move the will rather than the mind. Perfect clarity would help the mind and harm the will. Humble their pride.[5]

Another *pensée*, which shifts the metaphor from one of God blinding sinners to one of God hiding himself from them, sheds light on these thoughts:

> If there were no obscurity man would not feel his corruption: if there were no light man could not hope for a cure. Thus it is not only right but useful for us that God should be partly concealed and partly

---

3. Blaise Pascal, *Pensées*, trans. A. J. Krailsheimer (London: Penguin, 1966), #835 (p. 286).

4. Ibid., #232 (p. 101).
5. Ibid., #234 (p. 101).

revealed, since it is equally dangerous for man to know God without knowing his own wretchedness as to know his own wretchedness without knowing God.[6]

As is often the case with Pascal's *pensées*, this one needs some explaining. What people need more than anything is to know and to love God. For this to happen, they need both to acknowledge the sin (corruption, wretchedness) that separates them from God and to humbly repent of this sin. If God were clearly to reveal himself to *unrepentant* sinners, such people might know God but would not be capable of loving him. This possibility of knowing God without being able to love him is the first danger of which Pascal speaks. Therefore, God partly conceals himself in obscurity from such people. As a result, these people can feel the misery, restlessness, and wretchedness that attend their sin and separation from God. This negative experience can put them in a position to want their lives to be better and to want to be better people—to look for something to make them happy and good. In such a state, people are open to the possibility that God exists and that the Christian faith is true. If God did not reveal himself with an adequate degree of clarity, people in this position would not be able to hope that their desire for ultimate and lasting happiness will be satisfied. Such people would know that they are miserable (wretched) without knowing God. This knowledge of wretchedness without knowledge of God is the second danger of which Pascal speaks. But God does reveal himself to such people with some degree of clarity. People in this condition are capable of seeing and appreciating

the evidences God provides. Therefore, we can see that God has good reasons for deliberately making humans live in conditions of evidential ambiguity. This divine plan explains why reason alone is never *sufficient* to convince an unbeliever of the truth of the Christian faith.

As implied above, Pascal thinks that reason is not only insufficient, at least in the form of philosophical arguments, but also *unnecessary* to bring *some* people to saving faith in Jesus Christ.[7] For some people with certain intellectual needs, however, arguments of this sort *are* required. It was for the non-Christians in this group that Pascal developed his famous wager. Often this wager is discussed by Christian apologists as a strategy to employ with non-Christians *after* they have discussed the arguments both for and against the Christian faith with them, but they are unconvinced one way or the other. This post-apologetical maneuver may be effective. However, some Christian apologists overlook the effective role it can play relatively early in a conversation with non-Christians even *before* the theoretical arguments have been considered. This pre-apologetical strategy takes us back to the distinction made in the last section (on Augustine) between practical and theoretical reason.

Recall that practical reasoning is reasoning about what to do as opposed to reasoning about what to think (theoretical reasoning). Practical reasoning often appeals to what is in the best interest of

---

6. Ibid., #446 (p. 167).

7. Ibid., #380 (p. 138): "Do not be astonished to see simple people believing without argument. God makes them love him and hate themselves. He inclines their hearts to believe. We shall never believe, with an effective belief and faith, unless God inclines our hearts, and we shall believe as soon as he does so."

the reasoner. That is, a person engaged in practical reasoning will often reason on the basis of what he or she expects to get out of the courses of action he or she is considering. There are a number of reasons why a Christian apologist would do well to encourage an unbeliever to engage in practical reasoning about his or her life at the beginning of a conversation about the Christian faith. First, most people need a practical reason to be convinced that it is worth their while to spend time discussing abstract, theoretical, philosophical arguments, even about such important matters as the meaning of life and death and the existence of God. Second, sin makes people basically selfish, and so the most effective strategy is to enable people to see that a discussion of the rationality of the Christian worldview has something in it for them. Third, the principle of the primacy of the will over the intellect (the heart over the mind) shows that important truths about God can be sufficiently understood and appreciated only when a person wants to change his or her life. But reasons to want to change one's life are practical reasons; therefore, practical reasoning needs to occur before theoretical reasoning.

Pascal's famous wager is an example of practical reasoning. It is based on the assumption that the theoretical evidence for and against the existence of God is such that it is just as probable that God exists as that he does not exist (an assumption I will provide reasons to deny in part 2): There is a 50 percent chance that God exists and a 50 percent chance that God does not exist. Moreover, when it comes to belief in God and one's consequent way of life, there are really only two options: (1) to believe that God exists and to live

a life of devotion and service to God or (2) not to believe that God exists and to live however one wants to live (notice that this is consistent with atheism [the belief that God does not exist] and agnosticism [suspending belief about whether God exists], since what they have in common is not believing that God exists).[8] There are, therefore, two options for belief, each of which we assume is just as probably true as the other. Since it will turn out either that God exists or that there is no God, there are four possible combinations of belief and outcome. Let's talk about a person named Sam, who considers the wager:

1. Sam believes that God exists, and it turns out that God does exist.
2. Sam does not believe that God exists, and it turns out that God does exist.
3. Sam believes that God exists, and it turns out that God does not exist.
4. Sam does not believe that God exists, and it turns out that God does not exist.

A look at the Bible shows that if the Christian God exists, he will reward those who truly believe in him and live their lives for him (i.e., those who demonstrate true biblical faith in Christ) with an eternal, blissful life, and he will punish those who do not believe, trust, and obey with eternal damnation (see, e.g., Matt. 25:31–46). Given this, if we continue to think in terms of a bet or a wager, we can ask ourselves

8. A third possible option is to believe that God exists but to live one's life as if God does not. For the purposes of the wager, this can be categorized as a way of choosing the second option. This makes sense on the plausible assumption that how we live is an indication of what we *really* believe, regardless of what we may think or say we believe.

what the expected "payoff" would be for each of the four belief/outcome combinations enumerated above. The following table summarizes the payoffs (the numbers refer to the combinations):

	God Exists	God Does Not Exist
Sam Believes	1: An infinite positive expected payoff (Sam's eternal bliss)	3: At worst, a finite negative expected payoff (less fun here)
Sam Does Not Believe	2: An infinite negative expected payoff (Sam's eternal torment)	4: At best, a finite positive expected payoff (more fun here)

Should Sam take steps to believe in and live for God or not? The answer to this question can be determined by doing two simple calculations that take account of the equal probability of each of the two outcomes (God exists or God does not exist). What Sam stands to gain by believing in and living for God can be calculated by looking at the first row of the table. We will add together each of the two expected payoff values in that row multiplied by .5 (representing the 50 percent degree of probability that it is true): .5 (infinite positive expected payoff) + .5 (finite negative expected payoff) = an infinite positive expected value. We can do the same thing with the bottom row: .5 (infinite negative expected payoff) + .5 (finite positive expected payoff) = an infinite negative expected value. The operative principle here is that whenever you add a finite negative value to an infinite positive value, you wind up with an infinite positive value. Similarly, whenever you add a finite positive value to an infinite negative value, you get an infinite negative value. Clearly, Sam should take whatever steps he can to believe in and live for God rather than not to do so.

People who wager on God in this way are not acquiring theoretical reasons to believe that God exists. Instead, they are engaging in practical reasoning of the heart-changing variety. These people are doing more than merely betting that God exists. They are *wanting* it to be the case that God exists. They are *hoping* that God exists. They are therefore open to the possibility that God exists and consequently are able to appreciate evidence for God's existence that they would otherwise dismiss. Wagering on God in Pascalian fashion, therefore, is a good way to prime one's heart for maximal benefit from what Christian apologetics has to offer.

Christian apologetics is just as much about the heart as it is about the mind. Moreover, as the next chapter shows, the condition of one's heart affects not only what one thinks about the evidence available but also the way in which one asks questions about the Christian faith.

> **Wagering on God in Pascalian fashion is a good way to prime one's heart for maximal benefit from what Christian apologetics has to offer.**

Reflection and Discussion

1. Can you think of times in your life when your desire to sin hampered your belief in God or your ability to trust God? Do you know other people whose sinful choices have produced doubt or unbelief in their lives?
2. How have your personal struggles played a role in restoring or strengthening your relationship with God? How can reflection on life's challenges contribute to apologetical conversations?
3. In what specific ways could you use Pascal's wager to help someone become more open to the possibility of God's existence or the truth of the Christian faith?

Further Reading

Augustine. *Confessions*. Translated by Henry Chadwick. New York: Oxford University Press, 1991.

Pascal, Blaise. *Pensées*. Translated by A. J. Krailsheimer. New York: Penguin, 1966.

Schreiner, Thomas R. *Romans*. Baker Exegetical Commentary on the New Testament. Grand Rapids: Baker, 1998.

6

Critics, Seekers, and Doubters

Audiences for Apologetics

» **Outline**

- **Pilate: A Critic's Insincere Questions**
  - *Pilate Models an Insincere Question (What Is Truth?)*
  - *Appeal to the Mind or Appeal to the Heart?*
  - *How Practical Reasoning Can Make Insincere People Sincere*
- **The Ethiopian Eunuch: A Seeker's Sincere Questions**
  - *How Seekers Recognize Their Limits and Needs*
  - *The Role of Mind and Heart in the Birth and Growth of Faith*
  - *How Doubts Can Creep In Even after Faith Takes Root*
- **Thomas: A Doubter's Sincere Questions**
  - *How Doubters Differ from Critics and Seekers*
  - *Doubt as Intrinsically Bad but Instrumentally Good*
  - *How Doubt Can Be Instrumentally Bad*
  - *The Causes of Doubt and the Treatment of Doubt*

» **Summary**

Among those with questions about Christianity are critics, doubters, and seekers. Since the minds and hearts of critics are closed, they ask insincere questions about the Christian faith. Their questions are motivated by a desire to resist Christian claims. Critics can become seekers by means of practical reasoning that opens their minds and hearts. Seekers ask sincere questions about the Christian worldview. Because seekers recognize their intellectual limits and their dependence on others for understanding, they have humble hearts and an attitude that can lead to faith. Doubters are Christians who have sincere questions about Christianity that prevent them from sustaining confident Christian belief. Though doubt is intrinsically bad, it can be instrumentally good. Doubt is instrumentally bad when it leads to permanent unbelief. How doubt should be treated depends on whether it is based in the mind or rooted in the heart.

» **Basic Terms, Concepts, and Names**

critics
doubters
insincere questions
instrumentally good/bad
intrinsically good/bad
seekers
sincere questions

» **Reflection and Discussion**

» **Further Reading**

> What is truth?
>
> > Pilate (John 18:38)
>
> Tell me, please, who is the prophet talking about, himself or someone else?
>
> > the Ethiopian eunuch (Acts 8:34)
>
> Unless I see the nail marks in his hands and put my finger where the nails were, . . . I will not believe it.
>
> > Thomas (John 20:25)

Christian apologetics will be needed as long as there are questions, doubts, or concerns about the truth of Christian claims. There will be such queries, objections, and complaints until we see the Lord face-to-face. Until then, we "see but a poor reflection as in a mirror" (1 Cor. 13:12). Among the people with questions are critics, seekers, and doubters. *Critics* are those with criticisms of the Christian faith who are not open to the possibility of its truth. *Seekers* are people who are open to Christian belief but are prevented from making a commitment primarily because of honest concerns about Christian claims. *Doubters* are Christians who find it difficult to believe one or more Christian tenets with complete confidence. Christian apologetics is needed as long as there are people in any of these three categories.

Critics need to be answered both to neutralize the effects of their criticisms on seekers and doubters (and Christians who are potential doubters) and to try to persuade them to become seekers (though this persuasion will not be a purely intellectual task, as we saw in the previous chapter). Seekers need resources to remove intellectual obstacles to their faith and to set the stage for Christian commitment once the obstacles have been removed (that is, they need the weeding and watering provided by a Christian apologist). Doubters need to be restored to full Christian conviction by giving them the tools to remove their doubts. This may involve both undermining objections to Christianity that concern them and supplying them with more reasons, arguments, and evidences to shore up their commitment (again, weeding and watering). The ultimate goal in each case is to cultivate Christian commitment: to help people embrace the gospel of Jesus Christ as fully as they possibly can.

For our purposes, then, there are basically three kinds of people who raise questions about the truth, rationality, or credibility of the Christian faith. These are insincere non-Christians (critics), sincere non-Christians (seekers), and sincere Christians who have doubts (doubters). Three biblical characters illustrate these three types of people.

Pilate: A Critic's Insincere Questions

As reported in the Gospel of John, during his cross-examination of Jesus, Pilate asks him two questions: (1) Are you the king of the Jews? and (2) What is truth? In the context, Pilate does not really seem to be interested in knowing the answers to these questions. If anything, he is more interested in finding out what Jesus *claims* the answers to these questions are. In any event, Pilate's ultimate goal appears to be avoidance of having to deal with Jesus. Therefore, Pilate's questions are examples of *insincere* questions. A person asks an insincere question when that person is not really interested in knowing what the answer to it is.

Many non-Christians ask insincere questions about the truth, rationality, or credibility of the Christian worldview. In light of the points made in the previous chapter, their true motivation, whether they realize it or not, is often, like Pilate's, to avoid having to take the claims and commands of Christ seriously. Insincere questions with this sort of motivation are often covert *claims*: Though phrased in the form of a question, they are really asser-

> **A person asks an insincere question when that person is not really interested in knowing what the answer to it is.**

tions in disguise. For instance, consider the question, Why does God permit evil and suffering? This question is often a veiled attempt to imply that there is no God. A Christian's inability to answer the question satisfactorily is taken to mean that there is no reason for evil and suffering (a reason that would have to exist if there were a God).

Effective Christian apologetics requires discernment of the difference between insincere and sincere questions. A Christian apologist must decide in a given case whether to raise practical questions that address the heart or theoretical questions that appeal to the mind. As shown in the previous chapter, if a person enjoys a life of sin, then he or she will be motivated to suppress the truth and to dismiss evidence about God. In such a condition, the person will not benefit from considering a purely intellectual or theoretical case for the Christian faith. Such a person needs, as we saw, a change of heart. To bring about a change of heart, it is more effective to engage in practical reasoning of the sort involved in Pascal's wager, for practical reasoning is more closely tied to the emotions than is theoretical reasoning. If the question is, How should I live my life? and I reason as Pascal suggested, in the end I will be moved to adopt a given way of life on the basis of this practical reasoning not only because I have a reason but also because of a way I feel as a result of having this reason. The previous chapter offered a number of examples of relevant emotions. Misery, restlessness, and wretchedness are among the negative emotions. To these we can add fear and anxiety (ones that the Christian philosopher Kierkegaard discusses at length in his writings). Positive attitudes and emotions can also accompany practical reasoning of the Pascalian sort. Strong desire, hope, and humility are among them.

Combined with the appropriate attitudes and emotions, the right kind of practical reasoning can effect a change of heart that can turn an insincere questioner into a sincere questioner. A sincere questioner genuinely wants to know the answer to the question he or she asks. Such a person wants to know the truth. When it comes to questions about the truth, rationality, and credibility of the Christian faith, such a person is genuinely open to the possibility that God exists and that the Christian faith is true. Let us turn now to an example, from the New Testament, of such a person.

The Ethiopian Eunuch: A Seeker's Sincere Questions

While Pilate is a good example of a critic (one without faith in Christ who, though he asks questions about Jesus, does not really want to know the answers), the Ethiopian eunuch is a good example of a seeker (a non-Christian who asks sincere questions about God, the Bible, or Jesus because he wants to know the answers and is willing to act on them). The story of the Ethiopian eunuch is found in Acts 8:26–40. Philip, a member of the Jerusalem

Christian fellowship, was led by the Holy Spirit to a desert road south of Jerusalem. There he came in contact with an important Ethiopian official who was heading back to Ethiopia after having worshiped in Jerusalem. The eunuch was reading out loud from the book of Isaiah. When Philip heard him reading, he asked the Ethiopian if he understood what he was reading. The Ethiopian responded by saying, "How can I, . . . unless someone explains it to me?" (v. 31). He then invited Philip to join him in his chariot, and Philip proceeded to share with him the good news about Jesus, starting with an interpretation of the passage in Isaiah the eunuch had been reading. Their encounter culminates in the Ethiopian's request to be baptized and his resultant rejoicing.

Let's try to glean from this story a profile of this representative seeker that we may apply to a broader range of seekers. In the first place, the Ethiopian was engaged in activities that manifested some level of faith in God even if not yet a specific faith in Jesus, God incarnate. These activities include worship at the temple in Jerusalem and reading God's Word in the form of the prophet Isaiah. These outward behaviors suggest an inner positive orientation of heart and mind toward God and the truth about God. Second, the Ethiopian invites Philip to help him understand the passage of Scripture he is reading. He admits that he does not understand it and that he needs help interpreting it. This admission implies two important things about seekers in general, one that concerns an assumption they make about their minds and another that concerns an attitude of their hearts. Both distinguish them from critics. First, the intellectual assumption made by seekers is that they are incapable of understanding on their own everything it is important for them to understand. The Ethiopian admits that he is incapable of understanding Isaiah on his own. A critic would claim either that he does not need help understanding or that if there is something he does not understand, it is not important enough to understand. The second, related point is that the Ethiopian shows by what he does and what he says that he has a heart attitude of humble awareness of his need for God and others. Even before Philip came along, he was worshiping God. To worship God is, in part, to express one's dependence on God and God's superiority. The Ethiopian was also reading the Scriptures, presumably not merely for entertainment or even just for instruction but also for edification. This purpose is suggested by the manner in which he interacts with Philip and the joyful way in which he responds to being baptized. A critic does not recognize or acknowledge a need for God in this way.

These two characteristics of seekers—an acknowledgment of their intellectual limitations and a humble openness to help from God and others—are aspects of an attitude of *faith*. Again, this is not necessarily faith in Jesus Christ. It is also not even necessarily faith in God. It could be merely a receptivity to some higher power or supernatural reality. Of course, this kind of faith is not sufficient for salvation, but something like it does seem to be at least minimally necessary. Moreover, this faith is a response to an encounter of some kind with God. In the person of the Holy Spirit, God initiates such "meetings," and those to whom God reveals himself in this way can choose to respond favorably or unfavorably. As sinners, our natural re-

sponse will not be a positive faithful one but instead a negative and rebellious one. Before our hearts are softened by God's gracious love, we will resist turning from sin and submitting to God. In such a state, our hearts and minds will be affected by sin, as already discussed. This influence of sin will often manifest itself in a tendency to think we can figure things out for ourselves and that we really have no need for special help from others. In other words, a sinful and unfaithful response to God will be characterized by prideful and stubborn independence. It will involve effectively putting ourselves in the place of God in terms of our knowledge and abilities. But at times, perhaps times of suffering, doubt, or discouragement, we will be more open to responding to God with something very much like faith—a recognition of finitude and an attitude of dependence. Then we become, at least temporarily, seekers, like the Ethiopian eunuch.

This discussion illustrates how it is that both the mind and the heart are involved in the *birth* of faith. The mind and the heart also have a role to play in the *growth* of faith as a means of discerning the truth about God and Jesus—a means of knowledge about spiritual things. The more our minds and hearts are transformed by God's grace, the more they can work together to enable us to discern God and truths about God. In the first place, the more we are freed by God from the power of sin, the more we will want to know about God and how he wants us to live (this is primarily a contribution of the heart). Second, the more we learn about God, the more we will learn about ourselves in contrast to God (this is primarily a contribution of the mind). The more aware we are of God's infinite power, knowledge, and love, the better we can understand the limits of our own abilities, wisdom, and concern. When we realize that we cannot know and understand everything we would like to know and understand, we will be more open to being taught by someone who knows more than we do. Third, the more we allow ourselves to be transformed by God's grace, the more we will become like God in what we love and value, and the more we are like God in this way, the better able we will be to recognize God and the things of God. This is because what we see, notice, or pay attention to is often influenced or determined by what we really care about.

I was just talking with a person who has very fragile bones. As a result, he cares very much about whether there are obstacles in his environment that will cause him to stumble and break a bone. He tends to notice potential obstacles much more frequently than he used to because he cares so much about preventing injury to his bones. In the same way, a person who loves God and cares about the things of God will be more attuned to the presence of God and more likely to discern truths about God. In this sense, faith is a skill—even an intellectual skill—as well as an attitude. It is an art, and like any art, it can be practiced, honed, and perfected as well as neglected, weakened, and lost.

Seekers whose sincere questions are answered to their satisfaction are in an excellent position to respond with faith to the preaching of the gospel and to give their lives over entirely to the lordship of Christ. After all, by the time they get to this point, it is likely that their minds and hearts have already been transformed by their ongoing faithful responses to God

as God has pursued them and met them in various ways in the person of the Holy Spirit. By that time, they will be like a garden expertly prepared by the master gardener to receive the seed that will grow into saving faith in Christ. But even after this preparation and reception, just as every garden is subject to attack by insects, drought, and other threats to healthy growth, a Christian may have additional sincere questions that will lead to doubt. The Ethiopian eunuch, who went on his way rejoicing, can become the doubting Thomas, who would not believe until he could see for himself.

Thomas: A Doubter's Sincere Questions

Thomas was one of the twelve original disciples of Jesus. So he was with Jesus throughout Jesus' earthly ministry and heard what Jesus said and saw what Jesus did. He was, however, not present with the other disciples to whom Jesus appeared after his resurrection (John 20:24). As a result, he had not actually seen the risen Lord with his own eyes as the others had. Instead of believing on the basis of his friends' testimonies that Jesus had been raised from the dead, he said he would not believe unless he saw and touched Jesus' crucifixion wounds (v. 25). About a week later, Jesus appeared to them again, and this time Thomas was included (v. 26). After greeting them, Jesus turned immediately to Thomas and invited him to see and touch his wounds so that Thomas would "stop doubting and believe" (v. 27). Instead of touching Jesus' wounds, Thomas responded simply by exclaiming, "My Lord and my God!" (v. 28). Then Jesus pointed out that, though Thomas believed as a result of seeing Jesus alive after having died, anyone who believed (that Jesus is Lord and God) without the benefit of physically seeing him would be blessed (v. 29). The implication is that these latter people (most Christians) would believe, at least in part, on the basis of the *testimony* of those who, like Thomas (and John), had seen Jesus alive again (v. 31).

I have classified Thomas as a doubter, a Christian who has sincere questions about the truth of an (important) aspect of the Christian faith. However, though he was a disciple of Jesus, it is not completely clear that he was a Christian (as we call believers in Christ today) at the time of his doubts. He had certainly been a loyal follower of Jesus (see John 11:16), but he had not yet responded in faith to an encounter with the risen Christ. But we do not need to settle this question for our purposes. Whether Thomas was a Christian at the time of his doubts or not, his plight at that time is similar to that of many Christians who find themselves with serious doubts about their faith.

Thomas was certainly not a critic, as I have defined this word, in spite of the emphatic nature of his demand for both visual and tactile evidence that Jesus was indeed alive (John 20:25). In other words, he does not ask whether Jesus is alive without really wanting to know the answer—as demonstrated by the spontaneous nature of his outburst of faith upon seeing Jesus. At the same time, his sincere question is not motivated merely by intellectual curiosity. Though he wants to believe, he is a serious doubter. His being a genuine doubter rather than merely a questioner is evidenced by the fact that he did not trust his associates' insistent testimonies that

they had seen the risen Jesus with their own eyes, even though he had lived with them intimately for three years. He also was skeptical enough to require, initially, that Jesus pass both a visual and a tactile test, even though his fellow disciples had come to believe solely on the basis of sight. He is, then, like many seekers and like many doubters, though not like all of these. Not everyone has the same standards of evidence, and some people may require more or less evidence at different times in their lives (Thomas had already stood out from his fellows as especially skeptical [see John 14:5]).

Interestingly, in spite of his initially stringent evidential standard, Thomas apparently is satisfied on the basis of seeing alone. As soon as Jesus invites him to see and to touch him, Thomas starts believing even though he does not touch Jesus. All his doubts evaporate merely as a result of seeing the risen Lord. As the New Testament commentator Leon Morris puts it when commenting on this encounter, "We often make a mistake about what will enable us to recognize what we are looking for."[1] These observations suggest the following principles that would seem to apply to doubters (sincere Christian questioners): (1) People have different evidential standards—different ideas about the kinds and amounts of evidence that are required to satisfy them that Christianity is true—and yet (2) people may end up being satisfied with less evidence (or a different kind of evidence) than they originally believed they needed. (3) It is okay for followers of Jesus to question and even to doubt in some circumstances (such as when the evidence or the ground for their belief is

1. Leon Morris, *Expository Reflections on the Gospel of John* (Grand Rapids: Baker), 716.

really inadequate). After all, Jesus does not criticize or scold Thomas for doubting but rather offers him the evidence he is looking for. However, (4) doubting (not believing with full confidence, not having complete faith) is not the ideal condition for Christians, and Christians should deal with their doubts by looking for and responding appropriately to the available evidence. This need to move beyond doubt is implied by Jesus' admonition to Thomas to "stop doubting and believe" (John 20:27). Also, (5) there is faith-producing power simply in being in the presence of Christ, but (6) since our current experience of the presence of Christ is not *physical* but *spiritual*, we need to rely as well on the testimony of those who were eyewitnesses of the resurrected Christ. This need for eyewitness testimony makes the New Testament, especially the Gospels, an important resource for producing and strengthening faith, as we will see in chapters 13–15.

Let's spend a bit more time talking about whether doubt can be a good thing for Christians. It is helpful here to distinguish between two ways in which something can be good. Something can be good in itself and for its own sake (intrinsically good) or good as an instrument or tool to get other good things (instrumentally good). Since ancient times, philosophers have debated about what things are intrinsically good, and that debate continues today. Among the things that have been defended as intrinsic goods are happiness, pleasure, and knowledge. A good, uncontroversial example of an instrumental good is money. Money is not the kind of thing that is worth having just for its own sake. Rather, what makes money valuable is that it can be used for the purpose of getting other good things.

Let's apply this distinction to doubt. Doubt seems not to be an intrinsically good thing. As a matter of fact, it seems to be an intrinsically *bad* thing. Considered by itself, it seems to be the kind of thing that, by its nature, is something people are better off not having. Nevertheless, it seems clear that doubt can be an *instrumentally* good thing. In other words, there are certain good things that experiences of doubt can help Christians to attain. The most obvious example is growth in faith. If our doubt is intellectual, we have a question about the Christian faith for which we do not have an answer. Doubting can be instrumentally good when our experience of it motivates us to seek, and hopefully find, an answer to such a question. Even if we do not find a completely satisfactory answer, our experience of searching for one may have the good result of helping us to learn to live with an unanswered (or not fully answered) question.

But doubt can be instrumentally bad too. It can lead to other bad things. At worst, it can lead a person to experience a complete loss of faith and to reject Christ (or at least to drift away from Christian commitment). I am sorry to say that I have seen this consequence occur occasionally with students of mine. When I first met these students, they were confident believers. As time went on, they became doubters. Unfortunately, their experience of doubt did not lead to a strengthening of their Christian commitment but to a weakening of it. In some cases, these former students have become critics of Christianity. Because of this potential outcome of doubt, it is important to deal with doubt and to deal with it in good ways.[2]

How best to deal with doubt depends on what is causing it. There can be intellectual causes (unanswered questions) and more practical causes (unfulfilled desires). We have already seen in chapter 5 how both the mind and the heart are operative in both belief and unbelief. It is important to see that they can both be factors in doubt as well. This psychological dynamic is why it is important, when experiencing doubts about the faith, to find ways to satisfy both our minds and our hearts. Christian apologetics can help us with our intellectual concerns, but Christian experience in the form of devotion, fellowship, worship, and service is important when it comes to the heart. Thomas provides a good example of a person who made good use of both of these sorts of resources. For intellectual purposes, he listened to alleged witnesses, clearly stated his own criteria of evidence, and continued to be open to a convincing presentation of more evidence. For experiential purposes, he stayed with the fellowship of believers. This is an important lesson for Christians who want to maximize their chances of strengthening their faith rather than losing their faith as a result of doubting.

Now that we have looked at three biblical characters who illustrate the general categories of critics, seekers, and doubters, it is time to turn to a discussion of the questions about the Christian faith that these people are likely to ask. These questions can be divided into questions about commitment to God (part 2), commitment to God in Christ (part 3), and

2. See Gary R. Habermas, *Dealing with Doubt* (Chicago: Moody, 1990), for more along these lines.

> **How best to deal with doubt depends on what is causing it. There can be intellectual causes (unanswered questions) and more practical causes (unfulfilled desires).**

Christian commitment and the Holy Spirit (chaps. 20–21 in part 4). In other words, we can organize the questions of critics, seekers, and doubters into questions about the three persons of the Trinity. Moreover, the responses of Christian apologists to the questions in each of these three areas can be separated into two groups depending on whether the appropriate strategy is to set the stage for Christian commitment (watering) or to remove obstacles to Christian commitment (weeding).

As we engage in this apologetical watering and weeding, we will be using both our minds and our hearts. The last two chapters discussed the need for both apologists and their audiences to have tender hearts. Apologists need soft hearts to earn a hearing, and their hearers need humble hearts to accept the claims of the Christian faith. At the same time, both need tough minds to engage in a sufficiently careful and critical presentation and consideration of the arguments and evidences for Christianity. Many of the arguments for and against the Christian faith are relatively abstract and sometimes difficult to understand and evaluate. I will attempt to make them as simple and as clear as I can without making them simplistic and shallow. Prepare to use your mind to think hard about them. Along the way, I will occasionally appeal to your heart as well, to remind you that our goal is not merely to solve an intellectual challenge but also to cultivate a commitment to Jesus Christ as whole human beings.

Reflection and Discussion

1. Can you think of times in your life when you have been a critic, a seeker, or a doubter? What did it take at the time to move you toward being a believer?
2. Are there ever good reasons to engage in intellectual conversations with critics about the Christian worldview? If so, what would some of these reasons be?
3. What specific steps can doubters take (in addition to those mentioned in this chapter) to make sure their experiences of doubt have good results rather than bad ones?

Further Reading

Habermas, Gary R. *The Thomas Factor: Using Your Doubts to Draw Closer to God.* Nashville: Broadman & Holman, 1999.

Lewis, C. S. *Surprised by Joy.* San Diego: Harcourt/Harvest Books, 1966.

Martin, Michael. *The Case against Christianity.* Philadelphia: Temple University Press, 1991.

Part 2

Commitment to God

7

The Global Village

Worldview Options

» **Outline**

- **A World of Difference: Worldview Families**
  - *How Apologists Are Limited in Their Attempt to Show the Rationality of the Christian Worldview*
  - *Three General Worldview Classification Questions*
  - *Four Major Worldview Families*
- **Carl Sagan's Lonely Cosmos: Naturalism**
  - *Naturalists on What the World Is Like*
  - *Naturalists on Why a World Exists*
  - *Naturalists on How Humans Fit into the World*
    - The Nature of Human Beings
    - The Origin of Human Beings
    - The Destiny of Human Beings
- **A "New" Age of Oneness with God: Pantheism**
  - *The History and Influence of Pantheism*
  - *Pantheists and What the World Is Like*
  - *Pantheists on Why a World Exists*
  - *Pantheists on How Humans Fit into the World*

» **Summary**

The Christian worldview is only one of a number of incompatible worldviews. The goal of ambitious apologetics is to show that the Christian worldview is rationally superior to all the worldviews with which it competes. Apologists should realize their limits in the achievement of this goal. All worldviews belong to one of three relatively abstract worldview families. The supernaturalism worldview family contains monotheist and polytheist worldviews. The other two worldview families are metaphysical naturalism and pantheism. Each of these worldviews has a view about what the world is like, why a world exists, and what place human beings have in the world. Naturalism gives an account of these things on the assumption that there is no divine reality, and pantheism characterizes the universe as identical with God.

» **Basic Terms, Concepts, and Names**

Democritus
Epicurus
Hegel, Friedrich
impersonal reality
materialism
metaphysical naturalism
monotheism
necessary being
panentheism
pantheism
personal reality
polytheism
process theology
Sagan, Carl
supernaturalism
Whitehead, Alfred North
world, the
worldview family

» **Reflection and Discussion**

» **Further Reading**

> They worshiped other gods.
>
> 2 Kings 17:7

A World of Difference: Worldview Families

Among the questions people are likely to ask about the Christian faith is whether a God exists of the sort that Christians claim to serve and worship. Christians believe specific things not only about what kind of being God is in and of himself but also about how God is related to the universe. Some non-Christians agree with Christians about these things, but others disagree. These disagreements reveal a number of alternative worldview families—various general ways of thinking about God and God's relationship to the universe. The *members* of worldview families are more specific major religious traditions (such as Christianity, Judaism, Islam, Hinduism, and Buddhism) and well-known philosophies of life or ideologies (such as secular humanism and Marxism). The chapters on religious pluralism (chaps. 18–19) say more about these particular faiths (though not these philosophies). This chapter and the next are only about the *families* of which these traditions are members. This section explains how these different worldview families can be classified by means

of how they answer a few basic questions about God and the universe. We then look at four of the families in more depth, two in this chapter and two in the next.

As already discussed, the purpose of Christian apologetics is to show that there are adequate reasons for believing that the Christian worldview is true. If a case of this sort can be made for Christianity, then it follows that adequate reasons exist for thinking that all the worldviews that are incompatible with the Christian faith (all the worldviews that contradict an essential doctrine of Christianity) are false. Therefore, if we can give adequate reasons for believing that Christianity is true, we will have thereby shown the rational superiority of the Christian worldview over all the worldviews with which it competes (this was called ambitious apologetics in chap. 1). It seems reasonable to think that giving adequate reasons for thinking that Christianity is true requires a comparison of the Christian worldview with the worldviews with which it competes. Of course, to do so, we need to know (1) what these other worldview options are and (2) how they differ from the Christian worldview. The purpose of this chapter and the next is to investigate these questions in a general and systematic way.

Before we proceed, however, it is worthwhile to consider briefly some important limitations to which Christian apologists are subject when they attempt to make a case for the rational superiority of the Christian worldview over all those with which it competes. The best possible case of this sort would be made by a person who has (1) studied each worldview thoroughly (so he or she would have a complete understanding of each perspective), (2) seriously endorsed each of these worldviews for a time (so he or she would have a full appreciation for each point of view), and (3) could be completely objective in the comparative assessment of these alternative visions of life and reality (so he or she would be as fair and rational as possible).[1] But it is clearly impossible for anyone to satisfy even one of these conditions. Christian apologists, therefore, have to do the best they can to understand, appreciate, and evaluate each worldview given the limitations that prevent them from realizing this ideal.

With this caution in mind, let us now consider two questions that will help us generate a classification of worldview families. The first question is, Does anything other than the universe (nature) exist? Let us call a worldview that answers this question affirmatively a member of the supernaturalism worldview family. This is the family of those worldviews that claim the existence of a divine reality or realities above and/or beyond nature (the prefix *super-* means "above" or "beyond"). There are two major subdivisions in this

---

1. See John G. Stackhouse Jr., *Humble Apologetics* (Oxford: Oxford University Press, 2002), for a similar list of qualifications for this purpose.

> **Christian apologists have to do the best they can to understand, appreciate, and evaluate each worldview.**

worldview family. These subdivisions are determined by how the worldview answers question 2: Is there only one ultimate and supreme supernatural reality? Those worldviews that answer question 2 affirmatively are members of the monotheism worldview family. Those worldviews that answer question 2 negatively are members of the polytheism worldview family. These titles are easy to explain by looking carefully at the parts that compose them. Theism is a label for any view that affirms the existence of some kind of divine reality. *Mono-* means "one," and *poly-* means "many," so monotheism is the view that there is only one God above and/or beyond nature, and polytheism is the view that there is more than one god above and/or beyond nature. The next chapter briefly explains why monotheism is rationally superior to polytheism before making a case for the version of monotheism of which Christianity is an instance.

Worldviews that answer question 1 negatively agree that nothing exists above and/or beyond nature or the universe. These worldviews fall into two major categories, depending on how they answer question 3: Is nature divine? Those worldviews that see nature as divine are members of the pantheism worldview family. Pantheism is the view that all or everything (pan-) is identical to God (-theism) or is a part of God. Those worldviews that deny both the existence of a separate God above and/or beyond nature and that nature or the universe is itself God (or a part of God) are members of the metaphysical naturalism family.[2]

The characterizations of these worldview families are relatively abstract and ideal. They are primarily a result of philosophical thinking about the nature of the world and its inhabitants. As such, they do not necessarily reflect both accurately and completely what people in different religious traditions or who subscribe to different ideologies actually think or say. Nonetheless, it is important to begin an evaluation of the Christian worldview by placing it within its general philosophical framework and comparing and contrasting this framework with those of other religious traditions and ideologies. In doing this comparative and evaluative work, it is only fair to describe these frameworks in as complete, clear, and charitable a way as possible so as to consider them in the best possible light, even if those who hold these ideas do not always formulate and express them as fully, consistently, or abstractly as done here.

Carl Sagan's Lonely Cosmos: Naturalism

Before his untimely death, Carl Sagan was professor of astronomy and space studies and director of the Laboratory for

Planetary Studies at Cornell University. He created a TV series about the universe titled *Cosmos*. He later wrote a book with the same title based on the series. The premise of both the TV show and the book is Sagan's pronouncement that "the Cosmos is all that is or ever was or ever will be."[3] Since he was not a pantheist, this remark is a clear statement of metaphysical naturalism. A naturalist says that only nature exists: There is nothing, like God for instance (or gods or the divine), above and/or beyond nature.

In addition to the three questions already asked and on the basis of which we classified the worldview families under investigation, there are three additional questions that every worldview family (and worldview) answers. A worldview is a view or perspective on the world. *World* here means not the planet earth or even the entire universe (which we called nature) but everything that exists (so for the monotheist, the world contains both the universe and God). These three additional questions, therefore, are each about the world in the sense of everything there is: (1) What is the world like? (2) Why does the world exist? and (3) How do human beings fit into the world?[4] How do naturalist worldviews answer these three questions?

First, what would naturalists say the world is like? All naturalists are materialists. That is, all naturalists believe that the only reality there is—nature (the uni-

2. Metaphysics is the branch of philosophy that studies the nature of ultimate reality. Metaphysical naturalism, then, is the worldview family according to which a godless nature is the only reality there is. All the worldview families are, of course, metaphysical views, at least in part. This one features the word *metaphysical* in its name to distinguish it from other kinds of naturalism, such as methodological naturalism, which is discussed in chaps. 10, 14, and 22.

3. Carl Sagan, *Cosmos* (New York: Random House, 2002), 1. This is the very first sentence of the book.

4. See Peter van Inwagen, *Metaphysics* (Boulder: Westview, 1993), 4–5, for a more extensive discussion of these questions and both monotheistic and naturalistic answers to them.

verse)—consists in matter in motion.[5] According to this view, everything is (nothing but) a material or physical object moving around in empty space.[6] This was the view of the ancient Greek atomists such as Democritus (460–370 BC) and Epicurus (341–270 BC). It has also been the view of a number of other thinkers throughout history. Today, it is perhaps the dominant secular (nonreligious) worldview family (the members of which include secular humanism and Marxism, for instance).[7] Materialists (also sometimes called physicalists) believe that, ultimately, all facts about the world are physical facts, just as all things in the world are physical things; everything that is and happens in the world is ultimately explainable in terms of the interaction of physical things. Given this view of the world, physics is the most basic of all the sciences, and the other sciences (like chemistry, biology, and the social sciences) are in some sense dependent on or derivative from physics. Consequently, the ultimate laws governing the world are physical laws. Some believe these laws are deterministic—that everything that happens in the world at a given time is the inevitable result of the overall state of the universe just prior to that time and the natural or physical laws governing what happens in the universe. Others think the laws are not deterministic. But even they would say that what happens in the world happens with a high enough degree of regularity to be predictable—at least it would be from the standpoint of someone who knew everything about the universe at a given time. The world, therefore, according to naturalists, is a big, regular, material machine—and nothing else.

Second, how would naturalists explain *why* a material world exists (this question is about the *cause* of the world rather than the *purpose* of the world)? Here naturalists have a choice between (1) taking the position that a material world has always existed—in some form or other—and (2) opting for the view that at some point a material world just began to exist for no reason at all without having been caused by something else (after all, according to their view, there *is* nothing else). This latter alternative, which some naturalists have recently endorsed,[8] would mean the material world came to exist out of absolutely nothing. A material world could not have brought itself into existence, since that event would have required it to have existed before it existed, which is obviously impossible. Other natural-

5. Though it is conceivable that nature consists in immobile and/or immaterial things, most naturalists—if not all—would reject these possibilities. Also, matter in motion is a relatively loose way of talking about the ultimate constituents of physical reality posited by contemporary physicists. These include not only material particles but also at least forces, fields, energy, and space-time.

6. The theory of relativity has challenged commonsense ideas about what it is for a material object to "move around in empty space."

7. An indication of the prevalence of naturalism today, at least in academic circles, is the following statement in the preface of a recent short introduction to the scientific field of physical cosmology: "The subject matter of cosmology is everything that exists" (Peter Coles, *Cosmology: A Very Short Introduction* [Oxford: Oxford University Press, 2001]). This claim, reminiscent of Sagan's pronouncement quoted above in the text, entails metaphysical naturalism by assuming that it is not a part of cosmology to study God or any other supernatural reality. The author could easily have worded this sentence so as not to imply metaphysical naturalism by saying that the subject matter of cosmology is everything *physical* that exists.

8. Such as Quentin Smith in William Lane Craig and Quentin Smith, *Theism, Atheism, and Big Bang Cosmology* (Oxford: Clarendon, 1993), 135.

ists say that a material world has always existed, perhaps not in its present form or even close to its present form, but in some form or other.[9] In this case, the question, Why does a material world exist? does not really have an answer—at least if it is taken to be an inquiry about what reality outside the material world brought this world into existence in the first place (since, according to these naturalists, it has always existed). If the question is instead interpreted to mean Why does a material world *continue* to exist? then of course it cannot be answered in terms of something outside it that sustains its existence, since the material world, according to naturalists, is the only reality there is. Therefore, the only kind of answer naturalists can give to the question, Why does a material world exist? is either Because it does! or Because it has to! The first response is not really an explanatory answer. The second one is, however. Later, we will have an opportunity to decide whether it is a *good* explanatory answer.

Finally, what is naturalists' answer to the question, How do human beings fit into the world? We can make this question more precise by reformulating it to ask about the (1) nature, (2) origin, and (3) destiny of the human species (and of individual members of this species). As for human nature, given that naturalists have already said that the entire world consists only of material objects in motion, they are committed to the claim that the same is true of human beings as well. Therefore, human beings are—like everything else that exists—nothing but relatively complex configurations of matter in motion. It is true that humans differ from other kinds of composite physical objects in various ways. Unlike rocks and like plants and non-human animals, humans are living, biological organisms capable of nourishment, growth, and reproduction after their own kind. Unlike plants and like nonhuman animals, humans are capable of self-initiated motion in response to information about their environment that they receive by means of their senses. And unlike non-human animals, humans are capable of thinking and acting on the basis of *reasons* of which they are consciously aware. Thus, humans are distinctive among the world's inhabitants in virtue of being living, sensing, self-moving, and *reasoning* material objects.[10] But this distinctiveness of humans, according to naturalists, does not make them fundamentally different *in kind* from the other things that exist in the world. They are only different in kind

9. The relatively recent version of the big bang theory of the origin of the universe should not be thought of as a theory explaining why there is a material world rather than nothing at all. It should instead be considered an attempt to explain why the material world exists in its present dynamic form (i.e., why the material objects that compose the world are distributed the way they are and are moving in relation to one another the way they are). The big bang theory is a *scientific* theory that purports to explain the current behavior of the parts of the world relative to one another in terms of an initial arrangement of matter rather than a philosophical (metaphysical) theory that explains the origin of matter in the first place. The question, Why does a material world exist? is this latter sort of question.

10. Some naturalists downplay or even discard reason and consciousness as being either unimportant or illusory. They instead explain reason and consciousness in purely physical and/or chemical terms. Many philosophers think that a purely physical account of consciousness is impossible, and some Christian apologists formulate an argument for God's existence as the best way to explain the existence of human consciousness (see Lee Strobel, *The Case for a Creator* [Grand Rapids: Zondervan, 2004], chap. 10, for an argument along these lines).

in a more superficial way or merely *in degree*. Everything in the world is fundamentally the same *kind* of thing: a moving (or potentially moving) material object. But things of this kind exist with differing degrees of the organizational complexity of their component physical parts. There is a connection between complexity and function: Things can be put on a continuum from the relatively simple (e.g., subatomic particles) to the relatively complex (human beings) in such a way as to show that there is a correlation between degree of organizational complexity and possession of increasingly sophisticated kinds of capacities (e.g., life, self-motion, sensation, rationality). A large part of naturalists' theoretical project is to explain how all these capacities can be accounted for entirely in terms of differing degrees of organizational complexity.

What is the origin of these sophisticated material machines? What accounts for their existence? Where did they come from? There is both a general naturalist answer and a specific naturalist answer to these questions. The general answer—an answer given by those naturalists who deny that the world came from absolutely nothing—is that since a material world has always existed and consists in nothing but matter in motion, there has been an infinite extent of time during which it has been possible for smaller bits of matter to move together in various ways so as to form larger composites of matter in a variety of configurations. During this eternal period of time, a large number of such different combinations has existed. Because the parts of these complex objects continue to move in various ways, the existence of the wholes made up of these parts is only temporary. Just as they came

into existence at a certain time, so also at a certain time they will go out of existence. Their parts will simply move in such a way as to compose new configurations, which themselves will exist temporarily before coming apart to form still other kinds of complex material things. Moreover, these ongoing migrations and recombinations of bits of matter (and energy) are entirely accidental, since there is no agent moving them together and apart for a purpose. If the world is deterministic, then there is only one possible state of the universe at each instant given the prior overall state of the universe and the laws of nature. But it is possible for things to (1) be caused by events that necessitate them and yet (2) not happen for a reason or purpose. Therefore, the general answer to the question about the origin of human beings is that they are accidental temporary results of the ongoing motions of matter—as are all the other composite things that exist.

But how did these specific sorts of things—these living, sensing, self-moving, and rational material objects—come to exist at this specific time? What is the specific process by means of which the material parts that compose human beings moved together to constitute a composite material object with these capacities? The naturalist answer to this specific question about the origin of human beings is, of course, biological evolution by means of random mutation and natural selection. I will not explain and discuss this answer now, since we consider it in chapter 10, to some extent, and then more thoroughly in chapter 22. For now, it will suffice to say that naturalistic evolutionary theory is the only theory currently available to naturalists as a specific explanation of the origin of human beings.

We finish the description of naturalism by examining what naturalists say about the *destiny* of human beings. So far we have seen that naturalists characterize human beings as nothing but accidental, evolved, and temporary highly complex biological (and therefore physical) organisms capable of rational thought and action (and therefore also sensation and self-motion). Where will objects with such an origin and nature end up? As for *individual* human beings, it is clear that their existence will terminate at the point of physical death (the cessation of biological functioning essential for life). If to be an individual human being is to be nothing but a functioning biological organism of a certain sort, then a human must cease to exist when the organism with which he or she is identical stops functioning. Moreover, the body or corpse that remains will inevitably be annihilated as a result of undergoing the ravages of decomposition, decay, and disintegration. According to naturalists, eventually the material parts that compose humans will be distributed throughout the biosphere. At some point, they will enter into other composite material things, and the cycle of composition and decomposition will continue forever—even if the universe as we know it should cease to exist.

It is less clear what naturalists would say about the destiny of human beings as a *group*. This depends to some extent on the choices humans make, the eventualities of the process of biological evolution, and the destiny of planet earth, the solar system, and the universe itself. Though there is disagreement among naturalists about specific outcomes in these areas, all agree that the universe will not always continue to support living systems and consequently that the human species will eventually cease to exist.

It is difficult to rehearse these implications of naturalism for the destiny of human beings without pausing to shift from the relatively abstract and intellectual focus of our discussion so far to a more personal and emotional orientation. If some member of this worldview family is true, the deep hunger of the human heart for ultimate meaning, lasting love, and eternal fulfillment will remain unsatisfied and will one day cease to exist along with all those who have experienced these fundamental yearnings. This extinction of human hopes and dreams would leave a vast, silent, and indifferent cosmic wilderness as the only reality forever. Instead of the everlasting light and warmth of God's unquenchable love, there would be only the darkness and coldness of a dying and uninhabited universe. Though these reflections do not provide theoretical reasons for believing that naturalism is false, they do offer heart reasons for hoping that there is more to the world than a godless nature.

> **This extinction of human hopes and dreams would leave a vast, silent, and indifferent cosmic wilderness as the only reality forever.**

A "New" Age of Oneness with God: Pantheism

Though metaphysical naturalism is at least as old as ancient Greek atomistic materialists such as Democritus, it was not widely accepted until quite recently. Pantheism is a worldview family that is at least as old as naturalism but has been more generally endorsed from early on in the form of various ideologies and religious traditions. It continues to be a dominant perspective among many people today. Recall that pantheism is the claim that there is a God or divine reality but that nature (the universe) is either identical with God or a part of God. Therefore, according to the pantheist, the world (everything that exists) is really ultimately only one thing, and this one thing is God.

In the history of thought, pantheism has been propounded by thinkers in both the West and the East. In the West, philosophers such as Heraclitus (c. 535–c. 475 BC), Parmenides (c. 515–c. 450 BC), the Stoics, Plotinus (AD 204–70), Spinoza (1632–77), and Hegel (1770–1831) had pantheistic views about the nature of ultimate reality. In the East, the philosophers/theologians Sankara (AD 788–820) and Ramanuja (1017–1137) developed pantheistic Hindu views of reality.[11] The relatively marginal status of these Western pantheistic philosophers and the substantial influence of these Eastern thinkers on common understandings of Hinduism have led many to think of pantheism as primarily, if not exclusively, an Eastern perspective. However, at least two things have led to the increasing influence of pantheistic thinking in the West. First is the relatively recent introduction of Hinduism to the Western world as a result primarily of the British colonization of India. Second, the more recent emergence of New Age spiritualities that employ pantheistic language to characterize the world and human experience has made pantheism a viewpoint to be reckoned with in the West.

It is convenient to think of pantheism as being halfway between naturalism and supernaturalism. This is because naturalists say that the world is just *one* thing: nature. Pantheists say that the world is just *one* thing: nature and God.[12] And supernaturalists say that the world is at least *two* things: nature and a separate God (or gods). From a Christian standpoint, there is an important sense in which pantheism is a move in the right direction. However, there are good reasons for thinking that it does not go *far enough* in the right direction. Why is it a move in the right direction? There have always been a number of important things about the world and human beings that naturalists have had a tough time explaining adequately. These include the existence of a material world, the apparent design of the universe and of many things within it, the existence of living things, and various characteristics of human beings such as consciousness, sensation, rationality, intelligence, voluntary action, meaningful communication, morality, and the enjoyment of beauty for its own sake. How can we explain the existence of these things if the world is nothing but a big material machine? It would be much easier to explain such things if the world itself had similar attributes from which these characteristics somehow come. If nature is really a divine reality of some kind rather than merely matter in motion, then it seems that these features of the world and of human be-

11. Chap. 19 discusses these Hindu theologies.

12. Spinoza preferred to say that the world is nature *or* God. He believed that what it is best to call it at a given time depends on the perspective with which one is thinking about it.

ings can be much more easily accounted for. Divinizing nature would also seem to provide a basis for hope that there is something in the world that can fill the emptiness of the human heart.

But can a pantheist worldview account for these features of the world and support this hope for human fulfillment? We will be in a better position to answer this question if we apply the same questions raised about the naturalist worldview family to the pantheist worldview family. What do pantheists say about (1) what the world is like, (2) why the world exists, and (3) how human beings fit into the world?

The most general pantheist answer to the first question is, of course, that the world is divine. Pantheists also agree that the world is eternal in the sense of being uncreated and indestructible. Here they agree with many naturalists. But pantheists have a reason for this position that is not available to naturalists. Whereas many naturalists hold that the world is eternal because otherwise it would have had to come out of absolutely nothing, pantheists affirm the eternality of the world on the grounds that it is divine and that it is essential to the nature of what is divine to be immortal or eternal.

Beyond this general and abstract summary, it is difficult to find a list of more specific characteristics of this eternal divine world about which pantheists concur. However, unless we say something about what it means for the world to be divine beyond its eternality, we have not really provided a meaningful distinction between pantheism and the version of naturalism that affirms the eternality of the world. An additional important attribute of the divine that will help to distinguish these perspectives is unity. According to naturalists, there

is only *one* material world, but it is one *material* world. A material world is, by its nature, actually or potentially multiple. It either consists in many things, or it can be divided up in such a way as to be constituted by many things. Contemporary physics tells us that the universe and the things in it consist of a staggering number of very small particles in addition to a lot of energy and some fundamental forces and fields. These disparate kinds of things are unified only in the sense that they are subject to a relatively small set of physical laws that are the same throughout the universe. According to the naturalist view, there is no single absolutely unified *thing* or *being* to which everything is identical or of which everything is a part. In contrast, the kind of unity pantheists attribute to God (and so also ultimately to the world) is a true absolute unity that allows no possible division into separable parts. Indeed, in the case of some pantheists, the divine world is ultimately devoid of all qualities whatsoever.[13] What is the nature of this simple, unified, indivisible, eternal, divine world?

Perhaps the only additional agreement among pantheists is that it is *conscious*. If it is conscious, then it must have or be a mind or something like a mind. As a mind, it is capable of rational thought and knowledge. It is natural to think of such a minded being as a person or "personal." However, some pantheists, such as the Hindus who follow Sankara, think of the divine ultimate real-

13. This is the view of Sankara, who formulated a Hindu theology called Advaita Vedanta. Vedanta is a philosophical theory about ultimate reality (Brahman) based on the Hindu Vedic texts. Advaita means nondualist. Therefore, the basic idea of this Hindu philosophy is that there is only one reality—Brahman—which is the ultimate divine reality. See chap. 19 for more about Sankara's Hindu theology.

ity as impersonal. It is difficult, therefore, to articulate how the divine is conscious in a way that would meet with universal approval among pantheists. If we settle for what we have come up with so far, then, we can summarize the pantheist view of the world as being ultimately one indivisible, eternal, divine, conscious reality.

What do pantheists say about why this world exists? As shown, they share with many naturalists the idea that the entirety of the world (everything that exists) is eternal. So they have the same two answers to this second question that were available to naturalists: The world exists either because it just does or because it has to exist. Again, the first answer is really to say that there is no explanation for the existence of the world. Therefore, if this question has an explanatory answer, it must be the second answer: The world *must* exist. Unlike naturalists,[14] pantheists have a plausible reason available for this answer. According to their view, the world is God. If we add to that the assumption that God, by nature, *has* to exist (that God is a necessary being, a being that cannot possibly not exist), then we have a good reason for thinking that the world has to exist.

Finally, what is the pantheist answer to the question concerning the place of human beings in the world?[15] It is natural to think of human beings as a collection of real individuals that can be distinguished from one another and from other things in the world, including God. However, this commonsense idea is difficult to sus-

tain from a pantheist viewpoint. This is because pantheists say that the world is really only one thing—God. If that is the case, if humans really exist, they must be identical with (one and the same thing as) God. But then the appearance of human beings (and other things in the world) as separate and distinct individuals is just an illusion. That is not all. We also think of humans (and other things in the world) as being finite and imperfect. Indeed, human life is characterized by much pain, suffering, and evil. But then if pantheists are right and humans are identical with God, then either God is evil or evil does not really exist at all—it is just an illusion, like the illusion of multiple individuals. Neither one of these alternatives seems satisfactory. Some pantheists have simply chosen to deny the reality of evil. Others have concluded that God is not perfect after all. These seem to be the only two options for pantheists: (1) God is perfect, and there is no evil, or (2) there is evil, and God is imperfect. The latter view is held by pantheists who are called process theologians.[16] Process theology draws on

14. See chap. 9 for a full explanation of why naturalists cannot plausibly hold that the universe has to exist.

15. Chap. 19 says more about the origin and destiny of human beings from the standpoint of Hindu pantheistic philosophy.

16. Actually, these types of pantheists are also called pan*en*theists, since they think that the universe is *part* of God (like God's body) but that God's reality also extends above and beyond the universe. Thus, everything is either God or something *in* God. The reason God is said to be in process or to change is that a part of him—the universe—continually changes. Some choose to distinguish panentheism from pantheism. These are people who characterize pantheism as the view that the universe and God are absolutely identical. I have chosen to define pantheism more broadly and inclusively as the view that everything that exists is God or a part of God. This definition allows for panentheism to be classified as a form of pantheism. But the labels do not matter as long as the ideas are clear. Ramanuja's Hindu philosophy can be interpreted as an instance of panentheism (see chap. 19).

the philosophies of Hegel and Alfred North Whitehead (1861–1947) and characterizes the God/world as being in the process of becoming perfect.

This concludes our survey of the two worldview families that are the main competitors of the worldview family of which Christianity is a member. The next chapter looks carefully at the supernaturalism worldview family, especially the monotheism subfamily. The investigation of this family includes a critical comparison of polytheism and monotheism (many gods or just one God?), a distinction between the kind of monotheism endorsed by Christians and non-Christian kinds (concerning primarily the issue of God's sovereign creation of the universe out of nothing), and a discussion of the traditional monotheistic conception of God's nature or essence.

Reflection and Discussion

1. Try to name a representative person alive today for each of the worldview families introduced in the first section of this chapter. Do you know someone personally from some or all of these different groups? Discuss.
2. Do you know of any metaphysical naturalists? Why do you think some people are attracted to metaphysical naturalism?
3. What are specific ways in which members of the pantheist worldview family are becoming more influential in culture and society today?

Further Reading

Harrison, Paul. *Elements of Pantheism: Religious Reverence of Nature and the Universe.* 2nd ed. Tamarac, FL: Llumina Books, 2004.

Russell, Bertrand. "A Free Man's Worship." In *Why I Am Not a Christian: And Other Essays on Religion and Related Subjects.* New York: Touchstone, 1967.

Sire, James W. *The Universe Next Door: A Basic Worldview Catalog.* 4th ed. Downers Grove, IL: InterVarsity, 2004.

8

The Lord Our God Is One

Monotheism

» **Outline**

- **Many Gods or One God? Polytheism versus Monotheism**
  - *Apparent Polytheism versus Real Polytheism*
  - *Two Arguments against Real Polytheism*
    - Real Polytheism Is Insufficiently Supported
    - Real Polytheism Is Overly Anthropomorphic
  - *The Rational Superiority of Monotheism over Ideal Polytheism*
    - The Doctrine of the Trinity versus Ideal Polytheism
    - Why There Can Be Only One Omnipotent Being
- **A Trio of Monotheisms**
  - *Creation Monotheism*
  - *Contingency Monotheism*
  - *Dualistic Monotheism (Cosmological Dualism)*
  - *An Initial Case for the Rational Superiority of Creation Monotheism*
- **What Is the Monotheistic God Like?**
  - *Perfect Being Theology*
  - *Four Objections to Perfect Being Theology*
  - *Some Important Attributes of a Perfect God*

» **Summary**

The supernaturalism worldview family contains polytheism and monotheism. Some merely apparent polytheistic religions are really pantheistic. Real polytheism is rationally unfounded and overly anthropomorphic. Monotheism is rationally superior to ideal polytheism. Of the three versions of monotheism, creation monotheism is rationally superior to contingency monotheism and dualistic monotheism. The perfect being theological approach to the nature of the monotheistic God can rationally resist objections and identify some specific attributes of a perfect being.

» **Basic Terms, Concepts, and Names**

anthropomorphic
apparent polytheism
contingency monotheism
contingent existence
cosmological dualism
creation *ex nihilo*
creation monotheism
dependent existence
great-making properties
ideal polytheism
immaterial
immutable
independent existence
Manichcanism
monotheism
necessary existence
omnibenevolence
omnipotence
omniscience
perfect being theology
perfections
polytheism
real polytheism
supernaturalism
Xenophanes of Colophon
Zoroastrianism

» **Reflection and Discussion**

» **Further Reading**

The LORD our God, the LORD is one.

Deuteronomy 6:4

Many Gods or One God? Polytheism versus Monotheism

Naturalists say that a godless nature is the only reality. Pan(en)theists say that everything that exists is God or a part of God. Supernaturalists say that God (or gods) exist(s) above and beyond the universe in such a way that the universe is neither divine nor a part of the divine. As indicated in the last chapter, there are two branches of the supernaturalist worldview family: (1) monotheists, who say that there is only one God, and (2) polytheists, who say that there is more than one god. We begin our investigation of monotheism by considering a case for its rational superiority over polytheism. This case requires a more careful characterization of polytheism.

First of all, we need to distinguish between apparent polytheism and real polytheism. In some religious traditions, such as some branches of Hinduism, earlier polytheistic perspectives and practices have been reinterpreted in pantheistic terms. In this way, the many "gods" worshiped by different Hindu devotees are seen instead as different manifestations of

the one true divine reality. Therefore, according to this view, the existence of more than one divine reality is only apparent but not real. We are interested instead in real polytheism: The belief in more than one distinct divine and ultimate reality. We find real polytheism in ancient Mesopotamian, Egyptian, Greek (and Roman) religion and in Norse mythology, with its pantheons of gods. But polytheism was also widespread throughout the entire ancient world, and polytheistic belief and practice continue to exist throughout the world today.

Traditional polytheistic gods are like human beings in many ways. They have bodies, they engage in sexual intercourse, and their procreative activities produce additional gods. They are often engaged in conflicts with other gods or groups of gods, and they are motivated by jealousy, revenge, the desire for glory, and other human-like emotions and attitudes. They are also each characterized by having a special personality and a distinctive function or area of expertise or influence (such as love or war). What then makes them gods rather than merely superhuman beings? For one thing, they are *immortal*. Once created or procreated, they do not die. Moreover, they have a degree of knowledge and power that surpasses what humans can know and do. They are also objects of human worship. Human beings pray to them and offer them sacrifices.

From an apologetical perspective, we need to ask two questions about such alleged divine entities. First, is there a good reason for thinking that such beings exist? Second, whether or not there is evidence of the reality of these sorts of superhuman persons, is there adequate reason for classifying them as *gods*?

In answer to the first question, it seems clear that there are no good philosophical arguments for the existence of many beings of the sort classified as gods by polytheistic religions.[1] Though there are certainly polytheistic traditions and stories, there is no good reason to believe that these customary conceptions and myths are based on a true picture of the way the world really is. Whenever people in polytheistic contexts have begun to think carefully and critically about the supernatural, they typically have rejected polytheism in favor of pantheism, monotheism, or naturalism. The philosophical impulse among human beings has usually led to the conclusion that the alternatives for divine reality are either one or none.

But then why have so many people in so many places and at so many times believed that there are many gods? This psychological, sociological, or anthropological question is best answered by these social sciences. However, it seems reasonable to think that polytheism has been pervasive in human history because it meets a deep human need. Polytheistic beliefs are embodied in myth and story, and stories are the language of the human heart. Polytheistic narratives are tales about local human-like gods who protect and provide for their people in a hostile and uncertain world. The stories of the gods give those who believe them a sense that their lives have meaning, that they are connected with something transcendent, and that they can understand and explain the events of their lives in terms of something larger than themselves. The response of a Christian apologist to these aspects of polytheistic belief should be to affirm the human needs that gave rise to them (needs of the sort discussed in chap. 4) but to invite people to consider the possibility that Christianity can meet these needs of the human heart in a way that polytheism cannot. This was Paul's apologetic strategy when he spoke to the polytheists and idolaters on Mars' hill (see Acts 17:16–31). Christian apologists should follow his example.

But suppose there were good philosophical reasons to believe in superhuman beings of the sort featured in polytheistic perspectives on reality. In that case, the second question arises. Would such beings be genuine *gods*?

A long philosophical tradition that begins with the Greek philosopher and poet Xenophanes of Colophon (560–478 BC) answers this question negatively. Xenophanes criticizes the dominant polytheistic Greek religion of his day on two grounds. First, he argues that the "gods" of the Greek pantheon are not worthy of admiration, reverence, or worship. A look at the classic accounts of these gods in

---

1. Though it could be argued that polytheism is true because it explains diverse natural phenomena (e.g., lightning is thrown by Zeus), science can explain these better in natural terms. Also, monotheism provides a simpler and therefore better explanation of the existence and design of the universe.

the works of the Greek poets Homer and Hesiod bear this out. Morally speaking, the alleged residents of Mount Olympus are no better than a band of ruffians and thieves. In their relationships with humans and other gods, they lie, cheat, steal, and murder to secure their own selfish advantage. They are also constantly engaged in petty squabbles with their rivals. This is not the sort of behavior that ought to inspire praise and a desire to emulate their actions or to seek their guidance. Xenophanes' second reason for rejecting polytheism as it was manifested at the time was that it is easy to explain each culture's gods as mere fictional projections of that culture's distinctive characteristics. In making this point, Xenophanes says, "The Ethiopians make their gods snub-nosed and black; the Thracians make theirs gray-eyed and red-haired."[2] This cultural-relativity argument makes it reasonable to conclude that there are no superhuman beings of the sort postulated by Greek religion. The moral argument supports the idea that even if we had good reason to think such persons existed, it would not be rational to think of them as gods.

These criticisms are effective against extremely anthropomorphic polytheistic traditions. An anthropomorphic religious tradition characterizes its god or gods in primarily human terms. Most actual religious traditions contain conceptions of deity that are anthropomorphic to some degree (how could we understand what God is like if he was not like human beings in any way whatsoever?). However, most if not all polytheistic traditions are anthropomorphic to a relatively high de-

2. See John Manley Robinson, *An Introduction to Early Greek Philosophy* (Boston: Houghton Mifflin, 1968), 52.

gree. But might there be a much less anthropomorphic form of polytheism that would be reasonable to endorse? To avoid an objectionable form of anthropomorphism, such a version of polytheism would have to posit gods that are at least uncreated, immaterial, and sufficiently great. Otherwise, what good reason would we have for calling them gods? Let us call such a theoretical form of polytheism ideal polytheism.

Belief in the existence of many *created* supernatural beings would not be ideal polytheism. Angels and demons are, in some sense, supernatural (at least in virtue of being nonphysical or immaterial), but they are not really gods since they are dependent for their existence on the existence of something outside them that created them. Ideal polytheism, therefore, would be an affirmation that there are multiple uncreated supernatural beings. To count such beings as *gods*, they must also be immortal (incapable of ceasing to exist) and therefore eternal (at least in the sense of being everlasting). Moreover, to distinguish them from naturalists' "matter," which is also eternal, they must be immaterial. If there are eternal immaterial things, would they necessarily be gods? It seems not. According to some philosophical views, *numbers* are eternal and immaterial things (as distinct from *numerals*, which are temporal and material symbols for numbers). But numbers are clearly not gods (even the ancient Greek Pythagoreans, who apparently believed that numbers are the ultimate constituents of the universe, did not say that numbers are gods). It seems that the main additional characteristic required for an eternal immaterial thing to have the status of a god is *personality* (the property of being a person).[3] At minimum, a person is something that is capable of thinking and acting.

Therefore, ideal polytheism posits the existence of more than one ultimately distinct, eternal, immaterial, divine person. But we need to be careful here to distinguish ideal polytheism from the Christian doctrine of the Trinity. According to that doctrine, God is a trio of divine persons who exist as one divine substance. These three persons are eternal and immaterial. However, they are not individually *ultimate,* and this is an important part of what distinguishes the Christian doctrine of the Trinity from polytheism. According to Christians, the divine reality is ultimately one individual substance or being. The three persons of the Trinity are fundamentally unified in a number of important respects (we will discuss these in more depth in chap. 16). According to ideal polytheists, however, the many divine persons are unified only in the sense that they are all members of the same species: divinity. But this is to say only that they are the same *kind* of thing, not that they are the same *individual* thing. With this important distinction between Christian trinitarian monotheism and ideal polytheism, we are now in a position to appreciate the rational superiority of the former over the latter.

According to some monotheistic worldviews (such as the general theistic worldview shared by many Jews, Christians, and Muslims), the one God is not only eternal, immaterial, and personal but also infinite and perfect in every respect. Among other things, this means that God is infinite in power, knowledge, and goodness. God is all-powerful, all-knowing, and all-good (or to use the Latin terms, *omnipotent, omniscient,* and *omnibenevolent*). Though there is not complete agreement among monotheists about this description (since some question the possibility of an absolutely infinite and perfect being), all monotheists agree that the one God is the greatest possible being. And this seems right, doesn't it? The word *God* is not merely a descriptive term (a label for a being that satisfies a certain description) but also an evaluative or honorific term. It legitimately applies only to a kind of being that is sufficiently *great* in a variety of respects. A being worthy of the name God would have to be at least superior to humans in every respect. Moreover, it seems reasonable to think that the better a being is in every respect, the more appropriate it would be to call this being God (or a god). Also, for such a being to be worthy of worship (and not merely an object of worship whether worthy or not), it (or he or she) must possess an extremely high degree of greatness—perhaps excellence or even perfection—especially with respect to goodness. It seems that the more worthy of worship a being is, the more suitable it would be to call this being God. Therefore, it seems reasonable to think that only the

3. This is another reason to conclude that the supernaturalist conception of God as personal is rationally superior to the pantheist idea of God as impersonal.

> **The word *God* is not merely a descriptive term (a label for a being that satisfies a certain description) but also an evaluative or honorific term.**

greatest possible being is (or beings are) deserving of the label God.

Given all these assumptions about the characteristics required of something for it legitimately to be called a god, ideal polytheism can be true only if there can be more than one god possessing exactly the same degree of greatness. Though we may choose to call inferior beings "gods" ("lesser gods"), it is really the beings with more power, wisdom, and goodness that are deserving of the name in a completely unqualified sense. As we have seen, many monotheists posit the existence of a being that is *all*-powerful, *all*-knowing, and *all*-good. Such a being, if it exists, would be as great as it is possible to be and so appropriately called God. Could there be more than one such being? If so, then it would be possible for there to be more than one god (in the most honorific sense of the term). If not, then either there is only one God, or there is no God at all (except, perhaps, one or more than one lesser god, if that is not a contradiction in terms). Good reasons exist for thinking that there cannot be more than one all-powerful (omnipotent) being. If this is right, and if there is a good reason to think there is one omnipotent being, then there is a good reason to think there is *only* one.

Here is the argument for these claims. If there is more than one god (rather than merely more than one divine person, as posited by the doctrine of the Trinity), then there is more than one ultimate and fundamentally distinct divine center of thought and action. To say that they are fundamentally distinct is to say, at least, that they can think and act separately. What they think and how they act depend on what they individually *choose* to think and to do. They have their own wills. What they will is, to at least some extent, up to them. If their choices were determined by forces outside their control, then they would be inferior to human beings, who seem, at least some of the time, to be capable of willing freely. But gods are supposed to be superior to human beings. So the gods must have free will. But if they have free and radically separate wills, then it must be possible for them to have a conflict of wills. For instance, let's suppose that the goddess Athena wants the Greeks to win the war, and the god Apollo favors the Trojans. Assuming that there can be only one victor, only one of these divine persons can get what he or she wants. But to be all-powerful (omnipotent) is (at least) to be able to get whatever one wants. So Athena and Apollo cannot both be all-powerful. Notice that this is true of any two alleged gods as long as it is *possible* for them to experience a conflict of wills of this sort. Moreover, a part of what it means for two persons of any kind to be ultimately separate is that it is possible for them to experience a conflict of wills (if their wills cannot possibly conflict, then in what sense is it true that they are the wills of genuinely distinct beings?). As a result, there cannot be more than one all-powerful being. Consequently, if being as great as it is possible to be, and therefore all-powerful, is required to be a god (this was argued above), then there cannot be more than one god. If there cannot be more than one god, then no version of polytheism can be true. If polytheism cannot be true and monotheism can be true, then, for this reason alone, it is more reasonable to accept monotheism than polytheism. Is it possible for some version of monotheism to be true? No one has been able to show that the idea of a perfect (and therefore infinite, eternal, immaterial, omnipotent, omniscient, and omnibenevolent) personal being is contradictory.[4] Consequently, it is reasonable to believe that there may be such a being.

The argument for the rational superiority of monotheism over polytheism lays the groundwork for the case considered in the next two chapters: the rational superiority of monotheism over both naturalism and pan(en)theism. Before we are ready to look at those arguments, however, we must first distinguish among three major versions of monotheism and then say more about the nature of the one God who actually exists.

A Trio of Monotheisms

This section discusses the differences among creation monotheism, contingency monotheism, and dualistic monotheism. The differences among these versions of monotheism have primarily to do with what they entail about the relationship between God and the universe.

Creation monotheism is the thesis that the one eternal God created the universe *ex nihilo* (out of nothing). According to this view, the universe not only depends on God to sustain its ongoing existence but was also brought into existence by God in the first place. Moreover, when God created the universe, he did not make it out of any preexisting material. Rather, like a magician feigns to do when pulling a rabbit out of a hat, God made the

4. See Richard Swinburne, *The Coherence of Theism* (Oxford: Oxford University Press, 1977), for a sustained argument for the claim that the monotheistic concept of God is logically coherent.

universe materialize out of literally nothing. Creation monotheists normally add to this the claim that it was not *necessary* for God to create a universe. Instead, God freely chose to do so. Therefore, the universe is not only dependent on God for its initial and continuing existence but is also *contingent*: It is possible for it not to have existed, not to exist currently, and not to continue to exist in the future. Thus, its past, present, and future existence is due entirely, and explained completely in terms of, God's sovereign and free decision to will it to exist. All three of the major Western monotheistic religions (Judaism, Christianity, and Islam) traditionally subscribe to creation monotheism.

Contingency monotheism agrees with creation monotheism that the universe is both contingent and dependent on God for its existence. However, this view holds that the universe did not have a beginning in time but has instead always existed. According to this view, God has freely *and eternally* willed the existence of the universe. Both creation and contingency monotheism, then, agree that the universe did not have to exist and depends for its continuing existence on God. It is interesting to note that these monotheistic positions agree with pan(en)theism that the universe is dependent on God for its existence. Where they differ with this latter worldview family is in affirming God's freedom in willing the existence of the universe and the corresponding contingency of the universe. According to pan(en)theism, the universe is dependent on God because it is God (or a part of God). It is also *necessary*, since God (with whom it is identical or of whom it is a part) is a necessary being. Contingency monotheism has been affirmed by some philosophers, even though it is not a traditional and orthodox doctrine of any religious tradition.[5]

Finally, according to dualistic monotheism (also called cosmological dualism), God did not create the universe *ex nihilo*. Instead, the universe and God are coeternal, and the universe does not depend on God for its existence. The easiest way to explain this independence of the universe's existence from God is to attribute to the universe the property of *necessary existence* (the property of being such that it must exist or cannot fail to exist). This view clearly makes the universe a lot like God in some respects, at least in being eternal, independent, and necessary. The main difference is that the universe is material and impersonal, whereas God is immaterial and personal. Moreover, according to many traditional cosmological dualistic views, God is inherently good, and the universe is inherently evil. The ancient Persian religion of Zoroastrianism is a form of cosmological dualism, as is Manicheanism, a religion that combined Zoroastrian and Christian themes and with which Augustine was associated before he became a Christian. These two versions of dualism affirm that God is good and the universe is evil. This dualistic idea seems to have been captured to some extent in the *Star Wars* films, with their two cosmological principles of the force and the dark side. (To the extent that the latter is the dark side of the force, however, the theology of *Star Wars* may instead be a kind of pantheism that posits the existence of a godlike ultimate reality that is both good and evil.) The Hindu

theology of Madhva is also a version of cosmological dualism. But this theology does not make the God-universe dualism also a dualism of good and evil.[6]

Which of these versions of monotheism is most likely to be true? There are both theological and philosophical reasons for eliminating contingency monotheism from contention at the outset. The theological reason is that all the major monotheistic religious traditions (those mentioned above), at least in their more orthodox manifestations, traditionally subscribe either to creation monotheism or to dualistic monotheism. The arguments formulated later in this book provide good reasons to think not only that God exists but also that God is an infinite and loving personal being who initiates communication with human beings about his will. The best place to look for such a communication is among the existing religious traditions whose adherents claim to have had experiences of and revelations from God. Thus, we should restrict ourselves to those forms of monotheism endorsed by these traditions. The philosophical reason is that the universe had to have a beginning in time and could not have always existed. The next chapter investigates this reason in the form of an argument for God's existence.

If the theological reason for preferring worldviews endorsed by existing religious traditions is a good one, then we are left with a choice between the creation and the dualistic version of monotheism. The main problem with the dualistic view is that it assumes that the universe is eternal, independent, and necessary. As just mentioned, one of the arguments

5. One interpretation of Ramanuja's Hindu theology, however, construes it as a version of contingency monotheism. See chap. 19.

6. See chap. 19 for more on Madhva's version of Hinduism.

for God's existence considered in the next chapter attempts to show that the universe could not be eternal. The other is based on the conviction that the universe is both contingent and dependent. If either of these arguments is sound, then creation monotheism is rationally superior to dualistic monotheism. The bottom line here is that, on careful reflection, the universe does not seem to be the kind of thing—given its materiality in particular—that could possibly be independent and necessary as opposed to contingent and dependent.

What Is the Monotheistic God Like?

All three versions of monotheism generally agree on the nature of the one God who exists independent of the universe. Many monotheistic theologians and philosophers have embraced what has become known as perfect being theology, which takes God to be, essentially and most generally, an absolutely perfect being. We see this assumption at least as early as the Greek philosopher Aristotle, who thought of God as "fully actualized" and therefore without any potential to change for the better. The Christian Augustine employs the assumption that God is, by definition, "that to which nothing is superior," and the later Augustinian thinker Anselm considered God to be, similarly but more awkwardly, "that than which none greater can be conceived." Thomas Aquinas concurs, as do many other later philosophers, including Descartes, Spinoza, and Leibniz (though Spinoza was a pantheist). These latter three thought of God as a supremely or absolutely infinite and perfect being. I follow their lead here in sketching a general

account of the kind of being the theistic arguments conclude actually exists.

It is true that some monotheistic thinkers have balked at this way of thinking and talking about God, calling it the God of the philosophers in a disparaging way. Pascal seems to have been among these detractors, since in one of his *pensées* he says, "'God of Abraham, God of Isaac, God of Jacob,' not of philosophers and scholars."[7] Their reasons have varied, but among them are the claims that (1) the language of the Bible (and the Qur'an) does not support this view of God; (2) there is much more to God than the attributes entailed by the idea of a perfect being; (3) it is not metaphysically possible for an absolutely perfect being to exist of the sort posited by perfect being theology; and (4) even if God is a perfect being, the human intellect is too limited to know that this is true. These are important concerns, and we need to take account of them and reply to them before developing an account of God as a perfect being and arguing for the existence of such a being.

The Bible employs a number of terms to describe God's nature and character. A look at the book of Psalms reveals quite a few. God is referred to as "the Maker of heaven and earth" (121:2), he is addressed as "Most High" (92:1), and he is said to be "from all eternity" (93:2). God is "holy" (99:3), "righteous in all his ways and loving toward all he has made" (145:17), and "most worthy of praise" (145:3). The psalmist also calls God "Lord Almighty" (84:1), says that "the plans of the Lord stand firm forever" (33:11), and affirms that "the Lord knows the thoughts of man" (94:11). The book of Psalms ends with an

7. Blaise Pascal, *Pensées*, trans. A. J. Krailsheimer (London: Penguin, 1966), #913 (p. 309).

> **Reason and revelation work hand in hand to provide us with as complete a knowledge of the nature of God as it is possible for us to have.**

invitation to "praise [God] for his surpassing greatness" (150:2).

This sampling from various psalms of God's characteristics does not add up to a description of an absolutely perfect being, though a couple of phrases ("Most High" and "surpassing greatness") do tend to move us in this direction. A case could be made for the claim that the language used of God in the Bible supports only the view that God is *very, very* great in goodness, knowledge, and power. The degree of the greatness of God in these respects need be only high enough to enable God to have created and to sustain the universe and to bring about his purposes at the end of history. We can grant this and yet have good reason to think that what the Bible says about God is *consistent with* the view of God as absolutely perfect. If God is absolutely perfect, then God is also very great in every respect as well.

But why doesn't the Bible affirm God's absolute perfection if it is indeed real? The best answer to this question is that, just as the Bible is not a science book (an important point discussed in chap. 22), it is not a philosophy book either. The Bible's primary purpose is *practical* rather than *theoretical*. As Galileo said, "The Bible tells us how to go to heaven rather than how the heavens go."[8] From a Christian standpoint,

it makes sense to see the Bible as having been written using language that would be as accessible as possible to the widest range of people. Therefore, we are most likely to find language about God that is relatively concrete and poetic rather than relatively abstract and prosaic. But philosophical language of the kind employed to express perfect being theology falls into the latter category. Since the language of perfection is not ruled out by the Bible's language about God, it may be a more abstract but helpful way of thinking and talking about God that supplements what the Bible reveals about God.

But doesn't perfect being theology fall short of providing a complete account of God? Yes. *Every* theology is inadequate to give us a thorough description of God. But the Bible tells us more about God than we could discover by means of reflecting on the specific attributes a perfect being would have. Just as philosophical perfect being theology can enhance what we know about God from the Bible (by providing us with more abstract concepts and literal language about God), so also biblical theology can tell us more about God than we can discover on the basis of human reason alone. Reason and revelation work hand in hand to provide us with as complete a knowledge of the nature of God as it is possible for us to have. Among the things we learn about God from the Bible that we could not have known about God on the basis of reason alone is that God is triune in nature and that God the Son, the Second Person of the Trinity, became incarnate as a human being to accomplish our salvation. Nothing about God's per-

8. See Galileo, "Letter to the Grand Duchess Christina of Tuscany," 1615, quoted in Charles E.

Hummel, *The Galileo Connection: Resolving Conflicts between Science and the Bible* (Downers Grove, IL: InterVarsity, 1986), 9.

fection requires that the doctrines of the Trinity and the incarnation be the case. In sum, perfect being theology may tell us some important things about God even if we need to turn to the Bible to learn other important things about God.

The third objection is that it is not possible for a perfect being to exist. But why would someone think that a perfect being is impossible? Here is one way to think about this objection. If we think of a perfect being as the greatest possible being, whether such a thing is really possible depends on whether the greatest possible being is like the greatest possible angle (which does exist: 360 degrees)[9] or like the greatest possible number (which does not exist and could not possibly exist). Into which category does the greatest possible being fall? Though many attempts have been made to show that the greatest possible being cannot exist, most agree that these efforts are not clearly successful. Every claim that the concept of a perfect being entails a contradiction has been countered by good arguments to the contrary.[10] Though the conversation along these lines continues, it seems reasonable to affirm the possibility of a perfect being in the absence of a clearly successful case to the contrary. Moreover, as we will see, the specific contents of this concept can be articulated in such a way as to increase the reasonableness of believing that it is coherent.

9. Anything above 360 degrees is an angle, but such an angle is also equivalent to an angle less than or equal to 360 degrees. So the higher angles are not really *different* angles.

10. See Thomas V. Morris, *Our Idea of God: An Introduction to Philosophical Theology* (Downers Grove, IL: InterVarsity, 1991), for arguments of this sort.

The fourth and final challenge to the perfect being theological approach is the claim that we are too limited intellectually to know that God is a perfect being. In responding to this charge, it is important to reiterate that Christian apologists must acknowledge both that they cannot know the complete truth about the nature of God and that they cannot have complete objective certainty that anything they say about God is true. Theological beliefs are necessarily somewhat limited in content and rational confidence. Nonetheless, there are good reasons for thinking that we can know *a lot* about God with *a high degree* of assurance. Moreover, there are also good reasons to think that *if God exists,* then God is a perfect being.

First of all, if the Christian God exists and created human beings in his image, then there are good theological reasons to think that God would have made us capable of knowing him to some extent, even apart from what the Bible reveals about him. The Christian God is a personal being who created humans for the sake of eternal, loving fellowship with him. Genuine fellowship requires significant mutual knowledge of the loved one, and many human beings (among those who have died) did not have or (among those still alive) do not have access to Scripture. Therefore, it is reasonable to believe that if the Christian God exists, humans can know something about God apart from the Bible. The Bible itself affirms that we can have knowledge of God through creation (Rom. 1:20), and the arguments for God's existence considered in the next two chapters support this claim.

But, of course, the universe is imperfect in many respects, and according to perfect being theology, God is perfect. Can we conclude that the Creator is perfect in every respect solely by observing and reasoning about the imperfect creation? No. But some Christian thinkers, such as Augustine, Anselm, Descartes, and others, believed that God created human beings with the capacity to know, just by reflecting rationally on the concept of God and the concept of perfection, that if God exists, then God is a perfect being. What reason is there for thinking so? If we have the idea of a perfect being, and yet God is not absolutely perfect, then we have the ability to conceive of something that is even greater than God. But how could it be possible for anything to be greater than God? And how could God be worthy of our worship if we could imagine something or someone more exalted than God? Anyone who (1) has the concept of perfection, (2) believes that this concept is coherent, and (3) thinks that nothing could be better than God has good reason to believe that if God exists, then God is a perfect being. Moreover, the tendency to think that only a perfect being would be worthy of worship suggests that there are reasons of the heart that would prevent us from being satisfied with a God who was anything short of being absolutely perfect. Our disappointment with the various kinds of imperfections we encounter in our lives and in the created order is a sign that our hearts long to be connected with something free from all defects and deficiencies. In short, our hearts seem to yearn for union with a perfect God.

If God is a perfect being, then God has all the perfections. Perfections are specific properties or attributes that something needs to have to be perfect. More precisely, they are "great-making properties" that are possessed in the maximal way or to the maximal degree. A great-making property is a property that it would be better to have than not to have. We can easily generate a list of great-making properties just by asking ourselves what characteristics satisfy this criterion. The hard part is to provide a thorough and precise analysis of the concepts of each of these properties, but for our relatively limited purposes here, that will not be necessary. We can start an investigation of specific perfections by considering what properties of things with which we are familiar it is better to have than not to have.

Among existing natural things, it seems clear that those that are living are superior in value to those that are not. For instance, a plant is better than a rock, because it is alive, and the latter is not. Moreover, animals as a whole are more valuable than plants as a group. Why? Because animals are capable of sensation and independent movement, and plants are not. But human beings are even better than animals, plants, and rocks because they are existing, living, sensing, and moving persons capable of rational thought and action. Since humans have all the properties that make other kinds of natural things valuable and other value-enhancing properties as well, it follows that humans are at the top of nature's value hierarchy. Notice that this is true even of human beings who are extremely wicked and sinful. The very thing that has enabled them to become as evil as they are—their free wills—is what makes them more valuable than other inhabitants of the universe. A free will is a valuable tool, even when it has been misused as a source of great evil. The improper use of a tool does not diminish the value of the tool itself.

The characteristics that give humans an edge over other natural things provide a basis to determine many of the perfections possessed by a perfect being. A perfect being would be a personal being that thinks, wills, and acts in the best possible way. As for thinking, knowledge is better than ignorance, a great deal of knowledge is better than just a little, and knowing everything that it is possible to know is the best. Therefore, the perfection in the area of thought and knowledge is to be all-knowing (or to use the Latin term, *omniscient*). When it comes to willing and acting, we can think in terms of both quantity and quality. The quantitative aspect of willing and acting concerns power: how much a person is capable of doing. It is better to have some ability than to have none. It is even better to be capable of doing a lot rather than just a little. The best, however, when it comes to power, is to be capable of doing anything it would be logically possible to do. The perfection in this case, therefore, is to be all-powerful (Latin: *omnipotent*). Finally, the quality of willing and acting has to do with good and evil. It is better to be good than to be evil. Better even still is to be very good rather than just moderately good. The best is to be as good as it is possible to be: absolutely good and therefore not evil to even the slightest degree. This perfection is to be all-good (Latin: *omnibenevolent*).

In addition to this trio of perfections, we can add to the list some characteristics we have already been attributing to God. If God is a perfect being, then God is an independent being (he does not depend on anything outside himself for his ongoing existence or eternal attributes), since it is better to be independent than dependent. In addition, for something to be perfect, it must be a necessary being rather than a contingent being. That is, it must not be possible for it not to exist. Something that *has* to exist has a "firmer grip" on existence than something that does not, and so the former is better than the latter. Also (though more controversially among monotheists), if God is perfect, then God exists outside time (atemporal) and space (aspatial), since to exist in time and space is to be limited by them and therefore not absolutely unlimited or perfect. If God is atemporal and aspatial, then God is also immaterial, since material objects necessarily exist in space and time. So immateriality is a perfection as well. Since a perfect being is timeless, then it would also be unchanging and unchangeable (immutable) in some respect, since change is a temporal process (though it is difficult to articulate exactly what immutability means in the case of a personal being like God who acts in time).

These are among the properties traditionally considered perfections and therefore attributes of God, assuming that God is a perfect being. Though other properties have been proposed, this list is enough for our purposes. The next two chapters consider some arguments that purport to demonstrate the existence of a being with at least some of these characteristics. Though there are many kinds of arguments that attempt to establish this conclusion, this discussion focuses on those in the cosmological and teleological theistic argument families.

Reflection and Discussion

1. What do you think polytheists find appealing about the idea that there are many gods? How would you try to persuade a polytheist that the perceived advantages of polytheism are either disadvantages or are more likely to be found in a monotheistic religion like Christianity?
2. Name one thing about each version of monotheism that is difficult to explain. With which of these mysteries would you be most willing to live? Why?
3. Do you agree that Christian apologists should try to defend the existence of a *perfect* God? Why or why not?

Further Reading

Chesterton, G. K. *Everlasting Man*. San Francisco: Ignatius, 1993.

Morris, Thomas V. *Our Idea of God: An Introduction to Philosophical Theology*. Downers Grove, IL: InterVarsity, 1991.

Swinburne, Richard. *The Coherence of Theism*. New York: Oxford University Press, 1993.

9

In the Beginning

Cosmological Explanations

» **Outline**

- **Nothing Comes from Nothing: The Cosmological Arguments**
  - *The Principle of Universal Explanation (the PUE)*
  - *What Explains God's Existence?*
  - *Originating and Sustaining Efficient Causes*
  - *Two Versions of the PUE*
  - *A Defense of the PUE*
- **The *Kalam* Cosmological Argument**
  - *The Impossibility of an Actual Infinite Series of Times*
  - *What the Conclusion of the* Kalam *Argument Entails*
  - *The Rational Resistibility of the* Kalam *Argument*
- **The Contingency Cosmological Argument**
  - *The Universe as a Contingent and Therefore Dependent Thing*
  - *Why There Cannot Be an Infinite Regress of Sustaining Causes*
  - *What the Conclusion of the Contingency Argument Entails*
  - *The Rational Resistibility of the Contingency Argument*

» **Summary**

Cosmological arguments for God's existence conclude that the best explanation for the existence of the universe is that God exists as its cause. All cosmological arguments assume the principle of universal explanation (the PUE), according to which everything has an explanation for its existence. God's existence can be explained by the fact that he is perfect in nature and therefore necessarily existent. Things that are not necessary must be explained in terms of efficient causes. What comes into existence has an explanation in terms of an originating efficient cause, and every nonnecessary thing has an explanation of its ongoing existence in terms of a sustaining efficient cause. The *Kalam* cosmological argument concludes that God is the originating cause of the universe on the grounds that the universe began to exist, and the contingency cosmological argument concludes that God is the sustaining cause of the universe on the grounds that the universe is a contingent thing.

» **Basic Terms, Concepts, and Names**

actual infinite series
contingency cosmological argument
contingent thing (existence)
cosmological arguments
creation *ex nihilo*
dependent thing (existence)
efficient cause
Hume, David
independent thing (existence)
infinite regress of sustaining causes
Kalam cosmological argument
necessary thing (existence)
originating efficient cause
potential infinite series
principle of universal explanation
self-evident truth
sustaining efficient cause
truth of reason

» **Reflection and Discussion**

» **Further Reading**

> In the beginning God created the heavens and the earth.
>
> Genesis 1:1

Nothing Comes from Nothing: The Cosmological Arguments

There are a number of versions of both cosmological and teleological arguments for the existence of a monotheistic God. What they all have in common is (1) the observation of the existence of a cosmos—an ordered universe—and (2) an affirmation of the principle that everything that exists or happens has an explanation for its existence or occurrence (even though we may not always be in a position to *know* what that explanation is). Let's call this the principle of universal explanation (the PUE for short).[1] If we put these two assumptions together, it follows that there is an explanation for the existence of the cosmos. These arguments all conclude that the explanation for the existence of the universe and its features is that these things were and/or are caused by God. The difference between cosmological and

1. This principle is similar to the principle of sufficient reason employed by the philosopher G. W. Leibniz (1646–1716) in his version of the cosmological argument, but it is formulated somewhat differently in an attempt to avoid certain problems with Leibniz's principle.

teleological arguments is that the former argue that God is the ultimate cause of the *existence* of the universe, and the latter conclude that God is the ultimate cause of the *order* of the universe. This chapter and the next discuss two members of each of these two families.

The PUE entails not only that the existence of the universe has an explanation but also that we can explain the existence of God. After all, the PUE says that there is an explanation for *everything* that exists. But God cannot be caused to exist by something else (because then he would not be God by virtue of being dependent on something else for his existence), and God cannot cause himself to exist either (at least in the sense of bringing himself into existence). So how can God's existence be explained? If God exists, then God is the kind of being that *must* exist (could not fail to exist) because it is the nature of a perfect being to exist *necessarily*. If God only *happened* to exist (so that he might not have existed), then God could not be perfect (how could something that is possibly nonexistent be perfect?). If God exists, God is a *necessary being*. So even if God is *uncaused*, God's existence can be explained by appealing to his nature as a perfect and therefore necessary being.[2]

The cosmological arguments start with a question that has probably occurred to every reflective human being at one time or another: Why is there something rather than nothing? This sort of question—a Why? question—is most appropriately answered by means of a statement starting with the word *because* (as the parents of every inquisitive toddler know only too well). The question is a request for an explanation, and the answer is an attempt to provide it. An explanation of something is, in a broad sense of the word *cause,* an account of that thing in terms of its cause or causes (that is why explanations start with the word be*cause*). There are different kinds of causes (the philosopher Aristotle identified four). What kind of cause do we have in mind here?

The kind of cause the questioner of the cosmos is hoping to discover is a cause of the *existence* of the universe. This is the sort of cause that Aristotle called an "efficient" cause (that *by means of which* something is, occurs, or is the case). The PUE, as it applies to efficient causes, is grounded in the fundamental and apparently undeniable metaphysical maxim that nothing comes from nothing. Given this, if we have *something,* and the existence of this thing cannot be explained solely by appealing to its nature, then there must be something else from which it comes—something that has produced or

> **The cosmological arguments start with a question that has probably occurred to every reflective human being at one time or another: Why is there something rather than nothing?**

is producing it, something that is its efficient cause.

Before we see how the PUE is employed in theistic arguments, it will be helpful to distinguish between two kinds of efficient causes. Some things capable of having efficient causes have "originating" efficient causes, and all things capable of having efficient causes have "sustaining" efficient causes. For example, let's suppose we are wondering why it is light in a particular room rather than dark. In asking this question, we could be expressing curiosity about either how the room got to be illuminated in the first place or why the light in it continues to exist (or both). In the former case, we are asking about the *originating* efficient cause of the light in the room (that by means of which the light was brought into existence in the first place), and in the latter case, we are wondering about the *sustaining* efficient cause of the light in the room (that by means of which the light continues to shine without going out). A simple and incomplete answer to the first question might be, "Because I just flipped the light switch to the on position." A more complicated and exhaustive answer would also refer to such things as the completion of electrical circuits and the nature of electricity. Similarly,

---

2. Some philosophers such as Spinoza have held that God is a "self-caused" being. What they mean by this seems to be what I mean by saying that God's existence can be explained by his nature as a perfect and necessary being. Perhaps in some sense of the word *cause,* we can say that God's existence is caused by God's nature.

an entirely adequate physical explanation of what causally *sustains* the light in the room would appeal to the ongoing flow of electrons through the complete electrical circuit of which the light source is a part.

This distinction between originating and sustaining causes suggests the need for two corresponding versions of the PUE as it applies to things that have efficient causes:

PUE_O Everything that comes into existence has an originating cause (something that brought it into existence) that explains its coming into existence.

PUE_S Everything that exists but does not have a nature that *requires* it to exist has a sustaining cause (something that enables it to continue to exist) that explains its ongoing existence.

Notice that the PUE_O applies only to things that come into existence. But doesn't *everything* come into existence at a certain time? Interestingly, insofar as they presuppose the PUE, all the worldview families considered up to this point (metaphysical naturalism, pan(en)theism, polytheism, and monotheism) agree that the answer to this question is no. Assuming the PUE, each of these worldviews asserts that something about the world is eternal, whether it is the universe itself or God or the gods. If that is the case, then not everything in the world began to exist at a certain time.

Can we prove that the PUE is true? It does follow from the metaphysical maxim that nothing comes from nothing. Can we demonstrate the truth of this maxim?

No. Any proof we might offer for it would be no more certain than the principle itself. That nothing comes from nothing is a *foundational* belief. It is one of the claims on the basis of which we argue for other things rather than an assertion for which we can argue. After all, the only way to prove that it is true would be to show with respect to every single existing thing in the universe—past, present, and future—that it came from something. But this is obviously impossible. If we cannot prove this fundamental claim, then how can it be reasonable for us to believe it is true?

Some, like the agnostic empiricist philosopher David Hume (1711–76), have concluded that it is *not* reasonable to accept this principle, the PUE in general, or the two versions of it stated above. As a result, these philosophers have rejected the cosmological and teleological arguments as proofs of the existence of God, since, as said above, all the arguments in these two families depend essentially on the assumption that the existence and order of the universe must have an explanation in terms of either an originating efficient cause or a sustaining efficient cause. However, many other philosophers have endorsed the claim that nothing comes from nothing, the PUE, and its two versions as truths of reason—propositions that are *self-evidently* true. Recall from chapter 2 that a self-evident truth is a proposition that is knowable solely on the basis of our understanding what it means and seeing (on the basis of rational reflection alone) that it *has* to be true. Other examples of self-evident truths are "everything that has a color has a shape" and "a part cannot be bigger than the whole of which it is a part." Unlike a statement such as "all bachelors are unmarried," these statements are true not only by virtue of the meaning of the words in the sentence but also because they describe ways the world *has* to be.

We can choose to follow Hume and refrain from endorsing the PUE as it applies to efficient causes. However, if we do, we will pay a heavy price. This is because we will not only forfeit the cosmological and teleological arguments for God's existence but also surrender the right to believe anything else that is based on the assumption that whatever happens in the world has an explanation in terms of an efficient cause. This includes virtually everything that is ordinarily considered to be known or knowable on the basis of scientific investigation and commonsense reasoning. Much of what we take ourselves to know about the world is based on inferences from things we have observed to things we have not observed. For instance, we believe there are such things as electrons, not because anyone has ever directly observed an electron but because the theory that electrons exist provides us with the best explanation of things we do observe (such as vapor trails in a cloud chamber). Here is where the PUE comes in. Scientific inferences of this sort presuppose that everything that happens in the world has an explanation in terms of an efficient cause. Given this, it is reasonable to believe that electrons exist because their existence is needed to explain how something we have observed has been caused to occur. If we do not accept the PUE, or at least the two versions of it that apply to efficient causes, we have no good reason to posit the existence of theoretical entities that no one has ever directly observed.

But this sort of reasoning is not restricted to science. Whenever we get a letter in the mail, we engage in causal reasoning of the same sort (reasoning that presupposes the PUE). Though all we can see directly is the letter itself, we infer that it wound up in our mailbox as a result of a causal chain of events initiated by a sender unseen by us and perpetuated by a process we did not witness. Even the simple matter of hearing a friend's voice in a dark room and inferring that our friend is in the room as the cause of this sound requires an acceptance of the PUE. Hume was actually aware of all this and yet accepted the skeptical consequences of rejecting the PUE as it applies to efficient causes. Do we really want to follow Hume and say that we are justified in believing only what we can directly observe at the present time?

The *Kalam* Cosmological Argument

If nothing can come from nothing, and therefore something about the world (everything that exists) must be eternal, could this something possibly be the material universe itself? According to one member of the cosmological argument family, the *Kalam* cosmological argument, the answer to this question is no.[3] Here is the argument in a nutshell:

1. Everything that comes into existence has an originating cause (this follows from the PUE_O).

3. *Kalam* is an Arabic word that literally means "speech" but also acquired the meaning "logic" or "philosophy" in association with the attempt on the part of some medieval Muslim philosophers to prove God's existence on the basis of the sort of argument that has acquired this label.

2. The material universe came into existence (began to exist).
3. Therefore, the material universe has an originating cause.

We have already considered reasons for accepting the first premise of this argument. What about the second one? What reasons are there for thinking that the material universe began to exist and therefore is not eternal? If this premise is true (and if we continue to accept the PUE), then both metaphysical naturalism and pan(en)theism are false, since both of these worldview families entail that the material universe is eternal (but for different reasons, of course). Notice that the second premise is not merely a claim about the coming into existence of the material universe *as we know it today.* If that were all it claimed, then it could be established scientifically by means of the confirmation of the big bang theory of the origin of the universe. Instead, premise 2 is a claim about the existence of any material universe at all, whether arranged as this one currently is or not.

Premise 2 follows from a central Christian doctrine—that of God's creation of the universe *ex nihilo* (out of nothing). This doctrine is consistent with the principle that nothing comes from nothing. The principle rules out the possibility that something came into existence from *absolutely* nothing. The doctrine states that the universe came into existence by an exercise of God's will, and this is not absolutely nothing. The doctrine of creation *ex nihilo* requires that God did not make the material universe out of any preexisting *stuff.* It does not require that nothing whatsoever (not even God) existed prior to the existence of the universe.

If the doctrine of creation *ex nihilo* is true, then creation monotheism is true and the two alternative monotheistic worldview families are false. These worldview families are contingency monotheism and dualistic monotheism. The former is the view, discussed in the last chapter, that there is one God who has coexisted eternally with an eternal contingent universe that depends on God for its existence. The latter is the view, also discussed in the last chapter, that both God and the universe are eternal, independent, and necessary entities. As we have seen, Judaism, Christianity, and Islam, as religious traditions that subscribe to creation monotheism, all agree that God created the universe *ex nihilo.*

The scriptures of these three religious traditions all support creation monotheism. Is there also philosophical support for it? The *Kalam* cosmological argument is certainly a significant step in this direction, but we still need a reason to accept its second premise. The following is an argument for premise 2:

4. If the material universe did not come into existence, then the material universe has existed during an actual infinite series of times.
5. But the universe could not have existed during an actual infinite series of times.

Therefore, premise 2 is true (the material universe came into existence).

Premise 4 should be obvious. If the material universe did not come into existence, then it has always existed. If this is the case, then it has existed forever, and there has actually transpired an infinite number of instants or moments during which it has existed. These moments, taken together, would constitute an *actual infinite series*. But premise 5 states that there cannot be such a series during which the universe has existed. Why is this? The main reason has to do with the concept of an infinite series. An *infinite series*, by definition, is a series with no last member, a series that never ends. But the present moment, whenever it is (right this very instant, while you are reading these words), is (at least temporarily) the very last instant in a series of instants during which the universe has existed. It follows that the series of times leading up to the present time, during which the universe has actually existed, cannot be infinitely long. So premise 5 is true.

But what are Christians to make of this in light of the beliefs that (1) God exists and yet never began to exist and (2) those who trust in Christ for salvation will enjoy everlasting life? One answer to the first question is that God does not exist in time but instead *outside* of time. If this is the case, then the fact that God never came into existence does not mean that God has existed in and during an actually infinite series of times (since God does not exist in and/or during *any* times). As for 2, to say that we will enjoy everlasting life with God is to say that our lives with him will never end. But it does not follow from this that we will ever exist long enough to have completed an actual infinite series of times (which, as we have seen, is impossible). Instead, at any future time during our endless existence, we will have existed only for a finite period of time, no matter how long. To say our existence will be endless is only to say that it is *potentially* infinite. It is not to say that an infinite series is ever *actually* complete.

With these arguments for premises 1 and 2 of the *Kalam* cosmological argument, we have good reason to endorse the conclusion of the argument, that the material universe has an originating cause. But this is not yet to say that this cause must be God. What reasons are there for thinking that it is? In the first place, there is good reason to think that the universe's originating cause must be something eternal. If it were not eternal, then it would have come into existence, and given the PUE_0, something else would have to exist to be *its* originating cause. But if we keep moving in this direction (assuming that this other thing also came into existence and therefore must also have an originating cause, etc.), we will have to posit the existence of an actual infinite series of originating causes, and as we have seen, that would be impossible. So at some point there must be an ultimate originating cause that is eternal. But we have also seen why this eternal cause must be timeless, at least in the sense of not having existed during an actual infinite series of times, since that would be impossible. If it is timeless, then it must also exist outside space as well, since whatever exists in space also exists in time. If it exists outside space, then it must be immaterial, because a material object must be located in space. It must also be sufficiently powerful to have created the material universe without making it out of any preexisting material. All these conclusions about the nature of the cause of the universe follow necessarily from the premises of the *Kalam* argument (and the premises of the arguments for those premises).

We can also conclude, though more tentatively, that the cause of the universe is *personal* as well. For one thing, the only possible kind of thing that is both immaterial and has causal powers is a person. Moreover, if the cause of the universe were impersonal and timeless, it would be hard to explain why the existence of such a thing alone would not be sufficient to bring about the existence of the universe. But then it would be hard to explain why the universe came into existence rather than having always existed. On the other hand, this is explicable on the assumption that the cause of the universe is a person who brought the universe into existence by freely willing it to exist. Therefore, the ultimate originating cause of the universe must be at least eternal, timeless, spaceless, immaterial, and very powerful, and it may well be personal. Though these are not *all* of the attributes of God, they are certainly among the essential ones.[4]

The *Kalam* argument, like all arguments, is like a chain. It is only as strong as its weakest link. In this case, its weakest link is probably premise 5, according to which the universe could not have existed during an actual infinite series of times. Though I have offered some reasons for thinking this is true, my argument is only an opening move in a potentially much more involved series of interactions between a Christian apologist and his or her conversation partner. Whether or not the material universe could have existed forever is controversial, and there is more that can be said on both sides of the argument. Fortunately, there is another version of the cosmological argument that, though it is also rationally resistible, does not rely on

4. See J. P. Moreland and William Lane Craig, *Philosophical Foundations for a Christian Worldview* (Downers Grove, IL: InterVarsity, 2003), 468–80, for a more thorough treatment of the *Kalam* cosmological argument.

this controversial and somewhat complicated assumption. The contingency version of the cosmological argument seeks to establish that God is needed as the sustaining cause of the universe, *even if the universe has always existed.*

The Contingency Cosmological Argument

Let's suppose for the sake of argument (even though Christian theology denies it) that the universe never came into existence—that it has always existed. According to the PUE_S, assuming that the existence of the universe cannot be explained by the universe's own nature, such an eternally existing universe would have to have a sustaining cause, something that explains what enables it to *continue* existing:

6. Everything that exists but does not have a nature that requires it to exist has a sustaining cause that explains its existence (this is the PUE_S).
7. The universe exists.
8. The universe does not have a nature that requires the universe to exist.
9. Therefore, the universe has a sustaining cause.

Naturalists may well be happy to concede *the conclusion* of this argument, because they may claim that the universe—or something within it—is the sustaining cause of the universe. But could the universe sustain itself in existence? Anything that can sustain its own ongoing existence is an independent thing, since its continuing existence does not depend on the existence of anything outside it.

The opposite of an independent thing is a dependent thing, which is, by definition, something that depends for its existence on the existence of something else. Notice that only eternal things (either things that exist outside time or things that have always existed in time) can be independent things. Anything that comes into existence depends for its initial existence on something else, since nothing can bring itself into existence (since it would have to exist before it existed in order to do so, and this is obviously impossible).

We are assuming now for the sake of argument that the universe is an eternal thing. Could the universe also be an independent thing, as some naturalists think it is? According to the proponents of the contingency version of the cosmological argument, the answer is no. The reason for this is their conviction that the universe is a contingent thing. A contingent thing is something that might not have existed. If an existing thing is not a contingent thing, then it is a necessary thing, something that *has* to exist. Another way to express premise 8 above is to say that the universe is a contingent thing. If the universe is a contingent thing, then it did not have to exist, and if it did not have to exist, then it does not have a nature that requires it to exist. So we can restate premise 8 as premise 10 and then draw out the implications of this claim (we will continue to assume premises 6–9):

10. The universe is a contingent thing.
11. If the universe is a contingent thing, then it is a dependent thing.
12. If the universe is a dependent thing, then its sustaining cause must be something other than the universe and the things in the universe.

13. Therefore, the sustaining cause of the universe must be something outside the universe.

If the argument succeeds to this point, then clearly, naturalism is ruled out, since the conclusion states that something other than the universe (nature) exists. But does the argument succeed in establishing that this conclusion is true? Since premise 12 follows directly from the definition of a dependent thing, this question can be answered only by looking more carefully at premises 10 and 11. What follows provides additional explanation of and justification for these two premises.

First of all, let's consider the case for premise 10. What reason is there for thinking that the universe is a contingent thing rather than a necessary thing (it has to be one or the other)? Is a material universe such as the one in which we live the kind of thing that has to exist, or is it instead the kind of thing that is such that it is possible for it not to have existed? This is an abstract question that may seem difficult to answer with complete confidence. It will help to think a bit more about how a material universe can be characterized. The two PUE principles apply at least to individual things (like the book you are holding in your hand right now), collections of things (such as the pages in this book), and properties (for instance, the property this book currently has of being read by you). Which of these kinds of things is the material universe? If the pan(en)theist is correct, then the universe is either God or a part of God. But then, as we have seen, either the universe is perfect in every respect (since God is perfect and so also every part of God is perfect), or God is imperfect (since the universe is imperfect). The pan(en)theist seems unable to say both that God is perfect and that the universe is imperfect given that God (or a part of God) and the universe are one and the same thing.

Physicists and cosmologists tell us that the universe is a collection of material particles, energy, forces, fields, and various kinds of composite objects that are made out of these sorts of things—all located in space and time. If this is true, then the universe is an *imperfect collection* of things rather than a perfect individual thing. Since God cannot be an imperfect collection of things, it follows from what these scientists tell us that pan(en)theism is false. But why think that this collection of physical things we call the universe is imperfect? A perfect thing would be completely unlimited in every respect. But the universe has all kinds of limitations. For one thing, all the things of which it is composed are limited by their location in space and time. For another thing, each of these physical things seems pretty clearly to be a contingent thing. This is certainly true of *composite* physical things, which, as we have seen, come into existence and go out of existence as their simpler parts move together for a while and then move apart. But this also seems to be true of the simplest physical constituents of the universe as well. There is nothing about the nature of these things that forces us to conclude they had to exist. Though they actually do exist, and even if we assume (as we do for the present) that they have *always* existed, it seems reasonable to believe that they might not have existed. This makes them more limited than something that exists of necessity, if there is such a thing. So the material universe is an imperfect collection of contingent things.

Though it does not follow directly from this that the universe itself is contingent, it is hard to see how there could be a collection of contingent things that was not contingent itself. Therefore, it is reasonable to believe that premise 10 (and so premise 8) is true.

Moreover, it seems reasonable to think that if something is contingent, then it is also a dependent thing. This is the general principle from which premise 11 follows. If the universe is contingent, as I have just argued that it is, then it did not have to exist. Since it does exist, it follows from the PUE_S that it has a cause that explains its ongoing existence. This would be something that would explain why it continues to exist rather than never having existed at all or going out of existence. If the universe were a necessary thing rather than a contingent thing, then it would be a straightforward matter to explain these things in terms of its nature. Since a necessary thing is something that by its nature *must* exist, such a thing would have within its own nature the resources to explain its ongoing existence. But since a contingent thing does not have the nature of being the kind of thing that has to exist, there does not seem to be anything about its nature to which we can appeal in explaining its existence. Consequently, if the universe is a contingent thing, then it seems reasonable to conclude that we need to look outside its nature for an explanation of its existence—something else must be its sustaining cause. Therefore, if the universe is a contingent thing, then it is also a dependent thing. This is premise 11.

We have argued for the existence of something outside the universe that causally sustains it. What is this thing like? Is it also a dependent thing? If so, then according to the PUE_S, there must be something outside it that causally sustains it as well. If that thing were also dependent, then there would need to be still another thing, and so on. It must be the case that

14. If all sustaining causes are dependent things, then the ongoing existence of the universe is explained by an *infinite regress* of sustaining causes.

This sets the stage for the completion of the contingency cosmological argument:

15. But nothing can be explained by an infinite regress of sustaining causes.
16. So not all sustaining causes can be dependent things, and the ultimate sustaining cause of the universe must be an independent thing.
17. If something is an independent thing, then it must also be a necessary thing.
18. Therefore, the ultimate sustaining cause of the universe is a necessary thing.

Is premise 15 true? Perhaps the best way to make a case for this premise is to use an analogy. Just as some cards in a house of cards must rest on something that is not made up of cards, so also a series of dependent sustaining causes must eventually be explainable in terms of a cause that is not dependent. This analogy highlights an important feature of the kind of infinite regress of causes ruled out by premise 15. The kind of infinite regress of causes in question here is such that *all the causes exist simultaneously*. This is importantly different from the kind of infinite series

precluded by the *Kalam* cosmological argument discussed in the previous section. That kind of series involved an infinitely long sequence of temporal stages during which the universe has existed. Notice that this is just the sort of infinite sequence we are now assuming to have been actualized in the past, since we have granted for the sake of argument that the universe has existed eternally. But the assumption that the universe has existed during an infinite series of times does not entail that it can be causally sustained at a given time by an infinitely long chain of sustaining causes. According to premise 15, it cannot. Let's see why this is the case. The relation of one thing causally sustaining another thing is *transitive*. This means that if something A causally sustains another thing B, and B causally sustains C, then A causally sustains C. Given this, what *ultimately* causally sustains the universe must be the very last in the regress of simultaneous causes. But if this regress is *infinitely long*, then there is no ultimate sustaining cause of the universe. If there is no last member of the regress, then the explanation of what sustains the ongoing existence of the universe is never complete. We will forever need to appeal to an additional link in the chain, and therefore we will eternally put off the completion of the explanation. Thus, premise 15 is true: Nothing can be explained by an infinite regress of sustaining causes.

Since 16 follows from 14 and 15, which I have already explained and defended, the only other premise left to discuss is 17, which says that all independent things are necessary things. Recall that an independent thing is something that contains within itself—within its own nature—the resources that enable it to sustain its own

Though the argument does not *force* anyone to accept its conclusion, it does force a rational person to decide which set of convictions he or she believes it would be most reasonable to have.

ongoing existence. Premise 17 claims that there can be such a thing only if it is a necessary thing as well, that is, only if it is the kind of thing that *must* exist, that could not have failed to exist. We have already provided a case for this claim above where it appeared in another form. Premise 11 (that all contingent things are dependent things) is logically equivalent to premise 17. Thus, the argument offered in support of 11 makes it reasonable to accept 17.

The contingency cosmological argument supports the claim that the sustaining cause of the universe is an independent and necessary thing. As seen above, this means that it is also eternal. We can conclude that it is immaterial as well, since all material things are part of the contingent universe. It may also be reasonable to conclude, as we did with respect to the *Kalam* argument, that the sustaining cause of the universe is personal, since this cause is both a causal agent and immaterial. Would an independent, necessary, eternal, and immaterial personal being automatically be God (or even more, the *Christian* God)? No. These are all traditional attributes of God, but there are other essential divine attributes that are not supported (or at least not easily supported) by the argument (such as, most generally, the property of

being perfect *in every respect*). However, if what we have argued so far is correct, then the naturalism worldview family, the pan(en)theist worldview family, and the cosmological dualist version of the monotheism family are excluded from consideration. In addition, if the *Kalam* argument is sound, then contingency monotheism can be eliminated as well. Thus, we are left with at least nondualist monotheism in general and perhaps creation monotheism in particular.

This chapter ends by affirming that the contingency cosmological argument, like the *Kalam* version, is rationally resistible. After considering the argument and all its components, a critic could give a reason to reject its conclusion. He or she could do this by giving a reason to deny (1) that the universe has a sustaining cause that explains its ongoing existence (the PUE$_S$), (2) that the universe is contingent, (3) that all contingent things are dependent things (and thus that all independent things are necessary things), or (4) that nothing can be explained by an infinite regress of sustaining causes. In such a case, a Christian apologist might point out that, though the argument does not *force* anyone to accept its conclusion, it does force a rational person to decide which set of convictions he or she believes it would be most reasonable to have. In particular, one needs to decide whether it would be more reasonable to deny at least one of claims 1 through 4 or instead to affirm the conclusion of the contingency cosmological argument. Though the critic will want to deny at least one of the premises of the argument, it is important for the critic to consider the possibility that it would be more reasonable to accept the argument's conclusion.

It may also be useful to appeal to the *heart* of a person who resists endorsing the conclusion of the contingency version of the cosmological argument. As we have seen, a worldview that characterizes the universe as unexplained, independent, or necessary would be a worldview devoid of resources for satisfying the deepest needs of the human heart. Though pointing this out to critics would not give them theoretical reasons to accept the contingency cosmological argument, it would nonetheless give them a practical reason to give the argument a second chance.

Reflection and Discussion

1. Do you agree that the principle of universal explanation is true? If not, would you agree at least that the existence of the universe must be explained and has an explanation?
2. Do you agree that an actual infinite series of times is impossible? If so, how would you supplement the argument in the text for this conclusion? If not, why not?
3. What do you think are the best ways to try to convince someone that the universe is contingent and dependent rather than necessary and independent?

Further Reading

Craig, William Lane. *The Cosmological Argument from Plato to Leibniz.* Eugene, OR: Wipf & Stock, 2001.

———. *The* Kalam *Cosmological Argument.* Eugene, OR: Wipf & Stock, 2000.

Davis, Stephen T. *God, Reason, and Theistic Proofs.* Grand Rapids: Eerdmans, 1997.

10

What the Heavens Declare

Teleological Explanations

» **Outline**

- **The Traditional Design Argument**
  - *An Example of Teleology in Nature*
  - *Thomas Aquinas's Argument from the Governance of the World*
  - *The Argument from Analogy*
- **Darwinian Evolution versus Intelligent Design**
  - *Darwin's Naturalistic Explanation of Biological Teleology*
  - *A Darwinist Argument against the Design Argument*
  - *Michael Behe's Argument against Darwinism*
  - *The Limits of Apologetic Arguments Based on Scientific Claims*
  - *Michael Behe's Argument for Intelligent Design*
- **Fine-Tuning and Wider Teleology**
  - *A Version of the Design Argument Consistent with Darwinism*
  - *The Fine-Tuning of the Universe*
  - *The Fine-Tuning Version of the Teleological Argument*
  - *Objections to the Fine-Tuning Argument*

» **Summary**

Teleological arguments for God's existence conclude that God is the designer of the universe and of teleological systems in nature. The traditional design argument focuses on things in nature that appear to be designed. The tra-ditional design argument is based on observed similarities between artifacts and some natural systems. Darwin's theory of biological evolution by natural selection pur-ports to explain the appearance of design in nature without appealing to God. Critics of the teleological argument can appeal to Darwinism to conclude that this argument fails. Michael Behe argues against Darwinism on the grounds that some biological systems are irreducibly complex. He also argues that such systems can be explained only by appealing to an intelligent designer. Whether or not Behe is correct, the fine-tuning version of the teleological argument can succeed even if Darwinism is true because it appeals to a wider teleology in the universe as a whole: The universe is fine-tuned in such a way as to support life.

» **Basic Terms, Concepts, and Names**

apparent design
Aquinas, Thomas
argument from analogy
Behe, Michael J.
Darwin, Charles
Darwinism
evolution, biological
fine-tuning of the universe
intelligent design
irreducibly complex system
many-universes hypothesis
methodological naturalism
natural selection
teleological system
teleology (wider and narrower)
Tennant, F. R.

» **Reflection and Discussion**

» **Further Reading**

> The heavens declare the glory of God; the skies proclaim the work of his hands.
>
> Psalm 19:1

Just as there are different versions of the cosmological argument for God's existence, there are also various kinds of teleological arguments. This chapter considers two members of this family. Recall that, whereas the cosmological arguments conclude that God must exist as the cause of the universe's *existence*, the teleological arguments are intended to support the claim that God exists as the cause of the universe's *order*. The key idea in any version of the teleological argument is that the existence of order in the universe is best explained by the universe's having been designed by an intelligent designer. This is because the order we observe in nature appears to serve a purpose, and it seems reasonable to think that things can serve purposes only if they were intentionally designed to achieve these ends by a being capable of having intentions and goals—an intelligent designer. This focus on purposes is why this type of argument is labeled teleological. The Greek word *telos*, from which this word comes, means "purpose," "end," or "goal." We begin an examination of teleological arguments by considering the traditional design argument for God's existence.

> **The key idea in any version of the teleological argument is that the existence of order in the universe is best explained by the universe's having been designed by an intelligent designer.**

The Traditional Design Argument

The best place to start in discussing this version of the argument is with specific observations of nature, especially the constitution and behavior of living things. Take for instance the migratory behavior of the famous swallows of the San Juan Capistrano Mission. At some point after the founding of this mission by Father Junipero Serra in 1776, cliff swallows began to build their mud nests in its eaves. In subsequent years, the swallows returned every spring from their winter in the Southern Hemisphere to occupy the same nests or to rebuild them if they had been destroyed. It seems clear that the purpose of this remarkably regular behavior is to enable these birds to reproduce in a context that provides them with adequate resources for the successful achievement of this goal (the mission is near two rivers, needed for the mud out of which the nests are made, and, at least until recently, also by open fields with insects needed for food). But it also seems clear that cliff swallows are not the kind of creatures capable of conscious intelligent purposive behavior. They do not have conscious plans, intentions, and strategies for the satisfaction of their needs and desires. Instead, they seem to be "programmed" to engage in behavior that automatically brings about these ends, which are beneficial to them and their offspring.

Thomas Aquinas, like his favorite philosopher, Aristotle, noticed that nature is full of relatively unintelligent things like this that engage in goal-directed behavior. However, unlike his teacher, Aquinas believed that these natural teleological phenomena can be used as a basis for demonstrating the existence of an intelligent designer who made these things. His argument to this effect, which is one of his celebrated "five ways" to prove that God exists, is worth quoting in full. His title for it is "The Argument from the Governance of the World":

We see that things which lack knowledge, such as natural bodies, act for an end, and this is evident from their acting always, or nearly always, in the same way, so as to obtain the best result. Hence it is plain that they achieve their end,

not fortuitously, but designedly. Now whatever lacks knowledge cannot move towards an end, unless it be directed by some being endowed with knowledge and intelligence; as the arrow is directed by the archer. Therefore, some intelligent being exists by whom all natural things are directed to their end; and this being we call God.[1]

Aquinas's example of the unintelligent arrow directed by the intelligent archer suggests that there is a *similarity* between God's design and governance of natural goal-directed behavior (like the migratory behavior of swallows) and the human design and employment of things made by us (like bows and arrows). This analogy serves as the basis for a variation on the traditional design argument that has come to be known as the argument from analogy. At the heart of this version of the argument is the idea that, since many natural things resemble human-made artifacts in certain important respects, and since these artifacts were caused to exist by intelligent design, it is probably also the case that the natural objects in question were produced by an intelligent designer—God.

In what respect are some natural objects analogous to human artifacts? I will use the concept of a teleological system to answer this question. A system is a complex object—something made up of parts—whose (often diverse) parts are interrelated in such a way as to work together. A *teleological* system is a system whose parts function together in such a way as to achieve a certain purpose, end, or goal.[2] What many natural things and

1. Thomas Aquinas, *Summa Theologica*, part 1, Q. 2, Art. 3.
2. Sometimes the word *system* is defined in such a way as to include the idea of parts working to-

artifacts have in common is that they are teleological systems. For instance, both eyeballs and watches are teleological systems. Eyeballs are highly complex natural objects that, when their parts function together in certain ways, together with the visual system with which they are naturally connected, serve the purpose of enabling the organism that has them to see. Watches are less complex artificial objects that can be used by people to figure out what time it is, at least when their parts are functioning together in the way they were designed to operate. So in spite of the many differences between eyeballs and watches (different chemical composition, different kinds of parts, different arrangement of parts, and different uses), they are generally and fundamentally similar or analogous insofar as they are both physical objects that are also teleological systems.

We all know that watches exist and function as they do because human beings designed and produced them. Humans are the *cause* of both the existence and the teleological nature of watches. Moreover, watches are the *effects* of this intelligent causal activity. Given this, we can explain the existence and character of watches in terms of intelligent human design. But what explains the teleological nature of eyeballs? What caused things like this to exist? This is the point at which the similarity or analogy between watches and eyeballs comes into play. As we have seen, they are both physical teleological systems. Moreover, it is clear that both watches and eyeballs are the effects of a causal process. So they are similar effects. We know what this process

gether in a unified fashion to bring about a certain end result. In that case, the term *teleological system* is redundant. However, *system* is sometimes used without this purposive element.

is when it comes to watches. We need to find out what it is with respect to eyeballs. To determine this, we need to affirm another philosophical principle concerning causation. This is the inductive principle that similar effects have similar causes.

Given this principle (which we have confirmed to be highly probable on the basis of much observation and inductive reasoning about the world), since the effects in question (watches and eyeballs) are similar (since they are both physical teleological systems), it follows that the sorts of things that caused them are similar as well. Watches are caused by intelligent designers. Therefore, the cause of eyeballs is probably an intelligent designer as well. Moreover, it is clear that this intelligent designer is not a human being. Eyeballs are not the product of human manufacture (the only part humans have played in the production of human eyeballs is the relatively unintelligent role of participating in the process of sexual reproduction). Therefore, a nonhuman intelligent designer is responsible for making eyeballs. One reason humans have not made eyeballs is that their intricate design exceeds our abilities. Therefore, the intelligent being that causes eyeballs must be *super*human as well. Indeed, it appears that such a being must be very intelligent and very powerful.

In sum, broken down to its bare bones, the argument is: (1) eyeballs and watches are similar effects, (2) similar effects have similar causes, (3) watches are caused by intelligent designers, and therefore (4) eyeballs are probably caused by an intelligent designer as well. Moreover, (5) humans are not sufficiently knowledgeable and powerful to make eyeballs, so (6) the intelligent designer of eyeballs possesses superhuman power and knowledge.

If this argument succeeds in establishing its conclusion, does it thereby demonstrate the probable existence of *God*? Like the contingency cosmological argument, which purports to prove the existence of an independent and necessary (and therefore also eternal and immaterial) being, the traditional design argument concludes that a being exists with *some* but not all of the attributes of God listed in chapter 8. In particular, it supports the existence of a powerful, intelligent, and *personal* being. If an argument has to conclude that a being exists with *all* the divine attributes (all the perfections) in order to demonstrate the existence of God, then neither of these two families of arguments shows that God exists. However, they do each support the existence of a being with *some* of the attributes of God, and they do not entail anything inconsistent with God's existence. Therefore, if they provide ample grounds for their conclusions, then they at least make an important contribution to establishing the existence of God. Moreover, when we put these two argument families together, the resulting combination of conclusions can be used as a basis for establishing the existence of a being with a wider range of divine attributes than either argument supports individually. The independent and necessary being of the contingency cosmological argument could be shown to be the intelligent and personal designer of natural teleological systems. In this way, the theistic arguments are like the strands that go together to make a rope. The whole is stronger than the parts.

But does the traditional design argument succeed in establishing that its conclusion is probably true? A better question is this: Does this argument support the claim that the intelligent designer hypothesis is *the most probable* explanation of the teleology of eyeballs and other natural teleological systems? Though there have been a number of challenges to this claim in the history of philosophical conversation about this argument,[3] the most formidable obstacle emerged in the nineteenth century with Darwin's theory of evolution by natural selection.

Darwinian Evolution versus Intelligent Design

Darwin published *The Origin of Species* in 1859. In it, he expounded his theory of biological evolution. This theory provides a completely *naturalistic* hypothesis that purports to explain the apparent design of natural teleological systems like eyeballs. If the theory is true, it can explain how natural teleological systems may *look* like they were designed by an intelligent supernatural designer when they are actually the result of a purely natural, impersonal, and random process. Darwin's theory does not mention a supernatural agent such as God. To the extent that Darwin's naturalistic explanation of the origin of natural teleological systems is plausible and prob-

3. In *Dialogues Concerning Natural Religion*, ed. Kemp Smith (New York: Bobbs-Merrill, 1947), David Hume argues that the analogy version of the design argument fails on the grounds that it is based on a bad analogy. An alternative version of the traditional design argument concludes that *the best explanation* of the apparent design in the universe is that it was actually designed by an intelligent designer. Darwin's theory challenges this conclusion by purporting to offer an explanation of apparent design in nature that does not appeal to an intelligent designer.

able, the intelligent design hypothesis is made less probable. So even if Darwin's theory is not proven true, as long as there is evidence for it, it compromises the claim that an appeal to God is needed to explain the apparent design of biological organisms and their organs.

How does a Darwinian explanation of natural biological teleology proceed? There are three important aspects to the explanation: (1) random genetic change, (2) natural selection, and (3) genetic inheritance. Here is, generally speaking, how such an explanation would go. Complex organisms and organs (like eyeballs) have evolved over a long period of time from simpler life forms. This process of biological evolution from simpler to more complex forms took place by means of random genetic changes (mutations) that occurred in simpler forms during the reproductive process. That is, an organism produced an offspring that differed from it in some important respect. In general, such accidental and unplanned alterations to the parts of biological organisms either have survival value for the organisms or they do not. If they have survival value, then the organism that acquired them will have a tendency to be better able to adapt to its environment. If they do not have survival value, then the organism will not be as likely to adapt and so will not be as likely to survive. This is the idea of the survival of the fittest. Natural selection is the name given to this process of weeding out organisms that naturally occurs as a result of the degree to which they are able to survive. The organisms that inherit traits that enable them better to adapt to their environments are "selected" by nature.

Since the traits of parents are transmitted genetically to their offspring, they inherit their predecessors' tendency to survive or not to survive. Thus, eventually, the organisms that inherit traits with less survival value have a tendency to die out, and those that inherit traits with more survival value are likely to continue to reproduce from one generation to the next. Throughout successive instances of this process of mutation, selection, and transmission, the surviving biological organisms become more complex and better able to survive and reproduce. The long-term end result is the existence of biological structures that possess a degree of complexity and adaptability that produces the appearance of design.

With all this in mind, a critic may argue as follows: (1) If Darwin's theory of evolution by natural selection (Darwinism) is true, then the teleological argument for God's existence is a failure; (2) Darwinism is true; (3) therefore, the teleological argument fails. Laying out the critic's argument in this way makes it clear that Christian apologists have a number of replies available to them. The first reply, and the least adequate from the standpoint of the goals of apologetics, is to accept the argument. Though this response is not ideal, it would still be acceptable from an apologetic standpoint. Even if the design argument fails to support God's existence, other theistic arguments, such as the cosmological ones discussed in the previous chapter, may still provide good evidential grounds for belief in God. The second reply, which many Christians believe is the only adequate reply, is to deny that Darwinism is true. This approach would require an apologist to weigh the scientific evidence both for and against Darwinism and to argue on scientific grounds that this theory of biological evolution is either not adequately supported by the evidence or, more ambitiously, is downright false. The remainder of this section investigates a recent scientific attempt of this sort to discredit Darwinism. The third reply to the critic's argument is to deny the first premise and to argue that, even if Darwinism is true, it does not follow that no version of the teleological argument can succeed. This approach, which is discussed in the next section of this chapter, grants that Darwinism can explain the appearance of design in biological organisms but insists that there is a wider teleology of a nonbiological sort in the universe as a whole that can best be accounted for by an appeal to God as its cause. Those who take this route do not have to believe that Darwinism is true (since they are only trying to show that it does not entail that all teleological arguments for God are unacceptable), but if they do, they are theistic evolutionists. (Chap. 22 considers the debate between creationists and theistic evolutionists more thoroughly.)

Darwinism is a threat to the traditional design argument only insofar as it is plausible to think it is true. Moreover, it is reasonable to believe that it is true only if it accounts for *all* instances of apparent design in biological systems. Darwin himself identified a means to falsify his theory by remarking, "If it could be demonstrated that any complex organ existed which could not possibly have been formed by numerous, successive, slight modifications, my theory would absolutely break down."[4] Recently, biologist and Christian

Christian apologists have a number of replies available to them.

apologist Michael J. Behe argued in his book *Darwin's Black Box: The Biochemical Challenge to Evolution*[5] that some such complex biological systems exist. Behe calls these systems "irreducibly complex." He defines an irreducibly complex system as "a single system which is composed of several well-matched, interacting parts that contribute to the basic function, and where the removal of any one of the parts causes the system to effectively cease functioning."[6] Behe says that a simple mechanical mousetrap is a good (nonbiological) example of an irreducibly complex system. These mechanisms, with which most people are familiar, consist of a few simple parts: a rectangular wooden base, a spring, a wire hammer, a holding bar, and a catch. What makes this a *complex* system is that it is made up of these parts. What makes it an *irreducibly* complex system is that each of these parts *must* be present and capable of functioning properly for the entire mousetrap to function properly (i.e., to trap mice). If at least one of these parts were missing, the mousetrap would not be capable of performing its basic function. Behe claims that many systems in biological cells are, like these simple mousetraps, irreducibly complex. As an example, he cites the bacterial flagellum, which he says is "quite literally an outboard motor that some bacteria use to

4. Charles Darwin, *The Origin of Species,* 6th ed. (New York: New York University Press, 1988), 154.

5. New York: Free Press, 1996.
6. Ibid., 39.

swim."[7] Behe takes up Darwin's challenge by arguing that the bacterial flagellum and other subcellular systems are irreducibly complex and therefore "could not be formed by numerous, successive, slight modifications."

In a nutshell, Behe's argument against Darwinism is this:

1. Some biological systems (like the bacterial flagellum) are irreducibly complex.
2. If a biological system is irreducibly complex, then it could not have come about solely by means of a process of evolution by natural selection.
3. If there are biological systems that could not have come about solely by means of a process of evolution by natural selection, then Darwinism is false.
4. Therefore, Darwinism is false.

Premise 3 is another way of stating Darwin's own comment, quoted above, about what would falsify his theory. It is true because Darwin's theory of evolution by natural selection, as pointed out above, is intended to apply to *all* biological systems. Notice that if Darwin's theory were falsified by showing that a biological system could not have originated by means of natural selection, it could still be the case that some *other* biological systems arose by means of this process. But then this would not pose a significant threat to the traditional design argument, because the hypothesis of an intelligent designer may well be needed to explain the origin

of biological systems that did *not* arise by natural selection.

Here is an argument for premise 2. Recall that an irreducibly complex system is a system that would not be able to perform its basic function if at least one of its parts were missing. But the supposition that the system evolved by means of natural selection implies that (1) it evolved from a simpler system that lacked at least one of the parts that currently contributes to this functioning, and yet (2) it was *capable* of performing its basic function. Therefore, no irreducibly complex system could have arisen by means of natural selection. The mousetrap provides a clear example of this. A mousetrap could not have evolved from simpler to more complex forms by means of natural selection, because any reduction of the mousetrap to a simpler form (i.e., a form missing at least one of the parts it presently contains) would result in a system that would be incapable of performing its function (even to a degree).[8]

Premise 1 is a scientific claim. As such, for one to know whether it is likely to be true, one must know the following presumably uncontroversial scientific facts: (1) what the composition of these systems is (i.e., what their parts are and how these parts are interrelated) and (2) how these interrelated parts work together to enable the system to perform its basic function. One must also be in a position to evaluate the *controversial* scientific claim that (3) if just *one* of these parts were missing, the system would not be capable of perform-

7. Michael Behe, "The Modern Intelligent Design Hypothesis," *Philosophia Christi*, series 2, vol. 3, no. 1 (2001): 168.

8. Premise 2 and the argument for it have been challenged. See, for instance, Paul Draper, "Irreducible Complexity and Darwinian Gradualism: A Reply to Michael J. Behe," *Faith and Philosophy* 19, no. 1 (January 2002): 3–21.

ing its basic function. This is the claim for which scientific evidence needs to be given to justify concluding that the system in question is *irreducibly* complex. This claim is controversial because a number of biologists have denied that some biological systems are irreducibly complex. Some have backed up their denials with attempts to demonstrate that systems Behe alleges are irreducibly complex—such as the blood clotting system—are actually reducible to simpler systems that perform similar functions.[9]

The fact that these are *scientific* claims limits the general usefulness of these types of arguments for two reasons. First, non-scientists are ill equipped to follow the intricacies of the scientific conversations about these things, and second, even those with the requisite scientific knowledge have to admit that every scientific hypothesis about irreducible complexity—both pro and con—is highly tentative in nature (as Behe himself affirms) and difficult to confirm. The first consideration means that nonscientists will need to trust what scientists say about these things. The second means that it will be difficult for scientists to make a conclusive and compelling case and for nonscientists to know whom to trust. It is for such reasons that C. S. Lewis, in his essay titled "Christian Apologetics," says:

> Science is in continual change . . . [and] for [this] reason, we must be very cautious of snatching at any scientific theory which, for the moment, seems to be in our favour. We may *mention* such things; but we must mention them lightly and without claiming that they are more

than "interesting." Sentences beginning "Science has now proved" should be avoided.[10]

However, though the apologetic value of scientific claims about irreducible complexity is limited by their tentativeness and inconclusiveness, they are still useful to some extent. For one thing, insofar as the irreducible complexity hypothesis is taken seriously by the scientific community and is debated by its adherents and its detractors, the probability that Darwinism is true is called into question, and its tendency to weaken the traditional design argument is thereby compromised.

Behe's argument against Darwinism is the *negative* component of his apologetic project. The *positive* element is his argument that the best scientific explanation of the irreducible complexity of some biological systems is that they were produced by deliberate intelligent design. Though Behe stops short of concluding that this intelligent designer is God, the success of his scientific argument would open the door to further *philosophical* argument along these lines (such as the sort involved in the traditional design argument). However, as with the negative part of his program, there are concerns about the positive part.

For one thing, even if irreducibly complex biological systems rule out their having originated by means of a process of evolution *by natural selection*, there may be a process of evolution that makes use of *other kinds* of purely natural mechanisms that are capable of producing irreducibly complex systems. Of course, until these

---

9. Behe, "Modern Intelligent Design Hypothesis," 174–77.

10. C. S. Lewis, "Christian Apologetics," in *God in the Dock: Essays on Theology and Ethics,* ed. Walter Hooper (Grand Rapids: Eerdmans, 1970), 92.

are specified and evidence is provided for their existence, the mere possibility of such mechanisms would not diminish the probability of the intelligent design hypothesis. Second, this inference to the intelligent design hypothesis, like Behe's argument against Darwinism, is both tentative and inconclusive. Nonetheless, it may well be the best explanation available. Finally, Behe's scientific method, which involves an appeal to a nonnatural cause to explain normal natural phenomena, is quite controversial. Many scientists, including both theists and nontheists, agree that scientific hypotheses should be formulated only in terms of purely natural causes. This is the thesis of methodological naturalism, which is discussed at more length in chapter 22. Methodological naturalists argue that any postulation of a nonnatural cause to explain a normal natural phenomenon prematurely ends the search for a natural cause and is scientifically unproductive and ultimately untestable. Chapter 22 discusses this objection.

Fine-Tuning and Wider Teleology

Even if it should turn out that the case for irreducible complexity in nature cannot be sustained, in which case (1) Behe's argument against Darwinism would fail to establish its conclusion, and (2) the basis for his scientific hypothesis of the intelligent design of biological systems would be undercut, it would not follow that there is no good version of the teleological argument for God's existence. There may well be, as F. R. Tennant (1866–1957) argued, a wider teleology manifested by the universe as a whole (as opposed to a narrower teleology exhibited by living organisms within the universe), for which the best explanation is the existence of an intelligent designer of the universe. This would be consistent with the use of the process of evolution by natural selection by this designer to bring about, indirectly and gradually, the existence of the living organisms that populate the earth today. But what reasons are there for thinking that the entire cosmos exhibits the marks of design? Do features of the universe *as a whole* suggest that it is a teleological system—a complex arrangement of objects that functions in such a way as to serve a specific purpose, end, or goal?

Recent scientific conclusions support an affirmative answer to this question. There is remarkable agreement today among scientists who study the universe that there are numerous separate, specific features of the universe that (1) must all exist in order for life to be possible and (2) are such that it is highly improbable that any one of them arose by chance. Scientists call this collection of life-permitting cosmological characteristics the fine-tuning of the cosmos. This language makes it natural to employ the metaphor of a universe-generating machine with a number of dials on it that can each be set precisely at any number of a wide range of specific settings. We can imagine such a machine being capable of generating a large number of universes that differ from one another in various ways. These qualitatively distinct universes would be the result of the dials on the machine being set at different points. If we assume that each dial has a large number of settings and that there are a large number of dials, then there would be a large number of combinations of dial settings that would result in a large number of possible universes. What the actual fine-tuning of the universe means, when described in terms of such a fictional machine, is that only a small proportion of dial setting combinations—out of all those possible—would lead to the generation of universes that would have the conditions required for the existence of living organisms.

Among the examples of the fine-tuning of the universe are the following: (1) If the initial explosion of the big bang had been either weaker or stronger by a tiny amount, the universe would have either quickly collapsed or expanded too rapidly for the formation of stars, and in either case, life would not have been possible. (2) If the strong nuclear force that binds protons and neutrons together in the nuclei of atoms had differed minutely in strength, life could not have existed. There are a number of additional fine-tuning facts like these, and they add up to a conjunction of factors that had to be just right, and could easily not have been so, for living systems to exist.[11]

The previous section of this chapter discussed the scientific irreducible complexity hypothesis, which would provide strong support for the existence of intelligent design if it turned out to be true. The main problem with this hypothesis from the standpoint of Christian apologetics is that it is highly controversial among scientists. This, however, is not the case with respect to the claim that the universe is fine-tuned to support life. About this there is virtual consensus among contemporary physical cosmologists. The main disagreement has instead to do with whether the agreed-upon facts about the universe are

best explained by means of the philosophical hypothesis that an intelligent designer fine-tuned the universe for the purpose of making life possible. Are there reasons for thinking that the hypothesis of theism provides a better explanation of fine-tuning than does the metaphysical naturalist's claim that the fine-tuning of the universe is a result of chance?

A relatively simple philosophical argument, based on the uncontroversial claim that the universe is fine-tuned to support life, favors theism over naturalism on the assumption that the current universe is the only universe that has ever existed. Here is how the argument goes:[12]

1. On the hypothesis that God exists, the fine-tuning of the universe is not improbable.
2. On the hypothesis that God does *not* exist and that this is the only universe that has ever existed, the fine-tuning of the universe is very improbable.
3. If one hypothesis makes an observed phenomenon more probable than another hypothesis, then (other things being equal) the former hypothesis is rationally superior to the latter.
4. Therefore, the theistic hypothesis is rationally superior to the atheistic single-universe hypothesis.

There are good reasons to accept each of the premises of this argument. Premise 1 is supported by the consideration that

11. See John Leslie, *Universes* (New York: Routledge, 1989), for more examples, details, and explanations along these lines.

12. See Robin Collins, "A Scientific Argument for the Existence of God: The Fine-Tuning Design Argument," in *Reason for the Hope Within*, ed. Michael J. Murray, 47–75 (Grand Rapids: Eerdmans, 1999), for a similar version of this argument and a more thorough discussion of it.

if God exists, then a supremely good and powerful being exists. If such a being exists, given that conscious life is a good thing, it is not improbable that this being created a universe with the features required to permit life. We can appeal to our fabricated universe-generating machine to make a case for premise 2. If metaphysical naturalism is true, then there is no intelligent designer of the universe who deliberately set the dials on this machine to bring about the goal of generating a universe that supports life. If this universe is the only universe that has ever existed, then the probability that the dials on this machine could have been set randomly by chance only once to result in a combination of settings required for the possibility of life is exceedingly small, since the number of possible universes fine-tuned to support life is a very small fraction of the number of all the possible universes that could be generated by the machine. Finally, premise 3 is a principle on which commonsense and scientific reasoning are based.

Criticisms of this fine-tuning version of the teleological argument focus mostly on premise 2. What reasons can be given for thinking that the life-supporting fine-tuning of the universe (which virtually everyone agrees to be the case) is *not* very improbable given the assumptions that there is no God and that this is the only universe that has ever existed?

Objection 1: It is *necessary* in some sense that the universe be fine-tuned for life. According to this view, the universe can exist only if the universe is fine-tuned for life; there are no possible alternative universes that could have been generated instead. If this is the case, then given the existence of the universe, the universe's fine-tuning for life is maximally probable.

Reply: The main problem with this objection is that there is, at least currently, no good reason to think that the universe can exist only if it is fine-tuned for life, and there are, at least currently, many good reasons to think otherwise. For one thing, the physical cosmologists who have discovered the fine-tuning features of the universe have described and illustrated them by explaining ways the universe could have been if it did not have these specific features. These alternatives certainly *seem* physically possible, and unless there is good reason to think they are not, it seems reasonable to conclude that they are. Another difficulty with this objection is that it seems implausible, on the face of it, that the only structure the universe could have is a structure that would support the existence of intelligent living systems. This in itself seems highly improbable.

Objection 2: Since human beings exist, it should not be surprising or seem improbable that the universe is fine-tuned for life, since human existence *requires* such cosmological fine-tuning. More precisely, (1) it is highly probable (indeed, observationally certain) that humans exist, and (2) it is also highly probable that, if humans exist, then the universe is fine-tuned to support life. It therefore follows that (3) it is highly probable that the universe is fine-tuned to support life.

Reply: An assumption here is that both of the premises of this objection are acceptable from the standpoint of the atheistic single-universe hypothesis. However, this assumption is highly doubtful. The first premise in particular seems highly problematic from an atheistic point of view. The most reasonable account of human origins from that point of view is that human beings were not created by God but instead evolved by means of a long process of evolution by random mutation and natural selection. According to this hypothesis, it seems *improbable* that such a random unguided process should have resulted in the existence of human beings. It seems even more improbable that the only universe to have existed should be one that allows for such an evolution of *any* life form, including human beings. Therefore, this objection does not provide good grounds for denying the high degree of the improbability of a godless single universe having been fine-tuned for life. The reason the first premise of the objection seems plausible in spite of this is that it is shorthand for something like "given the observational data that confirm the existence of human beings, it is very likely that there are such beings." But then this is a claim about *evidential* rather than *objective* probability, and what is needed for the objection to succeed is the latter. That is, though our observations of humans provide strong evidence for the claim that humans exist (evidential probability), these observations by themselves do not make it highly likely that humans should have come to exist in the first place (objective probability).

Another critical response to the fine-tuning argument for God's existence is to accept the conclusion of the argument but to argue that the fine-tuning of the universe is not improbable—but instead quite likely—given an atheistic many-universes hypothesis. According to this hypothesis, there is no God, and the universe in which we live is only one of many—perhaps an infinite number—of actual universes that either have existed or (somehow) currently coexist. A long temporal series of universes could be due to an ongoing generation of universes explainable in terms of an oscillating universe model. According to this model, universes come into existence by means of a big bang, and then, after expanding, they contract into a big crunch, and the cycle begins again, with a different set of physical parameters resulting. If we continue to employ the pretense of a universe-generating machine to talk about this, we could say that this machine continues to generate universes in this fashion and that, before each generation, the dials on the machine are randomly reset. In this way, it becomes likely that, given enough such random resettings, a universe would eventually be generated that is fine-tuned to support life, even if there is no intelligent designer who sets the dials for this purpose. According to an alternative model, the machine generates a large—perhaps infinite—set of randomly different universes *simultaneously*. What makes these universes distinct from one another is that they are mutually spatio-temporally unrelated or discontinuous. Critics urge that, either way, this hypothesis is not clearly rationally inferior to the theistic design hypothesis.

A number of responses could be made to this argument. However, the most effective one is to point out that, though the theistic hypothesis and the atheistic many-universes hypothesis *might* be equally probable explanations of the fact that the universe in which we live is fine-tuned for life (though it is by no means clear that this should be granted), there are a number of good, independent reasons for thinking that theism is true, but there are *no* good, independent reasons to believe that the atheistic many-universes hypothesis is true. The additional grounds for theism include the two versions of the cosmological argument discussed in the last chapter. There are, as well, other arguments for God's existence that we have not yet discussed. One of these is the moral argument, which is articulated and defended in chapter 25. According to that argument, to the extent that we have good reasons to believe there is a universal and objective standard of morality, we have good reasons to believe that God must exist to be the ultimate ground of that moral standard. As for the atheistic many-universes hypothesis, not only is there no good reason to believe it is true, but it carries with it the additional burden of leaving unexplained how such a large temporal series or simultaneous set of universes could exist in the absence of an independent, necessary, personal, and

intelligent being such as God that could have created them. In sum, the hypothesis of theism is more probable than the atheistic many-universes hypothesis, given both the fine-tuning *and* the existence of the universe (in addition to such things as the existence of a universal moral standard and a host of other features of the world that resist ultimate explanation on purely naturalistic grounds).

There is, however, a pervasive feature of the world that, on the face of it at least, counts as evidence *against* God's existence and that many atheists believe can be employed to demonstrate that God does not exist. This theism-challenging characteristic is the existence of evil. We turn now to the problem of evil and the problem it presents to Christian apologists intent on defending the rationality of belief in a supremely good and all-powerful God.

Reflection and Discussion

1. What examples of apparent design in the biological world seem to require an explanation in terms of an intelligent designer (on the assumption that these things cannot be explained in terms of evolution by natural selection)?
2. Do you side more with the Darwinists or with the anti-Darwinists in the debate about irreducible complexity and intelligent design? Why?
3. What reasons would you give a defender of the atheistic many-universes hypothesis for the rational superiority of the hypothesis that God fine-tuned a single universe?

Further Reading

Behe, Michael J. *Darwin's Black Box: The Biochemical Challenge to Evolution.* New York: Free Press, 1996.

Darwin, Charles. *The Origin of Species.* New York: Signet Classics, 2003.

Hume, David. *Dialogues and Natural History of Religion.* Edited by J. C. A. Gaskin. New York: Oxford University Press, 1998.

Leslie, John. *Universes.* New York: Routledge, 1989.

11

Why Do the Righteous Suffer?

The Problem of Evil

» Outline

- **The Problem of Evil**
  - *The Practical and Theoretical Problems of Evil*
  - *Moral versus Natural Evil*
- **The Argument from Evil**
  - *The Basic Argument*
  - *An Inadequate Reply: Denying God's Omnipotence*
  - *The Possibility That God Has a Reason That Justifies Evil*
  - *The Revised Basic Argument*
- **Justifying the Ways of God to Men and Women**
  - *The Punishment Theodicy*
  - *The Free Will Theodicy*
  - *The Natural Consequences Theodicy*
  - *The Natural Law Theodicy*

» Summary

The existence of evil in the world poses two problems for theists. The practical problem of evil is the psychological problem of sustaining confident belief in God in the face of evil. The theoretical problem of evil is the philosophical problem of trying to understand why God allows evil or at least trying to show that it is reasonable to believe that God exists given the reality of evil. Apologists are concerned primarily with the theoretical problem. Moral evil is sin and the consequences of sin. Natural evil is pain and suffering that result from natural causes. The argument from evil concludes that God does not exist on the grounds that nothing would justify God in allowing evil. A theodicy is an attempt to explain why God allows evil. The punishment theodicy explains why people experience pain and suffering when they deserve to, but other theodicies are needed to explain the existence of undeserved pain and suffering. The free will theodicy explains why God permits some moral evil, but the natural consequences theodicy and the natural law theodicy are needed to explain why God allows both humans and animals to be subject to natural evils.

» Basic Terms, Concepts, and Names

Aquinas, Thomas
argument from evil
defense
free will theodicy
Hume, David
justifying reason for evil
Manicheanism
moral evil
morally significant free will
natural consequences theodicy
natural evil
natural law theodicy
problems of evil (practical and theoretical)
process philosophy
punishment theodicy
theodicy

» Reflection and Discussion

» Further Reading

> This is the evil in everything that happens under the sun: The same destiny overtakes all. The hearts of men, moreover, are full of evil and there is madness in their hearts while they live, and afterward they join the dead.
>
> Ecclesiastes 9:3

The Problem of Evil

We come now to what most people—theists and nontheists alike—consider to be the most formidable challenge to rational belief in the existence of God: the problem of evil. A good way to get an initial feel for this problem is to ask yourself, How can the kind of God that Christians and other theists believe exists—a perfect God—allow evils in the form of sin, injustice, pain, suffering, and death to exist in the world? After all, if God is perfect, then God is all-powerful, so he would be able to prevent these evils from occurring. Moreover, the fact that God is perfect also means that he is supremely good, and God would thus *want* to prevent the existence of evil. Here is how the agnostic philosopher David Hume put the problem in a nutshell:

Is he willing to prevent evil, but not able? then he is impotent. Is he able, but not willing? then he is malevolent. Is he both able and willing? whence then is evil?[1]

To facilitate understanding of this issue before trying to resolve it, the rest of this section discusses (1) the sense in which there is more than one kind of problem of evil and (2) the two major kinds of evil that these problems are about.

A distinction is often made between the practical/psychological problem of evil and the theoretical/philosophical problem of evil. Both of these problems can result from taking seriously the question posed above about why God would (or how God could) permit evil in the world. The former problem is the problem of trying to maintain or restore confident belief in God's existence or strong trust in God's providence when one is troubled by suffering, tragedy, or injustice, especially when

1. David Hume, *Dialogues Concerning Natural Religion*, part X, ed. Kemp Smith (New York: Bobbs-Merrill, 1947), 198.

one cannot explain why God would let these things happen. This is a *psychological* problem because it has to do with cultivating and/or sustaining the psychological states of belief, faith, and trust in God. It is a *practical* problem because it also concerns putting into practice or living out a relationship of trust with God. A book of this sort certainly ought to address this problem in some way, since the ultimate goal of Christian apologetics is to cultivate Christian commitment. However, since Christian apologetics has primarily to do with investigating the reasonableness of believing that Christianity is *true*, the focus will be on the theoretical/philosophical problem of evil. This is the problem of trying to figure out whether the existence of evil provides a good reason to believe that God does not exist (or is not perfect). This is a *theoretical* problem because it has to do with what theories we should adopt about the way the world is, that is, what we should believe to be true. It is a *philosophical* problem because it requires the use of philosophical tools both to articulate the problem and to solve it.

These two problems are often related in important ways. A person who does not know how to solve the theoretical problem (whether the existence of evil provides adequate reason to believe that God does not exist or is not perfect) can easily find himself or herself dealing with the practical problem of finding it difficult to sustain belief, faith, or trust in God. The likelihood of this sort of thing occurring provides a good *practical* reason to try to solve the *theoretical* problem (by at least finding good reasons to think that the existence of evil does not make theistic belief unreasonable). Moreover, a believer who begins to struggle with the practical problem of

evil, as a result of having experienced a tragic event of some kind, may by means of this become aware of the theoretical problem of evil, and this may result in an intensification and complication of his or her practical problem. Such a person can easily become a doubter and eventually a critic. Once again, this provides good practical reasons to tackle the theoretical problem. But even Christians who have not been faced with the practical problem of evil are well advised to think as carefully and thoroughly as possible about the theoretical problem and its potential solutions. This is because it is arguably the main theoretical objection to rational belief in God employed by critics to resist theism, experienced by seekers as an obstacle to belief, and encountered by doubters as a threat to their faith. Given the goals of Christian apologetics to defend the rationality of Christian belief and to contribute to the cultivation of Christian commitment, an honest and courageous examination of the theoretical problem of evil is a must.

To be in the best position to understand, appreciate, and attempt to solve this problem, it is important to be clear about a distinction almost always made in discussing it. This is the distinction between *moral* evil and *natural* evil. Moral evil encompasses both sin and the consequences of sin. An alternative nontheological way of defining moral evil is that it

> ## An honest and courageous examination of the theoretical problem of evil is a must.

involves anything a person or a group of persons freely chooses to do that is morally wrong or unjust. It also includes any pain and/or suffering that result(s) from such voluntary immoral behavior. Clear examples of moral evil include murder, rape, kidnapping, torture, and malicious slander and their consequences. Natural evils include the pain and suffering that are not an intended result of a person's deliberate choices but are instead the sorts of evils that are caused by what we typically categorize as natural disasters. Examples of natural evils include the pain, suffering, and death resulting from earthquakes, floods, tornados, and diseases.[2]

When we talk about evil in this chapter, we mean not only wickedness but also pain and suffering. Moreover, the pain and suffering include a range of intrinsically bad conscious experiences, some of which are exclusively or primarily psychological (like despair, depression, anguish, etc.) and some of which are predominately physical (like intense bodily pain of various kinds). Furthermore, any being that can and does experience pain and suffering—any sentient being—will provide potential instances of the problem of evil. This includes, of course, not only humans but also nonhuman animals of various kinds.

With these preliminary distinctions made, we are in a position to state the theoretical problem of evil more precisely: Does any philosophical argument exist, based on an observation of existing sin, pain, and suffering, that provides an adequate reason for believing that God does not exist (or is not perfect)? If there is such an argument, then it is unreasonable to believe that a perfect God exists, and thus it is unreasonable to believe that Christianity is true.

The Argument from Evil

To start our search for such a philosophical argument, let's consider a simple but ultimately unsatisfactory candidate:[3]

1. If God exists, then there is no evil.
2. But there is evil.
3. Therefore, God does not exist.

Since Christians will want to deny 3, the conclusion of this argument, Christian apologists must provide adequate reasons to deny either 1 or 2. But whereas some non-Christians may deny premise 2 (such as a pantheist who says that evil is an illusion on the grounds that everything is God and God is perfect), Christians are committed biblically and theologically to affirm premise 2 (at least on the basis of the doctrine of sin, since sin is moral evil). A Christian apologist, therefore, must make a good case for rejecting premise 1 or at least must show that it is reasonable not to affirm it.

Before formulating an argument against premise 1, however, we should ask what reasons anyone might have for believing it to be true. Such reasons can easily be

2. For various reasons, the ways I have defined these two kinds of evil in this paragraph may not clearly distinguish them in every case. This is not a problem, however, since it does not affect either the argument from evil or the replies to it. It is enough to have a rough and ready distinction between moral evil and natural evil.

3. In this chapter and the first section of the next chapter, I am indebted to Daniel Howard-Snyder, "God, Evil, and Suffering," in *Reason for the Hope Within*, ed. Michael J. Murray, 76–115 (Grand Rapids: Eerdmans, 1999).

found by reflecting on Hume's questions stated above. What Hume seems to have in mind is something like the following:

4. If God exists, then God is perfect.
5. If God is perfect, then God is omnipotent, omniscient, and omnibenevolent (omni x 3).
6. If God is omni x 3, then there is no evil.

Therefore, premise 1 is true.

We already discussed premises 4 and 5 in chapter 8. Most Christians will want to accept these premises (though the next paragraph considers attempts to resist premise 1 by denying premise 4). Therefore, the most questionable premise here, from a Christian perspective, is 6. Even though we will want and need to deny this premise, let's first provide as strong a case for it as we can so that we can be sure we are rejecting the strongest possible form of the critic's argument. Here is the case: If God is *omnipotent*, then God will be *able* to prevent pain and suffering from occurring. If God is *omniscient*, then God will *know in advance* when any pain and suffering is about to occur. If God is *omnibenevolent* (and, from a Christian standpoint, *supremely loving*), then God will *want* to prevent whatever pain and suffering he can. Moreover, if God has the ability, advance knowledge, and desire to prevent evil, then surely he would exercise this power, based on this foresight, to bring about his will that the evil not occur—*and there would consequently be no evil.* Given this argument for premise 6 (and the reasons to accept 4 and 5), we are faced with a strong rational basis for premise 1. How can a Christian apologist reply?

As just mentioned, some have chosen to avoid endorsing premise 1 by rejecting premise 4. In particular, they have sought to explain how both God and evil can coexist by denying that God has the perfection of omnipotence. According to this view, God allows evil because God is incapable of preventing it. This is the ancient Manichean solution to the problem of evil that temporarily satisfied Augustine before he developed an alternative orthodox Christian reply that affirmed God's omnipotence. It is also the solution offered by some today who combine process theology with panentheism. According to the former, God is not perfect but instead in the process of becoming better. According to the latter, the changing universe is a part of God. When we put these ideas together, we have a God who is limited by that part of him (the universe) that is imperfect and changing. Given this, the laws of nature are the laws of God's nature. Therefore, God cannot prevent evil from occurring by suspending the laws of nature (because God cannot change his nature).

Attempts to solve the problem of evil by denying that God has the perfection of omnipotence are problematic for a number of reasons. In the first place, if we set aside the process panentheist conception of God in favor of the creation monotheist claim that God created the universe *ex nihilo* (as we found good reason to do in chap. 9), then it is difficult to see how God could be powerful enough to have created the universe and all the laws that govern its operation without also having the ability to suspend those laws.

Second, even if we grant the process panentheist assumption that God cannot change the fundamental ways that nature works, there are still a staggering number of natural evils that it seems even a God limited in this way could have prevented. For instance, before Ignaz Semmelweiss, a physician in a Vienna hospital, discovered in 1847 that fatal infections were spread among patients by doctors who failed to wash their hands between examinations, much needless pain, suffering, and premature death were caused by this unfortunate practice. But surely these natural evils were preventable by any being worthy of the name "God," even if this being could not alter the laws of nature. After all, mere human beings eventually adopted hygienic practices that prevented additional pain, suffering, and death due to germ transmission. If God could not have done the same sort of thing early on, then there was a time when God was less powerful than human beings are now. But this is absurd.

Finally, there are distinctively Christian reasons for affirming premise 4 rather than denying it. If God is not omnipotent and thus not perfect, then it is not clear that God will be capable of accomplishing his ultimate redemptive purposes for humanity in particular and creation in general. But if God is not able in the end to rescue his creation from evil, then a fundamental and essential claim of the Christian faith is false. For all these reasons, it is best to affirm premise 4 and instead to look for good reasons to deny premise 6.

We can set the stage for a promising Christian response to premise 6 (and the argument provided for it above) by pointing out that human beings often justifiedly allow bad things to happen that they could have prevented but only if permitting these evils is necessary either (1) to prevent something worse from occurring or (2) to bring about a sufficiently great good. An example of the first case is the surgical removal of a gangrenous limb that would have resulted in the patient's death if it had not been amputated. An illustration of the second case is an athlete's sacrifice of a substantial amount of personal time and physical energy for the sake of winning an important competition. In each of these cases, there is a cost of some sort: the loss of a limb, an expenditure of precious time, an endurance of prolonged physical discomfort. These, considered by themselves apart from their consequences, are bad things. They are intrinsically evil things. Since legs, leisure time, and physical comfort are good things, it is bad or evil to lose them. However, something bad in itself may be good in relation to something else if the bad thing leads to the occurrence of something good. That is why we might reasonably say of an amputee that it is a good thing his leg was removed—not good in itself but good because it kept him from dying. In this case, the amputation is intrinsically evil and yet instrumentally good. Something is instrumentally good when it can be used as an instrument or means to bring about something good (or to prevent something evil). So also the athlete's rigorous and lengthy physical training may be bad in itself (because it tends to be painful, exhausting, and discouraging) but instrumentally good because it results in a victorious performance.

These examples may show that *humans* are sometimes justified in allowing intrinsically evil things to happen, but how do they provide us with good reason to think that *God* is ever justified in permitting evil? The previous paragraph showed that a person can have a reason that justifies allowing something evil to transpire only if it is not possible for him or her to prevent a greater evil or to bring about a sufficiently great good without allowing this evil to occur. But God is all-powerful. Doesn't this mean that God can do anything, including preventing great evils and bringing about great goods without letting anything evil happen? Aren't all things (including whatever would be impossible for anyone else) possible with God? Though there has been debate about this question, most philosophers throughout history who have considered the matter, including Thomas Aquinas, have held that God can do anything *as long as it is logically possible*. So God can suspend the laws of nature and raise a human being from the dead. However, God cannot suspend the laws of logic and make it the case that God both exists and does not exist at the same time (or that round squares or married bachelors exist or that $1 + 1 = 3$). To say this is not to place any real limits on God's power, since God would be limited in power only if there were something possible that God could not do.

Given this, it seems reasonable to say that a perfect God is morally justified in allowing evil to exist only if it *would not be logically possible* for God to prevent a greater evil or to bring about a sufficiently great good without allowing evil to occur. God may have a justifying reason for allowing evil, but only if this condition is met. Given the possibility that a perfect God could have a justifying reason for allowing evil, we need to change the argument from evil formulated above to reflect this. In particular, we need to revise premise 6:

6a. If God is omni x 3, then there is no evil *unless God has a reason that would justify him in permitting it.*

We also need to revise premise 1, which is based on 6:

1a. If God exists, then there is no evil *unless God has a reason that would justify him in permitting it.*

The argument from evil, based on this revised premise, will of course continue to affirm the existence of evil:

2. There is evil.

But now an additional premise is needed to establish the atheistic conclusion:

7. There is no reason that would justify God in permitting evil.

If 1a, 2, and 7 are true, then it follows that

3. God does not exist.

Justifying the Ways of God to Men and Women

Given this reformulated version of the argument from evil, it is clear that a Christian apologist's job is to provide either (1) good reasons to deny premise 7 or (2) at least good reasons to refrain from having to endorse it. There are, then, two ways to resist premise 7. One way is to show that premise 7 is false by providing a convincing account of the reasons that would justify God in allowing evil. Such an account would need to explain God's permission of evil by specifying the greater evils that God could not prevent and/or the sufficiently great goods that God could not bring about unless he allowed evil to occur. Any ambitious apologetic response to the argument from evil along these lines is called a *theodicy* (literally, a justification of God). The remainder of this chapter considers a few theodicies. The other way for a Christian apologist to provide good reasons to resist premise 7 is to offer a *defense* of theistic belief by arguing that there is no adequate reason to believe premise 7 is true. Clearly, this approach is much less aggressive than the former. In the former case, an apologist needs to show God's justifying reasons for evil (or at least show what these justifying reasons *might be*). In the latter case, an apologist needs only to show that the case for the claim that God has no such justifying reasons has not been made. So one can mount an adequate defense against the argument from evil without knowing what God's reasons for allowing evil are (though Christians need to be justified in affirming that God *has* such reasons).

Some theodicies make it reasonable to believe that premise 7 is false. This is because premise 7 implies that God is never justified in allowing *any* evil. Theodicies provide good grounds for the conclusion that God is at least sometimes justified in permitting at least some moral evils and at least some natural evils. However, many Christian apologists today believe that theodicies have only a limited value. Though they may explain why God allows *some* evils, they do not and cannot explain why God allows either (1) the amount of evil that actually exists or (2) certain especially horrible evils involving particular individuals. These two issues lead to a version of the argument from evil in the face of which we need to resort to a defense rather than to theodicies. The first section of the next chapter states this

alternative argument from evil and develops a defense against it. The remainder of this chapter, however, sketches a few theodicies that are intended to show that premise 7 is false.

Some have held that God is justified in allowing pain and suffering because those who experience it *deserve* to experience it as punishment for their sins. Let's call this the punishment theodicy. The Bible does, after all, affirm that "all have sinned and fall short of the glory of God" (Rom. 3:23) and that "the wages of sin is death" (Rom. 6:23). If all sinners deserve to die, then it might seem that they also deserve whatever other pain and suffering they may experience. There are a number of serious problems with this theodicy. First, the Bible also affirms the reality of undeserved human pain and suffering. This was the plight of Job, as recorded in the book that bears his name. Second, at the heart of the Christian faith is the claim that a sinless human being—Jesus—endured a substantial amount of pain and suffering. Since he was morally innocent, he did not deserve the evils inflicted on him. So even if the punishment theodicy could account for all other human suffering (which it cannot), it is not able to explain the suffering of Christ. Third, though it may be somewhat plausible that *adult* human beings deserve whatever pain and suffering they experience (as punishment for their sin), such a claim is much less plausible when it comes to infants and small children, many of whom undergo a degree of pain and suffering that far exceeds anything it is reasonable to think they would deserve (think of something horrible like the torture and rape of a toddler). Finally, even if the punishment theodicy could explain why God would be justified in allowing all *human* pain and suffering (which it cannot), it cannot explain the pain and suffering of nonhuman animals, which are not capable of sin and so not deserving of being punished for sinning. For all these reasons, it seems clear that a lot of pain and suffering exists for which the punishment theodicy cannot account, even if there is also much human pain and suffering that is deserved.

The question, then, is this: What explains God's allowance of *undeserved* pain and suffering? It is helpful to divide this question into two parts, each corresponding to the two types of evil identified: moral evil and natural evil. The goal is to show that premise 7 is false with respect to both of these kinds of evil.

Let's first attempt to explain why God would permit *moral* evil and the undeserved pain and suffering it brings about. The best explanation of moral evil available to Christian apologists is the free will theodicy. According to this theodicy, God created human beings (and angels) with *morally significant* free will. A person has a genuinely free will if that person is able to choose between at least two options in such a way that each option is within his or her power to realize. An action is within a person's power as long as, even if that person does not perform it, other things being equal, he or she *could have performed it*. Morally significant free will is the freedom to choose among a range of alternatives that include not only good behaviors but also evil, wicked, or sinful actions. What makes such freedom morally significant is that, in exercising it, one has the power to increase or diminish the moral goodness or moral evil in the world.

It is plausible to think that genuinely loving relationships require the persons involved to have free will. This is because people who are not free but are instead determined or forced to relate to each other (like puppets or robots) can at best act *as if* they love each other. Truly loving someone requires acting lovingly toward him or her because one has freely chosen to do so. Moreover, *meaningful* loving relationships require not only that the parties involved freely choose to love each other but also that they choose to do so when they could have chosen to refrain from loving each other or *to treat each other wickedly and unjustly*. Evidence for this can be found in the extent to which we tend to be moved when we witness former bitter enemies becoming loyal and loving friends. There is also a hint of this idea in Jesus' command to "invite the poor, the crippled, the lame, the blind" instead of one's friends, relatives, and rich neighbors to one's banquet (Luke 14:12–14). Choosing to love people one could more easily neglect or even harm is to do something more meaningful than loving those to whom one finds it natural to express affection. Therefore, meaningful loving relationships require the participants to possess morally significant free will.

But a person who possesses morally significant free will is capable of exercising it in such a way as to perform wicked actions that cause much pain, suffering, and injustice. Many people with morally significant free will are capable not only of an increased amount of individual moral evil but also of the production of evils that could exist only through the cooperative efforts of free people devoted to wickedness and injustice. War (at least *unjust* war) is a clear example of this latter sort of moral

> **At the heart of the free will theodicy is the claim that this divinely instituted, enabled, and governed community of love is such a great good that God is justified in allowing moral evil in order to bring it about.**

evil. So in creating the entire human race (and the angels) with morally significant free will, God made moral evil possible. Moreover, it is obvious that things have turned out in such a way that there has been a massive amount of individual and corporate moral evil throughout human history as a result of what we humans have done with the morally significant freedom God gave us. The moral evil that God made possible in giving humans such freedom has become a reality.

According to the free will theodicy, God is justified in allowing actual moral evil because the only logically possible way God could have guaranteed that there would be no moral evil is for God not to have given persons morally significant free will. This is because, *by definition,* a free will is morally significant only if the person possessing it is genuinely capable of using it to produce moral evil. Moreover, God is justified in having given human and angelic persons morally significant free will because doing so is the only logically possible way God could have made possible the exceedingly great good of the meaningful loving relationships of which a genuinely meaningful loving community consists. Such a community would

be characterized by a perfect realization of the two Great Commandments: (1) all created persons in the community loving God with all their heart, soul, mind, and strength, and (2) all created persons in the community loving one another as they love themselves (see Mark 12:30–31). All this creaturely love would be a response to God's great love for all created persons ("We love because he first loved us" [1 John 4:19]) made manifest in the death of Jesus on the cross ("For God so loved the world that he gave his one and only Son" [John 3:16]). Moreover, this ideal community could exist only if people exercised their wills not only to respond freely and lovingly to God's love and to love one another as God in Christ has loved them (John 13:34) but also to exercise their power of self-determination (which requires morally significant free will) to become the kinds of people who are capable of loving habitually in these ways.

At the heart of the free will theodicy is the claim that this divinely instituted, enabled, and governed community of love is such a great good that God is justified in allowing moral evil in order to bring it about. If this is the case, then premise 7 of the revised argument from evil is false, at least as applied to *moral* evil.

But what about natural evil? Recall that this involves the pain and suffering endured by human beings and animals that are not a direct result of sin but instead a consequence of the operations of natural laws. Though apologists have offered a number of theodicies over the years as attempts to explain why God allows natural evil, the most promising among these are those that are tied in some way to the free will theodicy. For instance, according to the natural consequences theodicy, the human pain and suffering due to natural causes such as earthquakes, floods, and disease are an indirect natural consequence of our being separated from God as a result of sin. The idea is that when humans exercised their free will to love other things more than God, their resulting loss of intimacy with God carried with it a diminishment in their ability to protect themselves from natural disasters and to avoid the pain, suffering, and death caused by them. An analogy may help to explain this. When children live at home, they are able to benefit from the guidance and protective oversight of their parents. If these children choose to leave home and to sever their relationship with their parents, they lose the protective advantages this relationship afforded them. As a result, they are more vulnerable than they were before to the dangers of the world. In such a case, loving parents may choose (if their child is old enough) to allow their child to suffer the consequences of his or her choice. Reasons that may justify such parental restraint are (1) respect for their child's autonomy, (2) a hope that their child's misfortunes will prompt him or her to choose to return home (as in the case of the prodigal son in Jesus' parable), and (3) a realization that this is likely to occur only if the child experiences a deep and lasting change of heart and mind as a result of his or her hardships. According to this theodicy, therefore, we can explain God's allowance of the evils of human pain and suffering due to natural disasters as a necessary (and potentially beneficial) by-product of human sin (and so human free will).

Notice that this theodicy has the advantages of (1) allowing for the existence of natural disasters before the arrival of human beings (and therefore human sinfulness) on the stage (and so allowing for the possibility of evolution by natural selection) and (2) not necessarily making natural evil a *punishment* for sin (though there may be many instances in which it is). However, this theodicy has some problems as well. For one thing, though it may explain why God allows the pain and suffering *humans* have freely put themselves in a position to experience, it does not explain *animal* pain and suffering—at least animal suffering that could not play a role in motivating humans to choose freely to become lovers of God so as to be reunited to God. For this purpose, the natural law theodicy—which is also tied to the free will theodicy—is more likely to succeed.

According to the natural law theodicy, the same natural laws that account for the occurrence of natural disasters are needed to make genuine freedom of the will possible. For our wills to be free, we need to be able to predict with a sufficiently high degree of confidence what the immediate outcome of our exercise of them will be. If nature were not governed by laws that made nature sufficiently orderly and regular, then we would not be able to make such predictions. For instance, I can freely choose to offer a thirsty person a cup of cold water in the name of Christ only if I can count on my arm cooperating with my will rather than arbitrarily and erratically punching the thirsty person in the stomach instead. Moreover, I need to have good grounds for believing that the water in the cup will not turn into poison as soon as the person begins to drink it. However, the same laws that prevent these random events also cause circumstances that lead to animal (and human) suffering. The same laws of momentum that enable me to exercise control over my limbs can also cause an avalanche to cripple a deer in the wilderness. According to the natural law theodicy, therefore, God is justified in allowing animal pain and suffering due to natural causes because this natural evil is a necessary by-product of the kind of world required for the existence of genuine free will.

If we put the free will, natural consequences, and natural law theodicies together, then we have a good reason to reject premise 7 of the argument from evil. There is a reason that justifies God in allowing moral evil (sin and the suffering it brings about). A community of meaningful loving relationships of the sort described above is possible only if the members of this community have morally significant free will, and the human exercise of this freedom has resulted not only in much moral goodness but also in a lot of moral evil. A natural consequence of this sin is a separation from God that has left humans subject to the pain, suffering, and death brought about by natural causes. However, God is justified in allowing humans to experience these consequences because such pain and suffering are required to enable us to see how miserable

we are apart from God and to motivate us to choose freely to become the kinds of people who love God above all else (and who love other human beings as we love ourselves). Moreover, for us to have the free will that makes such personal moral growth and loving relationships brought about by it possible, we need to live in a sufficiently predictable environment. Such an arena for human improvement and enrichment requires natural laws that also produce natural disasters that lead to animal pain and suffering. So God is justified in allowing animal suffering in order to make free will possible. Finally—and this is a new point—the existence of pain and suffering provides human beings with opportunities to develop moral virtues, such as compassion and a disposition to forgive, which are possible only if pain and suffering exist.

Though this case against premise 7 may undermine the version of the argument from evil we have been considering by explaining why God allows some (perhaps much) of the evil that exists in the world, there is another form of this argument that is resistant to theodicies and therefore requires a defense instead. The first section of the next chapter formulates this version of the argument from evil.

Reflection and Discussion

1. How do you think Christians should think and feel about the problem of evil?

2. Do you understand and can you appreciate why some people conclude on the basis of evil that God does not exist or is not all-powerful or all-loving—even if you do not agree with them that these conclusions are true?

3. Is it appropriate in all circumstances to try to explain to someone why God allows evil? Why or why not? Is it possible to explain why God allows *all* the evil that exists? Why or why not?

Further Reading

Adams, Marilyn McCord. *Horrendous Evils and the Goodness of God*. Ithaca, NY: Cornell University Press, 2000.

Howard-Snyder, Daniel, ed. *The Evidential Argument from Evil*. Bloomington: Indiana University Press, 1996.

Mackie, J. L. "The Problem of Evil." In *The Miracle of Theism: Arguments for and against the Existence of God*. New York: Oxford University Press, 1983.

12

A God Who Hides Himself

The Problem of Evidence

» Outline

- **Who Has Understood the Mind of the Lord?**
  - *The Argument for Atheism from the Amount of Evil*
  - *William Rowe's Case for the Claim That There Is No Reason for All the Evil*
  - *A Defense of Theism against This Claim*
    - The Typo Argument
    - The Extraterrestrial Argument
    - The No Justifying Reason Argument
- **The Argument from Divine Hiddenness and Silence**
  - *An Explanation of the Main Concepts of the Argument*
    - What Is Required for a Personal Relationship with God?
    - What Is Required for Reasonable Belief in God's Existence?
    - What Would Make Nonbelief Culpable?
  - *Arguments for the Premises of the Divine Hiddenness Argument*
- **A Defense of the Hidden God**
  - *God's Hiddenness, God's Silence, and the Psalms*
  - *Reasons to Think All Capable Nonbelievers Are Culpable*
  - *Reasons to Think a Perfectly Loving God Would Hide Himself*

» Summary

No combination of theodicies can explain why God allows the *amount* of evil in the world. The atheistic argument from the amount of evil concludes that God does not exist because if he did, we would know the reasons he allows so much evil, but there are no such reasons. Though some arguments of this sort do establish their conclusions (e.g., the typo argument), other arguments of this kind do not (e.g., the extraterrestrial argument). The argument from amount falls into the latter category. Some have also argued for atheism on the grounds that a perfectly loving God would provide adequate evidence for his existence, and yet the evidence for theism is inadequate. A defense of theism against this argument can either argue that the evidence for God's existence is adequate or that a perfectly loving God could have reasons to put some people in a position, at least for a time, not to have adequate evidence that he exists (i.e., a perfectly loving God could have good reasons to "hide" himself).

» Basic Terms, Concepts, and Names

argument from amount
argument from divine hiddenness
capable nonbelievers
culpable nonbelievers
defense
justifying reason for evil
Pascal, Blaise
Rowe, William
Schellenberg, J. L.
standards for reasonable belief
theodicy

» Reflection and Discussion

» Further Reading

> Truly you are a God who hides himself.
>
> Isaiah 45:15

Who Has Understood the Mind of the Lord?

The theodicies just discussed provide adequate grounds to believe God is justified in allowing *much* existing moral and natural evil. We can, therefore, with good justification, reject premise 7 of the argument from evil. However, on reflection, it seems pretty clear that the combination of these theodicies, along with a number we did not consider, cannot explain why God permits *all* existing evil. Though the free will theodicy may well account for much individual and corporate sin, wickedness, and injustice and their consequences, can it possibly explain why God allowed Hitler's holocaust, Stalin's purges,

> **It is certainly not obvious that God needed to let *all* these things happen in order to bring about the great good of an eternal loving community.**

or Pol Pot's killing fields? And these are just the most obviously horrible abuses of human free will in the twentieth century. There have been many more atrocities causing untold amounts of pain and suffering not only recently but throughout the history of the human race. It is certainly not obvious that God needed to let *all* these things happen in order to bring about the great good of an eternal loving community. Couldn't God create such a community without, for instance, having allowed the infamous events of September 11, 2001, to have transpired? Perhaps not, but perhaps so. It is hard to say.

Moreover, though the natural consequences and natural law theodicies may make sense of many natural evils, can they plausibly explain *all* the devastation, death, destruction, pain, and suffering brought about by centuries of loss caused by natural hazards? As long as there has been life on this planet (or at least since the fall), there has been human and animal pain and suffering from the loss of life and limb, health and home, and safety and security imposed by natural disasters of various kinds. There are also many kinds of evils that often have a mix of moral and natural causes such as birth defects, disease, famine, homelessness, injuries, and poverty. Did God have to allow *all* of this to accomplish his purposes? Couldn't God achieve his goals while preventing, for example, the recent earthquake and tsunami in Southeast Asia? Perhaps not, but perhaps so. It is hard to say.

These ruminations lead to another version of the argument from evil, the argument from amount:

1. There is no reason that would justify God in allowing *so much* evil (as much as there actually is) rather than a lot less.
2. If God exists, then there must be such a reason (for all the reasons already rehearsed in the last chapter).
3. Therefore, God does not exist.

In this case, a Christian apologist must find good reasons to resist having to accept premise 1. However, the strategy here will not be to prove that premise 1 is false by providing a theodicy that explains (or might explain) God's reason (or reasons). We have already tried that approach, and it seems reasonable to think that, at best, it enables us to show that God has reasons that justify him in allowing only *some* of the evils that exist. Instead, the goal here will be to *defend* Christian belief in God by arguing that no good case for premise 1 has been made (and thus that it is rational not to accept it).

What kind of case can be made for premise 1? The agnostic William Rowe has provided the following argument for it, which is among the best available:[1]

R1. Probably, if there were a reason that would justify God in allowing so much evil, we would know what it is.
R2. There are no reasons we know of that justify God in allowing so much evil.
R3. Therefore, probably, there are no such reasons (this is premise 1 of the argument from amount).

We have already granted R2, so our attention needs to focus on R1. Here is an argument for it: Probably, if there were a reason that would justify God in allowing so much evil, then the centuries of careful and imaginative philosophical effort expended by intelligent and philosophically skilled theists to find this reason would have been successful. Moreover, if these thinkers had discovered this reason, we would now know what it is. Therefore, probably, if there were a justifying reason for all the evil in the world, we would know what it is. Is this a good argument?

Some arguments of this sort are strong indeed. For instance, consider the claim that if there were any typographical errors on this page, you would be able to tell what they were. Here is an argument for this claim: If this page contained any typos, you could find out that this was the case by looking carefully and repeatedly at the text to tell whether each of the words is spelled correctly, whether all the words are in the right order, whether the proper punctuation is used, and so on. If you could find out in this way that the page contained a typesetting mistake, then you would be able to discover that it does. Consequently, if there were any typographical errors on

1. Rowe's argument is from "The Problem of Evil and Some Varieties of Atheism," in *The Evidential* *Argument from Evil*, ed. Daniel Howard-Snyder, 1–11 (Bloomington: Indiana University Press, 1996).

this page, you would be able to tell what they were. This is a strong argument, because each of the premises is highly likely to be true, and the conclusion clearly follows from the conjunction of these two premises.

But other arguments like this are much weaker. Take, for instance, an argument for the claim that if there were intelligent life in another part of the universe, we would know that this was the case: Probably, if there were intelligent extraterrestrials, then either our efforts to contact them would result in their replying to us or they would be successful in contacting us even if they did not receive our transmissions. If either of these types of communication occurred, then we would know that there was intelligent life in another part of the universe. Therefore, probably, if intelligent extraterrestrials were to exist, we would know that they did. What makes this argument weak is that, though the second premise is clearly true and the conclusion clearly follows from the premises, the first premise is not clearly true. That is, it is not clearly the case that if intelligent life forms exist elsewhere in the universe, we would have made contact with them in one way or another. As a matter of fact, there are good reasons to doubt this claim. For instance, even if such beings exist, our signals may not have been received by them, or perhaps they have been received but the receivers do not know how to interpret them (or do not even know that they are interpretable), or these beings may have interpreted them and yet chosen for some reason not to reply to them (or they may simply be unable to communicate with us in a way we could understand). All these possibilities (and others like them)—possibilities we have no

good reason to rule out—make it doubtful that this premise is true.

Is the argument formulated above for R1 more like the typo argument or the intelligent extraterrestrial argument? It is clearly more like the latter and therefore relatively weak. This is because the argument for R1, like the argument about extraterrestrials (but unlike the argument about typos), contains a premise (the first one) that is doubtful by virtue of there being too many relevant alternative possibilities that we do not have good reason to rule out. Recall that the first premise of the argument for R1 is that, probably, if there were a reason that would justify God in allowing so much evil, then the centuries of careful and imaginative philosophical effort expended by intelligent and philosophically skilled theists to find this reason would have been successful. But this is doubtful. God may have a reason that justifies him in allowing all the evil there is (and again, Christians are rationally committed to believing that God does), and yet it may nevertheless be the case that, in spite of centuries of ingenious attempts to find this reason, we do not (and perhaps cannot) know what this reason is. The possible reasons for this include the following: (1) Given the difficulty of the issues involved, we have not yet thought long and hard enough to have resolved them; or more likely, (2) our inherent limits as finite human beings may render an omniscient being's reasons inaccessible to us (just as—in a much lesser way—a scientifically illiterate person is not equipped to understand a difficult scientific theory); and similarly, (3) the sorts of reasons considered in the last chapter may be only a few of many potential justifying reasons that we could not even begin to know how to think of; because perhaps (4) the complexity of the sufficiently great good God intends to bring about by allowing evil exceeds our comprehension, at least in this life (it is reasonable to think that, at least sometimes, the better something is the more complex it is, as can be seen in the case of good music, good art, and good food).

Therefore, unless there is a better argument for R1, there is no good reason to accept this premise of Rowe's argument for premise 1 of the argument from amount. Moreover, if there is no better case for premise 1 than this, then there are also no good grounds for premise 1. Consequently, the argument from amount does not provide an adequate basis for concluding that God does not exist.

This completes the defense of theism against the argument from evil. None of the arguments from evil investigated has provided an adequate reason to believe that God does not exist. If we add this result to the outcome of the examination of some theistic arguments in chapters 9 and 10, then the overall tentative conclusion at this point is that we have good (though not conclusive) reasons to believe that God exists (or, more specifically, that creation monotheism is true) and no good reasons to believe that God does not exist. However, there is another type of argument for atheism (or at least for agnosticism) we have yet to consider. This is an argument that takes advantage of both the inconclusiveness of arguments for God's existence and our ignorance of a reason that would justify God in permitting so much evil. It is an argument that focuses on the extent to which it seems that the world is characterized more by God's absence than by God's presence.

The Argument from Divine Hiddenness and Silence

J. L. Schellenberg has formulated such an atheistic argument in his book *Divine Hiddenness and Human Reason.*[2] His argument focuses on perfect love, an important and essential characteristic of the Judeo-Christian God:

1. If there were a perfectly loving God, he would make sure that each person capable of a personal relationship with him reasonably believes that he exists, unless a person culpably lacks such a belief (i.e., unless a person's failure to have this belief is that person's fault).
2. But there are capable, inculpable nonbelievers.
3. Therefore, there is no perfectly loving God.

If we adopt the reasonable assumption that if God exists then God is perfectly loving (since either absolute perfection or supreme goodness requires perfect love), then this is an argument for atheism. The argument could be altered to support agnosticism by revising premise 1 to express a requirement for *reasonable belief* that a perfectly loving God exists. Neither conclusion is acceptable to a Christian apologist.

2. Ithaca, NY: Cornell University Press, 1993. See Daniel Howard-Snyder and Paul K. Moser, eds., *Divine Hiddenness: New Essays* (Cambridge: Cambridge University Press, 2002), for essays on the problem of divine hiddenness from the standpoints of atheism, agnosticism, and Christian theism. I am indebted to Howard-Snyder's introduction (1–23) to this volume for some of the ideas in this and the next section.

Before we consider how best to reply to this argument, let's consider how a proponent of it can clarify and defend it. The premises employ terminology in need of careful definition. Both premises make claims about people in terms of (1) their *capacity* for a personal relationship with God, (2) their *(non)belief* in God's existence, and (3) their *(in)culpability* in failing to believe that God exists.

First, what is required for a person to have the capacity to have a personal relationship with God? From a Christian standpoint, as shown in chapters 4 and 11, a personal relationship with God involves both God and a person giving and receiving love in ways appropriate to their status. A person is capable of receiving God's love in suitable ways only if that person can *understand* God's loving communications and *appreciate* God's loving sacrifice on his or her behalf. A person is capable of giving love to God only if that person is able to *respond* to God's mercy and grace with gratitude, worship, and continuing faith and trust. Moreover, these cognitive, affective, and behavioral capacities require, more fundamentally, a capacity for *consciousness* of God's reality, presence, and activity. This consciousness requires, in turn, a *concept* of God rich enough to make these psychological capacities possible. Consequently, it is clear that only human beings who have undergone a sufficient degree of psychological development and are sufficiently free from mental impairment are capable of a personal relationship with God. Thus, infants and severely retarded people are not capable of such a relationship.

Second, the strongest version of the divine hiddenness argument for atheism presupposes that believing that God exists requires consciously and explicitly accepting the proposition that God exists (and also that nonbelief in God requires not consciously and explicitly accepting this proposition). This is because if people could be said to believe in God *implicitly* and without realizing it, by, for instance, simply pursuing a moral life (and thus relating to God by means of relating to his attribute of moral goodness), then it would be difficult to make a plausible case for premise 2 of the argument, since it can reasonably be said that virtually all human beings (except, perhaps, psychopaths or sociopaths) are pursuing a moral life in some sense.

Given this, the *reasonable* belief in God's existence mentioned in premise 1[3] would require having reasons or grounds[3] for conscious and explicit belief that the proposition that God exists is true. A key question that needs to be answered in assessing this argument is, of course, what it is that would make belief in God reasonable. A person cannot merely have *some* reasons, regardless of their strength or relation to one's overall body of evidence, for believing that there is a God. This is because such reasons either may be too weak in themselves to justify belief in God or may be undermined by other reasons one has to believe that God does *not* exist. Instead, reasonable belief in God requires that, given all the evidence available both for and against God's existence, the net result is that one has *adequate* reason to believe that God exists. But what would count as enough evidence for belief in

3. Reasons and grounds include both beliefs and experiences. In the remainder of this section, when I refer only to reasons, or grounds, or evidence, I mean to include both beliefs and experiences, unless otherwise indicated.

God? It is clear that decisive, conclusive, or demonstrative proof would suffice, but part 1 of this book has already ruled out this possibility, and a careful and critical examination of the theistic arguments discussed in chapters 9 and 10 bear this out (the treatment of these arguments did not come even close to answering all the good questions that can be asked about them or replying to all the legitimate objections that can be raised against them).

Moreover, to make reasonable belief in God require an overwhelming demonstration of God's existence would make premise 1 implausible. It is unreasonable to think that perfect love would require God to make sure that capable and inculpable people have undeniable proof that God exists, because such a strong and clear indication of the reality of God would undermine the ability God has given people to enter into a personal relationship with him on the basis of a genuinely free choice. This eclipse of freedom would occur especially if one's knowledge of God's existence involved enough knowledge of God's nature to enable one to realize the dire consequences one could expect to experience if one chose a manner of being and living that was contrary to his righteous will. If someone has no reasonable way to deny that a holy God exists who will punish that person if he or she does not submit to God, then that person's deep desire for self-preservation and well-being would combine with a fear of God to compel him or her to surrender to God. This is not the position a perfectly loving being would want a loved one to be in. Consequently, the reasonable belief in God's existence mentioned in premise 1 must be consistent with a genuinely free response to God. The evidence that God supplies for his existence must be sufficient for reasonable belief without being so conclusive as to compel belief.

The third central concept is that of *culpable* or *inculpable* nonbelief. Again, people are culpable for doing something (or failing to do something) if and only if it is legitimate to blame them for their action (or inaction). Moreover, people are inculpable for doing (or not doing) something if and only if it would not be right to blame them for their activity (or inactivity). What are the circumstances in which it would be appropriate to blame a person when that person fails to believe in God (either by believing that God does not exist or by suspending belief about whether God exists)? A clear case of this would involve a person who is in possession of adequate evidence for God's existence and yet does not believe that God exists on the basis of this evidence. A somewhat less clear but arguably genuine case of culpable nonbelief would have to do with someone who does not possess such evidence, but for whom it is available, and who is capable of acquiring it without undue effort. In this case, the person would be to blame not for failing to believe something for which he or she has adequate evidence but instead for not believing something for which he or she is sufficiently able to acquire evidence. Given all this, nonbelief is *inculpable* when a person neither possesses nor could acquire (in a sufficiently easy way) sufficient evidence for belief.

Now that we have clarified the important terms in the atheistic argument from divine hiddenness, we are in a position to consider reasons to accept its premises. An argument for premise 1 is based on conceptual reflection about what perfect love requires: If there were a perfectly loving God, then he would do whatever it takes to at least make it *possible* for anyone capable of having a personal relationship with him to do so without overriding his or her free will. But it is not possible to have a freely chosen personal relationship with God unless one reasonably believes that God exists in a way that is consistent with one's freedom. So if there is a perfectly loving God, then he would provide people capable of personally relating to him with sufficient evidence to make it reasonable for them to believe that he exists so that if they do not believe this, it is their fault. Consequently, premise 1 is true.

Premise 2 affirms the existence of atheists or agnostics who are capable of having a personal relationship with God but who do not believe that God exists—through no fault of their own. Given what was said above, it follows that these people do not have in their possession adequate evidence for reasonable belief in God, nor is any such evidence available to them in a way that would be sufficiently easy for them to acquire. This is because if they had or could easily get such evidence, they would be culpable for not employing or acquiring it so as to believe that God exists on the basis of it. Whereas premise 1 is a conceptual claim about the nature of perfect love, premise 2 is an empirical claim about the existence of certain sorts of people. Is there good reason for thinking that such people actually exist? If there are any *seekers*, as chapter 6 defined this term, who do not believe there is a God, and if at least some of these people do not have sufficiently easy access to adequate evidence for God's existence, then premise 2 is true. This is because a seeker is an unbeliever who is genuinely open to the possibility that God exists and/or that

Christianity is true. Such a person sincerely *wants* to believe and *would* believe if he or she found adequate evidence for belief. There are certainly many nontheists who *seem* to be seekers in this sense. The proponent of the argument from divine hiddenness will urge us to take what these people say at face value—to give them the benefit of the doubt—as only seems fair. If we do, and we concede that they do not have evidence available to them sufficient to yield reasonable belief in God, then we will have adequate reason to endorse premise 2.

A Defense of the Hidden God

Christians are not rationally required to accept either premise of the argument from divine hiddenness. Consequently, a Christian apologist may choose to defend the rationality of belief in a loving God by arguing that an adequate case has not been made for both of these premises. Therefore, an adequate defense need only provide reasons for finding one of these premises doubtful. A stronger defense would argue that both premises are doubtful. That is what this section attempts to do (notice that as in the case of the reply to the argument from amount, it will not be necessary to show that the premises of this argument are *false* in order to make it reasonable to resist its conclusion).

In preparing to respond philosophically to this argument for atheism from divine hiddenness, it is worthwhile to point out that the Bible contains numerous acknowledgments of the problem on which this argument is based (as is also the case, of course, with the problem of evil). The psalmists in particular express much heartfelt anguish about God's hiddenness (for instance, "Why, O Lord, do you stand far off? Why do you hide yourself in times of trouble?" [Ps. 10:1]) and even indignation about God's apparently having forgotten them and their people as they are in the midst of their enemies ("Why do you hide your face and forget our misery and oppression?" [Ps. 44:24]). These complaints do not imply, however, that these biblical writers doubt the *existence* of God (though they do perhaps suggest the possibility of concerns about God's *love*).[4] Moreover, the psalmists and other biblical writers who sometimes lament God's hiddenness also often celebrate his presence with them and his faithfulness to them ("But you, O God, do see trouble and grief; you consider it to take it in hand" [Ps. 10:14]). The picture that emerges from the Bible, then, is that the experience of God's people includes both a sense of God's absence and a sense of God's presence.

But what about the claim of premise 2 that some people who are capable of relating to God do not believe that God exists—through no fault of their own—because they do not have or could not easily acquire sufficient evidence for God's existence? The discussion of the heart in chapter 5 provides good materials for casting doubt on this claim. Recall that Paul claims in Romans 1:18–23 that (1) God has made his existence and nature plain in the created order but that (2) some have suppressed these truths because of their desire to continue to sin so that (3) these people are without excuse for their unbelief and disobedience. This passage

strongly suggests that premise 2 is false. In particular, it implies that there *is* sufficient evidence for theistic belief and that therefore anyone who fails to believe in God is *culpable*. This argument from the Bible may well suffice to demonstrate the falsity of premise 2—at least to people who believe that what the Bible teaches is true. It may, therefore, persuade believers and doubters to reject this premise. But such a purely scriptural case is unlikely to convince a person to doubt or deny premise 2 if he or she does not accept the authority of the Bible, especially if this person considers himself or herself to be a capable and inculpable nonbeliever.

An adequate nonbiblical argument against premise 2 would need to (1) provide a good overall case for the existence of God and (2) show that this case provides sufficient reason to believe that God exists so that anyone who does not believe this would be culpable for not believing it. We have already made good progress in the construction of such an overall case for monotheism in chapters 7–11 (and we will be supplementing this case in various ways in later chapters). Therefore, the key question at this point is whether the case we are constructing is adequate for reasonable belief in God (or likely to be adequate after various adjustments and additions). To answer this question, we need to specify *standards* for sufficiently reasonable belief in God. These standards would provide general criteria that would enable us to determine whether a case for God's existence (that takes into account both arguments for and arguments against the reality of God) is successful. If we had such standards and we could show that our case for monotheism satisfied them, then

---

4. These questions about God's *existence* and *love* are not separable, however, on the assumption that if God exists, then God is loving.

we could reasonably conclude that there are no capable *inculpable* nonbelievers.

The main problem with this approach is that it is notoriously difficult to specify standards like this, and even when a specification is made, it is difficult to achieve a consensus among all interested parties that it is correct. What is likely to occur is that believers in God will formulate standards they believe the case for theism satisfies, and nonbelievers will propose alternative standards that they will argue this case fails to meet. Believers may suspect that nonbelievers are motivated to create these other, presumably higher or stricter standards by an unacknowledged and perhaps unconscious desire to sin. However, we have already set aside this response as lacking in apologetic value. It seems best, for apologetic purposes, to assume that there are sincere and open nontheistic seekers who would believe in God if they could but who do not find the case for theism sufficiently convincing.

So though we have provided reasons for believers and doubters to deny premise 2 and thus rationally to resist the argument from divine hiddenness based on it, we have yet to provide good grounds that might convince seekers and even critics that this argument fails. For this purpose, we will need to find reasons to doubt premise 1. Would a perfectly loving God make sure that everyone capable of having a relationship with him reasonably believes that God exists in a way consistent with his or her freedom? The answer to this question depends on the ultimate goal a perfectly loving God would have for such people and what means a perfectly loving God would choose to bring about this goal.

According to the Christian faith, God's ultimate purpose for human beings is for each of us to satisfy the two Great Commandments discussed in the last chapter: to love God with our entire being and to love our fellow human beings as we love ourselves. But the Bible also affirms that all human beings fall far short of this ideal (Rom. 3:23). Our shortcoming in this regard is not merely a behavioral matter but instead a deeper character issue; our motivational structure is deeply flawed in such a way that we are incapable of repairing it by purely natural means. As a result, without supernatural assistance, we cannot obey the two Great Commandments. This is because, in our sinful state, we are lovers of self rather than lovers of God and others. As Augustine put it, as sinners we have a "disordered love life." We do not love God, fellow humans, and other created things the way they ought to be loved. What we need is for God to transform our hearts and wills so that we have a "properly ordered love life." This is something God made possible by means of the death and resurrection of Jesus and the gift of the Holy Spirit to those who receive God's offer of salvation by faith (more on these themes in later chapters). From a Christian standpoint, therefore, God created us for perfectly loving relationships with him and other human beings, and God has acted on our behalf in Christ to enable us to overcome our sin in order to become the kinds of people who can love in these ways.

Would a perfectly loving God act in these ways? An analogy with human parents strongly supports an affirmative answer to this question. Genuinely loving parents choose to have a child primarily in order to bring someone into the world with whom they can have a loving relationship and who will be capable of making a loving contribution to others. Such parents will do whatever they can to enable their children to become the kind of people capable of loving them and others as they ought. Given the argument in the last chapter about the impossibility of forcing people against their will to love, the efforts of such parents in this regard will need to be consistent with an adequate amount of freedom on the part of their children. If these things are true of ideally loving human parents (and I believe they are), how much more would they be true of a perfectly loving God! Such a being would produce creatures to love him and one another and would enable them to become capable of such love in a way that is consistent with their freedom.

If these are the *ends* of a perfectly loving God, what *means* to these ends would such a being employ? In particular, and most relevant for our purposes here, would a perfectly loving God ever withhold evidence of his existence (and/or experiential grounds for his existence in the form of a direct awareness of his presence) so that a person capable of having a relationship with him would fail to have a reasonable belief that God exists through no fault of his or her own? There are a number of plausible reasons to think so. What they all have in common is the claim that God's "hiding" from a person by withholding evidence of or grounds for his existence from that person is necessary in order for God to put *that person* in a condition to be transformed into the kind of person who can fulfill the two Great Commandments—in a way consistent with *that person's* free will. We have already seen one argument along these lines in chapter 5. Recall that

> **If these things are true of ideally loving human parents, how much more would they be true of a perfectly loving God!**

Pascal argued that God sometimes partly conceals himself from people so that they will experience the misery, restlessness, and wretchedness that result from their sin and separation from God. God does this, Pascal thinks, to motivate such people to humbly repent of their sin and to become open to both the possibility that God exists and the necessity of submission to God as their Lord. If it is plausible that this is the sort of thing a perfectly loving God would do, and I believe it is, then we have reason to doubt the truth of premise 1 of the argument from divine hiddenness.

As a matter of fact, it is plausible to think that there are *many* specific ways that sinful people need to be transformed and that God may well "hide" himself from people to facilitate these types of changes—ultimately for the purpose of making these people lovers of God and others. Different individuals are likely to have needs for different kinds of changes, and one person is likely to need his or her character altered in different ways at different times. In addition to Pascal's idea, other specific ends God might try to bring about by hiding from an individual are (1) to make sure that a person does not respond to God in faith for the wrong sorts of reasons (e.g., a fear of hell); (2) to make sure that the individual's attitudes about God and his or her knowledge of God are appropriate (e.g., humility rather than arrogance, seriousness rather than flippancy); (3) to encourage *passionate* faith through a sense of risk that would be diminished if there were more and better evidence available; (4) to make it necessary for people to rely on one another in beginning and cultivating a relationship with God so that the second Great Commandment is more likely to be fulfilled by human beings; (5) to make it impossible (or at least difficult) for people to have a sense of being in complete control of their lives and destinies so that they need to depend on God in faith; and (6) in general to facilitate the acquisition and development of the virtues of faith, hope, and love and other more specific related virtues such as patience and compassion.[5]

These suggestions do not suffice to prove that premise 1 of the argument from divine hiddenness is false. However, they

seem sufficiently plausible to make premise 1 doubtful. If premise 1 is doubtful, then even if we grant the truth of premise 2, the conjunction of these two premises is inadequate to make it reasonable to accept the claim that there is no perfectly loving God. So neither the argument from amount (based on the claim that too much evil exists for there to be a God) nor the argument from divine hiddenness (based on the claim that too little evidence exists for there to be a God) succeeds in providing adequate grounds for its conclusion. Both of these arguments for atheism take advantage of the limits of human attempts to understand and know God. But Christians may reasonably believe that these limits are a part of God's loving plan for us. Christians can also insist that, though God may often conceal himself and his reasons for allowing evil, he has also revealed himself and many of his purposes for us in Jesus Christ. Whether it is reasonable to believe this claim is the primary question addressed in the next part of this book.

---

5. This list is based on a similar list in Howard-Snyder's introduction to *Divine Hiddenness,* 9–10. For discussions of these suggestions and others, consult the essays in that volume.

Reflection and Discussion

1. What are some reasons God might have for not revealing to us why he allows all the evil that exists?
2. Have you ever felt God's absence or silence in your life? Was it difficult for you to believe in God in those circumstances? Do you know anyone who sincerely wants to believe in God but says he or she cannot because of insufficient evidence or grounds? What would you say to such a person?
3. Reflect more thoroughly on the possible explanations suggested in the text for God's deliberately "hiding" himself from certain individuals. How would you develop or supplement these explanations?

Further Reading

Howard-Snyder, Daniel, ed. *The Evidential Argument from Evil.* Bloomington: Indiana University Press, 1996.

———, and Paul K. Moser, eds. *Divine Hiddenness: New Essays.* Cambridge: Cambridge University Press, 2002.

Schellenberg, J. L. *Divine Hiddenness and Human Reason.* Ithaca, NY: Cornell University Press, 1993.

Part 3

Commitment to God in Christ

13

Who Do You Say I Am?

The Person of Jesus

» **Outline**

- **The Gospels: Fact or Fiction?**
  - *The General Agreement about the Text's Reliability*
  - *The Controversy about the Authors' Reliability*
    - The Quest for the Historical Jesus
    - The Claims of the Jesus Seminar
- **Did Jesus Really Claim to Be Divine?**
  - *A Traditional Argument for the Reliability of the Gospels*
    - The Apostolic Eyewitness Connection
    - The Reliability of Eyewitness Accounts
  - *Recent Criticisms of This Argument*
    - Doubts about Apostolic Authorship
    - Doubts about the Reliability of the Gospels' Authors
  - *A Defense of the Traditional Argument against These Criticisms*
- **Liar, Lunatic, or Lord?**
  - *A Case for Jesus' Claim to Be the Messiah and the Son of God*
  - *Jesus More Likely Lord than Liar or Lunatic*
  - *Why This Argument Is Inconclusive as It Stands*

» **Summary**

A case for the rational superiority of Christianity over the other monotheist religions requires a defense of Christian claims about Jesus. The central affirmation in need of rational support is that Jesus is God the Son incarnate. One argument for the divinity of Jesus is that it is the best explanation of certain historical facts reported by the Gospels. Among these is the fact that Jesus claimed or implied that he is the Messiah and the Son of God. Though it is generally believed that the biblical text is a reliable record of what was originally written, some have questioned the reliability of the Gospels as accounts of what really happened. The traditional argument for the reliability of the Gospels assumes that they were written by apostolic eyewitnesses of the recorded events (or one of their associates) and are thus historically reliable. There are arguably reasonable replies to doubts about these assumptions. Therefore, Jesus probably did really claim to be divine, as reported in the Gospels. It is more likely that Jesus is Lord than that he is either a liar or a lunatic, but the possibility that he was sincerely and sanely mistaken needs to be ruled out as well.

» **Basic Terms, Concepts, and Names**

Gospels
higher criticism
historical reliability
inference to the best explanation
Jesus Seminar
liar, lord, or lunatic? argument
Papias
quest for the historical Jesus
textual criticism

» **Reflection and Discussion**

» **Further Reading**

> "But what about you?" he asked. "Who do you say I am?"
>
> Simon Peter answered, "You are the Christ, the Son of the living God."
>
> Jesus replied, "Blessed are you, Simon son of Jonah, for this was not revealed to you by man, but by my Father in heaven."
>
> Matthew 16:15–17

Part 1 of this book talked about Christian apologetics: its nature, purpose, benefits, limits, and strategies. Part 2 began to model the *doing* of Christian apologetics. That is, it began to construct an apology for the Christian faith by employing philosophical concepts and argumentation to define and defend the worldview family of which Christianity is a part: creation monotheism. I hope you agree, now that we have constructed a number of arguments for God's existence (of both the cosmological and the teleological sort) and replied to two types of arguments against God's existence (the argument from evil and the argument from divine hiddenness), that creation monotheism is at least cosmically competitive and perhaps even rationally superior to the worldview families with which it competes. This case for and this defense of creation monotheism are intended to contribute to the cultivation of Christian commitment by means of watering and weeding. They are meant to help critics of theism become seekers of God,

to assist seekers in becoming believers in God, to enable doubters to be restored to confident faith in God, and to reassure believers that a God exists who created the universe out of nothing. A commitment to God is an essential and foundational aspect of Christian faith. It is not, of course, all there is to Christian belief. Creation monotheism is a worldview family that includes the religious traditions of Judaism, Christianity, and Islam. What is needed to make it more reasonable to accept Christianity than these other two religious perspectives is a case for the distinctively Christian claims that center on the person of Jesus Christ.

These claims include the following: (1) Jesus is God the Son, the Second Person of the Trinity; (2) this person is not only fully divine in nature but also, as a result of the incarnation, fully human in nature; (3) this God-man died on a cross to save human beings from the penalty and power of sin and to reconcile them to God; (4) he was raised from the dead;

(5) he eventually ascended into heaven; and (6) he will return some day to earth to decide the eternal destiny of every human being—both living and dead. These distinctive Christian claims about Jesus represent the doctrines of the Trinity, the incarnation, sin, the atonement, the resurrection, the ascension, and salvation and damnation (heaven and hell). This part (chaps. 13–19) provides resources for defending the rationality of believing that these doctrines are true in the face of a number of objections to the contrary.

This chapter begins to build a case for the crucial claim that Jesus is God the Son incarnate. It is important to point out that philosophical argumentation alone will not provide adequate reasons to accept this thesis. Philosophy can take us no farther than to show that it is rational to believe that creation monotheism is the worldview most likely to be true. An argument for the divinity of Jesus needs to take the form of an inference to the best explanation of certain historical facts about Jesus. These historical facts (for which we will need to provide historical evidence) include the following: (1) Jesus said and did things that only a person who either believed himself to be God or at least wanted others to believe he was God would be likely to say and do; (2) Jesus is reported to have done things that only God could do (i.e., he is alleged to have performed miracles); (3) Jesus died and was buried in a tomb that was subsequently found to be empty, and Jesus was seen alive after this by a number of people; and (4) the facts summarized in point 3 led to certain dramatic and radical changes in the lives of Jesus' followers. This chapter and the next two argue that the best explanation of this conjunction of historical facts is

that Jesus is God incarnate. This chapter deals with fact 1, the next chapter focuses on fact 2, and chapter 15 examines facts 3 and 4.

Historical facts 1 through 4 are recorded in the Bible, in particular, in the four canonical Gospels[1] (Matthew, Mark, Luke, and John) and the book of Acts. These Gospels serve as the main source of historical information about Jesus because they are the only relatively developed biographies of Jesus available. They are the only extensive records of what Jesus said and did and experienced. But here, of course, we face an apologetical challenge. A common assumption of critics and a concern of many seekers and doubters is that the Bible is not a reliable source of historical information. The Bible is a very old collection of books that were written over a long period of time by a great number of people, some of whom are unknown. Moreover, in many cases, the authors of biblical books made use of a variety of sources, both oral and written, in writing the books, and it seems reasonable to think that their selection and use of these materials were influenced by their point of view and purposes for writing. Furthermore, the Bibles we use today are translations into modern languages that are based on copies of the original manuscripts, and many copies of the same book differ in

1. The four canonical Gospels are the accounts of the life, teachings, activities, death, and resurrection of Jesus included in the biblical canon. The canon is the collection of biblical writings accepted by the Christian church as the inspired Word of God. There are a number of other accounts of the teachings and/or life of Jesus that were not included in the canon, such as the Gospel of Thomas. Chapters 20 and 21 discuss questions that concern the reasonableness of distinguishing between canonical and noncanonical Christian writings.

The goal is to show that it is reasonable to believe that the New Testament provides reliable historical information about Jesus of the sort needed for apologetical purposes.

their wording. Given these facts about the composition and the preservation of the Bible, an apologist must answer two important questions. Q1: How do we know that the Bibles we use today contain a reliable record of what the original authors of the books of the Bible actually wrote? Q2: How can we be sure that any statement of historical fact made by a biblical writer is likely to be true?[2]

The next two sections discuss answers to these two questions (especially Q2) as applied to the Gospels (and other New Testament materials that contain historical claims about Jesus). The goal is to show that it is reasonable to believe that the New Testament provides reliable historical information about Jesus of the sort needed for apologetical purposes. The final section of this chapter presents the lunatic, liar, or Lord? (or mad, bad, or God?) argument for the claim that Jesus is God, which presupposes that it is historically true that Jesus claimed to be God (or at least said things and did things that implied that he believed himself to be God or at least wanted others to believe

2. The branch of biblical scholarship devoted to answering Q1 is sometimes called textual criticism or lower criticism. The area of biblical studies that focuses on Q2 is often called higher criticism.

this). The conclusion of this argument is that it is more reasonable to believe that Jesus is really Lord and God than to believe that he was either insane or dishonest. The following two chapters continue to strengthen the case for the divinity of Jesus by arguing that it is reasonable to believe that Jesus performed miracles (chap. 14) and that Jesus was raised from the dead (chap. 15), both facts that can best be explained by concluding that Jesus is God.

The Gospels: Fact or Fiction?

There is good reason to believe that what we read about Jesus in the New Testament is generally true only if (1) we have good reason to believe that our Bibles are reliable records of what the writers of the New Testament wrote about Jesus, and (2) we have good reason to believe that what these writers wrote about Jesus is generally true. As for requirement 1, it is relatively uncontroversial among both Christian and non-Christian scholars who study early Christian writings that the Greek texts on which modern translations are based are reliable records of the materials that comprised the documents of the New Testament in their final, original form. It is true that there are a number of variations among existing manuscripts of the same New Testament document, but it is generally agreed that these variations are relatively minor in the sense that they do not put the central claims of the New Testament in doubt. At any rate, for the apologetic purposes in the next few chapters, the existence of these textual variants does not compromise the effort to employ the

New Testament as a source of historical evidence about Jesus.[3]

The situation is quite a bit different with respect to requirement 2. The scholarly community is currently divided over whether we have good reasons to think that what the Gospel writers wrote about Jesus is generally true. Many scholars believe that the Gospel accounts of the life and teachings of Jesus are true—at least in general. Others believe instead that very little—if anything—of what the Gospels report about Jesus really happened. This radical disagreement is a result of the emergence over the last two hundred years of a critical historical approach to the reading of the Bible. Many scholars who employ this method treat the Bible as a collection of purely human documents rather than as the inspired Word of God. Moreover, they typically seek to distinguish elements in the text that are genuinely historical (reliable reports of things that really happened) from those that are not. They label as "myth" any biblical statement alleging that something transpired that they consider not to have occurred. Among the claims that many

have consigned to the myth category are various claims made about Jesus in the Gospels, especially claims involving an appeal to the supernatural (such as the claims that Jesus is divine, that he performed miracles and predicted the future, and that he was raised from the dead). This conclusion that not everything the Gospels say about Jesus was something Jesus really said, did, or experienced led to what has become known as the quest for the historical Jesus.

The goal of this intellectual quest has been to determine what Jesus was really like and what he really said, did, and experienced on the basis of those parts of the Gospels that are deemed to be historical. People who embark on this quest typically distinguish the Jesus of history from the Christ of faith. The Christ of faith is the portrait of Jesus allegedly constructed by his earliest followers on the basis of their seeing Jesus through the "distorting" eyes of faith. A standard idea here is that the Jesus of history was a mere human being who attracted followers on the basis of his countercultural and subversive stories and sayings, which were mainly about the kingdom of God. The claim is that after Jesus' death these followers, who had not adequately understood Jesus' teachings, gradually began to develop the mistaken view of Jesus as Messiah, Lord, and God. Moreover, the influence of Hellenistic mystery religions of that time, with their dying and rising gods, led to the belief that Jesus had been raised from the dead.

Among those who hold this view that the real Jesus was merely a human sage who was illegitimately made out to be the Lord of the universe by his followers are the members of the Jesus Seminar, which was founded by New Testament scholar

---

3. In spite of the general scholarly agreement that contemporary versions of the New Testament are highly reliable records of what the original writers of the New Testament documents wrote down, there are at least two groups of people who doubt that this is the case. One of these groups is Muslims, who believe that Jews and Christians corrupted the text of the Bible. The other group consists of people like Dan Brown, the author of the recent best-selling novel *The Da Vinci Code* (New York: Doubleday, 2003), who assert, without sufficient warrant, that the Bible has "evolved through countless translations, additions and revisions" (231). For good evidence that these people are wrong, see Lee Strobel's interview with New Testament scholar Bruce M. Metzger in *The Case for Christ* (Grand Rapids: Zondervan, 1998), chap. 3.

Robert Funk in 1985. This international (though mostly American) group of scholars adopted as their first major task the search for the authentic words of Jesus.[4] The results of this search are contained in their book *The Five Gospels,* which contains not only their translation of the four canonical Gospels (Matthew, Mark, Luke, and John) but also their translation of the gospel of Thomas, one of a number of extrabiblical accounts of the teachings and/or life of Jesus. *The Five Gospels* also contains an extensive commentary explaining and defending the decisions they made regarding whether the sayings and speeches attributed to Jesus by the Gospel writers (both canonical and noncanonical) were actually spoken by him. These decisions were made by means of a secret voting procedure involving colored beads being dropped into a box by each member of the seminar at the end of each of their biannual meetings. A vote on an alleged saying or speech of Jesus involving a *red* bead meant that the voter believed Jesus certainly said it (or something a lot like it) or that the saying could be employed with confidence in determining who Jesus was. Three other colors (pink, gray, and black) represented increasing degrees of skepticism about whether Jesus made the remarks in question (a black bead represented the judgment that Jesus definitely did not say what the Gospel reported him to have said and that the saying or speech tells us something about the early Christian church rather than something about who Jesus was).

As a result of employing this procedure over the course of eight years, the Jesus Seminar concluded that most of what

Jesus was reported to have said by the writers of the canonical Gospels was not really said by him. For the purposes of this chapter, it is important to point out that none of the alleged sayings of Jesus that could provide a rational basis for claiming that he believed himself to be divine passed the Jesus Seminar's test. All of these materials were rejected by them as inauthentic.

How can a Christian apologist reply to these serious and radical claims? There are at least three strategies we can consider. First, we could set out to *prove* on the basis of objective historical evidence that Jesus claimed to be divine (or implied that he was divine). However, the problem with this approach is that historical investigation can yield only probable conclusions at best. Moreover, no historical evidence is completely objective, since it is always subject to interpretation from a certain point of view (this is one reason why historical claims can be only probable). Second, we could attempt to show that there is a reasonable point of view from which it is more probable that Jesus claimed to be divine (or implied that he was) than that he did not. We could try to achieve this result by arguing, from the standpoint of creation monotheism (for which we made a case in the previous part of this book), that Jesus' having made such a claim is the best explanation of the fact that the Gospel writers reported that he did so. A successful use of this second strategy requires that we defend this thesis against arguments to the contrary by showing that these arguments do not establish their conclusions. Using the garden metaphor, the second strategy involves both a form of watering and a kind of weeding. The next section

---

4. This is the subtitle of their book *The Five Gospels* (New York: Macmillan, 1993).

outlines this approach. Finally, we could appeal to the witness of the Holy Spirit as a ground on which it is reasonable to believe that the biblical portrait of Jesus, including the claims he is alleged to have made about himself, is accurate. This is a good backup plan to use with people who are doubtful or critical about any kind of historical argument for claims about Jesus. This option is discussed in chapter 20.

Did Jesus Really Claim to Be Divine?

Christians who are looking for the best scriptural basis for an affirmative answer to this question are likely to turn to the Gospel of John. This is the Gospel in which Jesus responds to the Jews who ask him if he is the Messiah by saying, "I and the Father are one" (10:30). The audacity of this claim in that monotheistic context is underscored by the reaction of the Jews, who "picked up stones to stone him" (v. 31), most likely because they considered him to be blasphemous in having identified himself with God. John's Gospel is also the place where Jesus tells Philip that anyone who has seen Jesus has seen the Father (14:9).

The problem with using the Gospel of John for this apologetic purpose is that it was written later than the other three and seems clearly to involve more theological reflection on the person of Jesus. This makes it easy for a critic to theorize that these relatively explicit claims of identity to or equality with God were not really made by Jesus but instead were put in his mouth by John. A typical assumption made to justify this conclusion is that the longer the period of time between the events of Jesus' life and the date of writing, the more likely it is that myths and misunderstandings about him accumulated.

A natural reply to this charge is to point out that the Fourth Gospel was written by the apostle John, who was one of Jesus' twelve disciples and therefore an eyewitness to the events about which he wrote. Consequently, he would not have attributed words to Jesus unless Jesus had actually spoken them (or at least something synonymous with them). This reply is based on two general assumptions about the four canonical Gospels that were unquestioned before the rise of historical criticism. These assumptions are (1) the Gospels were written either by an apostle, who had been an eyewitness of the events he recorded (Matthew and John) or by a very close associate of an apostle (Mark, Peter's assistant; and Luke, Paul's coworker); and (2) if 1 is true, then either the Gospels recorded the career of Jesus as it really transpired, or, more cautiously, the Gospels can be relied on to give us at least a general picture of who Jesus was and what he said, did, and experienced. Unfortunately, both of these assumptions have come under serious critical attack, and the apologist's task has been complicated as a result. This is true not only of the later Gospel of John but also of the three earlier Gospels. We need to make a long but important detour from the main question of this section (Did Jesus claim to be divine?) to address the objections to these assumptions.

Let's first consider the case against assumption 1. We need to concede at the outset that none of the Gospels (each of which was written in the latter half of the first century) includes the name of its author in the text. The attributions to Matthew, Mark, Luke, and John are based instead on traditions dating back to the second century. In the case of Matthew and Mark, the tradition is that early in the second century a man named Papias, who knew some of the apostles' followers, said that "Matthew composed the *Logia* in the Hebrew tongue" and that Mark, an assistant of Peter, wrote down Peter's account of Jesus. These traditions provide good historical evidence that the Gospels were written by the men whose names have come to be associated with them. Is the evidence adequate to make it reasonable to believe that this is true? Skeptics of these traditional attributions argue, first, that the early Christian church ascribed the Gospels to apostles or their associates only to enhance these documents' credibility. However, there is no clear evidence that the church was seeking to do this, at least at the time of Papias. Moreover, though this argument may carry some weight when it comes to the apostles Matthew and John, it is much less plausible with respect to the non-apostles Mark and Luke, since there were a number of other apostles whose names would have been much more useful in increasing the reputation of the Gospels.

A second critical argument against the view that the authors were either associates of Jesus or companions of the apostles is that the Gospels were based on prior source materials and were shaped to some extent by the theological purposes of their authors. This objection assumes that eyewitnesses (or those in direct contact with eyewitnesses) would not need to make use of a wide variety of sources and would not have engaged in any editorial theological interpretation, an act that would more likely reflect the later concerns of the church than the reports of someone who experienced the events firsthand. Let's reply first to the issue of sources and second to the concern about interpretation.

Luke explicitly acknowledges in the introduction to his Gospel the existence of eyewitness accounts that were handed down to him. Since he was not an eyewitness, it makes sense that he would have employed whichever sources he considered acceptable as a result of his having "carefully investigated everything from the beginning" (1:3) (presumably by at least checking with eyewitnesses or people who had spoken with eyewitnesses, such as his companion Paul). He did so in order to write an "orderly account" for Theophilus (to whom Luke and Acts are addressed) to help Theophilus "know the certainty of the things . . . [he had] been taught" (1:3–4). It is clear to most scholars that among the sources Luke employed was the Gospel of Mark. Mark was therefore most likely among those Luke had in mind when he mentioned those who had "undertaken to draw up an account of the things that have been fulfilled among us, just as they were handed down to us by those who from the first were eyewitnesses and servants of the word" (1:1–2). This is an independent endorsement of the value of the Gospel of Mark by a person who explicitly stated what arguably amounts to a substantial concern for historical reliability. There is no evidence that Mark was an eyewitness to the events about which he wrote, so it seems probable that Luke valued the Gospel of Mark because it made use of eyewitness sources. This hypothesis is corroborated by Papias's comment that Mark wrote down Peter's account of Jesus.

Therefore, there is no good reason to doubt the traditional view that Paul's companion Luke wrote the Gospel of Luke, and there are good reasons to accept the traditional claim that Peter's assistant Mark wrote the Gospel that bears his name.

As for the Gospels of Matthew and John, the objection under consideration is stronger. Just as scholars tend to agree that Luke made heavy use of the Gospel of Mark, there is also widespread agreement that the Gospel of Matthew is based substantially on the Gospel of Mark. But why would an eyewitness to the events of Jesus' life depend to such an extent on the account of someone who was not an eyewitness (Mark), even if that person's account was based primarily on another eyewitness's account (Peter)? Though it is plausible that an eyewitness would make use of other sources in writing an account of what he had experienced, at least as a time-saving device, it may more likely be the case that another person (or persons) made substantial use of the eyewitness accounts of Matthew and John in writing the two Gospels that bear their names. This hypothesis squares with Papias's statement that "Matthew composed the *Logia* in the Hebrew tongue." Papias may well be talking about a Hebrew document on which the Greek Gospel of Matthew is based that consists primarily of Jesus' sayings or teachings (Greek: *logia*). Also, this hypothesis may fit better with the relatively sophisticated character of the Gospel of John and with this statement in John 21:24: "This is the disciple who testifies to these things and who wrote them down. We know that his testimony is true." The first sentence in this verse could reflect the written eyewitness record of John that was incorporated into the Gospel of John by the people who affirm the truth of John's testimony in the second sentence.

The Gospels' evident use of sources does not undermine the reasonableness of believing that Mark and Luke are the authors of the Gospels that bear their names and that the other two Gospels are at least based substantially on the eyewitness accounts of the apostles Matthew and John. Thus, it is reasonable to believe that all four Gospels are based primarily on significant eyewitness materials. Therefore, the first critical objection to the first assumption of the traditional view of the Gospels' authorship does not threaten the historical reliability of these documents.

But what about the concern that the authors edited their sources to fit their interpretations of the events they wrote about? This does not give us a good reason to doubt the conclusion to which we have just come. It would have been natural—even inevitable—for any concerned and thoughtful human being who was affected either directly or indirectly by Jesus to try to figure out for himself or herself what the words and works of Jesus *meant* and to communicate a conception of this to others. However, this phenomenon does provide a critic with a reason to reject the second traditional assumption stated above, that if the Gospels are rooted in the apostolic witness to Jesus, then they are historically reliable indications of what Jesus said, did, and experienced. Wouldn't both the passage of time and the faith presuppositions of the Gospel writers contribute to their twisting of the truth in the interest of persuading their readers?

Everyone agrees that the Gospel writers were not neutral scientific historians whose primary goal was simply to record the historical facts about Jesus. For one thing, at that time there was no such thing as a *science* of history, at least in the sense in which we mean it today. But it does not follow from this that these writers told the story of Jesus with no concern at all for what really happened. For another thing, these evangelists wrote the Gospels primarily for evangelistic, apologetic, and pastoral purposes. They believed that Jesus was the risen Messiah and the Son of God, and they wrote his story to proclaim this good news, to defend it from attacks of various kinds, and to encourage fellow believers by assuring them of the truth of what they believed. But again, it does not follow from this that they played fast and loose with the facts. As a matter of fact, their main objectives to preach, protect, and ponder what they considered to be the good news about Jesus *required* them to care about the historical basis of their stories in the life and teachings of Jesus himself.

But critics of the assumption that an eyewitness basis for the Gospels guarantees their historical reliability argue that, even if the Gospels are based on sources that go back to eyewitness accounts, there are various ways in which these traditions could (and perhaps even would) have been altered both during oral and written transmission and during eventual written collection and compilation in their final form. One has only to think of the characteristic results of the party game involving the transfer of a whispered message from one person to another to see the initial plausibility of this concern. Moreover, these modifications to the tradition could have

been relatively gradual and unconscious or relatively abrupt and deliberate. In the former category, we would find operative such psychological phenomena as lapses of memory, self-deception, and wishful thinking. The latter would contain efforts to place the story of Jesus in the best possible light so that it would be as well received as possible by one's readers. For instance, a critic may hold that, though Jesus himself never claimed to be the Messiah and the Son of God (or even implied that this was the case), either the tradition evolved over time to include such claims or the early church, believing Jesus to be divine on other grounds, purposely added this element to make Jesus more competitive with other alleged divine men of the time. In suggesting these hypotheses, critics need to avoid committing themselves to the extremely implausible view that the followers of Jesus did not believe he was the Messiah and the Son of God and deliberately fabricated the grounds for attributing divine status to him. It is unlikely that they would have subjected themselves (as they did) to ridicule, persecution, ostracism, imprisonment, and, in some cases, death for the sake of a claim they did not really believe to be true.

But if we assume, as we must, that the early Christians *believed* Jesus was Lord and God, we must look for the best explanation of this fact. In particular, could so many have come to believe this—including many eyewitnesses to the life of Jesus—within so few years of Jesus' death if Jesus himself had never explicitly claimed or implied that he was divine? There must have been some objective facts about Jesus that led to widespread conviction concerning his divinity. It is implausible to hold that merely subjective factors, such as self-deception and wishful thinking—especially among hardcore monotheistic Jews—could account for the worship of Jesus as God. It could be thought that the church's allegiance to the Christ of faith was based solely on their belief in Jesus' resurrection (and perhaps also their belief in his ability to perform miracles). But others had been reportedly raised from the dead (e.g., Lazarus), and still others had reportedly performed miracles (e.g., the disciples), but they had not been hailed as divine as a result. If, however, Jesus claimed or implied that he was divine—as the Gospels say—then his reputation for being a miracle worker would have buttressed this claim, and adequate evidence of his resurrection would have vindicated it. In short, if Jesus claimed or implied that he was divine, we can explain the early church's belief that he was, and if Jesus did not, we cannot explain this fact about the first Christians. Therefore, the critic's suggestion that these claims were either unconsciously or deliberately added to the tradition by the early church is implausible.

This concludes the defense of the claims that (1) the Gospels are based on apostolic, eyewitness accounts of Jesus and (2) that this means we have good reason to be generally confident in what the Gospels report about Jesus. Though it does not follow from this that everything the Gospels say about Jesus really happened, it is reasonable to conclude that the burden of proof is on a critic to provide good evidence for anything in the Gospels he or she believes to be inauthentic. This conclusion opens the door for us to take Gospel material about Jesus seriously in an attempt to show that it is reasonable to believe that Jesus is God the Son incarnate.

Liar, Lunatic, or Lord?

Given the arguments above, it is reasonable to think that John's portrayal of Jesus as identifying himself with God the Father is at least an instance of making explicit what was implicit in the words and works of Jesus himself or perhaps even based on the very words of Jesus (though in that case it is unclear why the other Gospels do not include such explicit claims to divinity on the part of Jesus). We can supplement these verses from the Gospel of John with other reasons for thinking that Jesus claimed or implied that he was divine and that he really believed what he claimed. We will then be in a good position to consider whether Jesus was a liar, a lunatic, or really the Lord he claimed to be. Consider the following argument:

1. Jesus' central message was that the kingdom of God had arrived and that his hearers should repent of their sins in order to share in the blessings of God's reign, which would be brought about fully by a future act of God (even the severest critics agree with this).
2. The character of Jesus' earthly ministry was such as to embody, enact, and anticipate this kingdom—as if Jesus himself were the one to usher in God's kingdom. Evidence for this includes the following (each of which it is reasonable to think really happened—in virtue of having been reported by a Gospel or Gospels—in the absence of a good reason to think otherwise):
   a. Jesus acted in the place of God in forgiving sins (Mark 2:5–12).

b. Jesus implied that he was greater than Moses by setting aside the levitical laws of ceremonial purity (Matt. 15:1–20).

c. Jesus claimed divine authority to exorcise demons ("But if I drive out demons by the finger of God, then the kingdom of God has come to you" [Luke 11:20]).

d. Jesus spoke authoritatively of God's judgment on sinners (Luke 13:28).

e. Jesus taught with unprecedented authority (Mark 1:27).

f. Jesus chose twelve disciples as the basis for the kingdom of God just as God formed the nation of Israel out of the twelve tribes of Israel in the Old Testament.

g. Jesus addressed God as "Abba" (Daddy) and invited his followers to do so as well—a novel and radically personal way to speak to God in a culture in which even speaking the name of God (Yahweh) was forbidden.

h. Jesus manifested the character of the kingdom by means of his alleged healings and miracles (more on this in the next chapter).

i. Jesus referred to himself as the Son of Man, the divine figure mentioned in Daniel 7:13–14 who would come at the end of the world to judge humankind and rule forever.

3. It is unlikely that Jesus could have acted as if he were the one through whom God was bringing about his kingdom in the ways indicated above (saying and doing things that only God had the right to say and do) un-

less he believed he was the Messiah and the Son of God; therefore, this is probably what Jesus believed about himself.

4. If Jesus really believed he was acting in the place of God to bring about God's kingdom, then it is likely that Jesus would have expressed this self-understanding in his teaching and in the ways he talked about himself to others, though it would make sense for him to be cautious about this with some people and in some contexts to avoid misunderstandings that could undermine his message. For instance, the Jews had a misconception of the Messiah as a military leader who would save them from their political oppressors, and explicit claims to be divine would have been met with charges of blasphemy.

5. Consequently, it is probable that Jesus both claimed to be and believed he was the Messiah and the Son of God.[5]

It remains to be seen whether there are good reasons to think that what Jesus believed and claimed about himself is *true*. This is the burden of the next two chapters. For now, it will suffice to argue that it is more likely that Jesus is Lord and God than that he was either lying or deluded.[6] First, it is more likely that Jesus is Lord than a liar because (1) from what the Gospels tell us about Jesus, he

5. The main structure of this argument is borrowed from I. Howard Marshall, *I Believe in the Historical Jesus* (Grand Rapids: Eerdmans, 1977), 228–30.

6. The following argument is drawn from Peter Kreeft and Ronald K. Tacelli, *Handbook of Christian Apologetics* (Downers Grove, IL: InterVarsity, 1994), 160–61.

is not the kind of person who would be likely to lie, especially about something as important as whether he is divine. Even people who do not believe that Jesus is God think of him as a good man whose ethical teachings demand unselfish love and moral integrity; (2) Jesus had no conceivable motive to lie in this way, and he had every reason to tell the truth about what he believed about himself. It makes no sense to think he would have persisted in such a lie in the face of "hatred, rejection, misunderstanding, persecution, torture, and death";[7] and (3) Jesus had no reason to believe that such a claim would lead to general acceptance on the part of his hearers if it was not true (again, without some vindication of this claim, Jesus could expect only to be branded a blasphemer who was deserving of death).

Second, it is more likely that Jesus is Lord than a lunatic because (1) there is no indication in the Gospels that Jesus fit the profile of a genuinely deranged person (e.g., inappropriate emotions, paranoia, being out of touch with reality, exhibiting unsuitable personal and social behavior, etc.); (2) the picture of Jesus in the Gospels is instead of someone who is wise, witty, creative, unselfish, sensitively attuned to the needs of others, and generally quite healthy psychologically; and (3) the reactions of people to him are more consistent with the view that he was not crazy. People admired him, were amazed by him, came to him for advice and healing, demonstrated great love for him, were challenged by him, and so on.

Some apologists would conclude at this point that Jesus is Lord. However, this conclusion is premature at this point. For one thing, even though it may not

7. Ibid., 160.

It is more likely that Jesus is Lord and God than that he was either lying or deluded.

seem plausible, an alternative hypothesis is that Jesus was an honest and sane person who believed he was divine and claimed or implied that he was but was tragically mistaken.[8] To rule out this possibility, we will make a case for the claims that (1) Jesus did things that only God or someone through whom God is working can do (i.e., performed miracles) and that (2) Jesus was raised bodily from the dead, never to die again. The former will provide good reason to think that Jesus was not mistaken in thinking he was divine, and the latter will provide good reason to think that *we* would be mistaken not to believe that Jesus is Lord and God.

The historical case for the divinity of Jesus, continued in the next two chapters, is meant to satisfy the mind. But critics, seekers, doubters, and believers alike can agree that the story of Jesus should appeal to the heart as well. Who can reasonably deny that the idea of "the king himself serving in the ranks like a common soldier" or "the master suffering instead of his servants"[9]—metaphors capturing the essence

8. Daniel Howard-Snyder argues in "Was Jesus Mad, Bad, or God? . . . or Merely Mistaken?" *Faith and Philosophy* 21.4 (2004): 456–79, that this alternative hypothesis can be made sufficiently plausible so as to render the standard mad, bad, or God? argument inconclusive. See Stephen T. Davis's reply, "The Mad/Bad/God Trilemma: A Reply to Daniel Howard-Snyder," in the same issue, pp. 480–92.

9. The British Roman Catholic apologist G. K. Chesterton uses these metaphors for the doctrine of the divinity of Christ in *The Everlasting Man* (San Francisco: Ignatius, 1925), 242–43.

of the incarnation—is an idea that ought to touch the human heart with wonder and admiration? Though many may insist that the story of God becoming human in Jesus is too good to be true, Christian apologists should be quick to point out that this tale of divine love is at least *good*—a story that one should try to find it in one's heart to *hope* is true even when one cannot bring one's mind to *believe* it is true.

Reflection and Discussion

1. Is it possible to be relatively objective in deciding whether the four New Testament Gospels are generally historically reliable? If so, if you were to adopt such a relatively objective stance, would it seem to you that the Gospels are fact, fiction, or a combination of both? Explain.
2. Do you think there is adequate historical evidence in the Gospels for thinking that Jesus claimed to be divine? Explain.
3. What are the apologetical advantages of having good reasons for thinking that it is more likely that Jesus is Lord than that he is a legend, a liar, or a lunatic? What more is needed—if anything—for it to be reasonable to conclude that Jesus is really God?

Further Reading

Howard-Snyder, Daniel. "Was Jesus Mad, Bad, or God? . . . or Merely Mistaken?" *Faith and Philosophy* 21.4 (2004): 456–79. See also the reply by Stephen T. Davis in the same issue, pp. 480–92.

Johnson, Luke Timothy. *The Real Jesus: The Misguided Quest for the Historical Jesus and the Truth of the Traditional Gospels.* San Francisco: HarperSanFrancisco, 1996.

Marshall, I. Howard. *I Believe in the Historical Jesus.* Grand Rapids: Eerdmans, 1977.

14

Lazarus, Come Forth

The Miracles of Jesus

» **Outline**

- **Miracles and Reasonable Belief**
  - *David Hume's Definition of Miracle*
  - *Hume's Argument against the Rationality of Belief in Miracles*
  - *A Defense of Reasonable Belief in Miracles*
  - *A Revision of Hume's Definition of Miracle*
- **Miracles and Historical Investigation**
  - *Objection 1: Miracle Reports Are Unreliable or Mythological*
  - *Objection 2: Historians Should Appeal to Natural Causes Only*
  - *Objection 3: Historical Objectivity Precludes Metaphysical Bias*
  - *Objection 4: Necessary Proof of Testimonial Reliability Is Not Available*
- **Miracles and the Son of God**
  - *Why It Is Reasonable to Believe God Would Perform Miracles*
  - *God's Interactions with Ancient Israel*
  - *Jesus and the Kingdom of God*
  - *How Jesus' Miracles Reveal His Divine Character*
    - Miracles Revealing Jesus as Creator
    - Miracles Revealing Jesus as Redeemer
  - *How Jesus' Miracles Support His Claim to Be Divine*

» **Summary**

An appeal to Jesus' miracles can strengthen the case for his divinity. But David Hume argues that it is never reasonable to believe that a miracle has occurred. Hume's argument loses its force given creation monotheism, for which a case was made in part 2. Four arguments purport to show that historical investigation cannot confirm particular miracle claims. However, it is reasonable to think that these arguments do not establish their conclusions. Monotheistic historians may take miracle stories at face value unless they have a good reason not to do so. It is reasonable to believe that God would perform miracles to facilitate communication with fallen humanity. Arguably, in his dealings with Israel, God set the stage for his revelation in Jesus, and Jesus' miracles were a sign of his messiahship. Both the existence and the nature of Jesus' miracles point to his divine status. A historical case for the authenticity of Jesus' miracles strengthens the argument for his divinity.

» **Basic Terms, Concepts, and Names**

creation miracles
Hume, David
kingdom of God
law of nature
methodological naturalism
miracle
redemption miracles
testimonial evidence

» **Reflection and Discussion**

» **Further Reading**

Your ways, O God, are holy.
What god is so great as our God?
You are the God who performs miracles;
you display your power among the peoples.
With your mighty arm you redeemed your people,
the descendants of Jacob and Joseph.

Psalm 77:13–15

Men of Israel, listen to this: Jesus of Nazareth was a man accredited by God to you by miracles, wonders and signs, which God did among you through him, as you yourselves know.

Acts 2:22

The previous chapter focused on Jesus' claim to be the Messiah, the Son of God, and the Son of Man. It argued that it is more likely that this claim is true than that Jesus was either mad (a lunatic) or bad (a liar). But there is still the possibility that Jesus was sanely and honestly mistaken. Though this hypothesis seems implausible, it is good to have reasons to rule it out. One of those reasons is that Jesus performed miracles. If this is true, then we have a good reason for thinking that Jesus was at least able to employ the power of God for the wise and loving purposes of God. Though this would not suffice to establish the divinity of Jesus (since the Bible also attributes miracles to mere humans), it would make the case for that claim stronger. Each of the four canonical Gospels includes stories in which Jesus is portrayed as acting miraculously. Do we have good reasons for thinking that any of these stories is true? We do, but the case for this claim can be made only by first removing doubts about the possibility of (1) a miracle actually occurring, (2) it being reasonable to believe that a miracle has occurred, and (3) formulating a good historical argument that something miraculous has happened. After giving reasons to set these doubts aside, this chapter makes a historical case for the claim that Jesus sometimes made use of supernatural power to supersede the ordinary course of nature. This case strengthens support for the thesis that Jesus is God.

Miracles and Reasonable Belief

Let's start by defining a miracle, as David Hume does, as an event that (1) is caused by God either directly or indirectly (through an agent of God such as Moses) and (2) violates a law of nature. Clause 2 of this definition distinguishes miracles from things that happen in the world as a result of God's regular, normal conservation of the universe in conformity with natural physical laws. Clause 1 entails that if disruptions of the natural order occur as the result of the activity of Satan or his demons, though these are supernatural events, they are not miracles. This definition leaves out some things often labeled miraculous, such as the birth of a child, since births are natural events in the sense that they conform to natural laws. It even leaves out possible cases in which God acts directly to save a person from death in answer to prayer, if God employs purely natural means to accomplish this. These restrictions are justified for our purposes, since only events that satisfy the definition (or similar ones like the revised definition introduced below) are likely to have apologetic value in contributing to a case for the deity of Jesus. This is because only events that do not have a natural explanation can be seen as requiring a supernatural cause.

Are miracles as Hume defines them *possible*? They are clearly not *physically* possible, since something is physically possible only if it conforms to natural physical laws. But they surely seem possible in the sense in which there is nothing logically contradictory in imagining them to have occurred. A round square is not possible in this sense, but the act of leaping tall buildings in a single bound is. Therefore,

miracles are at least logically possible, and since the fact that God is omnipotent means that he can do anything that would be logically possible for him to do, then God can perform miracles.

But can we ever have good reason for thinking that God has acted miraculously? Hume argued that the answer to this question is no. Here is Hume's argument (in my words):[1]

1. Reasonable people will always proportion their beliefs to the evidence they have for them.
2. Every law of nature is such that the evidence that it has never been violated is stronger than the evidence that it has been violated.
3. If a miracle has occurred, it would be a violation of a law of nature.
4. Consequently, it is never reasonable to believe that a miracle has occurred.

Premise 1 is a statement of the proportionalist version of evidentialism introduced in chapter 2. Premise 3 follows from the definition of miracle adopted above. What is Hume's reason for accepting premise 2? First of all, he says that the evidence for a law of nature is the sum total of the collective human experience of the past conformity of nature to this law. Second, he says that the only evidence ever available that a miracle has occurred (and therefore that there has been a violation of a law of nature) is the testimony of at most a relatively few human beings. But Hume wonders how the alleged experiences of so few could overturn the

1. David Hume, *An Enquiry Concerning Human Understanding*, ed. Tom L. Beauchamp (New York: Oxford University Press, 1999), sec. X.

confirmed experiences of so many. The word *alleged* is used here because, from Hume's point of view, there are a number of reasons why testimonial evidence for miracles is suspect. Hume says that testimony can be reliable only if the people providing it are (1) sufficiently numerous, (2) sufficiently intelligent, critical, and objective so as not to be deluded, and (3) sufficiently trustworthy and in need of preserving a good reputation so as not to be deceitful. In short, adequate testimony comes only from people who are unlikely to be mistaken or lying. Hume adds that religious belief makes a person too biased to count as a reliable witness in the case of an alleged miracle.

Christian apologists need to have a good reason to reject at least one of the premises of Hume's argument to safeguard the rational case for the divinity of Christ. This is because a historical argument for this claim is based not only on the thesis that Jesus performed miracles but also, and much more importantly, on the doctrine of the resurrection of Jesus, which, if it happened, was a miracle. One defensive strategy is to deny the statement of proportionalist evidentialism in premise 1, as we did in chapters 2 and 3 with respect to belief in God. However, there are good replies to Hume's argument that do not require this step. A better move is to deny premise 2.

A case against premise 2 begins with the observation that how one weighs the evidence for a miracle claim depends on the general worldview to which one adheres. If one considers a miracle claim from the standpoint of metaphysical naturalism, one will begin with the assumption that God does not exist and that therefore miracles have a zero probability of occurring.

A naturalist, therefore, will find premise 2 highly acceptable. Moreover, though an agnostic (someone who suspends belief about which worldview is correct) may be more open to the possibility of miracles than a naturalist, an agnostic will start with the assumption that miracles are relatively unlikely to occur. But as argued in part 2, it is reasonable to believe that the creation monotheist worldview is true, and from that point of view, miracles are not only possible but even likely.

If an omni x 3 God exists, then a being exists who could perform miracles and who would perform miracles if he had a good reason to do so. After all, according to creation monotheism, God freely created the universe out of nothing, and there is no good reason to think that the universe had to operate in one way as opposed to another. Though God's goodness and wisdom constrained him to make the operations of the universe sufficiently regular and predictable (at least for the reasons indicated in chap. 11), there is no good reason to think that God's goodness and wisdom require him always to run the universe in exactly the same way. As a matter of fact, there are good reasons to think that God would sometimes choose to diverge from his normal mode of managing the universe, as long as sufficient regularity and predictability could be maintained. Among these reasons is the likelihood that a supremely good, wise, and powerful God would choose a nonnatural (miraculous) means to get the attention of his intelligent but lost and alienated creatures for the immediate purpose of communicating with them and for the ultimate purpose of making it possible to commune with them (by providing them with indicators of his existence, nature, and will as a way to encourage an appropriate response from them). Therefore, if one is a creation monotheist, one has a good reason to doubt the assumption behind premise 2 of Hume's argument: that what usually happens is probably what always happens. Consequently, those who have a good reason to believe that God exists also have a good reason to resist accepting premise 2.

Creation monotheists also have a good reason to revise Hume's definition of a miracle. If laws of nature are simply descriptions of the ways in which God normally, typically, or usually manages the universe, then a miracle is an abnormal, atypical, or unusual way for God to make things happen. Understood in this way, a miracle need not be thought of as a *violation* of a law of nature. If God sometimes chooses to raise a human being from the dead, then it is still true that God normally works in such a way as to let nature run its course by arranging for dead people to stay dead. That is, if a natural law is that normally dead people stay dead, then it is no violation or suspension of this law if God sometimes decides to do something abnormal and raise a person from the dead.

Miracles and Historical Investigation

Miracles are possible, and it is reasonable for a creation monotheist to hold the *general* view that miracles sometimes occur. But do we ever have adequate reason to believe that a *particular* miracle claim or report is true? Nothing said so far shows that we do. This is because the case for the rationality of belief in miracles in the previous section was philosophical

> **If an omni x 3 God exists, then a being exists who could perform miracles and who would perform miracles if he had a good reason to do so.**

and theological, whereas a case for a particular miracle needs to be historical and to proceed on a case by case basis. This needs to be done by careful examination of each narrative or story that reports a miracle. But some critical historians have argued that it is not possible or legitimate to argue on historical grounds that a specific miracle report is true.[2] Why do they think so, and how can a Christian apologist reply?

Here is one argument for this claim about miracles and historical research:

5. Any narrative containing miracle stories (such as the four Gospels) is either historically unreliable or not a work of history at all but mythological.
6. If a narrative is either historically unreliable or mythological, then it is impossible to provide a good argument for the historicity of any story contained in the document.
7. Thus, historical investigation cannot confirm that a miracle has occurred.

Though this has been a popular kind of argument, it should be clear on reflection

2. See Van A. Harvey, *The Historian and the Believer* (New York: Macmillan, 1966), for the most recent extended attempt to make a case for this claim.

that the first premise is unacceptable in light of what was argued in the previous section. This is because the only good reason one could give for endorsing premise 5 is that either miracles are impossible or it is generally unreasonable to think that miracles could ever occur. But we have seen that there is good reason to deny this assumption from a creation monotheist standpoint. Miracles are both possible and even probable from that perspective. The presence of miracle stories in the Gospel narratives does not automatically render those stories either historically unreliable or mythological. They are clearly not mythological, because though their authors' primary aims are theological in a broad sense (evangelistic, apologetic, and pastoral), an important part of those theological aims is to provide a reliable historical account of the earthly career of Jesus. Whether there are good historical reasons to accept the truth of the miracle stories contained in them is not something to be decided on philosophical grounds.

A second kind of argument concedes that miracles are possible and that narratives that report them are not necessarily unreliable. However, it rules out the appropriateness of historical arguments for miracles on the ground that history is a *science*:

8. Scientific historians should appeal only to natural causes in formulating historical explanations of historical events.
9. If 8 is true, then it is illegitimate to explain any historical event in terms of supernatural (and thus miraculous) causes.

10. Therefore, no good historical case can be made for the existence of a miracle.

Premise 8 is an application of the thesis of methodological naturalism to the science of history. Chapter 22 discusses this thesis more thoroughly in connection with science in general. For now, we restrict our attention to its application to historical science. It seems that there are good reasons for historians to subscribe to this sort of principle, but its formulation in premise 8 makes it too restrictive. A more plausible and less restrictive version of the thesis allows for the legitimacy of historical arguments for the truth of particular miracle stories. According to this more acceptable version, historians should seek a natural cause for historical events unless there are sufficient reasons to think that these events do not have a natural cause. What makes this a (weak) variety of methodological naturalism is that it dictates that historical methodology should be guided by a *presumption* that historical events have natural causes. However, unlike its stronger cousin, it allows that this presumption could be overridden. What makes this less constraining principle more plausible is that it encourages a healthy but not overly extreme skepticism about miracle reports. We should be at least initially skeptical of any miracle story because miracles are, by definition, *rare* divine acts. However, we should not be *too* skeptical because from a creation monotheist perspective we have good reasons (as suggested in the last section) to think that God sometimes acts in history in extraordinary, nonnatural ways.

Some may object here that as scientists historians have an obligation to be *ob-*

jective in their work and that this means they need to set all their biases, presuppositions, and faith commitments aside. In the reply to the first argument against a historical approach to miracles, we insisted that miracles not be ruled out on metaphysical grounds by assuming, for instance, that metaphysical naturalism is true and that miracles are consequently impossible. But in the reply just now to the second argument, we appealed to creation monotheism as a reason to be open to the rationality of believing a miracle report on historical grounds. Isn't this a metaphysical and religious bias that should be ruled out as well? These considerations lead to a third argument against using historical evidence to support a miracle claim:

11. Historians have an obligation to be objective in formulating their historical explanations by not allowing their biases, presuppositions, and faith commitments to influence their judgment.
12. But it is reasonable to infer that a historical event requires a supernatural (miraculous) cause only if one assumes that God exists.
13. Therefore, historians have an obligation not to posit a supernatural cause to explain a historical event.

Here the problem is with premise 11. In spite of its superficial appeal (it is hard to deny that complete objectivity would be a good thing), it is arguably false in virtue of the reasonable assumptions that (1) we have an obligation to do only those things that we *can* do, and (2) we cannot be completely objective in historical investigation. For one thing, historians must have *faith* in the historical method as a reliable means of discerning and explaining historical facts. For another, historians cannot help but make value judgments about what questions are worth asking about the past, what counts as good historical evidence, and how best to interpret that evidence. Historians disagree about these things, and there is no completely objective way to settle these disputes. Moreover, there is no good reason for historians to leave their religious and metaphysical assumptions aside in doing history. If the goal of historians is to determine and explain what happened in the past, then it would make sense for them to make use of everything it is reasonable for them to believe to achieve this goal. Of course, this means that it is perfectly appropriate for metaphysical naturalists to assume that miracles do not occur. But this does not give them the right to insist (as in the first and second objections above) that creation monotheists cannot appeal to supernatural causes in a historical explanation if it seems appropriate from that metaphysical perspective. What is important is that one's metaphysical assumptions should not be allowed to settle historical questions without sufficiently careful and critical evaluation of the historical evidence available.

A fourth and final critique of a historical approach to the confirmation of a miracle report accepts the possibility of miracles, the weaker principle of methodological naturalism, the legitimacy of appeal to one's metaphysical assumptions in determining the best explanation of the historical data, and the probability that God would act miraculously in history at some time or other. But it holds that the evidence for the truth of a *particular* miracle claim is never adequate to make it reasonable, on historical grounds, to believe that it is. This argument focuses on the status and the quality of *testimonial evidence*:

14. A successful historical case for a miracle depends on adequate testimonial evidence that the miracle has occurred.
15. Testimony can provide adequate evidence for the truth of a claim only if there is adequate *independent* evidence that the testimony is reliable.
16. But there is never adequate independent evidence to accept the reliability of testimony on behalf of a miracle claim.
17. Therefore, no historical argument for a miracle can be successful.

An objector will offer reasons in support of premise 16 similar to those rehearsed by Hume (see above). Generally speaking, the claim is that there is inadequate reason for thinking that those who claim to have witnessed a miracle have sufficient competence, caution, and character to be trusted as reliable. When the people in question are ancient sources, such as the people who contributed to the writing of the four Gospels, it is often also added that such premodern people generally cannot be trusted because of their prescientific cultural context and therefore their overly credulous and uncritical acceptance of superstition and myth. It is generally assumed that only modern people (and especially trained scientific historians) are sufficiently objective and critical to be in a position to pass judgment on a miracle report.

This case for premise 16 seems both overly critical of ancient people and insufficiently critical of moderns. A more plausible view is that the ancients were more reliable than this *in spite of* their preconceptions and that modern people are less reliable than is assumed *because of* their preconceptions. As said above, everyone approaches historical questions with preconceptions. A realistic degree of objectivity requires not setting these aside but instead being aware of them and making sure they are employed with appropriate caution. In view of our common humanity, it seems reasonable to think that both ancients and moderns are capable of this sort of critical employment of their presuppositions. The case an objector makes for premise 16, therefore, is problematic.

However, the real problem with the above argument is premise 15. To see why, consider what would count as adequate independent evidence for the reliability of the testimony of people as a general source for your beliefs. Such evidence would need to be absolutely independent of what other people tell you, either directly or indirectly (through written communication, for instance), because evidence that consists in what *others* say is itself a form of testimony, and this is the kind of evidence that premise 15 says we need to *show* to be reliable. The only kind of evidence left over for this purpose is evidence you acquire by means of your own observations, memories of your own observations, and inferences from this evidence. But it seems clear that this kind of evidence will never be enough to justify your belief in the reliability of another person's testimony, especially when this other person is no longer alive. So if testimony is to have any evidential value at all, we must take it as a *basic or foundational source of evidence* that does not require independent evidence for its reliability. We must treat the testimony of others as having a presumption of reliability unless we have good reasons for thinking that it is unreliable. That is, we must take an innocent unless proven guilty approach to testimony as evidence. Thus, the burden of proof is on someone who claims that a particular witness is unreliable. This strengthens the case made in the previous chapter for the historical reliability of the Gospels, which are, after all, extended testimonies of the words and works of Jesus.[3]

Miracles and the Son of God

The goal of this chapter is to appeal to miracles to strengthen the case for the claim that Jesus is God the Son incarnate. The previous chapter argued that it is reasonable to believe that Jesus himself claimed to be the Son of God. We have seen that, from the standpoint of creation monotheism, miracles are possible, probable, and potentially historically discernible. As said earlier in this chapter, God is capable of performing miracles, and it is reasonable to believe that God would perform miracles if he had a good reason to do so. It seems clear, as suggested ear-

> ## We must take an innocent unless proven guilty approach to testimony as evidence.

lier, that God does have such a reason: to prompt lost humans to pay attention to his communications with them in order to save them.

Since God is supremely good, it is reasonable to believe that God is also eminently just, loving, and merciful. As a matter of fact, all three religious traditions that subscribe to creation monotheism (Judaism, Christianity, and Islam) agree that this is the case about God. Moreover, as argued in chapter 4, human beings have a number of needs that it seems reasonable to think can be fulfilled only by God. Among these needs are the needs for meaning, transcendence, forgiveness, reconciliation (with God and others), moral improvement, loving relationships, lasting happiness, and understanding. The discussion of the problems of evil (in chap. 11) and divine hiddenness (in chap. 12) also highlighted the needs for deliverance from sin, suffering, injustice, and alienation. In light of these serious human needs, it is reasonable to think that a just, loving, and merciful God would act so as to meet them.

But God's actions have to be consistent with human freedom. Consequently, God would not simply fulfill these needs without giving us a choice. God can invite us to make a choice about whether to accept his offer of assistance only by *communicating* in such a way as to *reveal* to us his nature, will, and plan. Moreover, a major part of the reason we humans are in such a fix is that, because of sin, we have failed

---

3. In *The Historical Christ and the Jesus of Faith: The Incarnational Narrative as History* (Oxford: Clarendon, 1996), C. Stephen Evans employs this sort of argument to criticize Harvey's assumption (in *Historian and the Believer*) that testimonial evidence needs independent evidential support. Evans attributes this critique of evidentialism about testimony to C. A. J. Coady, *Testimony* (Oxford: Oxford University Press, 1992), 79–100.

to acknowledge and have even forgotten God's role as Creator and Redeemer (we have, as Paul writes in Romans 1:18, "suppressed the truth [about God] by [our] wickedness"). So we need God to remind us of these things.

Christians claim that God's communication to humankind began in ancient Israel and that his initial revelation is recorded in the Old Testament (also called the Hebrew Scriptures). The Scriptures of the oldest living creation monotheist religion, Judaism, purport to tell the story of God's creation of the universe and of human beings in his image; the fall of humanity from its initial state of innocence and intimacy with God; God's selection of the Jewish people to be his ambassadors to all the nations of the world; God's giving of the moral law to these people and his covenant promise of rewarding their obedience to it and punishing their disobedience; his carrying out of this promise as his people lapse continually into idolatry and other forms of sin; and his continual loving and gracious redemption of a remnant of them to give them other opportunities to cultivate righteous relationships with one another and worshipful submission to God. Throughout this sacred history, there is recognition of the ultimate authority and rule of God even when human kings are on the throne. With the rise of the prophets, especially prophets such as Isaiah, comes a growing expectation of and hope for a Messiah—an ideal king in the line of King David who will inaugurate and rule an ideal kingdom that will succeed in bringing about peace and justice where the Davidic kingdom failed. Thus, many prophecies by many prophets predicted the coming of the Messiah to rule not only

Israel but all the nations of the earth as the vice-regent of God.

This religious and historical backdrop provides the context in which to understand the significance of Jesus' announcements at the beginning of his ministry that "the kingdom of God is near" (Mark 1:15) and that the messianic prophecy of Isaiah 61:1–2 had been fulfilled with his coming (Luke 4:16–20). But how could his listeners know that this was true? What evidence could Jesus provide to back up these momentous claims? Jesus provides the answer to this question in his reply to John the Baptist, who sent his disciples to ask Jesus if he was "the one who was to come" (i.e., the Messiah [Luke 7:20]). Jesus responded by saying, "Go back and report to John what you have seen and heard: The blind receive sight, the lame walk, those who have leprosy are cured, the deaf hear, the dead are raised, and the good news is preached to the poor" (Luke 7:22). Jesus implied that his miracles (or "signs," as the author of the Gospel of John likes to call them) are evidence that he is the Messiah, the one appointed and anointed by God to establish and administer the kingdom of God.

Thus, many of the things the Gospels report that Jesus did are not only supernatural in character (in virtue of being extraordinary events that are not explicable from a purely natural standpoint) but also alleged acts of God rather than works of Satan (because they accomplish the kingdom purposes of God). They are, therefore (if they really happened), miracles. Moreover, if Jesus really performed them (and we have yet to argue that he did), then Jesus' claim to be the Messiah and the Son of God receives substantial further confirmation. This confirmation is a result not only of the fact that it is highly likely that God is working in Jesus to perform the miracles but also of what the miracles communicate about the nature and character of Jesus as a person.

If Jesus really is the incarnate Son of God, then it would make a lot of sense for him to choose to call attention to himself during his earthly ministry in unusual and extraordinary (miraculous) ways.[4] Effective revelation of himself as God incarnate would seem to require not merely a claim of deity or even authoritative and godly teaching but also acts of the sort that only God could do. Moreover, it would make sense for him to choose miraculous deeds that reveal not only his identity as God but also the nature and character of God as Creator and Redeemer. A careful reading of the miracle stories in the Gospels strongly suggests that this is precisely what these miracles are intended to communicate.

Take, for instance, miracles that represent God as Creator. These include the water becoming wine (John 2:1–11), the feeding of the five thousand (Mark 6:30–44) and of the four thousand (Mark 8:1–13), and the calming of the storm (Matt. 8:23–27). If he performed these miracles, Jesus was arguably inviting us to identify him with the Creator who (1) makes wine from water more slowly and naturally with rain and grapevines, (2) multiplies grain and fish more gradually and normally in fields and oceans, and (3) brought about the atmospheric conditions responsible for weather patterns in the first place.[5]

Then there are miracles that represent God as Redeemer. These include the miracles of healing (Matt. 8:1–4), the exorcisms (Mark 1:21–28), the raising of people from the dead (John 11:17–44), the transfiguration (Luke 9:28–36), and, perhaps, Jesus and Peter walking on water (Matt. 14:22–33). If these miracles really occurred, it would seem that a major purpose for them was to identify Jesus with the Redeemer who will reverse the forces of sin, evil, suffering, pain, and death and will bring about a human community characterized by health, wholeness, righteousness, justice, peace, and eternal life. The transfiguration and the walking on water may look forward to the new powers of resurrected human bodies.[6]

It is interesting to note in this connection that the miracles that serve as bookends for the earthly life of Jesus—the virgin birth and the resurrection—are, respectively, a sign of God as the Creator of life and a sign of God as the Redeemer of life. Though these are not miracles that Jesus himself performed, they are miraculous signs of his divine status that invite us to pay special attention to the human being who lived on earth between them (just as Jesus' baptism and transfiguration do in the midst of his life as well).

In sum, if Jesus really performed the miracles the Gospels say he did, then both the existence and the character of these miracles add substantial confirmation to Jesus' claim to be the Messiah and one

---

4. It seems clear from the Gospels, however, that Jesus was careful to guard against the wrong kind of attention due to misunderstandings of the point of his miracles or the nature of his role as the Messiah (see e.g., Mark 1:43–45; John 6:15).

5. C. S. Lewis develops a similar line of thought, but for a different purpose, in "Miracles," in *God in the Dock: Essays on Theology and Ethics*, ed. Walter Hooper, 25–37 (Grand Rapids: Eerdmans, 1970).

6. Again, see ibid.

with the Creator and Redeemer God. This confirmation would make it unlikely that Jesus was honestly and sanely mistaken about being divine. But do we have good reason to believe that he actually did any of these things?

To show that we do, we need to pull together some strands from this and the previous chapter. In the first place, though the Gospels have primarily a theological purpose, they also have a historical aim (because they intend to portray Jesus as the eternal God who entered history as a human being). As a part of this historical aim, the Gospels present the miracle stories as accounts of what Jesus really did. Moreover, it is reasonable to believe that all four Gospels are based substantially (and perhaps completely) on apostolic eyewitness sources. In addition, there is no good reason to think that the Gospel writers imposed, either unconsciously or deliberately, a supernatural interpretation on what was originally the story of a merely human Jesus. Unless the Christ of faith is largely identical with the Jesus of history, we do not have an adequate explanation of the rapid and widespread rise of belief in Jesus as Lord and God by the early church.

Now we can add the argument of the previous section of this chapter: Testimony is a basic source of reasonable belief, and it should therefore be presumed to be reliable unless we have a good reason to think it is not. Since we have apostolic eyewitness testimony that Jesus performed many miracles of various kinds, and we have no good reason to believe that these stories were added by the early church to "supernaturalize" an otherwise purely natural Jesus, it follows that it is reasonable to believe that the miracle stories in the Gospels are true—at least with respect to their principal claims.

Let me now summarize the main argument of this chapter.

1. If Jesus really performed the miracles the Gospels report that he did, then both the existence and the character of these miracles add substantial confirmation to Jesus' claim to be the Messiah and one with the Creator and Redeemer God.
2. It is reasonable to believe that the miracle stories in the Gospels are largely true.
3. Thus, both the existence and the character of Jesus' miracles increase the degree of confirmation we have that Jesus was correct in claiming to be (or at least implying that he is) God.

We can conclude that it is highly likely that Jesus was not sincerely and sanely mistaken in claiming to be the Son of God. However, if he had died and stayed dead, this conclusion would be highly doubtful in spite of the argument given for it. Therefore, we need to turn now to the final step in the case for the divinity of Jesus. Is it reasonable to believe that Jesus was raised from the dead?

Reflection and Discussion

1. Do you have trouble believing in miracles? Why or why not?
2. Think more thoroughly about what reasons there are for believing that testimonial evidence needs to be accepted at face value without a demonstration of its reliability unless there are good reasons to reject it.
3. Do you agree that both the existence and the *character* of Jesus' miracles strengthen the case for his divinity? Why or why not?

Further Reading

Evans, C. Stephen. *The Historical Christ and the Jesus of Faith: The Incarnational Narrative as History.* Oxford: Clarendon, 1996.

Hume, David. "Of Miracles." In *An Enquiry Concerning Human Understanding,* edited by Tom L. Beauchamp, 169–86. New York: Oxford University Press, 1999.

Lewis, C. S. "Miracles." In *God in the Dock: Essays on Theology and Ethics,* edited by Walter Hooper, 25–37. Grand Rapids: Eerdmans, 1970.

15

He Is Risen Indeed!

The Resurrection of Jesus

» **Outline**

- **What Is the Resurrection of Jesus?**
  - *Four Models of Jesus' Resurrection*
    - The Existentialist Model
    - The Resuscitation Model
    - The Spiritual Immortality Model
    - The Physical Resurrection Model
  - *Why the Physical Resurrection Model Is Preferable*
- **Evidence and Explanations**
  - *Jesus' Historical Existence*
  - *Jesus' Genuine Death*
  - *The Burial of Jesus' Corpse*
  - *The Empty Tomb*
  - *The Post-death Appearances of Jesus*
  - *The Disciples' Radical Transformation*
- **Consequences and Implications**
  - *The Problem of Divine Hiddenness*
  - *The Problem of Evil*
  - *The Problem of Death*
  - *The Problem of Religious Diversity*

» **Summary**

The Bible claims that Jesus experienced a real physical resurrection. The alternative views that Jesus "lives on" in his life-changing message, that Jesus was merely resuscitated, and that only Jesus' spirit survived his death are less adequate models of his resurrection. The Gospels report a number of historical facts about Jesus and his disciples that are better explained by the hypothesis that Jesus was raised physically and gloriously from the dead than by a number of alternative hypotheses. The doctrine of Jesus' resurrection makes a number of problems less serious than they would be if Jesus had stayed dead. The problem of divine hiddenness is mitigated by the act of God revealing himself in the risen Christ; the problems of evil and death are diminished by God's demonstration of his ability and willingness to defeat sin and death in the resurrection; and the problem of religious diversity is alleviated by the vindication of Jesus' claim to be divine.

» **Basic Terms, Concepts, and Names**

Bultmann, Rudolph
existentialism
Joseph of Arimathaea
mass hallucination theory
principle of multiple attestation
resuscitation
spiritual immortality
stolen body theory
swoon theory
wrong tomb theory

» **Reflection and Discussion**

» **Further Reading**

> God has raised . . . Jesus to life, and we are all witnesses of the fact.
>
> Acts 2:32

We have come to the central event of the Christian faith, which, if it really happened, is also the turning point of all human history. There are three main questions about the resurrection of Jesus that a Christian apologist must address:

1. What is supposed to have happened?
2. What reasons do we have for believing that it really occurred?
3. What is the significance of Jesus' resurrection for human beings?

What Is the Resurrection of Jesus?

Theologians have differed in their understanding of the nature of Jesus' resurrection. This section talks about four such understandings. Only the fourth is defensible. The other three have serious problems from the standpoint of the apostolic Christian faith.[1]

Let us call the first inadequate idea about the nature of the resurrection of Jesus the existential model. This conception was developed by some theologians in the early part of the twentieth century, most notably Rudolph Bultmann (1884–1976). Though he was a theist of sorts, he labeled the supernatural cosmology presupposed by the New Testament mythological. He is famous for insisting that modern people cannot believe in "the New Testament world of spirits and miracles."[2] Moreover, according to Bultmann's view, nothing of significance can be known about the historical Jesus. Therefore, he believed that the quest mentioned in chapter 13 is a fruitless enterprise. But instead of rejecting Christianity, Bultmann held that what Jesus actually said, did, and experienced does not matter for Christians. All that matters is that the gospel of Christ provides an opportunity for human beings to make a decision to actualize their potential to become their "authentic" selves. This approach to Christianity effectively reduces

1. I am indebted to Stephen T. Davis, *Risen Indeed: Making Sense of the Resurrection* (Grand Rapids: Eerdmans, 1993), chap. 3, for many of the ideas in this section.

2. Rudolph Bultmann, "The New Testament and Mythology," in *Kerygma and Myth*, ed. Hans Werner Bartsch (New York: Harper & Row, 1961), 5.

its content to that of twentieth-century existentialist philosophy (Bultmann was highly influenced by the agnostic existentialist philosopher Martin Heidegger). According to this view, to say that Jesus is risen is simply to say that Jesus is the source of the life-changing opportunity for existential decision. Clearly, if this is all that Jesus' resurrection amounts to, then Jesus can be resurrected without having been brought back to real personal, biological, or even spiritual existence.

The first problem with Bultmann's approach (which is representative of others in this category) is that his rejection of a full-fledged supernaturalism that includes spiritual beings and miracles is unjustified. He provides no argument for this view other than to insist that moderns cannot believe it. However, though many today *do not* believe in these things, it is far from clear that they *cannot* believe in them. Moreover, many contemporary intelligent and rational people do affirm the existence of the supernatural. Furthermore, as argued in chapter 14, the case for the creation monotheist version of supernaturalism makes it rational to believe in miracles. It also makes it reasonable to believe in spirits and souls. If God is an omnipotent, infinite Spirit, then surely God can create finite spirits.

Second, the historical skepticism on which Bultmann's view is based is unwarranted, as argued in chapter 13. There is no good reason to think that the Gospel writers imposed a supernatural interpretation on the story of Jesus, and there is good reason to think they did not. There is good reason to think that the Jesus they portray is, at least for the most part and in the most important respects, the historical Jesus. Moreover, even if this were not the

case, an interpretation of the gospel message in terms of twentieth-century existentialist philosophy is implausible. Though the gospel challenges people to make a life-changing decision, it is *essentially* rooted in the historical claim that Jesus died and rose again to save them from their sins and reconcile them to God. To deny these historical claims is to deny the gospel. Bultmann's brand of existentialism is much more plausibly viewed as an *alternative* to Christianity than as a *version* of Christianity. The same conclusion holds for other variations on the existentialist model of Jesus' resurrection.

The second conception of Jesus' resurrection that can be ruled out is the resuscitation model. A human being is resuscitated if and only if that individual (1) has really died, (2) is somehow brought back to life with the same body that died, (3) continues to live after that point in the normal biological way in which he or she was living before dying, and then eventually (4) dies again. Depending on how one defines biological death, there may well have been many resuscitations in history brought about by humans (such as doctors) employing purely natural means (e.g., CPR). The Gospels contain a few stories about Jesus bringing people back to life. These are arguably cases of *miraculous* resuscitation, especially in the case of Lazarus, since he had been dead for four days (John 11:38). Clearly, Jesus' resurrection does not fit the resuscitation model, since, although it satisfies conditions 1 and 2, it does not meet requirements 3 and 4. The Gospels report that after his resurrection, although Jesus could be seen and touched, and although he could walk, talk, eat, and drink, he was also somewhat difficult to recognize, could appear and disappear at will (even when the doors were locked), and eventually ascended into heaven. His body had been altered and *glorified* in some sense. Moreover, when his postresurrection time on earth was over, he did not die but, as just mentioned, "was taken up [into heaven] before their very eyes, and a cloud hid him from their sight" (Acts 1:9). Jesus' resurrection, therefore, was not resuscitation.

Third, there is the spiritual immortality model of Jesus' resurrection. This conception presupposes the ancient Greek philosophical conception of human persons as essentially immaterial, nonphysical souls or spirits who are temporarily embodied during their sojourn on earth. The Platonic tradition also contains the nonbiblical assumption that material bodies are a relatively evil prison for the soul and that death involves the permanent liberation of the soul from the body. The heretical Gnostic theologies prevalent in the early Christian church presuppose this view of the body. This view is nonbiblical because the Old Testament book of Genesis affirms that God created the material world, including human bodies, and pronounced his creation "very good" (Gen. 1:31). But a dualistic view of human persons that identifies them with their soul or spirit whether embodied or not does not have to take this negative perspective on physical bodies (Augustine seems to have had such a Platonic but non-Gnostic view of human persons). According to this sanitized dualistic view, bodies are not evil, but they are not necessary for personal survival of death either.

According to the spiritual immortality model of Jesus' resurrection, what came back to life in the resurrection was Jesus' soul or spirit but not his physical or material body. According to this view, it does not matter if Jesus' body remained in the tomb, and thus it does not matter whether the empty tomb stories in the Gospels are true. All that matters is that Jesus survived his death as a person. If the Greeks were correct in thinking that souls are *naturally* immortal, then there would be nothing special about Jesus' resurrection, since his experience of survival would be simply a result of human nature. Given this natural immortality thesis, the point of the resurrection of Jesus would seem to be simply to reassure human beings that there is life after death for all humans. The unusual thing would be Jesus' *appearance* to them rather than his survival.

But this is clearly not how the New Testament writers think of Jesus' resurrection. For one thing, they do not consider it something that would happen to a person in the normal and natural course of events. It was something that God did (Acts 2:24), and it was completely unexpected, amazing, and extraordinary (see, e.g., Luke 24:22, 41). In short, it was a miracle. Was the miracle simply that God continued to sustain Jesus' spirit or soul in spite of the death of his body? This is not how the Gospel writers see it. Even in Mark, the earliest and briefest Gospel account, the women who visited Jesus' tomb find that his body is missing, and the "young man dressed in a white robe" (16:5) who is there tells them that Jesus "has risen" (16:6). This language (in addition to the language of resurrection) is more naturally used of bodies than of souls. Matthew says that the eleven disciples "saw" Jesus in Galilee after this and that he spoke to them (28:17–18). But aren't there apparitions of ghosts who can speak, like the deceased Jacob Marley in Dickens's

Christmas Carol? Perhaps so, but Luke explicitly rules out this interpretation. He reports that when the resurrected Jesus suddenly appeared among the disciples, "They were startled and frightened, thinking they saw a ghost. He [Jesus] said to them, 'Why are you troubled, and why do doubts rise in your minds? Look at my hands and my feet. It is I myself! Touch me and see; a ghost does not have flesh and bones, as you see I have'" (24:37–39). Luke goes on to say that Jesus ate a piece of broiled fish (24:42–43). Finally, in John, we learn from Jesus' encounter with Thomas (discussed in chap. 6) that the wounds from Jesus' crucifixion were visible (and tangible, since Jesus invited Thomas to touch them). It seems clear, therefore, that Jesus has not merely *a* body but the *same* body as the one that died—only his body has been transformed and glorified in certain ways. In conclusion, if these Gospel accounts are reliable (and we have seen that there is good reason to think they are), then the spiritual immortality model of Jesus' resurrection is highly unlikely to be true.

The discussion of the shortcomings of these three models of Jesus' resurrection provides a good case for the model that best squares with the New Testament conception: the physical resurrection model. According to this view, God brought Jesus to life again with a physical body that (1) was identical with Jesus' premortem body and yet (2) was glorified in such a way as to provide him with new powers and also (3) would never die again. But does Paul's description of resurrection bodies in 1 Corinthians 15:44 as "*spiritual* bodies" undermine this claim? No. It is probable that Paul is arguing in that chapter for the physical resurrection model against

> **The discussion provides a good case for the model that best squares with the New Testament conception: the physical resurrection model.**

a (probably proto-Gnostic) version of the spiritual immortality model. That is why he takes such great pains to emphasize the resurrection of the *body*. Bodies are essentially things that take up space and so are physical or material things (even if they do not obey the physical laws that govern *this* physical world). Thus, the expression "spiritual body" would be a contradiction in terms if spiritual here meant immaterial or nonphysical. It is more likely that what Paul means by a spiritual body is a body that is suited for or equipped with nonnatural abilities to facilitate the accomplishment of spiritual purposes, such as the goal of sinless and loving communion with the Triune God and fellow glorified believers.

Evidence and Explanations

What historical evidence is there for the claim that Jesus enjoyed a physical resurrection? The New Testament contains a wealth of historical data that is arguably best explained by the hypothesis that Jesus was raised from the dead. However, there is space here only for a summary of it. This summary includes primarily historical facts about Jesus, but it also mentions some historical facts about the first disciples and the early church. At appropriate points, it offers reasons for rejecting alternative hypotheses that are inconsistent with the claim that Jesus came back to life.

The first important historical fact about Jesus is that he really existed as a human being. Though some have denied this,[3] even the most radical of the current historical critics affirm it (and we have seen that there is good reason to do so). Second, Jesus really died on the cross on which he was crucified. Mel Gibson's recent movie *The Passion of the Christ*, which was based on a careful investigation of the history of Roman torture and execution, should convince anyone who views it that this is likely the case. Indeed, it is hard to see how anyone could have survived the flagellation Jesus endured before he was even hung on the cross. And once on the cross, the Roman guards responsible for overseeing the crucifixion would surely have confirmed his death before taking him down from the cross. The Gospel of John observes, "But when they [the Roman soldiers] came to Jesus and found that he was already dead, they did not break his legs. Instead, one of the soldiers pierced Jesus' side with a spear, bringing a sudden flow of blood and water. The man who saw it has given testimony, and his testimony is true. He knows that he tells the truth, and he testifies so that you also may believe" (19:33–35). From the standpoint of contemporary medical science, the water that came out of Jesus' side was probably a fluid that collects around the heart and/or the lungs only after a person has died.[4]

3. For instance, G. A. Wells, *Did Jesus Exist?* rev. ed. (London: Pemberton, 1986).

4. See Lee Strobel, *The Case for Christ: A Journalist's Personal Investigation of the Evidence for Jesus* (Grand Rapids: Zondervan, 1998), chap. 11,

Some who have denied that Jesus died on the cross have proposed the swoon theory as an explanation of what happened. According to this hypothesis, Jesus fainted on the cross due to exhaustion or the narcotic effect of the wine vinegar on the sponge offered to him (Mark 15:36), was taken down by soldiers who thought he was dead, and was revived by the coolness of the tomb. Though this may seem to explain why his crucifixion was relatively brief (Mark 15:44 reports Pilate's surprise that he was dead so soon), it is highly implausible that he could have survived given his probable physical condition. Furthermore, even if he had, it is unlikely that he could have rolled away the heavy stone in front of the tomb and been able to convince his disciples, while in that condition, that he was raised to a glorious and victorious state.

The third fact about Jesus is that his corpse was buried in a tomb. When Paul reminds the Corinthians of the gospel he had preached to them, he says, "For what I received I passed on to you as of first importance: that Christ died for our sins according to the Scriptures, *that he was buried*, that he was raised on the third day according to the Scriptures" (1 Cor. 15:3–4, emphasis added). This is the beginning of a passage to which we will return shortly because of its importance as evidence for the postresurrection appearances of Jesus to his disciples. The language ("received" and "passed on") implies the transmission of a formal early Christian tradition.

Before discussing additional evidence for Jesus' burial, let us first pause to consider the value of this tradition received by Paul. When and from whom did he

for an extensive discussion of this and other medical evidence that Jesus really died on the cross.

receive it? Paul wrote 1 Corinthians in AD 54 or 55 after having founded the Corinthian church during his second missionary journey around AD 51. Paul would have acquired this historical tradition (on which he based the gospel he preached) sometime before that. It is likely that he received it before AD 47, which is around the time his first missionary journey began (he would not have begun to preach until he had something to preach about). In his letter to the Galatians, which was written sometime between AD 49 and AD 54 or 55, Paul mentions a fourteen-year period after his conversion to Christianity and before his missionary journeys began (2:1). This means that Paul's conversion experience occurred around AD 33 or 34 and was thus only a few years after Jesus died (in AD 30). Since Paul began to preach that Jesus is the Son of God right away (Acts 9:20), it is likely that he already had the historical basis for this gospel in mind. Thus, there is good reason to think that the tradition goes back to within *just a few years* of the events it is about and that Paul received it from eyewitnesses to these events (or perhaps even from Jesus himself, as Paul seems to imply in Galatians). Even if this early date is incorrect, from the date of 1 Corinthians, it follows that Paul certainly received the tradition within twenty years or so after Jesus died. Either way, we can draw two important inferences: (1) Many eyewitnesses to Jesus' death, burial, and postresurrection appearances would still have been alive to confirm or disconfirm the tradition; and (2) it is extremely unlikely that the tradition contained any mythological elements in addition to the historical facts, since such alterations would take much more time to occur. This bolsters the case made

for the reliability of the Gospels in chapter 13. Therefore, an extremely early tradition was that Jesus was buried.

Moreover, all four Gospels agree that the tomb in which Jesus' body was placed was owned by Joseph of Arimathaea, and no competing tradition exists. It is unlikely that the early Christians fabricated this story, since (1) the specific use of Joseph's name means that the story could easily have been falsified if it were not true, and (2) Joseph was a member of the Sanhedrin, the group of Jewish authorities partially responsible (with the Romans) for Jesus' crucifixion. It is unlikely that Jesus' followers would have attributed such a noble act to a member of this group unless it really happened (especially in light of the disciples' failure to stay devoted to Jesus when the going got tough). Since Joseph was a prominent and wealthy man, his tomb would likely have been located in a well-known spot and would have been relatively secure. This makes the wrong tomb theory (that the women who went to anoint Jesus' body with spices on Sunday morning went to the wrong tomb) unlikely and the stolen body theory (that Jesus' disciples stole his body from the tomb) problematic. Moreover, the three synoptic Gospels[5] each report that the women saw Jesus' body being laid in this tomb on Friday.

The fourth important fact about Jesus is that the women who went to the tomb on Sunday to attend to Jesus' body did not find it there but instead found an empty tomb. Some argue that this is a later addition to the tradition since it is not in-

---

5. The synoptic Gospels are Matthew, Mark, and Luke, so-called because their high degree of similarity to one another becomes evident when they are set side by side and seen (-optic) together (syn-).

cluded in Paul's summary in 1 Corinthians 15:1–8. However, just because Paul does not explicitly mention that the tomb was empty does not mean that it was not. For one thing, given that Paul subscribed to the physical resurrection model (as argued in the previous section), the death, burial, and resurrection of Jesus (all of which Paul does mention) *require* the tomb to have been devoid of Jesus' body. But if the tomb was empty, and Paul believed it was, then why didn't he mention it? Why does the empty tomb story show up only later in the Gospels (which were written sometime between the 50s and the 90s)? A plausible answer to this question is that initially, when those to whom the resurrected Christ appeared were still alive and relatively numerous, their collective testimony that they had seen Jesus alive would have sufficed for evangelistic and apologetical purposes, especially since it was probably common knowledge that the tomb was empty (and so not worth mentioning). Later on, when such eyewitnesses were fewer and farther between, and when the empty tomb story ceased to be taken for granted, it became important for apologetic purposes to emphasize the absence of Jesus' body.

Another possible reason for the omission of the empty tomb story from the gospel tradition Paul received and passed on is that the witnesses to the empty tomb were all women (at least as reported by the earlier synoptic Gospels),[6] and the testimony of women was not considered credible at that time. If people would tend not to believe a story told by women, then such a story (and the claim based on it)

6. The mention of Peter witnessing the empty tomb in Luke 24:12 is not contained in all the manuscripts of this Gospel.

would not have sufficient apologetic value to be included in an official confession of faith communicated for the purpose of persuading unbelievers. Interestingly, this observation can be employed to provide support for the historical reliability of the Gospel accounts of the empty tomb in particular and the resurrection of Jesus more generally. If women were not considered reliable witnesses at the time, then why would the Gospel writers feature female testimony concerning the empty tomb unless the story were really true? If they had cared more about persuasion than about truth, it seems likely that they would have altered the empty tomb stories so as not to involve women.

The stories about the women at the empty tomb do, however, contain an element that is initially apologetically awkward. This is the problem of discrepancies of various sorts among the stories. The stories differ on the number and identity of the women who visited the tomb, what happened to them when they arrived, and other details. Moreover, attempts to harmonize these accounts are implausible. Some have argued that these conflicting accounts show that the Gospel accounts of the resurrection cannot be historically reliable. However, this aspect of the stories is not necessarily a problem and may actually be apologetically advantageous. For one thing, the differences have only to do with relatively minor details. All the stories agree on the basic facts (the facts we are in the process of discussing). Moreover, eyewitness accounts or reports of eyewitness accounts are likely to differ in these ways because people have different points of view and exercise selective attention and memory, especially with respect to details. If the stories agreed more on the details, then it would be harder to rule out the possibility that they all went back to only one source. But the principle of multiple attestation holds, rightly, that the more independent sources one has on the basis of which to confirm a historical fact, the more likely it is for that fact to be confirmed by those sources. If there is only one source, the chances of mistakes or deliberate falsehoods concerning the important matters are increased. Discrepancy in details suggests a basis of multiple independent sources—a basis that makes the main features of the overall story more likely to be true.

One significant difference in detail among the accounts is that only Matthew mentions the guards at the tomb (27:62–66) who were later paid by the Jewish authorities to say that Jesus' disciples stole his body while the guards were asleep (28:11–15). Some have argued that Matthew made this up to combat the charge that the disciples stole Jesus' body. However, whether he fabricated this or not (and there is no strong evidence that he did), the mere inclusion of the story tends to confirm that the tomb was empty. If Matthew *did* make up the story to prove that the disciples could not have stolen Jesus' body, then the tomb must have been empty for that charge to have arisen. If he *did not* make up the story, then the incident with the authorities and guards can be explained only if the tomb was empty. Moreover, if Jesus' body had still been in the tomb, the Jewish authorities would not have claimed that it had been stolen; they would instead simply have produced the body. But they did not do that because they could not.

But could the disciples have stolen Jesus' body? If the guards were present, it is unlikely. But even if the guards were not there, it is also unlikely. In the first place, they had no motive to do this. In spite of Jesus' prediction to them that "on the third day [the Son of man] will rise again" (Luke 18:33), Luke says that "they did not know what he was talking about" (18:34). They did not expect the resurrection. But if they did not conspire to give the impression that Jesus had been raised from the dead when he really had not been, what possible motive could they have had to steal his body? Moreover, it is highly unlikely that Jesus' followers would have faced persecution and death for something they knew to be a lie.

The fifth important fact about Jesus is that many people claimed to have seen him alive after he died. The remainder of the tradition Paul passed on to the Corinthians summarizes the specific main appearances:

> He appeared to Peter, and then to the Twelve. After that, he appeared to more than five hundred of the brothers at the same time, most of whom are still living, though some have fallen asleep. Then he appeared to James, then to all the apostles, and last of all he appeared to me also, as to one abnormally born.
>
> 1 Corinthians 15:5–8

As already mentioned, many of these people would still have been alive at the time of Paul's writing to confirm what Paul was saying (this may well be the reason Paul says, "Though some have fallen asleep"; all the rest would have been available for questioning). Critics have claimed that even if these people *claimed* to have seen Jesus alive after his death and *believed* that he was, an alternative explanation does not commit us to the truth of what they claimed. This is the mass hallucination theory. According to this hypothesis, all of the alleged postresurrection appearances of Jesus were nothing but purely subjective hallucinations experienced by the people Paul mentions (and others, whom he does not mention, such as Mary Magdalene [see John 20:14–18]). But this suggestion is highly improbable. Though it is true that some of Jesus' followers may well have been experiencing posttraumatic stress disorder (which can cause hallucinations) as a result of having witnessed Jesus' flogging and execution, there is no evidence that any of the other typical causes of hallucination (fever, drugs, dementia, organ failure, etc.) were present. Even more damning to this idea, however, is that, even if these causes were present in some people, it is highly unlikely that they would have been experienced by *all* the people purported to have seen Jesus. The appearances are reported to have occurred to many people at a number of times and places. Clearly, the mass hallucination theory can be ruled out.

The sixth and final important historical fact has more directly to do with Jesus' followers and the early church than with Jesus. This is the fact that their lives were quickly and radically transformed as a result of what happened on the first Easter.[7] Luke's story of the two disciples on the road to Emmaus that day portrays the mood that was probably characteristic of all of Jesus' followers at the time between the crucifixion and their knowledge of the resurrection. Luke says that when the unrecognized risen Christ questioned

them, "they stood still, their faces downcast" (24:17). In telling Jesus about the events of the last few days, they say, "We had hoped that he [Jesus] was the one who was going to redeem Israel" (24:21). The clear implication is that they had lost hope. The remarkable thing is that in the space of a few days the formerly dejected and despairing disciples were full of joy and amazement (24:41), began to worship Jesus (24:52), and started to preach to all who would listen that God had raised Jesus to life (Acts 2:32) and made him "both Lord and Christ" (Acts 2:36). Moreover, they continued to preach this message even when they were threatened (Acts 4:18–21), persecuted and scattered (Acts 8:1–3), imprisoned (Acts 12:1–18), and put to death (Acts 7:54–60). The only thing that can explain these facts is that they were absolutely convinced that Jesus had been raised from the dead. The best explanation for this conviction is that they had seen him alive after he had died.

Consequences and Implications

This concludes the historical case for the claim that Jesus is God the Son incarnate. Jesus explicitly claimed to be divine or at least implied that he was by what he said and did. It is more likely that this claim or implication is true than that Jesus was either lying or insane. It is reasonable to believe that Jesus performed miracles and that his miraculous acts reinforce the case for his deity both by their mere existence and also through their character as signs of Jesus' role as Creator and Redeemer. This argument that Jesus employed supernatural power makes the possibility that he was sanely and honestly

---

7. See chap. 18 for more about how the first Jewish disciples and converts experienced dramatic changes in belief and lifestyle as a result of their belief that Jesus was raised from the dead.

mistaken about his identity less plausible. Finally, the historical facts are arguably best explained by the hypothesis that Jesus was raised from the dead. This conclusion provides the strongest grounds to conclude that the wonder-working claimant to the messianic throne is none other than God incarnate.

Before the next chapter defends this claim against a philosophical objection, it is good to summarize briefly some ways in which the doctrine of the resurrection of Jesus provides additional apologetical advantages. In particular, at least four problems faced by Christian apologists and discussed in this book are rendered less serious by the fact of the resurrection of Jesus as it is interpreted in the New Testament (based on the teaching of Jesus himself).

The Problem of Divine Hiddenness. Jesus' resurrection gives us reason to believe that, though God often seems hidden, "God was reconciling the world to himself in Christ" (2 Cor. 5:19). As Charles Wesley's hymn "Hark the Herald Angels Sing!" puts it, "Veiled in flesh the Godhead see; hail the incarnate Deity!" Though Jesus' divinity was "cloaked" to some extent by his humanity, the resurrection removes the cloak in part, at least for seekers, open-minded doubters, and believers. As a result, we can trust Jesus when he says to Philip (and to us), "Anyone who has seen me has seen the Father" (John 14:9; see also Heb. 1:3). God may be hiding, but he is not absent, and he invites us in the resurrection to look to Jesus to find him. Moreover, the crucifixion shows that Jesus himself felt forsaken by God (Mark 15:34), but in the resurrection this alienation gave way to joyful exaltation (Heb. 12:2). The experience of the disciples and the promises of Jesus (e.g., Mark 8:34–35) make it reasonable to believe that following him will eventually lead to the same result.

The Problem of Evil. Jesus' resurrection gives us reason to believe that, though it looks at present as if sin, evil, and injustice are getting the upper hand, God can and will eventually win out over the powers of darkness. We may not currently know why he allows evil or exactly how he will overcome it, but God's victory over the evil of the cross by means of the power of the resurrection demonstrates that he was willing and able to bring the greatest triumph ever achieved out of the greatest injustice ever wrought. If this is the case, how much more will he be willing and able to eradicate *all* sin and evil when he brings about his kingdom in its fullness! The resurrection of Jesus provides a reasonable basis for the assurance that, though we do not know what God's reason is for allowing all the evil that exists, we can trust that he has such a reason and that he will eventually rescue all who trust in him for deliverance, as he rescued Jesus. Moreover, the crucifixion itself shows that God was willing to suffer and die unjustly on our behalf. Therefore, the God who

> **God's victory over the evil of the cross by means of the power of the resurrection demonstrates that he was willing and able to bring the greatest triumph ever achieved out of the greatest injustice ever wrought.**

allows pain and suffering is also the God who endured it for our sake.

The Problem of Death. Jesus' resurrection gives us reason to believe that, though each of us is certain to experience biological death as the end of our life on this earth, those who turn from sin to Jesus will also be raised to eternal life with God and other Christians. As Paul says in 1 Corinthians 15, "Christ has indeed been raised from the dead, the firstfruits of those who have fallen asleep [died]. . . . For as in Adam all die, so in Christ all will be made alive. . . . The last enemy to be destroyed is death" (vv. 20, 22, 26). This can happen only if we are saved from the penalty and power of sin, since "the wages of sin is death" (Rom. 6:23). But this is what Christ's atonement has accomplished for us (we talk more about this doctrine in chap. 17). That is why "the gift of God is eternal life in Christ Jesus our Lord" (Rom. 6:23). It is through our appropriation of the benefits of the atonement that our needs for forgiveness, reconciliation (with God and others), and moral transformation are met (as discussed in chap. 4). As a result, we can also meet our need to live a meaningful life in loving service to and enjoyment of God and others. We can also have a confident hope that our relationships with God and others will continue for eternity as a result of our postmortem experience of "the resurrection of the body and the life everlasting."[8] At that time, our joy will be made complete through the ongoing worship of God and fellowship with others who love God. Then we will also understand more fully what we understand only partially now (1 Cor. 13:12). Since the resurrection of Jesus makes it reasonable for us to hope for all this, it also gives us good reasons not to fear death.

The Problem of Religious Diversity.[9] Finally, Jesus' resurrection gives us reason to believe that, though a number of religious traditions claim to possess the way of salvation for human beings, Jesus can be trusted when he says, "I am the way and the truth and the life. No one comes to the Father except through me" (John 14:6). No other religious figure in human history has both claimed to be divine and risen from the dead. This makes Jesus stand out in the crowd. Whoever asks with the Philippian jailor, "What must I do to be saved?" (Acts 16:30), has good reason, given the resurrection of Jesus, to follow the advice of Paul and Silas: "Believe in the Lord Jesus, and you will be saved" (16:31). Paul writes to the Romans that Jesus "was declared with power to be the Son of God by his resurrection from the dead" (1:4). In the resurrection, God vindicated Jesus' claims and proved that Jesus is the divine Savior of humankind. In Paul's sermon to the Athenians, he tells them that God "commands all people everywhere to repent. For he has set a day when he will judge the world with justice by the man he has appointed. He has given proof of this to all men by raising him from the dead" (Acts 17:30–31). He also tells the Philippians that "God exalted him [Jesus] to the highest place and gave him the name that is above every name, that at the name of Jesus every knee should bow, in heaven and on earth and under the earth, and every tongue confess that Jesus Christ is Lord, to the glory of God the Father" (2:9–11). God raised Jesus from

---

8. See chap. 23 for more on the resurrection of believers and life after death.

9. See chaps. 18 and 19 for an extended discussion of this problem.

the dead in order that everyone on earth would worship him and acknowledge that he is Lord.

A reflection on these four consequences and implications of the resurrection of Jesus can both remove doubts from one's mind and fill one's heart with joy and gratitude. In short, meditating on this central doctrine of the Christian faith and pivotal event in human history is an important means by which to cultivate Christian commitment.

Reflection and Discussion

1. Is it important to affirm the physical resurrection model of Jesus' resurrection rather than any of the other three models? Why or why not? If it is important, what are some things people care about (or *should* care about) that are at stake in this debate?
2. How strong do you think the historical case for Jesus' resurrection is? Is it strong enough to contribute to the goal of *ambitious* apologetics or only strong enough to achieve the objective of *moderate* apologetics? Explain.
3. Expand on the consequences of Jesus' resurrection discussed in the text or supplement them with other implications. Explain the bearing of Jesus' resurrection on each of the human needs discussed in chapter 4.

Further Reading

Davis, Stephen T. *Risen Indeed: Making Sense of the Resurrection.* Grand Rapids: Eerdmans, 1993.

Swinburne, Richard. *The Resurrection of God Incarnate.* New York: Oxford University Press, 2003.

Wright, N. T. *The Resurrection of the Son of God.* Minneapolis: Augsburg Fortress, 2003.

16

The Word Became Flesh

The Trinity and the Incarnation

» **Outline**

- **God and Logic**
  - *Epistemological versus Logical Problems*
  - *A Defense of Logical Coherence versus Proof of Truth*
  - *A Critique of the Orthodox Doctrine of the Incarnation*
  - *A Critique of the Orthodox Doctrine of the Trinity*
- **The Logic of God Incarnate**
  - *A Defense of the Doctrine of the Incarnation*
    - Our Limited Knowledge of What Being Fully Human Requires
    - Two Important Distinctions
  - *The Two-Minds Model of the Incarnation*
- **The Logic of the Triune God**
  - *A Defense of the Doctrine of the Trinity*
  - *An Attempt to Satisfy the Demands of Both Orthodoxy and Logic*
    - The Heresies of Tritheism and Modalism
    - Social Trinitarianism

» **Summary**

The orthodox doctrine of the incarnation is that Jesus is one person who is fully human and fully divine. The orthodox doctrine of the Trinity is that God is three persons in one substance. Critics argue that both of these doctrines are logically incoherent and therefore not possibly true. Christian apologists can defend the rationality of believing that these doctrines are true. A defense of the doctrine of the incarnation emphasizes the limits of our knowledge of what is required to be fully human and the possibility that Jesus limited his access to his divine omniscience during his earthly existence. A defense of the doctrine of the Trinity stresses the proper interpretation of what the doctrine claims and some distinctive ways in which the persons of the Godhead are interrelated.

» **Basic Terms, Concepts, and Names**

epistemological problem
essential properties
eternal necessary relations
fully human
identity (and transitivity of)
incarnation, doctrine of the
logical problem
merely human
modalism
predication
social trinitarianism
substance
Trinity, doctrine of the
tritheism
two-minds model of the incarnation
universal property

» **Reflection and Discussion**

» **Further Reading**

> The Word became flesh and made his dwelling among us. We have seen his glory, the glory of the One and Only, who came from the Father, full of grace and truth.
>
> John 1:14

God and Logic

The historical argument of chapters 13–15 makes it reasonable to believe that Jesus is divine—as long as there are no good reasons to the contrary.[1] But some have argued that the traditional orthodox conception of the incarnation is logically contradictory. They hold that it is not logically possible for one person to be both fully human and fully divine. If it is reasonable to believe that this is the case, then we no longer have adequate grounds for accepting the deity of the human being Jesus of Nazareth. In that case, though it may still be rational to believe that Jesus was a human being through whom God worked in unique ways, he could not be God himself. Alternatively, one could consistently affirm Christ's divinity but deny

his humanity. Both of these approaches have been branded heretical by the historic Christian church. But the task laid out in the introduction to this book is to defend the orthodox Christian faith. The second section of this chapter shows how to defend the traditional orthodox doctrine of the incarnation against the charge of logical incoherence. That is, it supplements the watering done in the first half of this part with weeding.

If we can defend the doctrine of the incarnation against this logical objection, then it is reasonable to believe that Jesus is God. But some would argue that this means that, though we are out of the frying pan, we have jumped into the fire. How could both the Son and the Father be God? How can two be one? This question is complicated, of course, by the addition of the Holy Spirit. The traditional orthodox doctrine of the Trinity is that the Godhead is three and yet one. But how can this be? Even if it seems there is no logical contradiction in affirming the incarnation, it looks as though there is a contradiction in the case of the Trinity. Since contradictions

1. I am indebted to both Thomas V. Morris, *The Logic of God Incarnate* (Ithaca, NY: Cornell University Press, 1986); and Thomas D. Senor, "The Incarnation and the Trinity," in *Reason for the Hope Within*, ed. Michael J. Murray, 238–60 (Grand Rapids: Eerdmans, 1999), for many of the ideas in the first two sections of this chapter.

are necessarily false, if the doctrine of the Trinity is contradictory, then it cannot be true. But then the traditional doctrine of the incarnation would also be false insofar as it assumes the distinction between the Father and the Son. The third section of this chapter explores a way to defend the doctrine of the Trinity against the logical incoherence charge as well.

The problems faced in this chapter are different from those discussed so far in this book. The primary questions we have been dealing with to this point are *epistemological*. They concern whether we can know or at least be justified in believing that it is true that God exists and that Jesus is the Son of God. The questions in this chapter are instead *logical*. Such questions have to do with *possible* truth rather than *actual* truth. The objections we face here are not merely that we have no good reason to think that the doctrines in question are actually true. They are rather the claims that we have good reason to believe that these propositions are not even *possibly* true. If these essential Christian beliefs are not possibly true, then they are certainly not actually true. If that is the case, then the Christian worldview is false at its very heart and should be rejected. It is clearly important for Christian apologists to formulate an adequate reply.

It is important to clarify here that it is one thing to defend these two doctrines against charges of logical incoherence and another thing altogether to prove they are true. It is still another thing to explain thoroughly how they are to be understood. Our job here is restricted to the first, relatively modest task. We will have accomplished all that can reasonably be expected if we can show that a person does not have to sacrifice his or her intellect to

> **It is one thing to defend these two doctrines from charges of logical incoherence and another thing altogether to prove they are true.**

endorse these central Christian doctrines. The doctrines of the incarnation and the Trinity are great mysteries that we are not fully able to understand.

The remainder of this section clarifies the basic content of these two doctrines and then constructs arguments that purport to show they are logically contradictory.

The orthodox doctrine of the incarnation was formulated at the Council of Chalcedon in AD 451. Basically, the doctrine states that Jesus Christ is one person who is both fully human and fully divine. Put another way, Jesus of Nazareth, a fully human being, is one and the same person as God the Son, the Second Person of the Trinity. There is more to the Chalcedonian definition than this, but this is enough to generate the alleged logical contradiction.

The argument against the logical coherence of this doctrine is based on the assumption that it is logically impossible for one person to be both fully human and fully divine. To be fully human, a person must have all the properties that an individual has to have to be human (all the essential human properties); to be fully divine, someone must have all the properties required to be divine (all the essential divine properties). But it is reasonable, as argued in chapter 8, to think that a being can be divine only if it is perfect and therefore completely unlimited in every respect. It also seems reasonable that an individual can be human only if that individual is limited in at least some, if not all, of those same respects. If both of these assumptions are correct, then it follows that nothing can possibly be both fully divine and fully human.

Let's pick a specific property of God that it seems clear humans cannot have to illustrate this in the form of a numbered argument (the incarnation argument). One way in which God is unlimited is that God is eternal and therefore uncreated. But it seems clear that humans must be created:

1. If Jesus is fully divine, then Jesus must be uncreated.
2. If Jesus is fully human, then Jesus must be created.
3. It is not logically possible for anything to be both uncreated and created.
4. Therefore, it is not possible for Jesus to be both fully divine and fully human.
5. If the orthodox doctrine of the incarnation is true, then Jesus is both fully divine and fully human.
6. Consequently, the orthodox doctrine of the incarnation is not (possibly) true.

This is a deductively valid argument. That is, if 1 through 5 are each true, then 6 has to be true too. Christian apologists must find a good reason to reject at least one of the premises of this argument. That is the goal in the next section of this chapter.

According to the orthodox doctrine of the Trinity (discussed in chap. 8 to distinguish it from polytheism), the Godhead is three persons in one divine substance. The word *substance* here does not mean "stuff," which is what it often means today. Instead, it is based on Aristotle's use of the word to mean "individual being or thing." An Aristotelian substance is a distinct thing that can exist, in some sense, on its own. It is also something that has properties or attributes. Water in a cup is stuff rather than a substance. The cup holding the water is a substance (though it is, of course, made out of some kind of stuff). Therefore, the doctrine of the Trinity is that God is a community of three persons who are also one individual being.

A simple-minded objection to this doctrine is that it implies that 3 = 1, and since it is logically impossible that 3 = 1, it follows that the doctrine is logically false. But this criticism is based on an inadequate conception of the doctrine. The objection would succeed only if the doctrine implied that God is both three and one *in the same respect*. For instance, it would be obviously false if it stated or implied that God is both three *persons* and one *person*. But it does not say or imply this. Instead, it states that God is three *persons* in one *substance*. The assumption here is that this substance is not itself a person, so the doctrine does not imply that God is both three and one *in the same respect*. But a more sophisticated objection purports to show that the doctrine is logically contradictory. Here is a formulation of it (the Trinity argument):

1. If the orthodox doctrine of the Trinity is true, then (a) the Father is God, (b) the Son is God, and (c) the Holy Spirit is God.

2. According to the principle of the transitivity of identity, for any A, B, and C, if A = B and B = C, then A = C.
3. Therefore, the Father = the Son = the Holy Spirit.
4. But according to the orthodox doctrine of the Trinity, the Father, the Son, and the Holy Spirit are *distinct* persons and therefore *not* identical.
5. Therefore, the doctrine of the Trinity is not possibly true (since it entails that the three persons are both identical and distinct [not identical]).

This argument needs a bit of explanation. The principle employed in premise 2 is a necessary logical truth about the relation of numerical identity, which is represented by the = symbol. To say that A and B are numerically identical is to say that they are not really two things but one and the same thing. A and B, in this case, are two different names for the same individual thing. An instance of the principle of the transitivity of identity is that if Santa Claus is numerically identical to Kris Kringle, and Kris Kringle is identical to Father Christmas, then Santa Claus is identical to Father Christmas. Premise 3 of the above argument is a result of the application of this principle to claims a, b, and c in premise 1 on the assumption that each of these claims is an identity statement. For instance, if the Father = God, and God = the Son, then the Father = the Son. One can generate the remainder of 3 by further applications of the principle. Again, the Christian apologist cannot accept 5 and so must provide adequate reasons not to accept one of the set of premises that entails it. The third

section of this chapter discusses how this can be done.

The Logic of God Incarnate

Take a look again at the incarnation argument stated above. Which premise is the most vulnerable to criticism? We cannot dismiss premise 5, since it follows directly from the Chalcedonian definition of the incarnation we are trying to defend. We do need to deny premise 4, but our strategy is not to *show* that it is possible that Jesus is both fully divine and fully human but rather, less ambitiously, to give good reasons to think that the argument does not succeed in showing that this is *not* possible. So we need to deny premise 1, 2, or 3. Moreover, we must continue to affirm premise 3, since it is a logically necessary truth, and the goal is to try to show that we do not have to deny logical truths to accept the doctrine of the incarnation. This leaves only premise 1 or 2. Chapter 8 argued that God is perfect, and it seems clear that only an uncreated being can be perfect. This is beyond dispute. How can a person be genuinely divine if that person is a *created* person (created beings are limited to a temporally finite duration of existence and are dependent for their existence on what created them)? We must, then, find good reasons to avoid having to accept premise 2.

Premise 2 states that if Jesus is fully human, then Jesus must be created. This may *appear* true, but careful reflection shows that there is no good reason to think that it is. In the first place, the name "Jesus" refers to a single person. According to orthodoxy, this one person is an eternal divine person: God the Son, the Second Person of the Trinity. Moreover, this eternal divine person *became* a human being by *taking on* a human nature, and he also *acquired* the Hebrew name "Jesus" at a certain time in human history. What Jesus took on (a human nature) and acquired (a Hebrew name) are clearly created. However, it does not follow from this that the eternal divine person who received this nature and this name is also created. When one acquires some things one did not previously have, one does not necessarily lose anything that one already possessed.

However, what if what one acquires is something that has characteristics or properties that *logically preclude* the possibility that one can continue to possess all the characteristics or properties one had before? For instance, if I weigh 150 pounds and then I gain 20 pounds, I no longer have the property of weighing (only) 150 pounds, since it is a logically necessary truth that $150 \neq 170$. This is what *seems* to be the case with the incarnation: If (a) something becomes a fully human being, and (b) whatever is or becomes a fully human being must be a created thing, then (c) that thing must be a created thing. Replace "something" and "that thing" in this sentence with "God the Son," and you can see the problem. But what reason do we have to think that premise b in this sentence is true?

We have good reason for thinking that premise b is true only if we know that "having been created" is one of the properties something is *required* to have to be fully human. But careful thinking reveals that we *do not* know this to be true and that we actually know very little about the requirements for being fully human. We *would* know all the requirements for

being fully human if the concept of humanness were like the concept of triangularity. Simply thinking about this concept reveals that a triangle is a closed plane figure with three interior angles that add up to 180 degrees. Another example of this sort is the concept of a bachelor as an unmarried adult human male. But the concept of humanness is not like this. It is more like the concepts of other kinds of things—naturally occurring kinds of things like aluminum, elm trees, and tigers. In the case of these sorts of things, the content of our normal concepts of them falls short of capturing their entire essential nature. We know that aluminum is a certain kind of metal, that elms are a particular sort of tree, and that tigers are a specific type of animal (more specifically, a kind of cat). But these descriptions fall short of telling us all the properties something has to have to be one of these kinds of things. To learn more, we need to turn to the special sciences that study these types of things (metallurgy, botany, and zoology in these cases). But scientific knowledge of this kind is somewhat provisional and incomplete as well. If the concept of humanness is more like these latter concepts than the former, and I believe it is, then we need to be skeptical about our ability to know what is required for something to be fully human. Neither conceptual nor scientific means are adequate to provide this knowledge.

Full knowledge of the essence of humanness depends not only on conceptual and scientific investigation but also on worldview considerations. Naturalists and supernaturalists have different ideas about what kinds of things human beings are (as we saw in chaps. 7 and 8). The final verdict about what is required to be human must be informed by the worldview that has the best chance of being true. So far, the Christian version of creation monotheism is the most reasonable worldview option. Thus, it is legitimate to draw conclusions about the essence of humanness from the Christian worldview in general and from the incarnation in particular. But if we need to *draw on* Christian doctrine to learn what it means to be human, then we are not in a position to *object to* Christian tenets (such as the doctrine of the incarnation) on the basis of the concept of humanness.

It seems clear that all *merely* and yet also *fully* human beings like you and me have all the limitation properties that distinguish us from God (such as being limited in power, knowledge, and goodness and having been created). However, the fact that a particular property (such as having been created) is *universally possessed* by a group of individuals does not mean that the possession of this property is *required* for anything to be a member of this group. For instance, at the present time in history, the property of having been born either on the earth or within the earth's atmosphere is a universal human property. However, it is certainly *possible* for a fully human being to be born in a space station in outer space. Therefore, this universal human property is not also an *essential* human property. That is, it is not a property something *must* have to be human. If we apply this distinction to the properties that distinguish mere human beings from God, it seems reasonable to conclude that, though these limitation properties are *universal* properties of mere humans, they are not necessarily *essential* human properties. At least we do not know enough about what is required for

someone to be human to be in a position to insist (with good reason) that these properties are not only universal among mere humans but also essential. Even if it could be argued that all *merely* human beings *must* be limited in these ways, it does not follow that all fully human beings who are not merely human (such as Jesus, who is also divine) are required to have these limitations to be human.

No one is in a position to have adequate reasons to claim that any limitation properties, such as that of having been created, are required for being fully human. Therefore, no one is in a position to have sufficient reason to believe that premise 2 of the incarnation argument is true. Consequently, it is legitimate for Christians not to accept premise 2 and therefore reasonable for them to conclude that the case for 6 has not been made. The argument does not give adequate reason to believe that the doctrine of the incarnation is contradictory and thus false.

But a defense of the doctrine of the incarnation against this argument has put us in a position to have to affirm that Jesus was a fully human person who was not only uncreated but also unlimited in every other respect in which God is (since versions of the incarnation argument could be formulated in terms of any of the limitation properties). Jesus, therefore, was a human being who was omniscient, omnipotent, omnibenevolent, omnipresent, and so on. This is certainly the result we needed (since if Jesus lacked any of these properties, he would not have been fully divine, and that would have rendered the doctrine of the incarnation false). However, it is now difficult to see what is left of the claim that Jesus was fully human. Moreover, in the Gospel of

Mark, Jesus reportedly says that the Son does not know either the day or the hour when heaven and earth will pass away (13:31–32). But then how could Jesus be omniscient?

Christian theologians have considered a couple of conceptions of the incarnation to try to meet these concerns. One of these ideas is that, although Jesus continued to *possess* all the attributes essential for divinity (such as the omni properties listed above), he voluntarily chose not to *exercise* all of his divine abilities during his sojourn on earth. It is easy to see how this works with the attribute of omnipotence. Jesus could have been *capable* of doing anything it would be possible for God to do without *exercising* this ability. (Of course, he did, however, exercise his divine power when he performed miracles.) Moreover, if we think of omnipresence as having the ability to know about and to control what is happening everywhere without having to be physically located everywhere all at once, then we can see that Jesus could have been omnipresent—even if his human body was located only in a particular place. Omnibenevolence is also not a problem, since the Bible affirms that Jesus was without sin (Heb. 4:15). However, the attribute of omniscience does pose a special problem, at least because of the limitation in knowledge claimed by Jesus in Mark 13:31–32, but also because it is hard to see how Jesus could fully "sympathize with our weaknesses" (Heb. 4:15) if he had full knowledge of his supreme goodness and power. Moreover, if as God Jesus is not only supremely good but also *necessarily* supremely good, then it would not be possible for Jesus to sin. If he knew this about himself, how could he have been genuinely *tempted* to sin?

To surmount these difficulties, some have suggested what has become known as the two-minds model of the incarnation. According to this view, Jesus had a fully omniscient divine mind, but after the incarnation and during his earthly life, he voluntarily and temporarily relinquished his access to this range of consciousness. What he was consciously aware of was a severely diminished subset of his divine mind. This subset constituted his human mind—a range of consciousness much closer to what was roughly characteristic of a first-century Palestinian Jew. Of course, there were times when Jesus seemed to manifest a knowledge of people's thoughts and of future events of which no normal human being is capable. A plausible explanation of this that is consistent with the two-minds model is that God the Father provided Jesus with access to his larger range of divine consciousness at these times. The two-minds model enables us to say that, though Jesus was fully divine and therefore omniscient, he did not exercise his full ability to access the entire range of this perfect knowledge. Thus, his conscious experience while on earth could have been much more like ours than like God's. Such a diminished consciousness would have allowed him to be genuinely tempted if it did not include knowledge of his inability to sin. It would also have allowed him to have an authentic experience of the full range of human emotions, including uncertainty, disappointment, anguish, and despondency: "a man of sorrows, and familiar with suffering" (Isa. 53:3). Of course, we cannot prove that the two-minds view is true, but if it is at least possibly true, it can help us understand how Jesus could have been both fully divine and fully human.

The Logic of the Triune God

Which premise of the Trinity argument (stated in the first section of this chapter) do we have good reason to deny?[2] We must affirm premise 4, since it follows from the orthodox doctrine. Therefore, we must deny premise 3, since it is clearly incompatible with this doctrine. Since premise 3 follows from premise 1 and premise 2, one of these latter two premises has to go. But premise 2 is a logical truth, and we are attempting to show that one can rationally affirm both the truths of logic and the doctrines of the Christian faith (even if we cannot prove that these doctrines are true or explain away all the mystery that attends them). So premise 1 is the problem. But how can this premise be false? Doesn't it follow clearly and directly from the orthodox doctrine of the Trinity? Yes, it does, *according to one interpretation of what it means*. But premise 1 has more than one meaning, and there is an interpretation of it that we need to reject.

Since the sentence used to state premise 1 has more than one meaning, it is ambiguous. Its two meanings are determined by two uses of the word *is*, which occurs in it three times. In general, the word *is* is sometimes used to express predication, and it is sometimes employed to express identity. An example of the "is" of predication is when it is used in a subject-predicate sentence such as "John is human." Here the name John is the subject term, and the word *human* is the predicate term. Predicate terms are used to attribute characteristics or properties to things. So the sentence says that John has the property of being human. An example of the "is" of

identity is "Santa Claus is Kris Kringle." The purpose of this sentence is not to attribute a property to Santa Claus but rather to express the claim that the individual called Santa Claus is numerically identical to (one and the same person as) the individual called Kris Kringle.

When the doctrine of the Trinity affirms that the Father is God, the Son is God, and the Holy Spirit is God, these statements are meant to be interpreted as *predications* rather than as identity statements. So the principle of the transitivity of identity does not apply to premise 1 when it is interpreted in a way that is consistent with the orthodox doctrine, and therefore the identity statement 3 does not follow from 1. What premise 1 is saying is not that the Father, the Son, and the Holy Spirit are each identical to God but rather that each of the three persons of the Trinity has the property of being divine. Thus, if premise 1 is interpreted in such a way as to make it true, then neither premise 3 nor 5 follows from it, and if premise 1 is interpreted in such a way as to support premise 3 and 5, then it is false. Either way, the Trinity argument does not succeed in establishing its conclusion. Instead, it exploits the ambiguity of premise 1 to give the appearance of there being a compelling case for its anti-Christian conclusion. But as we have seen, this appearance is deceptive.

If the Trinity argument does not show that the orthodox doctrine of the Trinity is logically false (in virtue of entailing a contradiction), then it is reasonable to believe that it is true (in the absence of another argument against it to which we have no adequate reply). But a defense of the doctrine against this argument has left us vulnerable to another type of objection.

---

2. This section draws substantially on Senor, "Incarnation and the Trinity."

If the word *is* in a, b, and c of premise 1 is the "is" of predication rather than the "is" of identity, then the doctrine affirms that the Father, the Son, and the Holy Spirit each have the property of being divine. But then how does this differ from attributing to Tom, Dick, and Harry the property of being human when we say that "Tom is human," and "Dick is human," and "Harry is human"? If there is no difference, then the doctrine of the Trinity would imply that there are three distinct gods in the way our claims about Tom, Dick, and Harry imply that there are three distinct human beings. In both cases, what is being said is merely that three distinct individuals are members of the same species (divinity in the first case and humanity in the second). But this would be tritheism, the view that the Trinity is three distinct gods, which is heretical. It is, after all, a version of polytheism. How can we stick with our response to the Trinity argument in such a way as to avoid this heretical result?

Tritheism emphasizes the plurality of the Trinity at the expense of its unity, so we need to add something to our description of the Trinity that affirms this unity. In doing so, we must avoid the opposite error of stressing the unity of the Trinity at the expense of the plurality. One example of this opposite error is modalism. According to this view about the nature of the Trinity, the Father, the Son, and the Holy Spirit are not really distinct persons but merely modes of God. That is, they are only ways in which the one God acts and manifests himself. This view has also been considered heretical by the historic Christian church. One reason is that it does not do justice to the way the Bible talks about the Father, the Son, and the Spirit (and the foremost requirement of

Christian doctrine is that it be as compatible with Scripture as possible). For instance, the synoptic Gospels relate the story of Jesus' baptism in such a way as for there to be a simultaneous and distinctive role played by each of the three persons of the Trinity. When the Son is baptized, the Holy Spirit descends on him like a dove, and the Father speaks from heaven to express his love for and pleasure in the Son (Matt. 3:13–17; Mark 1:9–11; Luke 3:21–22). The modalist view that in this circumstance the one God is merely manifesting himself in three different ways does not do justice to this story. For one thing, it does not allow us to account for the different points of view involved among the Father, the Son, and the Spirit.

One problem with some popular analogies employed by Christians to try to make sense of the Trinity is that they tend to suggest a modalist interpretation. An example of this is when someone says that God is like H_2O in that he is Father, Son, and Spirit in the way that H_2O can take the form of solid, liquid, or gas. But these are just modes or manifestations of one kind of thing, and therefore the real plurality is lost. Christian apologists need to be careful not to resort to convenient and easy illustrations like this when they can end up doing more harm than good.

One could say that the correct doctrine of the Trinity is whatever view of the Trinity (1) is consistent with the statement that God is three persons in one substance and (2) achieves the right balance between the plurality and the unity of the Godhead (whatever that balance should turn out to be). Perhaps this rather sparse statement would be adequate. However, the reason it is important to try to walk the tightrope between tritheism and modalism *and* to say a bit more about the Trinity than this is that, unless we do so, it is not clear that the doctrine has sufficient meaningful content to be the object of a genuine Christian *belief* (as opposed to a mere formula that can be spoken but is insufficiently determinate to be the content of a belief). It is important for Christian apologists to defend the Christian doctrine of God not only from the charge of logical incoherence but also from the charge of excessive vagueness and obscurity (without, of course, attempting to eliminate its mystery). But whatever we say must be both logically possible and orthodox. So we must be cautious.

A more complete model of the Trinity that seems promising is called social trinitarianism. This view affirms the plurality of the Godhead by recognizing the real distinction between the three persons as separate centers and initiators of thinking, willing, and acting. However, it also attempts to preserve the unity of the Godhead by specifying ways in which the persons are related to one another that make their connection more intimate than merely being members of the same species (divinity). Among these additional relations, which are grounded in biblical revelation, are the following: (1) The Son is eternally generated by the Father, (2) the Holy Spirit proceeds eternally from the Father and the Son,[3] and (3) the Father, the Son, and the Holy Spirit have necessarily harmonious wills.

3. The Eastern Orthodox branch of the Christian church omits the phrase "and the Son" from its creeds. Whether this clause should be included in the description of the Holy Spirit's relation to the Godhead was one of the issues that split the Orthodox Church from the Roman Catholic Church.

No merely contingent and/or temporary relations would be adequate to make the Triune God more than just three closely related but ultimately distinct gods.

One thing that each of these internal trinitarian relations has in common is that they are each *necessary* and *eternal*. That is, they are each such that the divine persons *must* be related in these ways and *have always been* and *will always be* related in these ways. No merely contingent and/or temporary relations would be adequate to make the Triune God more than just three closely related but ultimately distinct gods. What we need are relations that suffice to integrate the Godhead into one ultimate being. The necessary and eternal relations listed above make a significant contribution to that end. These three relations are also *distinctive* of the members of the Trinity. No other persons are related to anyone in any of these ways, and the persons of the Godhead are not related in any of these ways to any persons outside the Godhead.

Moreover, the relations do not imply any priority among the members of the Godhead in terms of time, being, or value. Each divine person is equally eternal, uncreated, divine, excellent, etc. Each is *fully* divine, and so each has all the essential divine attributes. But relations 1 and 2 are asymmetrical, and so they do imply a kind of *functional* priority. For instance, the Father generates the Son, but not vice versa. So the Father is prior to the Son in terms of his functioning as the eternal generator of the Son. Something similar could be said about the eternal procession of the Holy Spirit.

As for 3, two or more persons have necessarily harmonious wills if and only if it is not possible for them to have a conflict of wills. Two persons have conflicting wills when one of them wills to bring about a certain result and the other wills that the result *not* occur. For instance, if you want the door open at a certain time, and I want the door shut at that time, then we have conflicting wills. Of course, we can have *different* wills that are not conflicting wills if the different things we will to occur are mutually compatible (e.g., I want chocolate ice cream, and you want vanilla, and we are happy to let each other satisfy his or her own desire). Chapter 8 argued (in connection with polytheism) that if it is possible for the wills of two persons to conflict, then they cannot both be omnipotent. It seems reasonable in the present context to hold that, if it is *not* possible for the wills of more than one person to conflict (that is, if they have necessarily harmonious wills), then it is not clear how they can be *fundamentally* distinct from one another. Though they may be different persons, if their wills cannot conflict, it seems that they must be *the same fundamental being*. To be fundamentally separate personal beings would seem to require at least the *possibility* (though perhaps not the actuality) of conflicting wills. Therefore, the relation of necessarily harmonious wills provides a strong basis for claiming the fundamental unity of the plurality of divine persons in the Godhead.

This discussion of the persons of the Trinity has left open the possibility that they are equal in wisdom, power, goodness, and glory and yet play different roles or exercise distinctive functions. One of the roles of the Son is to be the Savior and Redeemer of the world. But what does this mean? From what and to what will the world (and the saved people in it) be saved? To answer these questions and to address the apologetic problems to which they give rise, we must turn to the doctrine of the atonement and the orthodox Christian views about heaven and hell.

Reflection and Discussion

1. Is it appropriate to ask whether the doctrines of the incarnation and the Trinity are logical? Why or why not? Should Christians be willing to accept claims that they believe are incompatible with the laws of logic and therefore self-contradictory? Why or why not?

2. Why is it so important to defend the orthodox doctrine of the incarnation against charges of logical incoherence rather than to deny that Jesus is both fully human and fully divine? What, if anything, is it that Christians care about (or *should* care about) that is at stake here?

3. To what extent should we try to *explain* the doctrine of the Trinity, and to what extent should we be willing to stop trying to explain it and just accept it? Is it reasonable to believe something is true that we cannot fully explain? Why or why not?

Further Reading

Brown, David. *Divine Trinity.* Peru, IL: Open Court, 1985.

McKim, Donald K. "Trinitarian Controversy: Who Is God?" and "Christological Controversy: Who Is Jesus Christ?" in *Theological Turning Points: Major Issues in Christian Thought*, 4–43. Louisville: Westminster John Knox, 1988.

Morris, Thomas V. *The Logic of God Incarnate.* Ithaca, NY: Cornell University Press, 1986.

17

The Sheep and the Goats

Salvation and Damnation

» **Outline**

- **Making Sense of the Cross**
  - *Sin and Salvation*
  - *The Doctrine of the Atonement*
  - *The Critic's Case against the Sacrifice Model of the Atonement*
  - *Two Alternative Christian Replies to This Argument*
- **Eternal Damnation and Justice**
  - *The Traditional Doctrine of Hell*
  - *Two Inadequate Alternatives*
    - Universalism
    - Annihilationism
  - *A Critic's Argument against Traditionalism Based on God's Justice*
  - *Two Alternative Replies to This Argument*
    - An Infinite Series of Finite Punishments
    - All Sin Deserving of Infinite Punishment
- **Eternal Damnation and Love**
  - *Two Types of People*
    - The Reached but Unsaved
    - The Unreached
  - *Why a Loving God Would Allow Some to Be Reached but Unsaved*
  - *A Case against Traditionalism Based on God's Love and the Unreached*
  - *Two Alternative Replies to This Argument*
    - Ways a Loving God Might Save Some of the Unreached
    - How a Loving God Might Not Save Any of the Unreached

» **Summary**

Jesus came to save people from sin. The doctrine of the atonement states that Jesus made salvation available through his death and resurrection. There have been various specific attempts to understand how the atonement works. Critics argue that a version of the sacrifice model of the atonement makes it either unethical or ineffective. Christian apologists can reply by exploring alternative understandings of Christ's sacrifice and/or by defending the morality and success of Jesus' death on the cross, given this model. The traditional doctrine of hell states that all unrepentant sinners will suffer eternal separation from loving communion with God. Critics argue that this doctrine is inconsistent with God's justice and also with God's love. The most serious problem concerns the fate of those unreached by the gospel. Christian apologists have more than one way to defend traditionalism against each of these charges.

» **Basic Terms, Concepts, and Names**

annihilationism
atonement, doctrine of
general revelation
middle knowledge
penal substitution
postmortem evangelism
premortem unevangelized salvation
reached but unsaved
sacrifice model of the atonement
salvation
satisfaction theory of the atonement
sin
traditional doctrine of hell
universalism
unreached

» **Reflection and Discussion**

» **Further Reading**

> When the Son of Man comes in his glory, and all the angels with him, he will sit on his throne in heavenly glory. All the nations will be gathered before him, and he will separate the people one from another as a shepherd separates the sheep from the goats. He will put the sheep on his right and the goats on his left.
>
> Then the King will say to those on his right, "Come, you who are blessed by my Father; take your inheritance, the kingdom prepared for you since the creation of the world." . . .
>
> Then he will say to those on his left, "Depart from me, you who are cursed, into the eternal fire prepared for the devil and his angels." . . .
>
> Then they will go away to eternal punishment, but the righteous to eternal life.
>
> Matthew 25:31–34, 41, 46

Making Sense of the Cross

According to traditional Christian theology, God the Son became incarnate as Jesus of Nazareth to reconcile the world to God by saving people from their sin and its consequences. The salvation of the human race (and the liberation of all creation from its "bondage to decay" [Rom. 8:21]) is the goal of God's plan of redemption. God created human beings for the purpose of eternal loving communion with them. However, all human beings have sinned (Rom. 3:23), and sin is anything that separates us from communion with God (nothing can be separated from God's *presence*, since things can exist only if God is present with them to sustain them [see Ps. 139:7–12]). Moreover, human beings are not only sinners; those who have not been reconciled to God in Christ are also slaves to sin (Rom. 6:17). They are incapable of being restored to fellowship with God without God's gracious assistance. Thus, unless God takes appropriate steps to save the lost from the penalty and power of their sin, they will continue to sin and to experience its consequences, chief among which is the misery that results from spiritual death in the form of separation from communion with God. But God wants to save everyone (2 Pet. 3:9), and so the Father sent the Son to provide people with an opportunity to enjoy eternal life with God (John 3:16). Jesus' life, death, and resurrection are the means by which God made salvation from sin possible.

Christian theologians have expended a lot of effort over the centuries in an attempt to explain *how* Jesus' crucifixion made the salvation of humankind possible. The Bible supplies the raw materials for this reflection by describing Christ as victor (Col. 2:13–15), as sacrifice (Rom. 3:25; Heb. 10:10–14), and as example (Rom. 5:6–8; Eph. 4:32–5:2).[1] The results of this theological thinking are typically labeled the doctrine of the atonement. There are two important points we need to make about this doctrine before we discuss its implications for apologetics. First, unlike the doctrines of the incarnation and the Trinity, the essence of the doctrine of the atonement has not been encapsulated in a simple formula that is universally accepted as the orthodox teaching of the historic Christian church. Therefore, since the goal of this book is to defend only "mere" Christianity, it does not take sides in the ongoing theological debate about the nature of the atonement. Second, like the doctrines of the Trinity and the incarnation, each account of the doctrine of the atonement falls short of providing a *complete* explanation of how Jesus' death and resurrection make the salvation of the world possible. An element of mystery requires that we take it on faith that there is salvation in Christ. A Christian apologist will be quick to add, however, that Christian faith in the efficacy of Jesus' saving work on our behalf is reasonable.

But this claim is challenged by critics who charge that the doctrine of the atonement is either unethical or incomprehensible. If it is unethical, then it is inconsistent with the creation monotheist picture of God as supremely morally good. Therefore, if this objection sticks, a commitment to creation monotheism will make it unreasonable to endorse the Christian version of this worldview family (since the doctrine of the atonement is a central and essential Christian teaching). If it is incomprehensible, then, though it may be reasonable to believe everything argued up to this point in this book, we will be unable to provide an adequate answer to someone who wants to know why these things matter for human beings. Unless we can make *some* sense of the doctrine of the atonement, we will be unable to explain to people how Christianity is relevant to the human needs discussed in chapter 4.

These criticisms are typically leveled against versions of the Christ as sacrifice model of the atonement. According to a popular variant of this model, which emphasizes Christ's death as penal substitution,[2] the penalty of sin is eternal separation from communion with God (2 Thess. 1:9). Moreover, God is a holy and righteous judge whose wrathful enforcement of his moral law and penalization of those who transgress it are entirely just and justified. Since all humans have sinned, all will suffer eternal damnation (eternal separation from communion with God) unless God's wrath can be appeased by means of a satisfaction or payment of the penalty

---

1. See Jonathan S. Wilson, *God So Loved the World: A Christology for Disciples* (Grand Rapids: Baker, 2001), part 2, for an extended theological treatment of these biblical images of Christ.

2. This development of the doctrine of the atonement is due, historically, primarily to John Calvin (1509–64). See his *Institutes of the Christian Religion*, II.xvi.5.

in some other way. It was for this purpose that God the Son became incarnate. Since Jesus lived an absolutely sinless life, he did not incur a penalty for sin of his own. As a result, Jesus was eligible to pay voluntarily the penalty on our behalf. He did this by dying on the cross and suffering alienation from God (as evidenced by his cry of dereliction: "My God, my God, why have you forsaken me?" [Mark 15:34]). His death substituted for our death, and thus his death paid the penalty for our sin. This is what, according to this view, makes Jesus' death an instance of penal substitution.

Critics object that this model makes the atonement either unethical or ineffective. Their concern is stated in the following argument (which is stated as a challenge not only to the doctrine of the atonement but also to the Christian faith):

1. If Christianity is true, then the doctrine of the atonement is true.
2. This doctrine is true only if Jesus' death was (at least) a *sacrifice* for the sins of humanity.
3. This sacrificial aspect of Jesus' death is best understood by the penal substitution model.

> **Jesus is the victor over sin and death because of his sacrificial death on the cross (and his resurrection), and Jesus is an example of how God wants us to live by virtue of his sacrificial life and death.**

4. If the penal substitution model is true, then the substitutionary death of one innocent person for many guilty people can be both moral and effective in removing the guilt of the latter.
5. But it would be either immoral or ineffective to sacrifice the innocent in place of the guilty.
6. Therefore, Christianity is false.

What is the best way for Christian apologists to reply to this argument? Though some liberal Christians have denied premise 1, adherence to historic orthodoxy forbids this. Moreover, Christianity without the atonement is Christianity in name only. It may seem as if we could reject premise 2, since at least two other models of the atonement mentioned above could be employed in place of the sacrifice model (Christ as victor and Christ as example). But there are at least two problems with this move: (1) The sacrifice model is both pervasive and deep in the Bible, beginning with the Old Testament practice of animal sacrifice and ending with various New Testament descriptions of the sacrificial work of Jesus, and (2) the other two models arguably depend on the sacrifice model: Jesus is the victor over sin and death because of his sacrificial death on the cross (and his resurrection), and Jesus is an example of how God wants us to live by virtue of his sacrificial life and death. Premise 4 is certainly true. An adequate understanding of the atonement must be consistent with morality and must make it reasonable to think that what Jesus did on our behalf was effective in bringing about salvation. Many Christians are tempted to reject premise 3, primarily on the ground that premise 5 is true. On the other hand, many Christians seek to preserve premise 3 by arguing against premise 5. As in the case of all such disputes about doctrine between Christians who adhere to the historic orthodox Christian faith, the best apologetical strategy here is to argue that it is reasonable to think that at least one of these options succeeds rather than to take sides.

First, let's discuss the problems with premise 5. It would be immoral to sacrifice an innocent person only if that person did not voluntarily agree to be sacrificed. But Jesus' submission to death on the cross on our behalf is portrayed by the Gospel writers as fully voluntary. For instance, after saying that he will lay down his life for his sheep, Jesus says, "No one takes it [my life] from me, but I lay it down of my own accord" (John 10:18). If a merely human person agreed to sacrifice his life for the sake of others, we might wonder if this decision was fully voluntary. But in the case of Jesus, who is not only fully human but also fully divine, we have good reason to believe that he was perfectly willing to lay down his life for us. Therefore, the Father's punishment of the Son is fully within the bounds of morality and justice.

Let's suppose the critic accepts this. A reason remains to think that the penal substitution model describes something immoral or unjust. How would justice be served by means of the (even willing) sacrifice of an innocent person in the place of someone who justly deserves the punishment? Moreover, if the demands of justice cannot be satisfied by means of an innocent person suffering the penalty owed by a guilty person, then the atonement is ineffective—it does not do what it is supposed to do. But if the best attempt to explain the atonement leads to the conclusion that it could not bring about the intended result, then we are left with a false or at least incomprehensible doctrine at the heart of Christianity. In that case, it seems we need to either reject Christianity or sacrifice reason at a crucial point in our faith.

In reply, it is important to remember that the sins for which Jesus' sacrifice paid the penalty are offenses against God. Since Jesus is God the Son, he is not merely an innocent human being who was sacrificed in place of the guilty. He is the one wronged by human sinners. As such, it is his prerogative to choose mercifully to endure the penalty owed to him by those who wronged him. Moreover, as a human being who lived a life of complete obedience to the Father, Jesus is the perfect one to represent the entire human race in paying the penalty for sin. Therefore, it is reasonable to think both that justice was served (the penalty was paid by someone who had the right to pay it) and that the sacrifice was effective (since Jesus paid the penalty, those who trust in Christ are saved from having to pay it themselves).

Steven Porter has developed a version of the penal substitution model that provides additional resources for reply.[3] According to his view, God has a right to punish sinners, but God is not morally required to do so. Consequently, there would be no violation of justice if God chose to forgive sinners rather than to punish them. That forgiveness without punishment is something that is morally permissible and even virtuous for *humans* to do is borne out by our moral intuitions and by Jesus'

3. Steven Porter, "Rethinking the Logic of Penal Substitution," in *Philosophy of Religion: A Reader and Guide,* edited by William Lane Craig (New Brunswick: Rutgers University Press, 2002), 596–608.

teaching and example (see Matt. 5:38–48; Mark 2:5; Luke 7:40–50; 15:20–24, etc.). Surely what is permissible and commendable for humans would also be so for God. However, it would be just and good for God to punish sinners (even though it is not necessary). It would be just because sinners are deserving of punishment. It would be good for three reasons: (1) Punishing sinners takes them seriously as responsible agents and their sins seriously as offenses against God; (2) punishing sinners demonstrates a correction of the inflated sense of their own value and their devaluing of God expressed by their sin; and (3) punishing sinners provides opportunities for them to acquire the humility necessary for them to affirm their subservience to God and to become the kind of people God created them to be.

So it is just and good for God to punish sinners. But it is just and a greater good for Christ to be punished as a substitute for sinners. It is just because, as argued, Jesus' punishment on our behalf is voluntary on his part, and it is not morally necessary for individuals to bear their own punishment. The reason for this is that, though we deserve to be punished and God has the right to punish us, God is not required by any principle of justice to punish us, as argued above. Jesus' punishment on our behalf is a greater good than our being punished for our sin for three reasons: (1) God's willingness to suffer the punishment due sinners shows how seriously he takes his relationship with us and the sin that has broken this relationship; (2) God's punishment of sinners would likely alienate us from him more, but God's willingness to suffer our punishment in Christ provides us with a reason to be grateful to him and a motivation to

be reconciled to him; and (3) the cross of Christ exposes the value distortion of sin mentioned above in a highly effective way by revealing the depth of human sin in crucifying the holy Son of God and the greatness of God's love and mercy in suffering this punishment on our behalf. Porter's penal substitution model provides good reason to affirm premise 3 and to deny premise 5 of the critic's argument.

An alternative way to defend the Christian faith against the argument for 6 is to deny premise 3. The penal substitution model is not the only specific way in which theologians have attempted to explain how Christ's sacrifice accomplished salvation. For instance, Anselm had already developed a version of the sacrifice model called the satisfaction theory before John Calvin's formulation of the penal substitution view.[4] Though Anselm's view is not free from problems, it does not seem entirely mistaken either. Contemporary theologians continue to work creatively to deepen understanding of the sacrifice model by drawing on both Anselm and Calvin in such a way as to preserve their good insights while avoiding the problems with their views.[5] They also draw on the victor and example models to supplement the sacrifice model where it is lacking. In the meantime, it seems reasonable for Christians to believe, on the reasonable ground that Jesus is the resurrected Son of God, that whatever he accomplished on the cross is both just and effective in making salvation available to human beings. Objections to the doctrine of the atonement, such as the one

4. See Anselm's *Cur Deus Homo* (*Why God Became Man*).

5. See Wilson, *God So Loved the World,* chap. 5, for a good example of this.

above, are based not so much on a *general* statement of this doctrine as on *specific* interpretations of it. But it is arguably reasonable for Christians to accept the doctrine without being able to interpret it fully and unproblematically.

Jesus himself provided a way to interpret his death when he said, "The Son of Man did not come to be served, but to serve, and to give his life as a ransom for many" (Mark 10:45). Though our minds may not be able to comprehend completely what this means, our hearts can acknowledge that such a divine rescue is precisely what we need and that such a loving sacrifice of God on our behalf is an inexpressibly wonderful thing.

Eternal Damnation and Justice

It is reasonable to believe that what Jesus achieved through his death and resurrection made salvation available to human beings.[6] But the Bible seems to teach that not all human beings will freely choose to appropriate Christ's saving work on their behalf. Moreover, according to Scripture, salvation for human beings is possible only through Jesus (John 14:6; Acts 4:12). As a result, those who are not rightly related to Jesus will continue to be enslaved to sin and to experience the consequences of sin, including separation from communion with God. Furthermore, it seems clear from Scripture that these unrepentant sinners will suffer *eternal* separation from communion with God as

the natural consequence of and penalty for their sin (see the passage from Matthew at the beginning of this chapter). That some humans will be damned to suffer this deserved eternal punishment is the essence of the traditional doctrine of hell.[7]

This traditional doctrine of hell is the source of a number of concerns people have about the Christian faith. What these concerns have in common is the assumption that God is either unjust or unloving in consigning people to hell. The problem of hell is really a special case of the problem of evil. The question with which Christian apologists need to wrestle is how a good (just and loving) God could either damn people to eternal suffering or at least allow anyone to experience eternal misery as a consequence of his or her own choices—when he has the power to prevent these things from happening. This section focuses on the accusation that it is unjust for God to inflict or allow eternal punishment, and the next section concerns the charge that this is unloving.

Before we look at these objections and consider how to reply, we need to acknowledge that some Christians deny the traditional doctrine of hell in favor of either universalism or annihilationism. According to universalism, everyone will eventually be saved, and so there will be no eternal punishment in hell. There may be *temporary* punishment of sinners in the afterlife, but God will persist in loving attempts to persuade the unrepentant to turn freely from sin to God until everyone

---

6. For this section and the next, I have drawn a number of ideas from Michael J. Murray, "Heaven and Hell," in *Reason for the Hope Within*, ed. Michael J. Murray, 287–317 (Grand Rapids: Eerdmans, 1999).

7. I assume here that the language used in the Bible to imply that hell involves experiences of intense *sensory* torment (e.g., fire) is metaphorical and is meant to communicate the horrible suffering that results from eternal separation from loving communion with God, for which God created us.

has been saved. Since it is clear that many in this life die without having accepted Christ, universalists believe that many of these ongoing attempts to convince unbelievers to accept the gospel take place in the afterlife. Annihilationists agree with traditionalists that not everyone will be saved. However, they deny that anyone will suffer eternal punishment. Instead, they hold that the damned will be annihilated or destroyed.

Both of these alternative views are attempts to avoid the problems with the traditional view (these problems have to do with the assumption that some will suffer *eternal* punishment). Though these options may be attractive, they are not considered here. For one thing, the traditional view seems to be the clear teaching of Scripture, even though some language in the Bible seems to suggest otherwise.[8] As a result, the traditional view has historically been the central teaching of the Christian church. For another thing, both universalism and annihilationism face serious philosophical and theological problems that make it unreasonable to endorse them. Therefore, this section defends the rationality of the traditional view.

Here is one argument against the Christian worldview that targets the traditional doctrine of hell as being inconsistent with God's justice:

7. If the Christian worldview is true, then the traditional doctrine of hell is true.
8. If the traditional doctrine of hell is true, then justice will be served by the deserved eternal suffering of the damned.
9. But no human being deserves *eternal* punishment, and so it is unjust for God to allow anyone to experience such a penalty.
10. Therefore, the Christian worldview is false.

We have already given reasons for endorsing premise 7, and premise 8 follows from the traditional view of hell. Thus, we need to find a good reason to refrain from accepting premise 9. But let us first consider why someone would endorse premise 9.

One reason critics may accept premise 9 is that they simply deny the doctrine of sin. If no human being has ever sinned, then no human being deserves to be punished for sin. Critics in this category need to be convinced of the reality of sin. But some who insist on premise 9 are equally insistent that all human beings are sinners. This group affirms premise 9 on the grounds that a principle of justice is that the punishment should fit the crime and that no human being's sins are sufficiently numerous or serious to warrant an eternal or infinite punishment. They point out that each human being has only a finite period of time during which to sin, and they claim that no matter how serious any of these sins is, it is evil only to a finite (though possibly very great) degree. These people conclude, therefore, that God would be unjust to impose or permit an *eternal* punishment for sin.

A reply needs to provide good reasons for thinking that eternal punishment does fit the crime of human sin (it seems unreasonable to deny the principle of justice on which premise 9 is based). There are two plausible ways to make a case for this

---

8. See Stephen T. Davis, *Risen Indeed: Making Sense of the Resurrection* (Grand Rapids: Eerdmans, 1993), chap. 8, for a good defense of this claim.

claim. First, we could agree with the objector that at the end of a finite period of time, the sins an individual human being has committed to that point are deserving of only a *finite* punishment. However, those who are damned to hell continue to sin in hell, and as a result, they deserve to suffer for an additional period of time for these additional sins. On the reasonable assumption that these people continue to sin forever, they end up deserving an endless series of finite punishments. Thus, the eternal punishment does fit the crime because the crime never ceases to occur.

The second reply involves saying that, though human sins are finite in number, they are infinite in degree of seriousness. This is because all sins are at least offenses against God (even if they also involve wrongs done to other people), and all offenses against God are infinitely serious by virtue of being offenses against an infinite being. Since God is an awesomely great and holy being, a sin against God is an infinitely serious offense and therefore deserving of an infinite punishment. Thus, an eternal punishment would fit the crime of sin in this case as well. Moreover, this argument is consistent with the plausible idea that some sins are more serious than others, and therefore deserving of a more stringent (thus more infinite) punishment, since there are greater and lesser degrees of infinity.[9]

Though both of these replies cannot be true, since they are based on mutually incompatible assumptions (one affirming and the other denying that every individual

sin deserves an infinite punishment), it is reasonable to think that one of them is true. If so, we have good reason to refrain from endorsing premise 9, and this argument against the Christian faith falls apart.

Eternal Damnation and Love

Some argue that even if it is just for God to punish people or allow them to suffer eternally, it is not loving for him to do or permit this. Let us respond to this charge by first distinguishing between two categories of people: (1) those who die having heard and adequately understood the gospel without having responded favorably to it (the reached but unsaved) and (2) those who die either never having heard the good news of Christ or having heard it but not having adequately understood it (the unreached).

As for the reached but unsaved, some (especially universalists) argue that a loving God would not consign *any* of his beloved human creatures to eternal misery in hell but would keep working until he had found a way to save each of them. Many add that the conditions of divine hiddenness discussed in chapter 12, which make it difficult to know and therefore respond to the truth about God in Christ, require this persistence of a genuinely loving God. But it is important to remember that God created human beings with free will. Whatever he does to try to save people needs to be consistent with this. Moreover, it is reasonable to think that God gave us freedom of choice primarily to enable us to decide our own destinies by choosing what kind of person we want to become. From the standpoint of the

9. For instance, though the set of whole numbers is an infinite set, the set of *real* numbers is also an infinite set but with *more members* (because there are an infinite number of real numbers between each whole number).

Great Commandment (Matt. 22:37–40), the most important choice facing human beings is whether to become the kind of person who characteristically loves God as he deserves to be loved or instead to become the kind of person who loves himself or herself more than anything else. Of course, as indicated earlier, human beings are unable to become God lovers without God's gracious assistance. But God has provided assistance through the incarnation, the atonement, and the gift of the Holy Spirit (who helps Christians to become more adept at loving God by helping to free them from the power of sin). The Holy Spirit also works in the lives of unbelievers to try to persuade them to accept Christ and to receive the benefits that come from trusting him.

If in spite of all this some people persist in resisting God and in making free choices that reinforce their self-loving character, then they may well eventually become people who would find eternal communion with God intolerable. This is because only a genuine God lover would be able to enjoy eternal communion with God and to be a God lover one must love oneself in such a way as to be a self-denier rather than a person who loves himself or herself more than anything else. In that case, it would be *loving* of God to give these people what has become the desire of their hearts through a lifetime of free choices: eternal existence in separation from communion with God. Thus, it is reasonable to believe that it would not be unloving of God to allow the reached but unsaved to spend eternity apart from him.

Probably the more worrisome case for the claim (that even if it would be just for God to punish people or allow them to suffer eternally, it would not be loving for

him to do or permit this) has to do with the unreached:

11. If the Christian worldview is true, then (a) God is perfectly loving, and (b) the traditional doctrine of hell is true.
12. If the traditional doctrine of hell is true, then only those who have heard, understood, and freely accepted the gospel of Christ in this life will be saved from the punishment of eternal separation from loving communion with God.
13. But at their deaths, many human beings throughout history either (a) had not heard the gospel (through no fault of their own) or (b) had heard but had not adequately understood the gospel (again, through no fault of their own).
14. So if the traditional doctrine of hell is true, then all these people will suffer the punishment of eternal separation from loving communion with God.
15. But it would be unloving (and, some would argue, unjust) for God to allow people in categories a or b to suffer this fate.
16. So the traditional doctrine of hell is inconsistent with God's love.
17. Therefore, Christianity is false.

Let's consider how best to reply to this argument. Christians must affirm that God is supremely loving (1 John 4:8) and that Christianity requires the traditional doctrine of hell (though both universalists and annihilationists deny this). So we must endorse premise 11. Moreover, there are overwhelming historical grounds for premise 13, and no one denies it. We clearly need to have good reasons to resist accepting premise 16 and the argument's conclusion, 17, but these two follow from the other premises of the argument. This leaves premises 12, 14, and 15. Since premise 14 follows from the conjunction of premises 12 and 13, we are down to premises 12 and 15. Thus, as before, Christian apologists have more than one response at their disposal. The existence of these options is due to the fact that Scripture does not put us in a good position to know for sure what God's plan is for those who died (and will die) without an opportunity to hear and understand the gospel message. Christians disagree about which of these options to select, but as long as it is reasonable to accept at least one of them, the argument under discussion fails to establish its conclusion.

First, Christian apologists may choose to affirm premise 15 and deny premise 12. That is, they may agree that it would be unloving for God to damn the unreached but then deny that he will do this. What reasons can be given for this position? One possibility (that seems to be neither taught by Scripture nor clearly ruled out by it) is that God will judge people on the basis of how they freely chose to respond to God and to live their lives based on what they were able to know about God and his will apart from a verbal communication of the gospel. Chapter 3 discussed the doctrine of common grace, according to which God graciously blesses all human beings with certain good things. Among these things is God's general revelation of his existence, nature, and will (Rom. 1:20; 2:14–15). Though unrepentant sinners have suppressed this knowledge (Rom. 1:18), it does not seem that they have completely eradicated it, as evidenced by the

> **Christians disagree about which of these options to select, but as long as it is reasonable to accept at least one of them, the argument under discussion fails to establish its conclusion.**

number of non-Christians who claim to believe in God (or at least a transcendent being or higher power much like God) as well as those who acknowledge their failure to live their lives as they know they should. Among these people are those in cultures that have not been influenced by the Judeo-Christian worldview. Such people are in a position to know (or at least believe) some rudimentary elements of the gospel message: that God exists, that a right relationship with God requires at least a high degree of moral goodness, that he or she falls short of this standard, and that reconciliation with God is somehow possible in spite of this. People who believe these things may well become genuinely sorry for their failures and repent of them in the hope of God's forgiveness and their eventual union with God. Might this be enough to justify God in saving them?

One major problem with this alternative is that it assumes that the salvation of an individual can be based entirely on what he or she does rather than on what God has done for that person in Christ. So if there is any hope for this alternative, we must add something that connects the unreached with the death of Christ for them on the cross. The first step in this direction is to affirm that what Jesus did in the atonement was entirely adequate to accomplish whatever is *objectively necessary* for the salvation of human beings. All that remains for salvation in the case of individual human beings is for them to receive the benefits of Christ's atonement in an appropriate, subjective way. In ideal cases, this involves a response of repentance and faith to a hearing of the gospel message. But we are now talking about cases that are less than ideal, cases in which a person has not heard the good news of Christ. The previous paragraph considered the case of unreached people who responded with repentance and a kind of faith to what they believed about God's will on the basis of general revelation. Can this repentance and faith be connected in some way with the gospel even if these people have never heard it?

Perhaps so. Suppose that because God is omniscient, God has what theologians call middle knowledge. If God has middle knowledge, then God knows not only what people *will* freely choose to do in the future (this is due to God's *fore*knowledge) but also what people *would* freely choose to do if they were in circumstances other than those they are actually in. If God has middle knowledge, then God knows how the unreached would have freely responded to the gospel message if they had had the privilege of hearing and understanding it. We can now suggest that God will save those who would have responded favorably and will damn those who would have freely rejected the gospel. In that case, the results are the same as they would have been if those people had really heard and responded to the gospel.

For those who are unhappy with this suggestion, there is still another possible way to affirm premise 15 and deny premise

12. This is to consider the scenario (again, not clearly taught by the Bible but not explicitly excluded by it either) that all unreached people have an opportunity to hear, understand, and respond freely to the gospel *after death* (but before the last judgment). Some believe that, between his crucifixion and resurrection, Jesus provided just such an opportunity for those who had died earlier (and who therefore could not have heard the gospel, since the historical events on which it is based had not yet occurred [see Eph. 4:8–10; 1 Pet. 3:18–20; 4:5–6]). After all, though the faithful Old Testament figures celebrated by the author of Hebrews "were . . . living by faith when they died . . . [and] did not receive the things promised . . . God is not ashamed to be called their God, for he has prepared a [heavenly] city for them" (11:13, 16). Moreover, even now they are surrounding us as "a great cloud of witnesses" (12:1), and they will be made perfect together with us (11:40). How could this be unless either God considered their faith adequate to save them once the atonement had occurred (as with the previous suggestion), or they had an opportunity to hear and respond to the gospel after death? If either of these possibilities is the case, then justice would seem to require that all human beings be treated in the same way. If so, then we have a reasonable way to affirm premise 15 and deny premise 12.

But as said earlier, some Christians may prefer to accept premise 12 and reject premise 15. By virtue of affirming premise 12, these people rule out both options just considered (both premortem unevangelized salvation and postmortem evangelism). As a result, those who accept this alternative must also accept the consequence that all unreached people will suffer the punishment of eternal separation from communion with God (this is premise 14). The burden of this approach is to show that it is reasonable to think that this is consistent with God's love. Some have suggested that this can be done by appealing, as we did above, to God's middle knowledge. The idea is that God has middle knowledge that all the people who died unevangelized would not have responded favorably to the gospel if they had heard and understood it. According to this view, this is what justifies a loving God in permitting them to spend eternity apart from loving communion with him. So there is more than one way to make a case for the claim that the argument against Christianity considered in this section fails to provide adequate reasons for the truth of its conclusion.

Reflection and Discussion

1. Can you articulate a version of the sacrifice model of the atonement that helps to explain how what Jesus accomplished on the cross was both effective in securing salvation and consistent with justice and morality? If so, what is it? If not, does your inability to do this pose an important apologetical problem for you? Why or why not?

2. Do you agree that Christians should defend the traditional doctrine of hell rather than annihilationism or universalism? Why or why not?

3. What is the best defense of the traditional doctrine of hell against the charge that a loving God would not allow unreached people to suffer eternally in hell?

Further Reading

Kvanvig, Jonathan L. *The Problem of Hell.* New York: Oxford University Press, 1993.

Sanders, John. *No Other Name: An Investigation into the Destiny of the Unevangelized.* Grand Rapids: Eerdmans, 1992.

Walls, Jerry. *Hell: The Logic of Damnation.* South Bend: University of Notre Dame Press, 1992.

Wilson, Jonathan R. *God So Loved the World: A Christology for Disciples.* Grand Rapids: Baker, 2001.

18

No Other Name

The Problem of Religious Pluralism I

» **Outline**

- **Do All Roads Lead to Rome?**
  - *Christian Exclusivism and the Scandal of Particularity*
  - *What Religious Pluralists Believe*
  - *A Pluralist Critique of Christian Exclusivism and Christian Replies*
  - *Five Reasons to Reject Religious Pluralism*
- **Jesus and Judaism**
  - *How Christianity Includes and Completes Judaism*
    - The Stories of the Old and New Testaments
    - The New Testament Fulfillment of Old Testament Patterns
  - *The Reaction of First-Century Jews to Jesus*
    - The Dramatic Transformation of Those Who Became Christians
    - Why Many Jews Did Not Believe Jesus Was the Messiah
  - *Christian Apologetics and Anti-Semitism*
- **Jesus and Islam**
  - *Muhammad and the Qur'an*
  - *What the Qur'an Says about the Bible and Jesus*
  - *The Case for the Qur'an as God's Final Revelation and Christian Replies*
    - The Testimony of Muhammad
    - The Content of the Qur'an
  - *The Need for Sensitivity in Relating to Muslims*

» **Summary**

The Bible teaches that salvation is possible only through Jesus. Religious pluralists hold instead that people can be saved through any legitimate religious tradition. Though pluralists reject religious exclusivists as arrogant and irrational, Christian apologists can resist their critique and turn it against them. Moreover, a number of good reasons exist to reject religious pluralism. A comparison of Christianity with its monotheist competitors shows that Christianity includes and completes Judaism and that there are both historical and theological reasons for affirming the superiority of the Bible over the Qur'an (and thus Christianity over Islam).

» **Basic Terms, Concepts, and Names**

anti-Semitism
Islam
Judaism
Muhammad
Qur'an
religious exclusivism
religious pluralism
scandal of particularity

» **Reflection and Discussion**

» **Further Reading**

> Thomas said to him, "Lord, we don't know where you are going, so how can we know the way?"
>
> Jesus answered, "I am the way and the truth and the life. No one comes to the Father except through me."
>
> John 14:5–6

Do All Roads Lead to Rome?

The previous chapter explored the possibility that people who die without having heard the gospel might be saved nonetheless because of their repentance and faith. This could be the case if God knows that their attitudes would have been supplemented by a favorable response to the good news of Christ if they had heard it. The chapter also mentioned the role of the Holy Spirit in drawing people to Christ. It seems reasonable to affirm that the Holy Spirit works in the lives and hearts of people for this purpose, even if they have not heard the gospel. It may well be the work of the Spirit that enables the unreached to experience genuine repentance and faith in God apart from their having heard the gospel. Among these people to whom the Holy Spirit ministers are many adherents of religious traditions other than Christianity. If God saves any of these people on the basis of their Spirit-induced repentance and faith and God's middle knowledge that they would

have accepted Christ if they had heard about him, then they are saved through the atonement and Spirit of Christ, even if they do not realize that this is the case (at least this side of heaven).

Even when Christians disagree about whether any unreached people in other religious traditions will be saved in this way, they can agree that salvation is possible only through Christ. This is because their disagreement is focused on whether explicit acknowledgment of Christ is necessary for salvation rather than on whether Christ must play an essential role in salvation (whether he is acknowledged consciously and explicitly or not). Let's call the claim that salvation is possible only through Jesus Christ (whether or not Christ is consciously recognized as Savior) Christian exclusivism.[1] This exclu-

1. Sometimes the label of Christian exclusivism is reserved only for the narrower view that someone can be saved only through consciously and deliberately acknowledging Jesus as Savior and Lord. Moreover, the view that people in other religious traditions can be saved through Christ without realizing it is often called inclusivism. However, I use

sivist assumption seems to be taught by Scripture. In addition to the passage from John quoted above, there is also Peter's bold affirmation about Jesus to the Jewish authorities that "salvation is found in no one else, for there is no other name under heaven given to men by which we must be saved" (Acts 4:12).

But exclusivist religious claims like this are currently unpopular. Christian exclusivism has been called by some the scandal of particularity. The idea that human salvation from eternal punishment and for the enjoyment of eternal life is possible only by being rightly related to a particular historical individual—Jesus of Nazareth—seems to some to be downright scandalous. The plight of the unreached (discussed in the previous chapter) is one of the reasons for this. Wouldn't a good and loving God make the means of salvation available to *all* human beings? If so, doesn't it make sense to think that the various religious traditions that have existed throughout history and that exist around the globe today all provide alternative ways to achieve salvation? Isn't this what the view sketched above in the first paragraph of this chapter comes down to anyway? Don't all roads lead to Rome? Religious pluralists answer these questions in the affirmative. Their view is that, though it is important to be connected with an authentic religious tradition (such as Judaism, Christianity, Islam, Hinduism, or Buddhism), it does not matter with which of these one affiliates oneself. They say that no one religion, such as Christianity, is *exclusively* the way to God.

Instead, there is a *plurality* of equally valid ways to attain salvation.[2]

One obvious exclusivist reply to the pluralist is to point out that, since the different religious traditions make mutually incompatible claims about the nature of ultimate reality, they cannot all be true. For instance, though the three creation monotheist religions (Judaism, Christianity, and Islam) share the same *general* conception of God as a perfect personal being who created the universe out of nothing, only Christianity holds that God is essentially *triune* in nature and that a member of the Trinity became *incarnate* as a human being to *atone* for the sins of humanity. Moreover, these three creation monotheist faiths disagree with all the versions of Hinduism and Buddhism about the nature of ultimate reality. The three dominant Hindu theologies are versions of pantheism (Sankara), panentheism or contingency monotheism (Ramanuja), and dualistic monotheism (Madhva).[3] As for Buddhism, some of its manifestations are polytheistic, and some seem best described as metaphysically naturalistic.[4]

A religious pluralist's response to this observation of religious incompatibility is to agree that this is the case but to insist on being both skeptical about religious knowledge and relativistic about religious truth. Such skepticism is based on the claim that there is no objective basis on which anyone can know or even be justi-

---

the former name more broadly to encompass both of these views. Both have in common a rejection of religious pluralism.

2. One proponent of the brand of religious pluralism considered in this chapter is John Hick. See John Hick, ed., *Problems of Religious Pluralism* (New York: St. Martin's Press, 1985).

3. See chaps. 7 and 8 for an explanation of these worldview families. Hinduism is discussed more fully in the first section of chap. 19.

4. See the second section of chap. 19 for more on Buddhism.

fied in believing that one religious tradition is rationally superior to all the others. Thus, all the philosophical and historical arguments constructed for Christianity so far in this book are powerless to demonstrate that Christianity is more likely to be true than the religious traditions with which it competes. A pluralist's relativism is expressed by the view that each religious tradition's conception of ultimate reality is true for that religious tradition's adherents. People in every religion claim to have had religious experiences of ultimate reality. Pluralists say that the differing (and incompatible) interpretations of these experiences are the result of the diverse cultures in which they occur. Pluralists also think that the best explanation of these widespread but differently conceptualized experiences is that ultimate reality (God, the divine, the transcendent, the One, etc.) exists, but no human can know what it is like. In sum, pluralists believe that no one knows the true nature of ultimate reality, but experience of ultimate reality is universal, and each religion has its own equally valid way of thinking and talking about these experiences.

However, in spite of this skepticism and relativism about the metaphysical tenets of the world's religions, pluralists believe that these traditions are in fundamental agreement about ethical ideals. In particular, they hold that for all legitimate religious traditions, the ideal goal of human existence is to be transformed from a basically self-centered person into a person centered on ultimate reality. Pluralists say this moral agreement makes the world's religions *practically* equivalent, even though they are *theoretically* incompatible. But since the fundamental religious problem is practical ("How can I be saved?"), how

one lives matters more than what one thinks—or so say the pluralists. According to their view, though we are not able to know what ultimate reality is really like in itself (because we can know only how it *appears* to us in our distinctive cultural settings), we can know how we ought to live. Religious pluralists conclude that the most effective way to become the sorts of people who can live this way is simply to follow the religious path into which one was born.

This positive picture of religious pluralism is usually combined with the following criticism of religious exclusivism:[5]

1. There is no objective basis on which it is both (a) reasonable to believe that one particular religion is the only means of salvation and (b) possible to convince reasonable, well-informed, and good-intentioned people that some version of religious exclusivism is true.
2. If 1 is true, then it is both arrogant and irrational to believe that a version of religious exclusivism is true.
3. Therefore, Christian exclusivists—people who say that salvation is possible only in Jesus Christ—are both arrogant and irrational.

Christians are committed to truth, moral virtue, and reason. For all these reasons, we must deny 3 and provide good reasons not to accept either premise 1 or 2 (or both). Since we are committed to the

5. This argument is based on a similar objection to religious exclusivism discussed in Timothy O'Connor, "Religious Pluralism," in *Reason for the Hope Within*, ed. Michael J. Murray, 165–81 (Grand Rapids: Eerdmans, 1999).

truth, and as Christians we believe that what the Bible teaches is true (a claim that Christians are justified in making, as chap. 20 argues), we must affirm that salvation for human beings is possible only through Jesus Christ. That is, we must be Christian religious exclusivists. Moreover, our call as Christians to be like Christ requires us to practice humility (Phil. 2:1–4) and to find good reasons to deny that our exclusivism is necessarily arrogant (because if it were, we would have Christian grounds both to deny and to affirm Christian exclusivism—an unhappy situation). Finally, the primary goal of Christian apologists is to show that Christian belief is not unreasonable or irrational.

Fortunately, there are good reasons for thinking that both premise 1 and premise 2 are unacceptable. Also, there are good reasons to reject religious pluralism. Let's start with premise 1. First of all, the arguments formulated in part 2 in defense of creation monotheism and the case made earlier in part 3 for the deity of Jesus are objective evidences for the truth of the Christian faith and, by implication, Christian exclusivism. These arguments contribute substantially to the claim that Christianity is rationally superior to the other religious traditions with which it competes. Thus, they make it reasonable to believe that Jesus is the only means of salvation. Would it be possible to employ these arguments to convince anyone who denies Christian exclusivism to change his or her mind and heart? It seems reasonable to think that such objective, rational grounds could be (and have been) employed by effective apologists or evangelists in partnership with the Holy Spirit to persuade seekers to become believers. Anyone who endorses premise 1 needs

to show that these arguments have not and cannot be used for these purposes. But this has not been shown, and I doubt that it could be. So premise 1 is doubtful at best.

But suppose for the sake of argument that premise 1 is true, or suppose at least that part b is true, that it is not possible to convince anyone on objective grounds to adopt some form of religious exclusivism. Would it follow from this that religious exclusivists would be both arrogant and irrational to persist in believing and espousing their exclusivist views? In other words, is there good reason to accept premise 2? There are at least three good reasons for thinking there is not. First, many Christian exclusivists (and exclusivists in other religious traditions) have demonstrated by their attitudes, manner of living, and thoughtful reflections that it is possible to be a humble and rational exclusivist. Second, many intellectual disagreements are tolerated, accepted, and even encouraged in domains other than religious belief (such as in science, politics, ethics, art criticism, etc.) in such a way that one's inability to provide rational arguments for positions that can change the minds of those with whom one disagrees does not justify charges of arrogance and irrationality. Why should things be any different when it comes to theological matters? Finally, if the general principle from which premise 2 follows applies to religious issues in general, then it applies to the position of religious pluralism itself. But religious pluralism is clearly an intellectual claim with which many reasonable, well-informed, and well-intentioned people disagree. Consequently, according to the principle on which premise 2 is based, religious pluralists are arrogant

The claim that one ought to live a life centered on ultimate reality is empty of meaning without a specific conception of the nature of ultimate reality.

and irrational as well. The principle religious pluralists employ to criticize religious exclusivists backfires in such a way as to apply the same critique to them. For all these reasons, premise 2 should be rejected.[6]

Not only does this argument against religious exclusivism fail to provide adequate reasons for accepting its conclusion, but there are also a number of good reasons to reject religious pluralism itself. First, as already pointed out, the case for the Christian version of creation monotheism provides a good reason for thinking that not all religious traditions are equally likely to be true. Second, even if the arguments are not adequate to support this claim, it would be preferable to conclude that we do not know which religious tradition is most likely to be true rather than to infer that they are all somehow relatively true (in spite of their fundamental metaphysical differences). Third, the pluralist's claim that it does not matter what one believes about the nature of ultimate reality as long as one strives to live a life centered on ultimate reality is arguably false. For one thing, how we ought to live our lives depends essentially on the kind of world in which we live. For instance, if meta-

physical naturalism is true, then there is arguably no good, objective reason for valuing one way of living over another (see chap. 25 for more on this). For another thing, the claim that one ought to live a life centered on ultimate reality is empty of meaning without a specific conception of the nature of ultimate reality. But this is just what pluralists say we cannot have. How can we strive to achieve an ideal that has no meaningful content? Fourth, religious pluralism is not as inclusive as it claims to be (nor can it be), since by definition it must exclude all forms of religious exclusivism. These include at least the traditional versions of Judaism, Christianity, and Islam. To be a traditional adherent of any of these faiths requires one to believe that salvation is possible only through one's own religion. Therefore, the pluralist's claim that salvation is possible in *any* religious tradition contradicts the teachings of these traditions. Finally, even apparently nonexclusivist religious traditions, such as some versions of Hinduism and Buddhism, nonetheless make specific claims about the nature of ultimate reality that are not considered merely relatively true by their adherents. This is inconsistent with the pluralist's insistence that we make no absolute claims about the ultimate.

This case against religious pluralism can be supplemented by looking closely and carefully at each of the major religious traditions with which Christianity competes. The purpose of doing so is to try to show that (1) there are objective grounds on the basis of which we can engage in rational evaluation of them and that (2) there is good reason to think that Christianity (with its claim of exclusivism) is rationally superior to its major competitors (or at

6. The replies in this paragraph are based on similar responses in ibid.

least rationally competitive with them). As cautioned in chapter 7, no one is sufficiently informed, experienced, and objective to accomplish this project completely and decisively. In addition, we have space here for only the most cursory reflections. The comments should be considered simply the opening moves in a conversation about religious diversity. Moreover, we should always look for common ground and things we can learn from other traditions. The goal is to be as confident in the superiority of Christianity as the arguments warrant while having the degree of humility required by the inconclusiveness of our reasons. This chapter considers Judaism and Islam, and the next chapter considers Hinduism and Buddhism.

As said above, the three major creation monotheist religious traditions of Judaism, Christianity, and Islam each adhere to a form of religious exclusivism. Each claims to provide the only means of salvation through being properly related to God. What good reasons can a Christian apologist provide for thinking that Christianity is more likely to be true than either Judaism or Islam? A better question, since this is really the crux of the issue, is What reasons can we give for thinking that Jesus is the only Savior and Lord in spite of the contrary claims of some Jews and all Muslims?

Jesus and Judaism

The Hebrew Scriptures (what Christians call the Old Testament) affirm that God chose Abraham to be the father of a nation through whom God would bless the world (Gen. 18:18–19). Abraham's grandson Jacob became the father of Israel—God's chosen people (Ps. 135:4). The historical writings of the Hebrew Scriptures record the blessings enjoyed by the Israelites under their kings David and Solomon but also the tremendous suffering they endured because of subsequent bad kings and eventual exile to foreign lands (misfortunes the biblical writers say were due to God's just punishment for Israel's disobedience toward him). The prophetic writings express their hope in God's rescue of them from their enemies by a divinely appointed Messiah King who would set up a kingdom in which God's people would enjoy justice and peace (Hebrew: *shalom*) forever.

Then a first-century Israelite named Jesus of Nazareth claimed to be the Messiah, God's chosen and anointed one and Israel's long-awaited Redeemer King in the line of the great king David. As shown, Jesus claimed that the kingdom of God arrived with his coming and that he was the only way to the Father. The New Testament book of Hebrews implies that, though God had spoken through prophets in the past, his final prophetic word came through his Son (1:1–2). Overall, the New Testament claims that in Jesus all the promises of God to Israel are fulfilled and that Jesus is the final prophet, priest, and king of the chosen people of God.

What reasons do we have for believing these New Testament claims? The arguments in part 2 provide grounds to look to religious traditions that endorse the creation monotheist conception of God and God's relationship to the universe. We have seen that Judaism, Christianity, and Islam are the only major faiths that do. Moreover, both Christians and to some extent Muslims endorse the Hebrew Scriptures as part of God's revelation to human beings. These Scriptures record God's acts in human history—acts of creation, judgment, and redemption in particular. They also preserve prophecies of God's future acts of the same sort. Those who study these Scriptures discern a general pattern of divine action—a pattern of God's accomplishment of his purposes for human beings.

The authors of the New Testament books argue in a number of places that various aspects of this pattern find their completion in Jesus Christ. Examples of these specific fulfillments include the following: (1) The sacrifice of Jesus on the cross fulfills the Jewish practice of animal sacrifice (Heb. 10:1–18); (2) the incarnation of God the Son in Jesus takes the place of the tabernacle or temple (John 1:14; 2:19; 4:19–24; Acts 7:44–50); (3) the life Jesus lived in obedience to God fulfills the righteous requirements of the divine moral law (Rom. 8:1–4); (4) Jesus is the high priest of a new covenant (Mark 14:22–25; Heb. 7–8); and (5) Jesus' life fulfills elements of the exodus story in that he was the sacrificed Passover lamb (1 Cor. 5:7), he resisted the temptations in the desert to which the Israelites succumbed in the wilderness (Deut. 6:13, 16; 8:3; Matt. 4:1–11), and his Sermon on the Mount affirmed the law given to Moses on Mount Sinai. These are just a few of the significant continuities, recognized by the writers of the New Testament, between God's acts in the history of Israel and God's acts in and through the person of Jesus.

Moreover, all the first Christians were Jews who came to faith in Christ either through witnessing an appearance of the risen Lord or by responding to the testimony and preaching of those who had (Acts 2:41). These Jewish believers experienced dramatic changes in belief and practice as a result of becoming Christians. They no longer offered animal sacrifices (since they believed that the sacrifice of Jesus rendered them unnecessary); they (eventually) no longer insisted on circumcision but practiced baptism instead as the rite of initiation into the family of God (a ritual that symbolizes Jesus' death and resurrection); they worshiped on Sunday (the day Jesus was raised from the dead) instead of on the Sabbath (a day they were taught from childhood to set aside as holy); they ate with Gentiles and declared all foods clean (a radical reversal of their traditional behaviors); and they worshiped a human being as Lord and God (something these monotheists would have considered blasphemous before the resurrection of Jesus). These deep changes in conviction and lifestyle on the part of these Jews can be explained only by the fact that they genuinely believed Jesus was the Messiah. Moreover, their revolutionary belief in a suffering and crucified Messiah can be explained only by their being convinced that he had been raised from the dead. Thus, many Jews saw becoming a follower of Jesus Christ (on the basis of their belief in his resurrection) as a fulfillment or completion of their Jewish faith.

But many Jews did not. Though the reasons for this are complicated, one plausible and prominent reason is that those who hoped for a Messiah to liberate them from their Roman oppressors were not willing to accept a Messiah whose ultimate victory over the forces of evil involved a shameful death by crucifixion. Paul says that his preaching of Christ crucified was "a stumbling block to Jews" (1 Cor. 1:23). In terms of Old Testament prophecy, these Jews did not identify the figure in Daniel's vision, who was "one like a son of man," who "was given authority, glory and sovereign power," and who was such that "all peoples, nations and men of every language worshiped him" and whose "dominion is an everlasting dominion" and whose "kingdom . . . will never be destroyed" (7:13–14), with the suffering servant of Isaiah 53, who "was despised and rejected by men, a man of sorrows, and familiar with suffering" and who "was pierced for our transgressions [and] was crushed for our iniquities" (vv. 3, 5).

It is reasonable to think that one important thing the believing Jews had that the unbelieving Jews lacked was a conviction that Jesus had been raised from the dead. Those who were convinced of this could interpret the crucifixion in light of the resurrection, and as a result, they could also interpret Old Testament prophecy as the writers of the New Testament did. This is what the risen Jesus helped the disciples he met on the road to Emmaus to do:

> He [Jesus] said to them, "How foolish you are, and how slow of heart to believe all that the prophets have spoken! Did not the Christ have to suffer these things and then enter his glory?" And beginning with Moses and all the Prophets, he explained to them what was said in all the Scriptures concerning himself.
>
> Luke 24:25–27

From the standpoint of faith in the resurrection of Jesus, it is reasonable to think that, with respect to the two testaments of the Bible, "the New is in the Old concealed, and the Old is in the New revealed."[7] So if, as argued in chapter 15, it is reason-

able to believe that Jesus was raised from the dead, then it is also reasonable to think of Judaism as a complement to Christianity rather than as a competitor with Christianity.

This is not, of course, how contemporary Jews see it. Centuries of anti-Semitism propagated by Christians who blamed Jews unfairly for the crucifixion of Christ have made it increasingly difficult for non-Christian Jews to see Jesus as the Messiah. This is tragic not only because of the suffering it has caused the Jewish people but also because in many cases it has prevented them—those who would otherwise be in the best position to understand and appreciate the gospel—from reconciliation with God through Christ. As conversations about the film *The Passion of the Christ* have shown, it is important for Christian apologists to be sensitive to the history and ongoing consequences of anti-Semitism among Christians. This is another way apologists should use their hearts in addition to their heads.

Jesus and Islam

In AD 610, an Arab named Muhammad (alleged to be a descendant of Abraham through his son Ishmael) is reported to have experienced a special revelation from God ("Allah" in Arabic) through the angel Gabriel. The initial message Gabriel is purported to have given Muhammad is that he should recite. This is recorded in the Muslim scriptures (called the Qur'an, which means "recitation") in Sura (chapter) 96. Eventually, Muhammad, the messenger of God, recited the contents of the entire Qur'an, considered by Muslims to be the infallible word of God. The Qur'an

---

7. St. Augustine, *Quaestiones in Heptateuchum,* 2, 73 (the Heptateuch is the first seven books of the Bible).

refers to Muhammad as "the Apostle of God and the Seal of the Prophets" (Sura 33:40). As the seal of the prophets, Muhammad is believed by Muslims to be the last and the greatest of the human beings who have had the authority to speak on behalf of God. "Muslims consider their Prophet Muhammad as the highest exemplar of humanity and his message a purification and fulfillment of Judaism and Christianity."[8]

Earlier prophets recognized by Muslims include all the Jewish prophets and Jesus, but Muslims think of Jesus as merely a human prophet. Muslims call Jesus the Messiah, but they deny his divinity and his resurrection (Suras 4:171–72; 5:72–76; 17:110), though they believe in a *general* resurrection of the dead and a final judgment (Suras 4:158; 23:15–16; 69). Consequently, they deny the trinitarian nature of God (Sura 5:73). They even reject the claim that Jesus died on the cross. This is based on a single verse in the Qur'an: "They [the Jews] denied the truth and uttered a monstrous falsehood against Mary. They declared: 'We have put to death the Messiah, Jesus the son of Mary, the apostle of God.' They did not kill him, nor did they crucify him, but they thought they did" (Sura 4:157).

In spite of these fundamental disagreements with Christians about doctrine, Muslims consider both Jews and Christians "people of the book," and Muslims respect and accept (sufficiently revised and interpreted) parts of the Old and New Testaments (the first five books of the Old Testament, the Psalms, and the Gospels). However, they also believe

that Jews and Christians changed their Scriptures from their original form so that they now contain falsehoods (corruptions) and can no longer be entirely trusted. They believe the Qur'an is God's final and perfect revelation that reveals these errors. That is how they can justify respect for the Gospels and yet a refusal to believe in the doctrines of the Trinity, incarnation, atonement, and resurrection and in the historicity of Jesus' death on the cross.

Clearly, Islam is both religiously exclusivist and inconsistent with Christianity in its teachings. Does it pose a rational challenge to Christian belief? There are good reasons to think it does not. We can start with the historical case sketched in the first three chapters of this part of the book for the divinity of Jesus. This case is based on evidence for (1) the general reliability of the canonical Gospels, (2) the claim that Jesus believed himself to be divine, (3) the authenticity of Jesus' miracles, and, most importantly, (4) the resurrection of Jesus from the dead. Chapter 16 also defended the doctrines of the incarnation and the Trinity from the charge of logical incoherence, and chapter 17 defended the doctrines of the atonement and hell from moral objections.

Though the Qur'an denies each of these historical claims (and all the doctrines based on them except for the doctrines of a general resurrection, a final judgment, and heaven and hell), these denials are credible only if we have good reason to believe that the Qur'an is God's final word to human beings. But what grounds do we have for thinking this? We have only two that carry any weight: (1) the testimony of Muhammad that he received the contents of the Qur'an from God through

8. S. A. Nigosian, *World Religions: A Historical Approach*, 3rd ed. (Boston: Bedford/St. Martin's, 2000), 311.

a series of revelations mediated by the angel Gabriel and (2) the content of the Qur'an itself.

Are these grounds adequate to justify the claim that the Qur'an, rather than the Bible, is God's final, authoritative word to human beings? They are not. Ground 2 is rendered evidentially ineffective because of the extent to which the general content of the Qur'an (other than its explicit denials of biblical claims) is consistent with much of the general content of the Bible. That is, the major themes of the Qur'an are also contained in the Bible as major themes. These include (1) the affirmation of creation monotheism and the denunciation of polytheism and idolatry; (2) the division of humanity into two groups, the righteous friends of God and the unrighteous enemies of God; (3) the compassion and mercy of God toward the righteous and his anger and judgment toward the unrighteous; (4) God's guidance of human beings through his messengers and prophets to help them both submit to God by repenting of their sin in order to receive divine forgiveness and perform deeds of righteousness to avoid God's wrath and incur God's favor; and (5) the eventual resurrection of human beings to face the consequences of God's judgment: bliss in heaven for the righteous and misery in hell for the unrighteous.

Noticeably absent from a Christian standpoint is both an emphasis on the impossibility of salvation by human effort alone (even with God's guidance), given the seriousness and power of sin, and a corresponding doctrine of salvation through faith in God's gracious, loving, and atoning self-sacrifice alone. In comparison with the Bible, what the Qur'an affirms is basically not new, and what it denies (about Jesus) leaves it seriously incomplete and inadequate to solve the deepest problems of human existence. A genuine divine revelation would provide a means for the solution to these problems. Therefore, we have a theological reason for thinking that the Bible, rather than the Qur'an, is more likely a revelation of God.

In addition, in denying the bulk of the New Testament picture of Jesus, the Qur'an undercuts all the important ways in which Jesus can be seen as the fulfillment of Old Testament prophecy and the culmination of the redemptive work of God in the history of Israel. Whereas the New Testament genuinely *completes* the Old Testament in many significant ways, the Qur'an merely *repeats* many Old Testament themes in a new key. Like the Old Testament, the Qur'an gives us wisdom to guide us and laws to govern us as we seek to worship and serve God and live in harmony with others. However, only in the New Testament do we find the wisdom of the cross (1 Cor. 1:18–2:5), which made possible the fulfillment of the law (Rom. 8:1–4) so that we might be reconciled to God (2 Cor. 5:16–21) and able to love one another as we ought (1 John 4:7–21).

Moreover, ground 1 for thinking that the Qur'an is God's final revelation provides only the testimony of one human being:

> **Whereas the New Testament genuinely *completes* the Old Testament in many significant ways, the Qur'an merely *repeats* many Old Testament themes in a new key.**

Muhammad. In contrast, the grounds for believing that the New Testament is historically reliable include a large number of human beings who claim to have been eyewitnesses to the events of Jesus' life, death, and resurrection. Since a greater number of independent, reliable witnesses makes historical claims more credible, we have a much stronger case for believing that the Bible is God's revelation (based on Jesus' resurrection, his treatment of the Old Testament as authoritative, the authority of his life and teachings themselves, and the authority of the apostles he commissioned to preach and explain the gospel) rather than the Qur'an (based on Muhammad's claim to have experienced revelations from God). Thus, we also have a historical reason for believing that the Bible, rather than the Qur'an, is God's Word to us.

As in the case of Judaism, these claims of the superiority of Christianity over Islam must be communicated carefully and humbly. Since the Crusades (discussed in chap. 21), Muslims and Christians have had a precarious relationship. Recent events have only intensified what has been the case for many centuries. This clash of civilizations is a genuine and serious problem that Christian apologists would do well to try to understand, at least for the sake of preventing further polarization between these two members of the family of Abraham. Perhaps the best approach is to downplay language of the superiority of Christianity over Islam and to avoid talking about Christians as being better than Muslims (since this latter charge is in many cases not true). As argued, it is more reasonable to think that God's final word to human beings was spoken by (and embodied in) Jesus than that it was delivered nearly six hundred years later to Muhammad. Therefore, we should urge our Muslim brothers and sisters to consider or reconsider the historical case for the superiority of Jesus over all human beings, a superiority that is grounded in the fact that he is the resurrected Son of God and Savior of the world. Though it is difficult for these strict monotheists to accept the incarnation, if they are devout, their deep faith in God as compassionate and merciful and their recognition of their need for forgiveness and assurance of salvation—something they share with committed Jews and Christians—may well provide the Holy Spirit with fertile ground in which to plant the seed of faith in Christ.

Reflection and Discussion

1. Are you convinced by the arguments in this chapter that it would not necessarily be irrational and arrogant to endorse Christian exclusivism and that there are good reasons to reject religious pluralism? Why or why not?
2. What advice would you give someone who is planning to talk to a non-Christian Jew about Jesus? Should Christians and Jews be having more conversations about anti-Semitism? If so, how should these conversations go? If not, why not?
3. Should Christians appeal to common historical and theological ground in conversations with Muslims in order to interest them in talking about Jesus? If so, what is this common ground, and what things about Jesus need to be discussed? If not, why not?

Further Reading

Accad, Fouad Elias. *Building Bridges: Christianity and Islam*. Colorado Springs: NavPress, 1997.

Brown, Michael L. *Answering Jewish Objections to Jesus*. Vols. 1–3. Grand Rapids: Baker, 2000, 2000, 2003.

Quinn, Philip L., and Kevin Meeker, eds. *The Philosophical Challenge of Religious Diversity*. New York: Oxford University Press, 2000.

19

East Meets West

The Problem of Religious Pluralism II

» **Outline**

- **Jesus and Hinduism**
  - *Sankara's Pantheistic Hinduism*
  - *Ramanuja's Panentheistic (or Contingency Monotheist) Hinduism*
  - *Madhva's Cosmological Dualist Hinduism*
- **Jesus and Buddhism**
  - *What All Forms of Buddhism Have in Common*
  - *Theravada Buddhism and Mahayana Buddhism*
  - *A Critique of Both Versions of Buddhism*
- **Every Knee Shall Bow**
  - *Monotheistic Religions Are Rationally Superior to Monistic Religions*
  - *Creation Monotheisms Are Rationally Superior to Other Monotheisms*
  - *Christianity Is Rationally Superior to Other Creation Monotheisms*
  - *Jesus and New Age Spiritualities*

» **Summary**

Hinduism and Buddhism have some fundamental doctrines in common. The three most prominent Hindu theologians are Sankara, Ramanuja, and Madhva. They interpret the Hindu scriptures in pantheistic, panentheistic (or contingency monotheistic), and cosmological dualist terms, respectively. These three versions of Hinduism are subject to the following kinds of problems: logical (Sankara), moral (Ramanuja), and philosophical (Madhva). Christian apologists can argue that Christianity is rationally superior in each of these respects. The two main versions of Buddhism are also subject to criticism from a logical, moral, and philosophical standpoint. Overall, it is arguable that monotheistic religions are rationally superior to monistic religions,

creation monotheisms are rationally superior to other monotheisms, and Christianity is rationally superior to other creation monotheisms. Any spirituality that does not acknowledge the lordship of Christ is deficient.

» **Basic Terms, Concepts, and Names**

Advaita Vedanta
anatta, doctrine of
Atman (and atman)
Bodhisattva
Brahman
Buddhism
eightfold path
Enlightenment
four noble truths
Hinduism
karma
liberation (moksha)
Madhva
Mahayana Buddhism
maya
monistic religions
nirvana
pan(en)theism
Ramanuja
reincarnation (samsara)
Sankara
Siddhartha Gautama (the Buddha)
Theravada Buddhism
Vedas, the

» **Reflection and Discussion**

» **Further Reading**

Great and marvelous are your deeds,
    Lord God Almighty.
Just and true are your ways,
    King of the ages.
Who will not fear you, O Lord,
    and bring glory to your name?
For you alone are holy.
All nations will come
    and worship before you,
for your righteous acts have been revealed.

Revelation 15:3–4

Both Hinduism and Buddhism originated on the Indian subcontinent.[1] Buddhism has spread throughout Asia, while Hinduism continues to be a predominately Indian religion. Unlike the three Abrahamic faiths just discussed, Hinduism has no identifiable historical founder or central figure. Hindus disagree about their origins, but they all look to their earliest sacred scriptures, the Vedas, for what they believe are eternal truths about the world, human existence, and salvation. Buddhism was founded by Siddhartha Gautama, the Buddha (Enlightened One), in the 6th century BC. The teachings of the Buddha are preserved in the Pali Canon. The Buddha both accepted and reformed Hindu teach-

1. The first two sections of this chapter draw on ideas in Robin Collins, "Eastern Religions," in *Reason for the Hope Within*, ed. Michael J. Murray, 182–216 (Grand Rapids: Eerdmans, 1999).

ings and practices, so there are important similarities and differences between the two religious traditions.

What they have in common is the view that the universe is both eternal and cyclical (undergoing cycles of evolution and decline). They also share a belief in reincarnation (samsara): All of us existed in a previous life, and each of us will most likely be reborn as another living creature after we die. They add to this the doctrine of karma, a principle of justice according to which the circumstances in one's life are determined by the moral worth of one's deeds and character in previous lives. Salvation for a Hindu or a Buddhist consists in liberation (moksha) from this cycle of birth, death, and rebirth. Both believe that salvation occurs by means of enlightenment, typically after many successive lives. Popular manifestations of both religious traditions tend to be polytheistic, but philosophical and theological articulations of them are often not.

Tremendous diversity exists within each of these traditions. The treatment here will be cursory, general, and relatively abstract. This chapter focuses on three major Hindu theologies and two main Buddhist traditions. The primary concern is to discern whether any of these pose a serious challenge to the claim that salvation is possible through Jesus Christ alone. There are, of course, a number of other less prominent religions around the world (such as Confucianism and Taoism) that we cannot consider here due to space limitations. Consequently, the conclusions will be somewhat tentative, and readers are encouraged to engage in a more thorough investigation of this question on their own.

Jesus and Hinduism

Hinduism may be the most metaphysically diverse of all religious traditions, since its practitioners have been polytheists, monotheists, pantheists, panentheists, atheists, and agnostics. This metaphysical diversity is grounded in the widespread Hindu conviction that the truth about ultimate reality is inexpressible and unknowable.

The Hindu name for ultimate reality is Brahman. In spite of the general skepticism just mentioned, many Hindu scholars have studied the Vedic texts (especially the Upanishads, the Bhagavad Gita, and the Brahma-sutra) to articulate an understanding of Brahman and Brahman's relationship to the universe. The philosophical/theological systems formulated

are called Vedanta. The three most influential vedantic thinkers are Sankara (788–820), Ramanuja (1017–1137), and Madhva (thirteenth century AD).

Sankara's view is called Advaita (nonduality) Vedanta. According to this worldview, reality is one, and the one is Brahman. It follows that the only absolute reality is Brahman, and therefore everything that exists is Brahman. Thus, each individual atman (soul) is identical with Atman (the world soul), and Atman is the same thing as Brahman. Though Brahman may seem to be a personal lord with a variety of divine attributes who is worthy of worship, Brahman is really impersonal (and so not appropriately worshiped) and completely without different and distinct qualities (except for being, consciousness, and bliss). This is clearly a version of pantheism, which accounts for polytheism at the popular level: The allegedly many gods are just manifestations of Brahman. Sankara says that the assumption that there are many real things (human beings, animals, plants, inorganic things, different qualities of things, etc.) is due to ignorance and that this ignorance is caused by maya (illusion). According to his view, salvation comes through eliminating maya and the ignorance based on it by becoming enlightened. Enlightenment involves grasping that everything (including oneself, of course) is really (distinctionless and impersonal) Brahman.

Sankara's interpretation of the Vedas is philosophically problematic, and because of this, it does not provide a plausible challenge to Christian exclusivism. The main problem with his view is that it says, on the one hand, that there is only one thing and thus no distinctions between different kinds of things, and, on the other hand, that there is a distinction between maya and ultimate reality, ignorance and enlightenment, bondage to samsara and liberation from it, and so on. In short, Sankara's Hindu theology is self-contradictory. Moreover, it does not help to distinguish, as Sankara does, between absolute reality (Brahman) and conventional reality (maya). This too is a distinction between two different things, and if Brahman is all, then there cannot be two different things. An additional problem is that Sankara's view is inconsistent with the wisdom of collective human sensory experience, which reveals a world of many real things. An appeal to mystical experience does not save his position. There is no good reason to trust such an experience, since insofar as it supports Sankara's view, it contradicts both reason and sense perception.

Ramanuja is a later Hindu thinker who tried to improve on Sankara's theology by attempting to be faithful to the theme of unity between Atman and Brahman in the Vedas while avoiding contradiction. His theology is a qualified nondualism. According to his view, the universe is Brahman's body, which emerges or emanates eternally out of Brahman and through which Brahman expresses itself. As such, the universe is coeternal with and dependent on Brahman, but it is not the same thing as Brahman. Therefore, the universe can consist in many different things, including souls, which are not identical with Brahman. If we take this to mean that the universe is part of Brahman, then Ramanuja's theology is a version of panentheism. If instead Brahman's body is not a part of Brahman, then Ramanuja's view is a version of contingency monotheism. Either way, Ramanuja avoids Sankara's pantheism. Moreover, whereas Sankara

conceives of Brahman as impersonal, Ramanuja believes Brahman is a personal God who has become incarnate in many forms (such as Rama and Krishna)[2] and who gives grace to save human beings who love him and are devoted to him (but this salvation does not involve atonement).

Though Ramanuja's picture of reality avoids the contradictory antirealism of Sankara's approach, and though it includes some Christian themes, it faces a problem of evil that is more serious than the one afflicting the Abrahamic faiths. In the first place, if his view is panentheistic, so that the universe is part of God and the universe contains evil, then a part of God is evil. But Ramanuja says that God is perfect. Therefore, the universe does not contain evil, or God is not perfect, or the universe is not a part of God. Since it seems best to affirm the last of these alternatives, it seems best to reject the panentheistic interpretation of Ramanuja's theology. Second, since Ramanuja affirms the eternality of souls (a consequence of his denial of creation *ex nihilo*), then those souls that have not yet been liberated from the cycle of death and rebirth have already suffered eternally. But this is an experience equivalent to eternal suffering in hell—at least with respect to length of time. Therefore, all of us still caught in the cycle of death and rebirth have no freedom of choice in this life to avoid eternal suffering. We have already endured it! According to the Christian view, all human beings suffer only a finite amount during the one earthly existence they are granted, and they are given an opportunity to choose freely whether to suffer eternally apart from God. Moreover, there is consequently

2. In Hinduism, an incarnation of God is called an avatar.

a much greater *amount* of pain and suffering for which Ramanuja needs to account than there is in the Christian view.

The third Hindu theologian is Madhva. According to his view, the universe is eternal and completely independent of God. His theology is a member of the cosmological dualism family. Thus, he avoids the problems facing Sankara's pantheism and the panentheist interpretation of Ramanuja. Moreover, he says God is the *designer* of the universe but not the *creator*. Therefore, his theology does not have to explain why God either created or eternally generates a universe that contains evil, pain, and suffering. Like Ramanuja, he also affirms that God is personal, has become incarnate in different forms, and offers salvation by grace.

But Madhva's account of God and the world has two serious problems. First, from the standpoint of Hinduism, it does not affirm the close relationship between God and the universe that is taught by the Vedas. Second, it can provide no satisfying philosophical explanation of the existence of the universe. Since Madhva's position is that the universe is both eternal and independent, the universe's existence is a brute fact. But the Abrahamic faiths and the other versions of Hinduism can all explain the existence of the universe as identical with God (Sankara), a part of or dependent on God (Ramanuja), or created by God out of nothing (Judaism, Christianity, and Islam). Therefore, these other theologies are superior to Madhva's theology in this respect.

Jesus and Buddhism

Though Buddhism comes in a variety of forms, there are two major Buddhist traditions. What they have in common is an adherence to the Buddha's basic teaching, the fundamental elements of which are encapsulated in the four noble truths:

1. Life is suffering.
2. Suffering is caused by desire.
3. Suffering can be eliminated by eliminating desire.
4. Desire can be eliminated by right action and right belief.

The Buddha used the word *suffering* broadly to encompass everything from mild dissatisfaction to intense misery. He believed that all forms of suffering are a result of desire (craving, thirst, attachment, etc.). Thus, we can avoid suffering by refraining from desire. Moreover, the means of extinguishing desire is to follow the eightfold path, which leads to right thinking and willing (wisdom); right speaking, acting, and living (morality); and right effort, mindfulness, and meditation (meditation). The goal, as in Hinduism, is to be freed from the cycle of death and rebirth by means of enlightenment. Those who achieve this goal reach a state of nirvana (which means "quenching" or "blowing out," as with a candle flame).

The Buddha believed salvation from suffering was a practical matter and accordingly avoided metaphysical speculation about the nature of ultimate reality and the fate of the enlightened at death. As a result, there is no ultimate divine reality in early Buddhist theology, and therefore, in some of its manifestations, it is more like metaphysical naturalism than a form of theism. In spite of the Buddha's antimetaphysical orientation, however, he did think there was practical value in endorsing the metaphysical doctrine of impermanence. According to this position, nothing endures for more than an instant; everything in reality is impermanent. When this view is applied to the nature of the self, it results in the Buddha's doctrine of anatta (no-self). According to this claim, there is no such thing as a stable, enduring, substantial self that remains the same throughout time. The self is like a candle flame that consists of gases that are dispersed as soon as they are produced. Realization of this truth is what leads to nirvana. The reason for this is that people desire things and become attached to them only because they are ignorant of their true nature and believe they will continue to exist from moment to moment as the beneficiary of the things they want to have. The Buddha believed that anyone who becomes fully convinced of his or her impermanence will cease to have the requisite motivation to desire anything. After all, what would be the point of wanting to be happy tomorrow if we know we won't exist tomorrow (even though something causally continuous with us will)?

The two main Buddhist schools are Theravada Buddhism (which developed first) and Mahayana Buddhism (which evolved later and claims to be based on later teachings of the Buddha). For our purposes, there are two main differences between them. First, the former sees salvation as primarily an individual matter that involves only one's diligent efforts to follow the eightfold path through an ongoing succession of lives until one attains enlightenment and nirvana. According to the latter, the ideal route to salvation involves compassion and self-sacrifice. Mahayana Buddhists believe that one should seek to eliminate suffering not only for oneself but also for all sentient beings. Moreover, one's compassion for others should be so great as to cause one to self-sacrificially postpone one's own attainment of nirvana to help others achieve it too. Those who strive to do this and are destined for enlightenment are called Bodhisattva (Buddhas-to-be). The Bodhisattva play the role of saviors, but only through friendship and example (and, according to some, the transfer of merit). They do not and cannot *redeem* others or *atone* for the sins of others as Jesus did. This emphasis on helping others attain salvation is the reason the latter form of Buddhism is called Mahayana (Greater Vehicle), and the former is called Hinayana (Lesser Vehicle).

The second difference between the two versions of Buddhism is that, whereas Theravada Buddhists say that distinct things are real even though impermanent, Mahayana Buddhists (such as Nagarjuna, who lived around AD 150) argue that there are no distinct, independent things in reality—not even momentarily. They would agree with Sankara that the appearance of real distinctions is an illusion. Others say that all the things that seem to exist independently are really *empty* of real being. However, they do not say that things such as rocks, plants, animals, and people do not exist in *any* sense. Rather, they claim that the true status of such things is midway between existence and nonexistence (this is Nagarjuna's "middle way"). Others say instead that what is ultimately real is a distinctionless and indefinable "something" (*tathata*: "suchness"), and still others affirm more positively that it is pure distinctionless consciousness.

Though Christians should applaud the Mahayana Buddhist emphasis on compassion, a Christian apologist can also raise some critical questions about Buddhist assumptions concerning salvation and reality. First, there is a tension between the doctrine of reincarnation and the doctrine of anatta (no-self). The former requires the existence of an enduring self to be reincarnated, and the latter denies that such a thing exists. This tension poses both a metaphysical problem and a moral problem. If samsara truly exists, and after people die they are reborn, then there is a self in an earlier life that is numerically identical to a self in a later life. That is, there is a single self that endures from one life to the next. But the doctrine of anatta denies this. Therefore, if this doctrine is true, then the doctrine of reincarnation is false (and vice versa). That is the metaphysical problem. The moral problem is that if we combine the doctrine of anatta with the doctrines of karma and samsara, then the circumstances of a person's birth and resulting life are due to the merits and demerits of *another* person in a previous life. But how is it just for one person to be rewarded or punished for the character and actions of another person, even if these two people are somehow closely causally related to each other?

Second, if there is no personal God to oversee the ongoing cycle of reincarnation so that people are rewarded or punished according to their karma, then what explains the existence and continual functioning of this cosmic process? Theistic religions can account for the survival of persons after they die and for their postmortem enjoyment or sufferance of the just consequences of their premortem lives. However, if there is either no divine reality of any kind or merely an impersonal emptiness, suchness, or consciousness,

Though Christians should applaud the Mahayana Buddhist emphasis on compassion, a Christian apologist can also raise some critical questions about Buddhist assumptions concerning salvation and reality.

then how can we account for the existence and management of such a teleological process? The teleological argument would account for it in terms of intelligent design, but an intelligent designer would arguably be a *personal* being.

Third, there is also at least an apparent tension between the Buddha's encouragement to eliminate desire and his affirmation of the eightfold path as a means to attain nirvana. Why would people follow this path to achieve that goal unless they were motivated by a desire to attain it? The Buddha advises people to eliminate desire for both existence and nonexistence. Perhaps nirvana is somehow a state in which one neither exists nor fails to exist (which is one way the Buddha describes it) so that in seeking to reach it one would not need to desire either existence or nonexistence. Nonetheless, one would strive to achieve the state of nirvana only if one *desired* to bring about *this* goal. True absence of desire ought to undermine *all* goal-directed behavior.

But perhaps the Buddha's four noble truths ought to be interpreted instead as affirming that only certain *bad* desires (whatever they might be) lead to suffering. If so (and some Buddhists insist on this interpretation), then there would be nothing wrong with desiring enlightenment and nirvana (and, as with the Bodhisattva, the salvation of all sentient beings). However, then we are back to an inconsistency with the doctrine of anatta. How could it make sense for one to desire eventual enlightenment and attainment of nirvana if one believes that one does not continue to exist from one moment to the next?

Fourth, if none of us is an enduring self, then none of us will survive to enjoy personal fulfillment and ongoing loving relationships (or the satisfaction of any of the needs discussed in chap. 4). But aren't these the fundamental things for which every human being longs? How can Buddhism be competitive with Christianity if it does not offer to *fulfill* our deepest desires but rather merely encourages us to *extinguish* at least our bad desires? It is true that desire can lead to suffering, and there are many desires that it would be better for us not to have. This is especially true of selfish desires and desires that are based on one's ignorance of what is truly good for oneself and others. Here Christianity and Buddhism can find common ground. But human beings need more than merely the elimination of suffering caused by bad desires. We also need to have our deepest needs satisfied. Moreover, much suffering seems to be due to unfulfilled good desires. The elimination of this kind of suffering would require the fulfillment of these desires. But the future fulfillment of desire requires the existence of an enduring self, and this is what the Buddhist says does not exist.

Fifth, there are a number of good things the achievement of which *require* suffering. If one followed the Buddha by making one's chief goal the elimination of one's suffering by the elimination of desire, then one would not be able to acquire these good things. Jesus is the prime example of someone who voluntarily took on suffering to bring about the good of salvation for the world. Moreover, Jesus calls us to take up our crosses and follow him (Mark 8:34). Christians look at some suffering as redemptive. Suffering that occurs for the sake of the welfare of others and for the sake of moral and spiritual improvement falls into this category. It is precisely here that Mahayana Buddhism, with its Bodhisattva ideal, is superior to Theravada Buddhism.

But sixth, if there are no real distinctions and therefore no real plurality of individuals, then there are no others to whom the Bodhisattva can be compassionate. The Bodhisattva cannot even care for *themselves* by caring for others (by virtue of not being individuals distinct from those others). The doctrine of anatta implies that there is not even a Cosmic Self. Ultimate reality is merely emptiness, suchness, or (impersonal) consciousness.

Finally, the Mahayana denial of real distinctions is subject to the same objections raised above against Sankara's similar claim. For all these reasons, there is good reason to think that neither version of Buddhism offers a serious challenge to Christianity's creation monotheism and its insistence that salvation is available only through the resurrected Christ.

Every Knee Shall Bow

We have now briefly summarized and evaluated four non-Christian religious traditions to see whether any of them is rationally competitive with or even rationally superior to Christianity. Given the discussion so far, arguably none of them is. But let's strengthen the case by concluding with some general observations about the similarities and differences among these faiths.

If we set polytheistic religious orientations aside, we can see that the great religions can be divided roughly into two general camps: (1) monotheistic religions, which affirm the existence of a personal God and a real material universe consisting of many nondivine things, and (2) monistic (pantheist and panentheist) religions, which assert that ultimate reality is fundamentally one and impersonal and that other things that seem to exist are illusions.[3] The former group includes Judaism, Christianity, and Islam and also Ramanuja's and Madhva's Hindu theologies. The latter group contains Sankara's Advaita Vedanta Hinduism and Mahayana Buddhism. Theravada Buddhists tend not to affirm (or deny) the existence of any kind of ultimate divine reality. This book has argued that, on philosophical (especially metaphysical) grounds, monotheistic religions are rationally superior to monistic religions. The reasons for this include the arguments for God's existence in part 2 and the problems monistic views have avoiding self-contradiction and accounting for the reality of both good and evil. Theravada Buddhism is also philosophically problematic, since it both fails to affirm the existence of God and encounters difficulties providing consistent accounts of its central doctrines.

3. Though panentheism can also be seen as an attempt to find a middle position between monotheism and monism.

The monotheistic faiths hold to the existence of a perfect, supremely good, and holy personal Lord. This picture of divine reality has consequences for the relationship between human beings and God and also for what is considered the most serious problem of human existence. As a majestic and holy personal being, God is worthy of worship and devotion, and humans are obligated to express their allegiance to him. Moreover, since God is morally perfect, the main thing separating human beings from God is human sin and wickedness. Insofar as we are sinful, we are unable to give to God the adoration he deserves. Consequently, the most serious and fundamental problem of human existence is sin. Monotheistic religions differ in the means they offer for solving this problem. The differences have primarily to do with the extent to which they emphasize the roles of divine grace and human effort. However, only Christianity holds that the problem of human sin must and can be solved by means of atonement accomplished by God.

Since monistic religions claim that ultimately reality is impersonal and in some sense beyond good and evil, they do not posit the existence of a being who is worthy of worship and devotion and from whom we can be separated by sin. Rather, since this impersonal reality is one, the basic human problem is ignorance of the

> **Only Christianity holds that the problem of human sin must and can be solved by means of atonement accomplished by God.**

true nature of reality (since our beliefs are based on how things appear to us, and things appear to be many). What humans need, therefore, is not so much to repent of their sins and to be forgiven on the basis of obedience or a gracious self-sacrificial divine atonement but to be enlightened. Whereas monotheists locate human failing in a misuse of the will, monists place it in a defect of the intellect. The means they recommend for repairing this defect is meditation and contemplation. When enlightenment occurs, the result is not a capacity to love, serve, and worship a personal God but absorption into an impersonal cosmic unity (if indeed there was ever anything separate to be absorbed in the first place).

The rational superiority of the monotheistic faiths carries with it good reason to favor a religious tradition with a personal God, who is worthy of worship, from whom humans are separated by sin, and from whom they need forgiveness from sin. But which monotheistic religion is most likely to provide both truth and an efficacious means to this end? As shown above, the monotheistic Hinduisms have philosophical problems that do not beset the creation monotheist traditions. Moreover, though the three Abrahamic traditions generally agree on a philosophically superior conception of God and God's relationship to creation, they disagree about the solution to the problem of sin.

It is at this point that the superiority of Christian exclusivism is best seen. There is both a theological and a historical reason for this. The theological reason is that Christianity is the only religious tradition that affirms both that (1) human beings are completely powerless on their own to remove the penalty and overcome the power of sin and that (2) God has acted so as to solve these problems of sin in a way that is both efficacious and just. According to claim 1, no amount of human righteousness, obedience, repentance, meditation, right action, right thinking, love, or self-sacrifice can remove sin and reconcile us to God. So neither Sankara's Hinduism nor either kind of Buddhism provides a means sufficient for salvation. With respect to claim 2, even divine love, grace, and forgiveness are not adequate by themselves to solve the problem of sin. This is because full reconciliation between human beings and God requires genuine human righteousness and obedience to God, and this requires an atonement accomplished by God. Therefore, neither Judaism nor Islam, Ramanuja's Hinduism, or Madhva's Hinduism offers an entirely satisfactory path to salvation.

Only a person who is fully divine (and so morally perfect) and fully human could pay the penalty for sin. As God, he would not owe a payment for sin, and as a human, he could represent the human race and pay the penalty on behalf of all human beings. As God, he could be a perfectly righteous and obedient human being, and as a human, he could inspire us to follow his example of service to God and others. As God, he could empower us to be able to do this. As a human, he would understand our weaknesses when we fail. Moreover, as both divine and human, he would be the perfect mediator between God and human beings. This is the kind of person who would be needed to provide a completely just and efficacious solution to the problem of sin.

This is where the historical basis for the rational superiority of Christian exclusivism comes in. The historical case made in the first three chapters of this part makes it reasonable to believe that Jesus of Nazareth is a person who fits the profile just described. As mentioned at the end of chapter 15, especially the historical evidence for his resurrection places Jesus head and shoulders above all the other religious figures and traditions that offer guidance for human salvation. If Jesus was really raised from the dead, then he really defeated sin and death. If he was not, then as Paul told the Corinthians, we are still in our sins (1 Cor. 15:17). There is no one else of whom it would be reasonable to say this.

This chapter ends with a brief word about New Age spiritualities. It is currently popular for many people to avoid commitment to established religious traditions and instead to piece together their own "spirituality" from a variety of religious sources. Therefore, what was argued in this chapter and the last about the major religious faiths of the world does not apply directly to them. However, insofar as these people have borrowed elements from these religions, they have also taken on whatever disadvantages they have (their advantages generally require a wholesale adherence to the entire tradition). Much New Age spirituality has a decidedly Eastern flavor to it in its employment of the themes of "the god within" (polytheism? pantheism?), reincarnation, salvation through meditation, and so on. As a result, New Age spirituality inherits the problems posed by these ideas. Moreover, insofar as a spiritual orientation leaves Jesus out of the picture, it omits the only genuine means for human fulfillment.

The fundamental questions facing all human beings, whether they are religious or spiritual or not, are, To whom do I owe my ultimate allegiance? To whom should I give my heart? People give many answers to these questions: No one, myself, and God are among them. Some live their lives in such a way as to suggest that they believe the answers are money, my country, or my career. As shown, there is good reason to believe that we all have a duty to serve God above all else. We have also seen that it is reasonable to think that the God to whom we owe everything became a human being, died on our behalf, and was resurrected to show his victory over the forces of evil and his superiority over all counterfeit saviors. As Paul wrote to the Philippians, "Therefore God exalted him to the highest place and gave him the name that is above every name" (2:9). May we do all we can to cultivate Christian commitment in ourselves and others so that we will be prepared to participate joyfully and gratefully when "at the name of Jesus every knee should bow, in heaven and on earth and under the earth, and every tongue confess that Jesus Christ is Lord, to the glory of God the Father" (2:10–11).

Reflection and Discussion

1. If the claims of Christianity are rationally superior to the claims of all three Hindu theologies discussed in this chapter, why has the Indian religious tradition survived so long (longer than Christianity), and why are there still so many devoted Hindu practitioners today?

2. What would you say to someone who claimed that Mahayana Buddhism is superior to Christianity because it not only stresses compassion for others but also provides—through meditation—a means to become compassionate that is more effective than any methods available in the Christian tradition?

3. Do you think the sorts of considerations summarized in the last section of this chapter can be developed and supplemented to show that Christianity is rationally superior to the other major world religious traditions? If so, try to explain how you would make such a case. If not, why not, and would this failure pose a significant apologetical problem?

Further Reading

Anderson, Norman. *Christianity and World Religions.* Downers Grove, IL: InterVarsity, 1984.

Burnett, David. *The Spirit of Hinduism: A Christian Perspective on Hindu Thought.* Tunbridge Wells, Eng.: Monarch, 1992.

Zacharias, Ravi. *The Lotus and the Cross: Jesus Talks with Buddha.* Sisters, OR: Multnomah, 2001.

Part 4

Contemporary Challenges to Christian Commitment

20

The Spirit of Truth

Commitment, Canon, and Community

» **Outline**

- **With a Demonstration of the Spirit's Power**
  - *Specific Ways the Holy Spirit Works in the Preaching of the Gospel*
  - *How the Holy Spirit's Work Makes Faith Reasonable*
    - Psychological versus Epistemological Role of Experiences
    - Analogies with Ordinary Perceptual Beliefs
    - Observation versus Inference in the Confirmation of Hypotheses
    - The Role of Testimonies
- **All Scripture Is Inspired by God**
  - *The Spirit's Role in Understanding and Accepting What the Bible Teaches*
  - *Elements of a Doctrine of Scripture*
  - *The Inerrancy of the Bible*
    - Two Problematic Arguments for *Absolute* Inerrancy
    - An Alternative: Inerrancy Relative to What the Bible Teaches
  - *A Circularity Problem and Two Ways to Avoid It*
    - Historical Reasons to Believe That What the Bible Teaches Is True
    - Rational Belief in the Witness of the Holy Spirit
- **And They Were Filled with the Holy Spirit**
  - *Why the Church Is Justified in Accepting the Biblical Canon*
  - *The Apologetical Importance of the Spirit's Work of Sanctification*

» **Summary**

The Holy Spirit provides people with experiences that create, sustain, and justify their Christian beliefs (in the absence of reasons to think these beliefs are unjustified or false). Support for this claim comes from analogies with perceptual experiences and beliefs. Therefore, Christian hypotheses can be confirmed by inference to the best explanation, observation, and testimony. The Spirit also helps believers reasonably affirm that the Bible is God's Word and to understand and accept what the Bible teaches. Christian apologists are wise to avoid insisting that the Bible is *absolutely* inerrant (even if this is true) and to claim instead that it is true in all it teaches. That the Bible is true in all it teaches can be argued for historically and grounded noninferentially in the witness of the Holy Spirit. The Holy Spirit also worked historically in the church community by guiding it to form the canon, and the Spirit's ongoing work of sanctification provides pragmatic support for Christianity.

» **Basic Terms, Concepts, and Names**

canon
circular argument
dictation model
epistemological role of experience
experience, religious and perceptual
Holy Spirit
inerrancy (absolute versus relative)
inspiration of the Holy Spirit
numinous experience
psychological role of experience
sanctification
special revelation
witness of the Holy Spirit

» **Reflection and Discussion**

» **Further Reading**

> I will ask the Father, and he will give you another Counselor to be with you forever—the Spirit of truth. The world cannot accept him, because it neither sees him nor knows him. But you know him, for he lives with you and will be in you.
>
> John 14:16–17

Christian apologists employ philosophical arguments to defend belief in God and historical arguments to provide grounds for faith in the deity of Jesus. They also attempt to counter the objections of critics and to answer the questions of seekers and doubters. But as argued in part 1, the use of such reasoning is neither necessary nor sufficient to produce and sustain confident and reasonable Christian commitment. We as Christians believe that God the Holy Spirit works in our hearts and minds to give us faith, to lead us to the truth that God wants us to know, and to enable us to interpret it. He does this directly by means of experiences of him and indirectly through experiences with the Bible and the church. This chapter argues that it is reasonable for Christians to believe that these experiences are means God uses to strengthen and warrant faith. The next chapter responds to objections aimed at casting doubt on the authenticity of religious experience, the authority of the Bible, and the presence of Christ in the Christian church.

The focus here and in the next chapter on the role of the Holy Spirit in Christian belief is mostly for the sake of believers and doubters. Many of the grounds, evidences, and reasons for faith in Christ discussed here are available primarily for Christians and only secondarily for non-Christians (through their observations of the life and testimony of Christians). Christians interpret the experiences discussed in terms of the Holy Spirit in light of what the Bible teaches about the manifold ministries of the Spirit in people's lives. Non-Christians who do not believe in the Holy Spirit interpret these experiences of Christians differently. The appeal to the Spirit here is meant to provide reassurance for believers and doubters and an alternative interpretative scheme for seekers.

With a Demonstration of the Spirit's Power

Paul reminds the Corinthians that when he first came to them to proclaim "the testimony about God," his "message and . . . preaching were not with wise and persuasive words, but with a demonstration of the Spirit's power, so that [their] . . . faith might not rest on men's wisdom, but on God's power" (1 Cor. 2:1, 4–5). Let's explore two questions about this. First, what are the specific ways in which the Holy Spirit's power is demonstrated in the preaching of the gospel (and in the ongoing cultivation of a believer's faith)? Second, what is involved in a believer's faith being *based on* the power of God the Holy Spirit?

How the Holy Spirit works in the lives of people to bring them to faith and to enable them to grow in faith is no doubt a highly individual matter that depends on the diverse needs of each person. In the end, exactly what the Spirit does in and for each human being is a mystery. This seems to be what Jesus suggests to Nicodemus when he tells him, "The wind blows wherever it pleases. You hear its sound, but you cannot tell where it comes from or where it is going. So it is with everyone born of the Spirit" (John 3:8). However, there do seem to be a few common features of the Spirit's ministry of leading people to faith in Christ and sustaining and strengthening their faith thereafter. Chapter 18 considered the possibility that the Spirit works in the lives of those who have not heard the gospel. The focus here is on the Holy Spirit's role in the minds and hearts of people to whom the gospel is being or has been preached.

First, the Holy Spirit convinces people of the reality of God (1 Cor. 2:5). Sometimes this is just a firm confidence in the existence of God. Other times it goes beyond that to involve a strong sense or perception of God's very presence. These latter sorts of experiences sometimes have distinctive features, including feelings of both overwhelming power and unconditional love. People who report encounters with God that have these features also often relate having been overcome with awe. Theologians call this kind of experience "numinous."[1] Blaise Pascal had an experience of this sort, which he recorded in a characteristically cryptic manner on a piece of parchment that was found sewn into his clothing after his death.[2] But not everyone's experience of God is this dramatic.

Second, the Holy Spirit convicts people of their sin (John 16:8). To a large extent, this is a natural consequence of being aware of God's reality or sensing the presence of God. A representative biblical example is Isaiah's reaction to his vision of the Lord on the occasion of his commissioning as a prophet: "'Woe to me!' I cried. 'I am ruined! For I am a man of unclean lips, and I live among a people of unclean lips, and my eyes have seen the King, the LORD Almighty'" (Isa. 6:5). Conviction of sin leads to sorrow for sin and a desire to repent (turn away) from it and submit to God. This is what happened to those to whom Peter preached at Pentecost. Peter ended his sermon by saying to the crowd, "God has made this Jesus, whom you crucified, both Lord and Christ" (Acts 2:36). Luke reports that

1. See Rudolph Otto, *The Idea of the Holy,* trans. J. W. Harvey (London: Oxford University Press, 1959). Numinous experiences are different in kind from mystical experiences (in a technical sense of this term), which are characterized instead by a sense of merging with ultimate reality—experiences that cohere better with pantheistic worldviews.

2. Blaise Pascal, "The Memorial," in *Pensées,* trans. A. J. Krailsheimer (London: Penguin, 1966), 309–10.

"when the people heard this, they were cut to the heart and said to Peter and the apostles, 'Brothers, what shall we do?'" (2:37). Peter told them to "repent and be baptized . . . in the name of Jesus Christ for the forgiveness of [their] . . . sins" (2:38). In this context, it is plausible to think that the Holy Spirit was acting to persuade people (1) through the behavior of the apostles, who were speaking in tongues, (2) through the words Peter was preaching to them, and (3) through their minds and hearts as they thought about and reacted to what they were seeing and hearing.

Third, the Holy Spirit confirms that Jesus is the crucified and risen Lord through whom salvation from sin and reconciliation with God are possible (1 Pet. 1:10–12). The word *confirms* is used here because this work of the Spirit depends on a person's having heard the gospel message. As Paul tells the Romans, "Faith comes from hearing the message, and the message is heard through the word of Christ" (10:17). The Holy Spirit can convince people of the reality of God by facilitating an encounter between them and God. The Spirit can convict people of sin by enabling them to understand the condition of their heart in light of their knowledge of God. But the gospel of Christ is based on particular historical events about which one needs to be told in order for one to accept that they occurred and that they accomplished one's salvation. The Spirit's role, therefore, is to provide an inward confirmation of the truth of what the gospel claims concerning what Jesus accomplished. If it were not for this work of the Spirit, it is reasonable to think that we could not explain the initial relatively rapid and widespread acceptance of the gospel message by those who were not eyewitnesses of the resurrection. These converts came from groups that considered the crucifixion of Jesus either a stumbling block (the Jews) or foolishness (the Greeks). Moreover, people throughout the world continue to accept the gospel today—just on the basis of hearing it preached.

Finally, Paul tells the Christians in the Roman church that "the Spirit himself testifies with our spirit that we are God's children" (Rom. 8:16). The author of 1 John agrees with Paul about this: "We know that we live in him and he in us, because he has given us of his Spirit" (4:13). This work of the Holy Spirit does two important things for Christians: (1) It provides us with ongoing assurance that God exists, and (2) it assures us of our salvation in Christ. Thus, this ministry of the Holy Spirit involves the activity of the Spirit discussed above: strengthening faith in God's reality, love, power, forgiveness, and ongoing presence.

We have addressed the question raised above about the specific ways in which the Holy Spirit's power is manifested in the preaching of the gospel (and in the ongoing cultivation of a Christian's faith). Let us turn now to examine what is involved in a believer's faith being *based on* the power of the Holy Spirit. The four roles of the Spirit just discussed clearly provide important psychological and practical advantages to those who respond favorably to the gospel. Faith is required for salvation. Moreover, it is difficult to love and serve God completely when one lacks confidence in God's existence or love. Therefore, a person whose faith is based on the power of the Holy Spirit benefits psychologically and practically. But will such a person also be better off epistemologically as a result of the Spirit's work on his or her behalf? That is, does the ministry of the Holy Spirit make a person's faith reasonable or increase a person's knowledge?

The answer to this question is yes. The ministry of the Holy Spirit creates or contributes to a variety of experiences that not only cause and strengthen Christian belief but also make Christian belief reasonable. Examples of such experiences can be found in the preceding discussion. One is the experience of sensing God's presence. Another is the experience of feeling guilty or ashamed of oneself for being a sinner. Still another is the experience of hearing the gospel. These experiences can produce, sustain, and make reasonable one's beliefs that God is here, that one is a sinner, and that the good news about Jesus is true. They do this in the same way in which perceptual experiences both cause and justify the beliefs based on them. For instance, when I have the visual experience of seeming to see a tree in front of me in circumstances in which I have no reason to think either that there is not or that there is something wrong with my eyes, I find myself with the *belief* that a tree is in front of me. Moreover, everyone agrees that when I have this belief in those circumstances my belief is reasonable, warranted, and justified. If this is true in cases of perceptual experience and belief, then it seems reasonable to think it is also true in cases of Christian experience and belief (see chap. 2 for more on this).

If it is sometimes reasonable to believe, on the basis of having an experience in which one seems to sense the presence of God, that God is present, then some religious experiences are like perceptual experiences. If so, then the hypothesis of God's existence (a hypothesis that part 2

> **The ministry of the Holy Spirit creates or contributes to a variety of experiences that not only cause and strengthen Christian belief but also make Christian belief reasonable.**

argued best explains the existence and design of the universe) can be confirmed to be true on the basis of observation. This is analogous to the way in which my hypothesis that the holes in my back lawn are caused by gophers can be confirmed by my actually watching a gopher dig one of the holes. Moreover, it is one thing to hypothesize, on the basis of historical evidences, that Jesus was raised from the dead. It is still another thing to come to know this on the basis of a personal spiritual encounter with the risen Lord. It is no accident that a standard way of asking people if they are Christians is to ask them if they know the Lord or have met Jesus.

If experiences can confirm belief in God in this way, then one's testimony about one's experiences can also do so, both for oneself at a later time and for others. When people share their testimonies of what God has done or is doing in their lives, they tell stories. These narratives can become powerful evidences of the truth of the Christian faith. Though such accounts are not usually considered part of a Christian apologist's tool kit (along with philosophical arguments and historical evidences), they ought to be. They can at least play the role of preventing the empirical and pragmatic falsification of the Christian hypothesis. Because of such stories, critics cannot reasonably argue that Christianity is false on the ground that it claims encounters with God and dramatic life-changing experiences that never occur. But stories about meeting God and being changed for the better as a result can also play a more positive evidential role. Millions of people throughout history and in the world today claim to have experienced Christ and to have been radically transformed as a result. It is arguable that the best explanation of this is that Jesus is the risen Christ and that God is in him reconciling the world to himself (2 Cor. 5:19).

All Scripture Is Inspired by God

Christians believe that the Holy Spirit works not only to enable people to believe that the gospel is true but also to help people understand and accept what the Bible teaches more broadly. The Bible provides the historical and theological context for the message of the gospel. Christians believe that it tells how God prepared the human race for the coming of Christ in his interactions with ancient Israel; what God did in the life, death, and resurrection of Jesus; and how the Holy Spirit guided the first Christians in their response to and interpretation of these events. In telling these things, the Bible provides a basis for mature Christian belief and practice. Therefore, this role of the Holy Spirit is an important one.

But here it looks as though we may have a circularity problem. The only way we can know about the existence and work of the Holy Spirit as a member of the Trinity

is by reading the Bible. But how do we know that what the Bible teaches about the Holy Spirit is true? It would be to argue in a circle (to assume the conclusion for which we are arguing) to respond by saying that the Holy Spirit tells us that what the Bible teaches about the Holy Spirit is true.

An objective historical case (one that does not appeal illegitimately to the Holy Spirit) can be made for the claim that what the Bible teaches is true. What follows sketches it after discussing the main components of a Christian doctrine of Scripture. This historical argument is not circular, but since it is historical, it can support its conclusion with at most a high degree of probability. Unfortunately, this alone does not provide an adequate basis for full conviction. We can also appeal, as John Calvin did, to the witness of the Holy Spirit as a ground for acceptance of the teachings of Scripture. He believed that the Spirit enables Christians to be confident that the Bible is God's Word.[3] But to avoid circularity, belief that the Spirit plays this role needs to be an article of faith rather than something for which we argue by appealing to what the Bible says about the Spirit. As argued below, it is reasonable for Christians to take it on faith that the Holy Spirit confirms that the Bible is the Word of God.

Christians believe that it is important to accept what the Bible teaches because the Bible is God's written, special revelation to human beings of himself and his will. Recall that God's *general* revelation is what

3. See Bernard Ramm, *The Witness of the Spirit* (Grand Rapids: Eerdmans, 1959), for an exposition of Calvin's views about the role of the Holy Spirit in convincing people that the Bible is the Word of God.

God has made known about himself and his will both in nature (e.g., the design of the cosmos) and in human nature (e.g., our consciences). God's general revelation is accessible to all human beings on the basis of observation and introspection. But according to Christians, God has also revealed himself in a *special* way both in Jesus Christ and in Scripture, which tells us about Jesus Christ. Therefore, God's special revelation is available today only to those people who have either direct or indirect access to a Bible. Moreover, people can benefit from a reception of God's special revelation only if they have an adequate understanding of what it teaches and they respond with faith in and obedience to God.

The traditional Christian understanding of how God chose to reveal himself in and through the Bible is that the Holy Spirit inspired the authors of the various parts of Scripture to write what God wanted them to write. Paul writes to Timothy about "the holy Scriptures, which are able to make you wise for salvation through faith in Christ Jesus." He goes on to affirm that "all Scripture is God-breathed and is useful for teaching, rebuking, correcting and training in righteousness, so that the man of God may be thoroughly equipped for every good work" (2 Tim. 3:15–17). The Greek word translated "God-breathed" here is also translated "inspired" in some versions of the Bible. Paul is clearly referring only to the Hebrew Scriptures (the Christian Old Testament), since he says that Timothy has known them "from infancy" (v. 15). But Christians have extended the concept to cover the New Testament as well. Some reasons for this are discussed below.

Exactly what was involved in the inspiration of the authors of Scripture by the Holy Spirit is a mystery. However, Christians typically reject a "dictation" model according to which the biblical writers were merely passive instruments who recorded only what the Holy Spirit dictated. In this way, Christians view the Bible differently from how Muslims think of the Qur'an (and Mormons the *Book of Mormon*), since the latter hold that their scriptures are entirely of divine origin. Just as Christians think of Jesus, the incarnate Word of God, as being both fully human and fully divine, Christians consider the Bible to be God's written Word, which is also both human and divine in nature.

The writer of 2 Peter does offer an important qualification here, however. Whatever freedom God granted the writers of Scripture was exercised within the limits implied by the following passage: "Above all, you must understand that no prophecy of Scripture came about by the prophet's own interpretation. For prophecy never had its origin in the will of man, but men spoke from God as they were carried along by the Holy Spirit" (1:20–21). Though God gave the biblical authors latitude in their expression, the core of what they expressed was God's Word rather than their own.

If the Bible is God's special revelation by means of the inspiration of the Holy Spirit, then it is authoritative in what it teaches about what we should believe and how we should live. Thus, whenever we have a correct interpretation of Scripture, we may (and we should) evaluate alternative truth claims in light of it. Of course, there may be legitimate questions about whether a given interpretation of the Bible is correct, and if there are, we should be only as confident about the interpretation as warranted by the strength of our reasons for adopting it and the quality of the evidence against it. Though the meanings of the primary teachings of the Bible are arguably relatively clear, there are a number of relatively difficult passages, and some sections are downright obscure. This is one thing that accounts for disagreement among Christians on secondary theological matters in spite of consensus on the central doctrines that have become enshrined in the church's historic creeds and confessions.

Some Christians insist that the Bible can be authoritative for matters of Christian faith and practice only if it is absolutely inerrant—wholly without errors or falsehoods of any kind. This is the absolute inerrancy claim. To many people, this absolute inerrancy claim seems to be inescapable for the Christian for both theological and epistemological reasons. The theological reason is that God would not employ falsehoods in communicating with human beings. A simple argument along these lines for the absolute inerrancy of Scripture is that (1) the Bible is God's Word, (2) God does not utter falsehoods, and therefore (3) the Bible does not contain any false claims. The epistemological reason is that we could not trust the Bible if it had any errors in it. An argument in this vein is that (1) the Bible is authoritative for Christian faith and practice, (2) the Bible can play this role for Christians only if Christians can confidently come to know what to believe and do on the basis of reading it, (3) we can be assured that we can acquire this doctrinal and ethical knowledge from the Bible only if we can be certain that the Bible does not contain any falsehoods, and therefore (4) the Bible is absolutely inerrant.

Though this doctrine of *absolute* inerrancy may be true, there are two reasons Christian apologists would do well to avoid having to affirm it, at least in the context of apologetical conversations. First, the above two arguments for it do not clearly succeed in establishing it. Second, it is difficult to defend. Let's consider the arguments for it first.

As for the theological argument, though it is true that the Bible is God's Word, it is also the case, as we saw above, that God inspired human authors to write it. If God allowed these authors a certain amount of freedom and creativity (and it seems reasonable to think that he did), then they were not merely God's mouthpieces. In that case, even if God does not ever say anything false, it seems possible that those he inspired to write the Scriptures did, at least about relatively unimportant matters.

The epistemological argument falters at premise 3. The only good reason one could give for accepting this premise is the general principle that something can be a reliable source of knowledge only if it is completely infallible (contains no falsehoods or errors whatsoever). But this principle is clearly false. Our five senses can be highly reliable sources of knowledge even though they sometimes lead us astray. Though our senses can and do deceive us, we learn from experience how to tell the difference between reality and illusion.

The doctrine of absolute inerrancy is also difficult to defend. To defend it, a Christian apologist would need to respond to each particular claim of biblical error (or contradiction) by showing that the alleged falsehood is really true (or the alleged contradiction is nonexistent). The problem with this is that over the years critics have come up with quite a few allegations of biblical error. Though in many (and perhaps most) cases it has been possible to respond with convincing reasons for thinking that an allegation of this sort fails (such as by pointing out that a biblical writer intended a claim to be taken metaphorically rather than literally), an apologist would be better off not having to enter this morass of controversy.

Apologists need not defend the claim of absolute biblical inerrancy. For the purpose of making a case for the reasonableness of believing that the central Christian doctrines are true, an apologist need only argue that whatever the Bible *teaches* is true. This would leave open the possibility that there is a false claim in the Bible that is not among the things the Bible teaches. An example of this is the classification of bats as birds in Leviticus 11:13–19. Since this occurs in a section concerning the Old Testament dietary laws (which were rescinded in the New Testament [see Matt. 15:10–11; Acts 10:9–15]), though it is something *claimed* (or at least implied) in the Bible, it seems reasonable to deny that it is something the Bible *teaches*. It is true that an apologist is now saddled with the task of distinguishing what the Bible teaches from what it does not, and this may not always be easy to do. However, the distinction is arguably clear enough in at least the most important cases. After all, the fact that the church has been able to agree on some creeds and statements of faith shows that it is possible to discern at least the most important teachings of Scripture.

In summary, the Christian doctrine of Scripture is that the Bible is God's written, special revelation produced by the

> For the purpose of making a case for the reasonableness of believing that the central Christian doctrines are true, an apologist need only argue that whatever the Bible *teaches* is true.

agency of human writers who were inspired by the Holy Spirit, and therefore it is authoritative for Christian belief and practice. Moreover, the Bible is true at least in whatever it teaches. But is it reasonable for Christians to believe these things about the Bible? Yes. There is an objective and yet inconclusive historical case for this claim. In addition, it is reasonable for Christians to accept this doctrine of Scripture by an appeal, in faith, to the witness of the Holy Spirit.

The historical argument presupposes the general philosophical claim that God could and likely would reveal himself to human beings in a special way (we discussed this claim above). It also builds on the case for the resurrection and deity of Jesus in part 3 (which did not presuppose this doctrine of Scripture but was based entirely on historical evidence). If Jesus is the risen Son of God, then we can trust what he says. We have good historical grounds for believing that Jesus regarded the Old Testament as God's Word, and therefore we have good reason to believe that it is. In addition, to the extent that we have good historical reasons to think that Jesus really said what the Gospel writers report, we have good reason to regard those dominical sayings as the Word of

God. Moreover, Jesus commissioned the apostles to preach the gospel about him to the world. He told them he would send the Holy Spirit to enable them to remember what he had taught them. Since we have good historical grounds for thinking that the New Testament documents were written by an apostle, someone closely associated with an apostle who would be able reliably to record his teaching, or at least someone who faithfully employed apostolic sources, it is reasonable to conclude that the New Testament is God's Word. That is the historical argument.

Is it reasonable for Christians to believe that their confidence that the Bible is God's Word (and thus true in all it teaches) is warranted by the witness of the Holy Spirit? Yes. Just as it is reasonable to believe—solely on the basis of certain kinds of experiences—that God exists (or is present), that we are sinners, and that we can be saved by faith in Jesus, it is also reasonable for us to believe that the Bible is God's Word when we find ourselves with this conviction upon reading or hearing Scripture. It is true that reasonable doubts can and do arise about this (as they do about God's existence, etc.), and when they do, philosophical and historical apologetical arguments may be needed to dispel them (the next chapter looks at such arguments). However, when we read the Bible without experiencing uncertainties of this sort, our belief that God is speaking to us through it is arguably rational. This is especially the case when the context in which we experience the Bible as the Word of God is the Christian community, the church. The next section discusses the role of the Holy Spirit in working through the church to help its members grow in faith.

And They Were Filled with the Holy Spirit

The Christian church has already been implicit in what was said above about the Spirit's work in evangelism and the reading of the Bible. The Holy Spirit is active in the preaching of the gospel (as in the example of Peter's Pentecost sermon). But the good news of Christ is proclaimed in and by the Christian church. Therefore, the Holy Spirit works in the context of the church when he confirms the truth of the gospel. Moreover, the gospel message is the heart of what the Bible teaches. But the Bible is a book that was written by God's people and for God's people. So when the Holy Spirit is active in and through the study of the Bible, he is working in and through the church.

Consequently, finding faith and keeping faith are not things that happen to people in isolation. They occur in the context of the Christian community, the body of Christ. Moreover, the church is not merely a group of people with whom one worships on Sunday or even the collection of all such local worshiping communities around the world. It includes all the people of God throughout history. So when one finds oneself believing that God is real, that Jesus saves, and that the Bible is the Word of God, one finds oneself believing this in a family of faith with a long tradition.

Since one's experience of the witness of the Holy Spirit takes place in this historical and communal context, the best way to describe it is not to say that the Holy Spirit is speaking to *me* about the authority of the Bible. Rather, it is better to say that my experience is that of seeing the Holy Spirit at work in the church. Moreover, one of the primary ways in which Christians normally see the activity of the Spirit in the church is through the church's exposition of Scripture. I believe that God speaks to me through the Bible as I read and hear it read in the context of study, fellowship, and worship with other Christians, each of whom is often having a similar sort of experience.

It is clear how this communal element can provide a powerful strengthening of one's faith in God, the Bible as the Word of God, and central Christian teachings that are based on the church's reading of Scripture throughout history. Human beings have a strong tendency to be influenced by their associates concerning what they believe and value. This is why doubters are best advised to continue fellowshiping and worshiping with a body of believers in spite of their doubt. As I shared in the introduction, my own participation with a group of Christians on a mission trip played an important role in the rehabilitation of my faith. Doubters who instead spend the bulk of their time with unbelievers are likely to experience a further erosion of their faith as a result of the negative influence of these non-Christians.

The Holy Spirit works through the church not only to provide Christians with the experience of confidence that God is revealing himself in the Bible but also to enable us to interpret the Bible more accurately. Though Christians have disagreed with one another about whether every individual Christian should have the authority to interpret Scripture rather than only a small group of church leaders, they have always agreed that the Holy Spirit enables individual Christians to understand the Bible primarily through the church.

Individuals who have shunned the church's teachings by insisting on their own alternative interpretation of Scripture have often (though not invariably) fallen into heresy and schism (division of the church). I say "not invariably" because there have always been reformers whom the Spirit has used to bring an erring church back to conformity with Scripture. But this seems more the exception than the rule.

We have seen that the Spirit plays a number of important roles relative to the Word of God. He inspired the original writers, he works in the church to strengthen the confidence of Christians that the Bible is God's special revelation and true in all it teaches, and he guides the community of faith as it seeks to discern what the Bible teaches and what it means for Christians in their specific cultural and historical contexts. But Christians also believe that the Holy Spirit guided the early church in its gradual discernment concerning which early Christian writings were the Word of God and which were not. The result of this Spirit-led process was the formation of the biblical canon, those writings accepted by the church as authoritative by virtue of being inspired by God. Today, all branches of the historic Christian church agree that the sixty-six books of the Old and New Testaments belong in the biblical canon.[4] As a result of this process of canon

4. However, the Roman Catholic Church and the Eastern Orthodox Church accept a number of books as canonical that were written in the intertestamental period after the close of the Jewish canon. They refer to these works as the Deuterocanonicals (secondary but with canonical status). Protestants call the collection of these works the Apocrypha and do not include them in the biblical canon. In light of this, we should concede that though the guidance of the Holy Spirit results in a substantial amount of agreement, it does not settle all controversies about

formation, a number of other Christian and quasi-Christian writings were passed over. As the next chapter shows, there is currently a fair amount of criticism directed at the church for this selectivity. For now, we will focus on the question of whether the early Christians were justified in limiting the canon as they did.

It will come as no surprise by now that I appeal to the *experience* of the early Christians to argue that their reliance on the Holy Spirit to guide them in forming the canon was reasonable. The experiences of individuals who see themselves as sinners to whom God is speaking through the preaching of the gospel justify them in believing that Jesus died for their sins. Moreover, the experiences of Christians hearing or reading the Bible with fellow Christians justify them in believing that they are hearing or reading the Word of God. In the same way, the experiences of the early Christians in various churches for whom some Christian writings came to play an authoritative role and some did not justified them in eventually coming to the consensus that some of these writings were divinely inspired and some were not. A verse in 2 Peter may reflect an early acceptance of (at least some of) Paul's epistles as authoritative in this way. The author refers to people who distort difficult passages in Paul's writings "as they do the other Scriptures" (3:16).

At the same time, various New Testament documents reflect the existence of false teachers and deceivers whose teachings were to be rejected. John is especially intent to warn his readers about these people: "Dear friends, do not believe every

spirit, but test the spirits to see whether they are from God, because many false prophets have gone out into the world" (1 John 4:1). In the next two verses, John states a criterion for Christians to employ in determining whether a spirit is from God: "This is how you can recognize the Spirit of God: Every spirit that acknowledges that Jesus Christ has come in the flesh is from God, but every spirit that does not acknowledge Jesus is not from God. This is the spirit of the antichrist" (4:2–3; see also 2 John 7). This criterion provided the early church with a doctrinal test of the sort they probably used to discern which writings were inspired (and so appropriately included in the canon) and which were not. In particular, it justified them in excluding what came to be known as Gnostic texts, which denied that God had really become incarnate in Jesus.[5]

This sort of criterion, which provides an objective basis on which to discern the guidance of the Holy Spirit, was not chosen arbitrarily by early Christians like John. After all, John starts his first epistle by affirming, "That which was from the beginning, which we have heard, which we have seen with our eyes, which we have looked at and our hands have touched— this we proclaim concerning the Word of life" (1:1). The Second Epistle of Peter makes a similar claim: "We did not follow cleverly invented stories when we told you about the power and coming of our Lord Jesus Christ, but we were eyewitnesses of his majesty" (1:16). Peter and John had seen the transfigured and eventually risen Jesus himself in the flesh and so knew that he was God incarnate. In light of this, it was reasonable for the early Christians to

---

what counts as Holy Scripture (and even about how best to interpret every part of what all agree belongs in the Bible).

5. The next chapter discusses such Gnostic writings.

follow the Holy Spirit's lead in denying the canonical status of any text that denied or cast doubt on this.

This chapter has argued that it is reasonable for Christians to believe that the Holy Spirit has been and continues to be active in the church. We focused on the Holy Spirit's role in initially leading the church to affirm the canon, in continuing to confirm to the body of Christ that the canonical Scriptures are the Word of God, and in guiding Christians in every generation to understand and apply the Bible's teachings. We also discussed the role of the Spirit in drawing people into the church in the first place. The church is important not only because it is the community to which both the gospel and Scripture were entrusted by God but also because it is the fellowship of people whose acceptance of the gospel and nurture in Scripture have resulted in their transformation by the Holy Spirit into people who manifest love for God, one another, and the world.

This work of the Spirit of sanctification (delivering Christians from the power of sin and making them progressively more and more like Christ) has substantial apologetical value. The Gospel of John reports that Jesus told his disciples during their last night together that "by this all men will know that you are my disciples, if you love one another" (13:35). The gospel of Christ promises to deliver from sin those who trust in Christ and to reconcile them in love to God and one another. The church is the community in which this love ought to be exhibited if there are ever people genuinely capable of it. Therefore, seekers who are wondering whether the gospel is true should pay close attention to the community of those who profess it to see whether they practice what they preach. Does the history of the church provide an adequate demonstration of positive life change? Have Christians improved the world in substantial ways as a result of their sacrificial love? The answer to both of these questions is yes, but we will not defend these affirmative answers until the end of the next chapter, which replies to objections to the claims argued for in this chapter.

Reflection and Discussion

1. What specific experiences have you had that have produced and sustained your confidence that God exists and that the gospel is true (and in some cases, perhaps, that God is present with you at a certain time)? Do you think these experiences can suffice by themselves to make your belief in God and the truth of the gospel reasonable? Why or why not?

2. Do you agree that Christian apologists need not defend the thesis of the *absolute* inerrancy of the Bible and that it would be good enough for apologetic purposes to defend the claim that the Bible is true in all it teaches? Why or why not?

3. As you think about both the history of the Christian church and the Christian church around the world today, in what ways does it seem that the Holy Spirit has been active in the church to do the work of God? Give as many specific examples as you can.

Further Reading

Alston, William P. *Perceiving God: The Epistemology of Religious Experience.* Ithaca, NY: Cornell University Press, 1991.

Cohn, Harvie M., ed. *Inerrancy and Hermeneutic: A Tradition, a Challenge, a Debate.* Grand Rapids: Baker, 1988.

Plantinga, Alvin. *Warranted Christian Belief.* New York: Oxford University Press, 2000.

21

The Spirit of the Age

Critiques from the Social Sciences

» **Outline**

- **The Future of an Illusion: The Challenge of Psychology**
  - *A Freudian Critique of Religious Belief*
    - The Psychological Explanation of All Religious Belief
    - Psychological Origins and Epistemological Deficiencies
  - *A Christian Reply*
    - The Explanation for Religious Belief Is Not Merely Psychological
    - The Critique Commits the Genetic Fallacy and Backfires
- **The Bible as Literature: The Challenge of Historical Criticism**
  - *The Challenge of Biblical Methodologism*
    - The Alleged Need to Rely on Experts to Understand the Bible
    - The Sufficiency of the Spirit for Basic Comprehension
  - *The Challenge of the Naturalistic Historical Critical Method*
    - The Alleged Need to Read the Bible as If There Were No God
    - How Criticism Lacks Objectivity and Needs the Spirit
- **The Dark Side of the Church: The Challenge of History**
  - *The Church's Alleged Abuse of Power in Canon Formation*
    - Objection: Motivation by Self-interest Rather than Guidance by the Spirit
    - Reply: The Church's Primary Interest in Serving God
  - *The Church's Actual Admitted Abuses of Power*
    - Objection: The Church Has Caused More Evil and Injustice than Good
    - Reply: The Church's Evil Due to Sin and Good Due to the Spirit

» **Summary**

Critics allege that Christian experiences can be explained in naturalistic terms rather than in terms of the Holy Spirit. A Freudian critique of religious beliefs purports to explain them solely in terms of psychological factors. But such arguments are unconvincing, fallacious, and applicable to nontheistic beliefs as well. The claim that the illumination of the Holy Spirit is both necessary and sufficient for Christians to understand the core teachings of the Bible is challenged by biblical methodologism (according to which expert methods are also required for understanding) and the naturalistic historical critical method (according to which the Bible should be studied as if God does not exist). But Christians can reasonably rely on the Spirit alone for basic understanding of the central claims of the Bible. Also, the work of the Spirit is arguably required for comprehending Scripture, because historical criticism is inadequate and insufficiently objective by itself. Finally, critics allege that the church abused its power in the formation of the canon and in other injustices in history. Apologists can provide good reasons to deny the former claim. They can accept and explain the latter and yet point to good things done by the church as well.

» **Basic Terms, Concepts, and Names**

biblical methodologism (strong and moderate)
canon
Freud, Sigmund
genetic fallacy
Gnostic documents
naturalistic historical critical method

» **Reflection and Discussion**

» **Further Reading**

> The time will come when men will not put up with sound doctrine. Instead, to suit their own desires, they will gather around them a great number of teachers to say what their itching ears want to hear. They will turn their ears away from the truth and turn aside to myths. But you, keep your head in all situations, endure hardship, do the work of an evangelist, discharge all the duties of your ministry.
>
> 2 Timothy 4:3–5

The previous chapter argued that it is reasonable for Christians to believe that the Holy Spirit works in the circumstances, minds, and hearts of people to produce and sustain the beliefs that God is real, that they are sinners, that the gospel is true, that the Bible is the Word of God, and that the Christian church is the primary context in which God is at work to enable people to mature in faith and to serve God, one another, and the world. Christians are justified in believing these things about the Spirit's activities on the basis of various kinds of experiences—at least when they do not have good reasons to think either that there are better explanations of them that do not appeal to the Holy Spirit or that the Spirit is not working in these ways. This chapter considers and criticizes such alternative explanations of Christian experience. It also states and replies to other objections

that tend to undermine Christian confidence in the role of the Holy Spirit in the cultivation of reasonable commitment to God in Christ.

The first section looks at the claim that experiences Christians believe have a supernatural cause are better explained in purely naturalistic (typically psychological) terms. The second section resumes the examination begun in chapter 13 of the employment of historical criticism in biblical studies. It focuses on uses of that method that are based on purely naturalistic presuppositions, which thus rule out the possibility that the Bible is the Word of God rather than a collection of merely human works. The third section responds to recent charges that the Christian church both (1) illegitimately excluded many Christian works from the canon and (2) has produced more evil than good in the world. What both of these claims have in common is the assumption that the church has been characterized throughout history by the human abuse of power rather than by the divine guidance and empowerment of the Holy Spirit. Like the previous two objections, this one purports to explain things that Christians attribute to God in purely naturalistic (e.g., sociopolitical) terms.

Before we turn to these objections, we need to address a concern that is not driven by naturalistic assumptions. Another sort of objection to the claims of chapter 20 is based on the observation that other religious traditions exist whose adherents attribute a divine origin to their religious experiences, sacred scriptures, and faith communities. In light of this, can Christians be justified in believing—solely on the basis of experience—that God is found exclusively or even primarily in their lives, the Bible, and the Christian church and not at all (or at least not equally) in these other religions?

In reply, the mere existence of these alternatives should not pose a serious threat to the claim that Christians have experienced God through the ministries of the Holy Spirit. After all, as already suggested, the Holy Spirit may be working to draw people to Christ in these other contexts as well. A problem does arise, however, when we affirm the Christian exclusivist thesis that salvation is possible only through Jesus Christ. This means that the body of Christ and the Scriptures that contain the gospel of Christ are the focal point of God's revelation and redemption. A case can be made for the superiority of Christian experience over non-Christian religious experiences along the lines sketched in chapters 18 and 19, so we will not say more about this objection here.

The Future of an Illusion: The Challenge of Psychology

Christians believe that their convictions about God and Christianity are a result of God's revelation of himself in nature and through the Bible and Jesus Christ. Some critics object that theistic beliefs in general and Christian beliefs in particular originated instead in the human psyche. According to this view, God does not really exist. Instead, the idea of God is one that human beings developed and then projected onto the world in the form of a belief that a supreme being really exists. These psychological processes of concept formation and belief projection are not conscious and deliberate. Rather, they are products of the unconscious mind. Various specific explanations have been offered concerning the psychological causes that account for this alleged work of the unconscious. What all these explanations have in common is the assumption that people believe in God and commit themselves to particular religious traditions only because doing so satisfies some of their important psychological desires. Let's put this psychological challenge into the form of an argument:

1. The best explanation for the existence of religious beliefs is that they satisfy some important human psychological desires.
2. If 1 is true, then religious beliefs are false, unjustified, or both.
3. Therefore, religious beliefs are false, unjustified, or both.

Before we evaluate this argument, let's look at a few of the theories that posit specific psychological desires alleged to be the cause of religious belief. Sigmund Freud (1856–1939) was one of the most influential proponents of this sort of objection to religious convictions. Though his theories are complex, we can extract some simple ideas from them to demonstrate the initial plausibility of this argument. Among the desires Freud identified as contributing to the formation of religious beliefs (and the adoption of religious practices) are the desire for security in a life that is full of potential harms and inevitably ends in death; the desire to control the world and one's own aggressive and sexual impulses; the desire (based on one's childhood experiences) to have an all-powerful father and a virgin mother; the desire to recapture the infantile experience of "oneness" with one's mother; the desire to avoid the helplessness one experienced as an infant; and the desire to make sense of the world.[1]

Though it is debatable whether all human beings possess each of these desires, it is clearly the case that we all desire, for instance, to find security in the face of death and to have an adequate degree of control over what happens to us. Given this, the question is whether these desires are the best explanation for the existence of religious beliefs (as claimed by premise 1). Do Christians believe in God and heaven only because doing so helps them cope with the fears of danger and death?

Perhaps some do, but it is arguable that not all Christians do. A much more plausible hypothesis is that people *hope* that God exists because they fear death. Arguably, the fear of death and the belief

that a number of desires could not be fulfilled if death were the end (such as the desire for ongoing loving relationships and the happiness produced by them) combine to cause us to hope that God exists and to make it reasonable for us to hope that there is a God. However, it would be irrational to *believe* that God exists simply because we *want* a God to exist to provide us with security in the face of death. This is to believe something solely on the basis of wishful thinking, and wishful thinking is not a rational basis for belief production. Is it plausible to think that human beings are this irrational? It is more likely that we believe God exists for other reasons or on other grounds and that this belief functions in such a way as to provide a sense of security about dangers and death.

A critic may object here, believing that whatever reasons we may provide for believing that God exists (whether philosophical or experiential) are merely rationalizations and that the true originating cause of belief in God is fear of harm or nonexistence. Though this claim does not do sufficient justice to human rationality, let's grant it for the sake of argument and move on to consider premise 2.

If a critic is correct in thinking that the best explanation of the origin of religious belief is the fear of death, does it follow that religious beliefs are false, unjustified, or both? No. It clearly does not follow that religious beliefs are false. If people believe that God exists only because they want to believe this, it does not follow that God does not exist. Suppose I believe that it won't rain on my picnic simply because I do not want it to rain. Does this mean it *will* rain? Obviously not. Does it follow that belief in God is unjustified? Not necessarily. Someone could have come to be-

---

1. Freud has other similar psychological explanations of religious belief. See especially *The Future of an Illusion* (New York: Norton, 1975).

lieve in God on an irrational ground (such as wishful thinking) and yet later could have acquired good reasons or grounds to continue to believe this (in the form, for instance, of the cosmological or teleological argument or of an experience of God's presence). Suppose my belief that it won't rain is initially based only on wishful thinking. At that point, this belief is unjustified. If I subsequently acquire good evidence for this belief (e.g., by reading the weather report in the newspaper), then my belief becomes justified.

A critic who employs premise 2 (when premise 1 is interpreted as having to do only with the origins of belief) commits the genetic fallacy. People commit the genetic fallacy when they argue that, because a belief has a certain psychological origin (a certain "genesis"), it follows that it cannot be justified. We have seen above that this is not the case. In sum, there are good reasons to reject premise 1, but even if we allow that some religious beliefs are initially caused by wishful thinking, there are good reasons to deny premise 2. Therefore, the argument does not succeed in providing adequate grounds for accepting its conclusion.

Moreover, the type of reasoning employed in the argument can cut both ways. A critic of atheistic or agnostic beliefs could argue that the best explanation for them is that their possessors are afraid of the prospect of there being a God to whom they are accountable and who would require them to change their lives. The idea is that unbelievers are motivated to adopt their intellectual positions because they do not want God to exist. Since both the argument against theistic belief and this argument against nontheistic belief have the same form, critics who accept the first will be obligated to affirm the second as well. But this would backfire on them and have the effect of neutralizing the force of their critique of theistic belief.[2]

The Bible as Literature:
The Challenge of Historical Criticism

The previous chapter argued that it is reasonable for Christians to think that the Holy Spirit enables them to believe that the Bible is the Word of God and therefore true at least in all it teaches. It also argued that Christians are warranted in thinking that the Holy Spirit guides them in their interpretation of Scripture. It is natural for Christians to be convinced that, when they read the Bible, God speaks to them in and through the words it contains. When Christians have this experience of confidence that God is communicating with them through Scripture, it is reasonable for them to believe that this is true, at least in the absence of any reasons to think otherwise.

But the rise of the science of biblical criticism brought with it the assumption that Christians cannot properly understand the Bible unless their reading of it is mediated by an application of certain critical methodologies. Since most Christians are not trained to employ such methods, it follows that they must rely on biblical experts to achieve a reliable interpretation

2. Notice that though chap. 5 argued on scriptural grounds that many people are motivated not to believe in God because of their desire to continue sinning, it did not claim that this psychological motivation for unbelief rendered agnostic or atheistic positions unjustified or false. On the contrary, agnostics and atheists usually have reasons for their unbelief such as the problem of evil and the problem of divine hiddenness.

of Scripture. To a certain extent, this assumption and its consequence are arguably right. The more a person knows about biblical genres, the historical and cultural context within which Scripture was written, and the theological purposes of the biblical authors (among other things), the better able the person will be to understand as fully as possible what the Bible teaches.[3] These characteristics of the Bible are things one must learn from other human beings. However, if Christians who are not experts in biblical criticism are *completely* dependent on biblical scholars for their understanding of Scripture, then the role of the Holy Spirit in nonexpert individual interpretation is completely eclipsed.

Some may argue that as long as the experts rely on the Holy Spirit for guidance in their use of critical methodology to understand what the Bible teaches, the Spirit can still speak to untrained Christians through these teachers. But this position presupposes a view about the relationship between most Christians and the Bible that is analogous to what evidentialism presupposes about how Christians are related to the truth about God's existence. Recall that an evidentialist says that it is not reasonable to believe that God exists or that Christianity is true apart from adequate philosophical arguments and historical evidences. In a similar way, a biblical methodologist holds that it is not reasonable for Christians to believe that they have interpreted the Bible properly apart from the employment of the proper historical and literary methods. But if this

3. A helpful resource for Bible study that provides a general discussion of topics like this is Gordon D. Fee and Douglas Stuart, *How to Read the Bible for All Its Worth: A Guide to Understanding the Bible*, 3rd ed. (Grand Rapids: Zondervan, 2003).

is true, it threatens to limit unduly the role of the Holy Spirit in the direct guidance of many individual Christians who are not biblical scholars.

According to *strong* biblical methodologism, Christians cannot understand the Bible at all apart from critical methodologies. *Moderate* biblical methodologism holds instead that reliance on such methods is needed only for a *complete* comprehension of the Bible. This latter view is consistent with the claim that the work of the Holy Spirit can suffice to enable untrained individual Christians to understand at least the core or central teachings of Scripture. It also allows for the possibility that Christians can *benefit from* expert help in their grasp of these central teachings even though they may not *need* such help. An important exception to the moderate view is that all untrained Christians must rely on the expertise of biblical translators to have a Bible they can read or hear in a language they can understand. But this minimal requirement still allows much room for the Holy Spirit's guidance. It is true that Christians claiming the Spirit's guidance sometimes disagree in their interpretation of the Bible. However, these disagreements tend to be about matters that are relatively secondary. The church's historic consensus about the central claims of Christianity provides a good reason to believe that the guidance of the Holy Spirit can suffice for a basic understanding of the most important teachings of the Bible. Therefore, the church's agreement also makes it reasonable to reject the strong version of biblical methodologism.

There are other good reasons to reject the strong version of biblical methodologism, which precludes the direct role of the Holy Spirit in guiding individual Christians in their interpretation of the central teachings of the Bible. For one thing, there are both biblical and experiential grounds for concluding that the Holy Spirit is given to every person who gives his or her life to Christ (see Acts 2:38). For another thing, biblical grounds exist for thinking that the Holy Spirit guides all Christians to know the truth (not just the apostles to whom Jesus announced in John 14:26 that he would send the Holy Spirit). First John says, "But you have an anointing from the Holy One, and all of you know the truth" (2:20) and "As for you, the anointing you received from him remains in you, and you do not need anyone to teach you" (2:27). Again, this does not mean that exegetical and hermeneutical methodology cannot be beneficial and even at least sometimes and to some extent necessary. It just means that these methods are not always necessary. A final point against strong biblical methodologism is that the central teachings of the Bible are plain enough to be understood without the use of critical methodology.

This section mentioned the possibility of biblical scholars' relying on the Holy Spirit in their use of critical methods to study the Bible. There is good reason to believe that many experts in biblical criticism do this, to the great benefit of the church of Christ. However, much of what goes today by the name of historical biblical criticism deliberately rules out this sort of partnership between human beings and God in the interpretation of Scripture. We have already considered this sort of approach in chapter 14 in connection with whether it is reasonable to believe the New Testament miracle reports. Recall that many historians who study the Bible adopt a strong form of methodological naturalism according to which scientific historians should appeal only to natural causes in formulating historical explanations of historical events. There is an analogous version of methodological naturalism that many biblical critics presuppose in their study of the Bible as a whole. According to a former biblical critic who was trained by Rudolph Bultmann, the basic principle here is that "research is conducted *ut si Deus non daretur* ("as if there were no God").[4] Even many biblical scholars who believe that God exists and that the Bible is in some sense the Word of God (or can *become* the Word of God in some circumstances) adopt this principle. Clearly, those who do cannot consistently rely on the Holy Spirit's guidance in their study of the Bible.

Let us call the method of biblical exegesis that presupposes this form of methodological naturalism the naturalistic historical critical method (biblical naturalism for short). Biblical naturalism differs from the biblical methodologism argued against above in that it rules out *completely* any role for the Holy Spirit in biblical interpretation for both those without special training in biblical exegesis and biblical scholars. The reasoning behind the adoption of biblical naturalism rather than a method that relies to at least some extent on the guidance of the Holy Spirit is something like this:

1. Biblical naturalism is more objective and scientific than any method of Bible study that involves reliance on the guidance of the Holy Spirit.
2. If 1, then biblical naturalism should be employed to study the Bible instead of any method that involves

4. Eta Linnemann, *Historical Criticism of the Bible: Methodology or Ideology? Reflections of a Bultmannian Turned Evangelical*, trans. Robert W. Yarbrough (Grand Rapids: Baker, 1990), 84.

reliance on the guidance of the Holy Spirit.

3. Therefore, biblical naturalism should be used for biblical interpretation rather than any method that involves reliance on the guidance of the Holy Spirit.

There are good reasons not to accept the premises of this argument.

A number of reasons exist for thinking that premise 1 is doubtful.[5] In the first place, the most objective approach to the study of an aspect of the Bible would take into account everything that others have written on the same topic. However, not all the relevant literature is (or could be) consulted by biblical scholars. There is just too much of it. As a result, scholars need to be selective in the use of their sources, and these choices are made on the basis of judgments about which studies are valuable and which are not. But these evaluations are often made on the basis of considerations such as the extent to which the researcher agrees with the methods employed and the conclusions reached by the authors of the studies. Once scholars adopt a certain approach and develop a certain point of view, they are unlikely to consider paths and positions with which they disagree. There is a substantial amount of disagreement among biblical critics about fundamental matters. Therefore, however "objective" they are in their study of Scripture, the result is not a growing consensus about how to interpret the Bible. These disagreements tend to persist because scholars become deeply entrenched in their perspectives. Scholars are unlikely to change their minds because their reputations are strongly tied to the

5. I rely on ibid., chap. 6, for most of these.

views they have defended in the literature. Moreover, there is a tendency to respect those with whom they have fundamental agreements and to dismiss those considered by their group to have less prestige (by virtue, for instance, of holding "uncritical" or "naive" views about the Bible).

Perhaps the most significant way in which scientific objectivity is compromised in the practice of biblical naturalism is through the way in which an interpreter's ideology often drives his or her methodology. We can see this most clearly in the study of the Gospels and in the quest for the historical Jesus discussed in chapter 13. For instance, New Testament scholars with socialist economic and political orientations can have a tendency to conclude that the historical Jesus was primarily a social reformer or revolutionary (rather than God the Son incarnate). They can justify this by arguing that only the sayings of Jesus that support this view are authentic and that anything suggesting otherwise was put into Jesus' mouth by the early church. But these sorts of decisions about what Jesus said are highly subjective, and it seems clear that they are often motivated by an interpreter's preexisting ideological biases. In most cases, a scholar's historical Jesus (and there are numerous incompatible accounts of the historical Jesus) is made in his or her own image—a reflection of the beliefs and values he or she brought *to* rather than found *in* the biblical text.

As a result, there are many reasons for thinking that biblical naturalism is not scientific and objective at all. Might it be at least *more* objective than any method that relies to at least some extent on the guidance of the Holy Spirit? A Christian apologist must concede that a reliance on the guidance of the Holy Spirit is not a fully objective method of biblical exegesis, since it is not a method that is accessible to anyone regardless of his or her faith orientation, it is not learned solely on the basis of human instruction, and it is not employable exclusively at the will of its user. It is instead a means of biblical interpretation available only to people in whom the Holy Spirit dwells, given as a gift from God, and operative only at the will of God himself. However, if we measure the degree of objectivity of a method by the amount of agreement it makes possible among a relatively large and diverse group of people, then a method of biblical interpretation that relies on the Holy Spirit arguably comes out looking more objective than biblical naturalism. A look at the experience of Christians in the church throughout history provides substantial evidence that, at least with respect to the fundamental tenets of the Christian faith contained in the creeds, there has been more agreement about what the Bible teaches among Christians who have relied on the Holy Spirit than among the community of scholars who practice biblical naturalism. Therefore, biblical naturalism is not very scientific and objective, and it is not clearly more objective than a method that relies on the Holy Spirit. As a result, there is good reason to doubt premise 1.

But suppose we assume for the sake of argument that premise 1 is true. Would it follow that biblical naturalism is preferable to any method that depends at least to some extent on the guidance of the Holy Spirit? That is, is there good reason to think that premise 2 is true? The answer to this question is no. From the standpoint of the case in parts 2 and 3 of this book for Christian creation monotheism, a method of biblical interpretation that involves the Holy Spirit is preferable to biblical naturalism. If there are good reasons to believe God exists and that this God became incarnate in Jesus Christ, then there is good reason to rely on God's help in understanding the book that is a revelation of God and a record of his incarnation. If it is indeed the case that the Bible is God's Word rather than merely a collection of human documents, then it is reasonable to think that, to be in the best position to discern the meaning of a passage of Scripture, one must be guided, at least in part, by God himself. So even if biblical naturalism is more objective than any method that includes the guidance of the Holy Spirit (and there are good reasons to doubt this claim, as argued above), it does not follow that the use of the former ought to be preferred to an employment of the latter.

There are good reasons to think that a method of Bible study that presupposes

> **If it is indeed the case that the Bible is God's Word rather than merely a collection of human documents, then it is reasonable to think that, to be in the best position to discern the meaning of a passage of Scripture, one must be guided, at least in part, by God himself.**

that God exists, that the Bible is God's Word, and that the Holy Spirit guides one to understand it is preferable to a method that requires one to set aside all these assumptions. A number of subjective experiences of various sorts that Christians believe are prompted by the Holy Spirit are arguably required for one to be in the best position to appreciate, understand, and accept what the Bible claims and teaches. For instance, the Bible teaches that all human beings are sinners (Rom. 3:23). The fullest understanding and appropriation of this truth arguably requires full, subjective access to the evil condition of our own hearts made possible only when the Holy Spirit convicts us of sin. Moreover, a personal, subjective experience of the risen Christ seems necessary to make us fully confident that he was resurrected, that he is God, and that he was (and is) capable of performing miracles and predicting future events.

A purely naturalistic and "objective" method of Bible study encourages one to withhold belief about these things and even to be downright skeptical about them. The critical spirit that goes along with this approach at least tends to dampen the enthusiasm with which one turns to the Word of God for instruction, direction, encouragement, and consolation. To the extent that Christians have good reason to believe that the Bible is God's Word, then, they have good reason to avoid the naturalistic historical critical method of reading the Bible. So there is good reason for Christians to reject 3, which is the conclusion of the above argument. What this means is that Christians are well advised to turn to the Holy Spirit for guidance in interpreting Scripture. It does not mean, however, that Christians should not make

use of any of the methods of historical biblical criticism. As said earlier, and as shown in chapter 22, it is important for Christians to employ these methods for the fullest possible understanding of the Bible. Rather, only the approach that presupposes methodological naturalism should be avoided.

The Dark Side of the Church: The Challenge of History

The previous chapter argued that Christians are justified in believing that the Holy Spirit has been at work in the church throughout history. This activity of the Spirit includes both guiding the church in confirming the canon of Scripture and then working through God's Word in the lives of individual people to transform them for the better and to use them to bring God's transforming love to the world. But critics argue that (1) the formation of the canon was a merely human process in which the church abused its power by suppressing some early Christian voices in favor of those that served its interests and that (2) the church has continued to abuse its power in various ways throughout history. The result has been so much pain, suffering, and injustice that it is unreasonable to believe that God is at work in the Christian church.

These sorts of charges have been leveled against the church in the guise of a best-selling novel by Dan Brown called *The Da Vinci Code*. Though the critique is embedded in a fictional narrative, the author presents his character's arguments in such a way as to blur the line between historical fact and fiction. The end result is to leave many readers with questions and doubts about both the central historical claims of Christianity and the work of God in and through the church. Christian apologists are well advised to familiarize themselves with the novel and to be prepared to reply to the historical arguments contained in it. What follows is a consideration of the general sort of critique contained in the novel (without, however, referring to its content).

Critics such as Brown and those on whom he draws often employ the following type of argument to reject the church's position that the Holy Spirit guided the early church to recognize an authoritative biblical canon as the entirety of the Word of God:

1. History shows that the Christian church formed the canon by including those materials that served its interests and excluding those that did not.
2. If 1 is true, then the biblical canon is not a result of the guidance of the church by the Holy Spirit, and therefore the Bible is not the only authoritative Word of God.
3. Therefore, the biblical canon is not a result of the guidance of the church by the Holy Spirit and is not the only authoritative Word of God.

The general idea is that the church had some kind of self-serving reasons to choose some writings rather than others and that its selection of works to honor as authoritative was motivated only by these reasons. Its claim that it was guided by the Holy Spirit in this process was, according to critics, only an attempt to render its decision immune to criticism.

A more specific case for premise 1 usually goes something like this. In the first few centuries after Christ, incompatible forms of Christianity emerged as a result of variant understandings of the events surrounding the life and death of Jesus. The groups adhering to these different versions of Christianity competed with one another to become the dominant and eventually exclusive interpreter of the Jesus story. In the end, the most powerful group won by suppressing the voices of the alternative groups. This victory made it possible for members of this group to reserve the title of the Christian church for themselves, to classify only those writings agreeing with their point of view as canonical and so authoritative, and to decide which theological positions were orthodox and which were heterodox by appeal to these favored writings. As a result, this group held the power to decide who would be incorporated into the community in order to be saved and who would be excluded or excommunicated, with the result of being damned.

A number of observations can be made in reply. First, though it is true that many incompatible interpretations of the Jesus story existed (among which was the dualistic Gnostic approach that followed Plato in denigrating matter and the body, thus making a genuine divine incarnation problematic), the eventual orthodox perspective resided primarily in the earliest documents that had the best historical claim of being rooted in genuine eyewitness apostolic sources. Writings with incompatible theological orientations (such as the Gnostic documents) are generally dated later and also less clearly associated with authentic apostolic traditions.

Second, the story told above implicitly excludes any significant role for God in guiding the church to think rightly about who Jesus was and what he did. It presupposes that a purely naturalistic historical explanation can be given of what shape the church, its canon, and its orthodoxy eventually took. But if the philosophical and historical arguments in parts 2 and 3 are cogent, then we have good reason to believe that God exists, that God was at work in Jesus, and that God guides his people to acquire an understanding of what he accomplished in Christ adequate for God to fulfill his purposes for human beings.

Third, the narrative characterizes the process of canon formation as a struggle for power. However, it is more reasonable to think that the first Christians were primarily motivated by a desire to know the truth about Jesus and that they responded most favorably to those writings that seemed most reasonably to tell the truth.

Fourth, the formation of the canon was arguably a gradual process that resulted from an emerging consensus on the part of most of the congregations that comprised the early Christian church. Accordingly, it was not a consequence of deliberate decisions made by a few powerful individuals or groups. Moreover, it is likely that the canonical materials were favored because of the way in which they facilitated the church's worship of God and service to the world rather than because of any way in which they served some self-interested goals of the church.

Finally, the above account leaves unexplained what reason the church would have had for wanting to exercise self-serving power over people. Though it is true that

the church has done some horrible things in the name of God throughout history (and we discuss some of these things below), there is no reason to think that the church's primary goal has been to amass power for itself so as to exploit and oppress people. But this is the sort of assumption that underlies the critic's reasoning.

In light of these responses, it is reasonable to resist accepting premise 1 if we interpret it, as the critic does, to mean that the Christian church limited the canon to those texts that served its interests—given a narrow and self-serving understanding of what those interests were. However, if we think of the church's interests as consisting primarily in the worship and service of God and the spread of the gospel of Christ for the salvation of the world, then it is reasonable to think that premise 1 is true. But given this reading of 1, premise 2 is arguably false. If the church formed the canon on the basis of recognizing which documents would enable it to glorify and obey God, then it is reasonable to think that the Holy Spirit was involved, guiding the church in this process, and that the end result is consequently the authoritative Word of God.

Though this may blunt the force of the first objection mentioned at the beginning of this section, we still have to consider and reply to the second. This is the charge that the Christian church has perpetrated so much pain, suffering, and injustice throughout its history that it is unreasonable to believe that it is the vehicle of the Holy Spirit's saving work. It is not difficult to find historical instances of church-instigated evils. Most educated people could easily construct a list of the general moral failings of the Christian church. Such a list would likely include the Crusades (military expeditions from Christian Europe to recapture the Holy Land [Palestine] from the Muslims in the eleventh to the fourteenth century), the Inquisition (a court set up by the Roman Catholic Church in the Middle Ages to seek out and punish heretics), witch hunts and trials (such as those in Salem, Massachusetts, in 1692), anti-Semitism (the persecution of Jews on the grounds that they were responsible for the death of Christ), and the sanctioning of slavery. More recently, the Christian church has become notorious for sex scandals and exploitation involving evangelical televangelists (among others) and a history of child molestation by some Roman Catholic priests (made worse by cover-ups and light penalties). The church has also been blamed for treating women and homosexuals unjustly.

The first thing a Christian apologist should do when confronted with accusations such as these is to admit that both the institutional Christian church and many individual Christians have done many wicked things throughout history and that the specific examples of the sort mentioned above are among them. Acknowledgment of these sins is important both for the sake of honesty and to find common ground with the person lodging the complaint.

Moreover, it is important to affirm that the church is without excuse and therefore to blame for these crimes. However, though the church has no *excuse* for these wrongs, it does have an *explanation* for them.[6] This explanation is based on the doctrine of sin. The Bible teaches not only that all human beings have sinned (Rom. 3:23) but also that individual Christians

Though the church has no *excuse* for these wrongs, it does have an *explanation* for them.

continue to sin (1 John 1:8). It also provides a strong basis for concluding that all Christian communities are flawed in some way (as evidenced by Paul's epistles to various churches and the letters to the seven Asian churches in Rev. 2–3). The Christian doctrine of sin leads us to *expect* Christians and Christian churches to be engaged in wrongdoing. The church's fulfillment of this expectation contributes to the confirmation of the Christian worldview.

But it is also crucial to point out the many good things Christians and Christian groups have done throughout history. Among these are contributions to the growth of science (by providing scientists with important presuppositions, sanctions, motivations, and regulations),[7] contributions to human freedom and welfare (by means of the abolitionist movement against slavery; legal and educational reforms on behalf of women; the civil rights movement; labor reforms, including child labor laws; prison reforms; etc.), and contributions to health care (such as the origin of the modern hospital in medieval monasteries, Florence Nightingale's influence on the nursing profession, and the establishment of the Red Cross by an evangelical Christian).[8] Moreover, many Christian or-

6. My thanks to church historian Jon Lemmond for this point.

7. See Nancy Pearcey and Charles Thaxton, *The Soul of Science* (Wheaton: Crossway, 1994), for an amplification of these points.

8. See D. Kennedy and Jerry Newcombe, *What If Jesus Had Never Been Born? The Positive Impact*

ganizations today are devoted to the alleviation of human miseries and ills around the world through relief work, health care, agricultural and economic development, legal reforms, peacemaking, reconciliation, prison ministry, food pantries, homeless shelters, the protection of refugees, the liberation of slaves (e.g., child laborers and sex slaves), and so on.

Given the clear, empirical evidence of universal human sin and selfishness throughout history, these positive contributions to society brought about by the influence of Christianity, individual Christians, and the Christian church are arguably best explained by means of an appeal to the supernatural work of the Holy Spirit. In spite of the good that human beings are capable of doing on their own, if we were left to our own wicked devices, it seems unlikely that we would have or even could have wrought such substantial beneficial changes in the world as those just listed. Though critics will point to the historic failings of the church as an instance of the problem of evil, Christian apologists can showcase the evident successes of the church as an example of the problem of good. This is the problem facing anyone who denies the redemptive work of the Holy Spirit in and through the church. How would such a person explain all the good things accomplished by Christians both individually and corporately throughout the centuries since the church was born on Pentecost?

Though it is good and potentially helpful to point out the benefits brought about by Christians after admitting the harms inflicted by the church, we must be careful not to resort to overly simplistic ex-

of Christianity in History (Nashville: Nelson, 1994), for more along these lines.

planations of the church's historic role in society. This warning should be heeded by both Christian apologists and critics of the Christian faith. History is both too complex and subject to too many alternative interpretations to warrant overly confident and simplistic accounts of either the church's failures or its successes. For instance, critics must be careful not to assume that the tragedies resulting from the witch hunts were entirely the responsibility of the church. A good historical case can be made for the involvement of the secular state in many witch trials. On the other hand, it would be illegitimate for apologists to presuppose that only Christians should be credited with major societal improvements. Historical explanation is complicated, and though some significant historical knowledge is possible, everyone should adopt a sufficiently cautious skepticism about the history of the impact of Christianity on society, especially given the strong biases on both sides of the issue.

However, even given such a modest approach to history, it is reasonable to conclude that the modern secular state has perpetrated far more evil than the historic Christian church. Even if we restrict ourselves to the twentieth century, it is evident that totalitarian regimes on both the right and the left of the political spectrum have brought about massive amounts of inhumanity, injustice, death, and suffering. For examples, one has only to think of the Holocaust wrought by Nazi Germany, Stalin's purges, the killing fields of Cambodia, and the ethnic cleansing in Rwanda and the former Yugoslavia. From a Christian perspective, it is reasonable to see these horrors as the result of both individual and corporate human wickedness and the neglect of the power of the Holy Spirit to transform sinful hearts and unjust institutions. From this point of view, it is reasonable to view the church throughout history as a fallen and yet moderately effective instrument of God's redeeming love in a lost and broken world.

Reflection and Discussion

1. Do you sometimes worry that the only reason you believe in God is that you are afraid of death and that you want to be secure and happy in this life? Did the discussion of psychological explanations of religious belief give you adequate resources to deal with this concern? Why or why not?
2. Is historical biblical criticism a friend or an enemy to Christians—or both? Explain.
3. What would you say to someone who rejects Christianity because of bad things done by the church or individual Christians (hypocrisy, injustice, abuse, etc.)?

Further Reading

Freud, Sigmund. *The Future of an Illusion.* New York: Norton, 1990.

Kennedy, D., and Jerry Newcombe. *What If Jesus Had Never Been Born? The Positive Impact of Christianity in History.* Nashville: Nelson, 1994.

Linnemann, Eta. *Historical Criticism of the Bible: Methodology or Ideology? Reflections of a Bultmannian Turned Evangelical.* Translated by Robert W. Yarbrough. Grand Rapids: Baker, 1990.

22

The Origin of Species

Christianity and Natural Selection

» **Outline**

- **Christianity and Science**
  - *The Book of Scripture and the "Book" of Nature*
  - *Theological Explanation versus Scientific Explanation*
  - *Ultimate Efficient Causes versus Proximate Efficient Causes*
  - *Methodological Naturalism Pro and Con*
- **The Challenge of Darwinism**
  - *Some Reasons to Doubt Darwinism*
    - Problems with the Thesis of the Inorganic Origin of Life
    - Questions about the Thesis of Common Descent
    - Challenges to the Thesis of Natural Selection in Light of the Fossil Record
  - *A Defense of the Compatibility of Darwinism and Christianity*
    - Biblical Arguments against Compatibility and Replies
    - Philosophical Arguments against Compatibility and Replies
- **The Interpretation of Genesis 1 and 2**
  - *General Observations about Biblical Interpretation*
  - *Replies to the Biblical Arguments against Theistic Evolution*

» **Summary**

Critics can argue against Christianity on Darwinist grounds. Apologists can reply by challenging Darwinism, affirming the compatibility of Darwinism and Christianity, or doing both (the dual strategy). Christians have faced challenges from science for a long time, but there is no inevitable conflict between science and Christianity. The Bible is not a science book, and theology generally answers questions different from those answered by science. Though Christians disagree about whether methodological naturalism is true, apologists who allow for both creationism and theistic evolution do not have to take sides on this issue. The Darwinist argument against Christianity can be undermined by showing that the case for Darwinism and the philosophical and biblical arguments against theistic evolution are inconclusive. Careful interpretation of the Genesis creation stories supports this latter claim.

» **Basic Terms, Concepts, and Names**

creationism
Darwinism
dual strategy
final cause
fixity of species
Galileo
genre, literary
God of the gaps
intelligent design
mechanistic explanation
methodological naturalism
microevolution versus macroevolution
practical versus theoretical purpose
proximate efficient cause
special creation
teleological explanation
theistic evolution
ultimate efficient cause

» **Reflection and Discussion**

» **Further Reading**

> So God created man in his own image, in the image of God he created him; male and female he created them.
>
> Genesis 1:27

Chapter 10 looked at the relationship between Darwin's theory of biological evolution by natural selection and the teleological argument for God's existence. It revealed that Darwinism challenges the traditional design argument for theism that is based on biological teleology but not the fine-tuning version of the teleological argument that appeals to a wider teleology in the universe. It also showed that some Christian apologists choose to argue against Darwinism and for scientific theories that appeal to intelligent design in nature. The success of this anti-Darwinist approach would open the door to a renewed employment of the traditional design argument. Other Christian apologists accept Darwinism and revert to the fine-tuning argument instead (though this argument is also employed by anti-Darwinists, of course).

This chapter considers the consequences of Darwin's theory for the Christian faith more generally. The discussion is shaped by the following argument:

1. If Darwinism is true, then Christianity is false.

2. Darwinism is true.
3. Therefore, Christianity is false.

Christian apologists have two obvious avenues of reply to this argument (as they did with the similar argument in chap. 10). One is to argue that premise 2 is either false or doubtful. Doing this requires entering the scientific debate about the theory of evolution by natural selection. This is the approach taken by adherents of the creation science perspective on the origin of biological species and also the proponents of the intelligent design research program in biology. The other obvious defense of Christianity against this argument is to give reasons for doubting premise 1. This is the route favored by those who hold a theistic evolution perspective, that is, those who think God created living organisms by means of a process of evolution by natural selection.

A third kind of response to this critical argument is perhaps not as obvious as the other two. This is the dual strategy of striving to build a case against both premise 1 and premise 2. This two-pronged effort makes sense for a number of reasons. First, in spite of what some on both sides of the debate think and say, the resolution of each of these issues is still an open question. No conclusive arguments settle the matter one way or the other in either case. Thus, it is wise to explore ways to deny both premise 1 and premise 2. Second, to the extent that it can be shown that premise 1 is doubtful and that Darwinism may be compatible with Christianity, there is less pressure on Christian apologists to provide a convincing case against Darwinism itself. This would make it easier for apologists to investigate Darwinism without feeling a strong need to falsify it. As a result, Christians would have more intellectual options open to them and would be able to consider them with an open mind. Third, to the extent that it can be shown that premise 2 is unacceptable, there is less need to argue against premise 1. If Darwinism is likely false, it does not matter whether it is consistent with the Christian faith. Finally, attacking both premise 1 and premise 2 makes it more likely that we will discover that at least one of them is false. Only one of them needs to be rejected to defend Christianity against the critic's argument.

This dual strategy is subject to an important qualification. As pointed out in chapter 10, Christian apologists must be cautious about taking sides in scientific debates for apologetic purposes. There are three reasons for this hesitation. First, apologists without scientific training in a particular area do not have the expertise required to make wise judgments about scientific theories in that area. Second, on a number of occasions in history, Christians have entered a scientific controversy by taking a side for apologetic reasons only to be proved wrong by subsequent scientific investigation. The church's response to Galileo (to be discussed in the next section) is an example of this sort of mistake. A third reason for circumspection applies specifically to the current creation-evolution debate. All working scientists who are nontheists and many who are Christians believe that some version of the theory of biological evolution is true and that there are no good reasons to doubt it. Accordingly, apologists who try to show that evolutionary theory is doubtful must provide very strong reasons for this claim. In light of these observations, Christian apologists are well advised to put more weight on their arguments against premise 1 than those against premise 2. Arguments against the former draw on philosophy, theology, and biblical studies and cannot be discredited by ongoing scientific research, whereas those against the latter make use of scientific claims, which are subject to change in light of subsequent scientific discoveries. Consequently, apologists who employ the dual strategy must be careful and tentative in their attempts to show that Darwinism is doubtful.

The second section of this chapter sketches this dual strategy. The first section takes up some general issues concerning the relationship between Christianity and science that characterize the wider conversation in which the discussion about evolution and creation takes place. The third section reflects on the relationship between this contemporary scientific debate about human origins and the proper interpretation of the first two chapters of Genesis, which concern God's creation of the universe and everything in it, including human beings.

Christianity and Science

The creation-evolution controversy is an important and relatively recent example of a number of tensions between Christianity and science that have challenged Christians for centuries. These tensions are created when a scientific theory seems to be at odds with the correct interpretation of the Bible and/or accepted Christian theology. Christian thinkers have always been challenged to reflect on whether and to what extent ideas and values in their wider cultures are compatible with their understanding of what the Bible teaches and requires. Augustine and Thomas Aquinas are among those who attempted to synthesize the Christian worldview with classical philosophy in late antiquity and the High Middle Ages. It was not until the rise of modern science around the time of the European Renaissance that Christians had to grapple earnestly with the consequences of scientific theories for the Christian faith. Galileo's condemnation by the Inquisition as a heretic because of his support of the Copernican view of the universe is viewed by many as the classic historical example of the inevitable incompatibility between science and religion. Moreover, Galileo's subsequent vindication has been employed by critics to discredit the Christian faith.

But there is no good reason to see the Galileo affair as a basis for rejecting the Christian worldview. What happened to Galileo involved a dispute between him and authorities in the Roman Catholic Church. It also had to do with a clash between his scientific approach and the Aristotelian approach that had been adopted by the church (and used by theologians in their interpretation of the Bible). But it does not follow that there is an inevitable conflict between Galileo's cosmological theory and the correct interpretation of the Bible or good theological reflection based on it. Instead, the case of Galileo shows that Christians need to be open to the possibility of rethinking their understanding of what the Bible teaches in light of advances in scientific theory (though it is also true that there are times when theories put forward by scientists require critical scrutiny from the standpoint of the Bible, and it seems reasonable to think that Darwinism is one of these at the present time, even if it should turn out later to be true).

The case of Galileo raises the important question of how to understand the relationship between the book studied by Christian theologians (the book of Scripture) and the "book" investigated by natural scientists (the book of nature). Before Galileo, Augustine had written that "the Spirit of God who spoke through them [the biblical writers] did not choose to teach about the heavens to men, as it was of no use for salvation."[1] As we saw in chapter 8, Galileo expressed the same idea in a catchier fashion: "The Bible tells us how to go to Heaven, not how the heavens go."[2] Galileo's version implies that the primary *purposes* of the Bible and science are different. Careful reflection on both Scripture and the discipline of science bears this out.

The main purpose of the Bible is the *practical* one of answering the question What must I do to be saved? The main

1. Augustine, quoted in Charles E. Hummel, *The Galileo Connection: Resolving Conflicts between Science and the Bible* (Downers Grove, IL: InterVarsity, 1986), 165.
2. See Galileo, "Letter to the Grand Duchess Christina of Tuscany," 1615, quoted in ibid., 9.

purpose of natural science is the *theoretical* one of answering the question How does nature work? Of course, the practical biblical question is answered on the basis of claims about the world—for instance, that God exists, that he created the universe and human beings, and that he has a plan for this creation. But none of these claims is of the sort investigated by the natural sciences. Also, answers to the theoretical scientific question lead to practical applications of them—for instance, insights in nuclear physics make nuclear reactors and nuclear warheads possible. But science alone cannot answer ethical questions about the proper use of such things, and it cannot solve the deepest spiritual problems of humankind. Clearly, the Bible is not meant to be a science book, and science is not intended to answer questions about the ultimate origin and purpose of the universe and human existence. The Bible and science have different primary purposes.

Modern science focuses on explaining nature in terms of efficient causation. Recall from chapter 9 that an efficient cause is *that by means of which* something exists or occurs. To ask for the efficient cause of a phenomenon in nature is to request a description of the mechanism responsible for bringing it about. It is to inquire about how something works or functions. Arguably, the Bible does not provide these kinds of explanations of natural events. Some will protest that the first two chapters of Genesis give an account of how God created the universe. However, there are good reasons for thinking that this is not the case, as we will see in the third section of this chapter. The Bible is more concerned with what Aristotle called final causes. A final cause

> **The main purpose of the Bible is the *practical* one of answering the question What must I do to be saved? The main purpose of natural science is the *theoretical* one of answering the question How does nature work?**

is *that for the sake of which* something exists or occurs. To state the final cause of something is to specify its purpose, end, or goal. For example, the Bible makes it clear that the goal of human existence is to glorify God and to enjoy eternal loving fellowship with God and others. The kind of how question the Bible answers is how will God accomplish this goal?

It is possible to answer questions about the efficient cause of something without addressing its final cause and vice versa. Imagine a person who has never seen an automobile before and does not know what they are for but who learns how one works by learning about each of its parts and how they interact. This person's knowledge of a car would be *mechanical* but not *teleological*. This person would know how it works without knowing what it is for. Most of us, on the other hand, understand the final cause or teleology of automobiles while having a very limited grasp of how they accomplish their purpose. We know that we use cars to get from one place to another, but we have to call on a mechanic who understands how they operate to fix them when they stop working properly. In the same way, a person can know that the universe was created by God as a setting within which humans can come to love God without knowing much at all of a scientific sort about the universe itself. Alternatively, a scientist can know a lot about natural mechanisms without knowing anything about their ultimate purpose. Of course, a scientist who is also a Christian can understand nature well both mechanically and teleologically.

But Christian theology also answers questions about the efficient cause of nature itself. We already addressed one of these questions in the second part of this book: What is the cause of the universe's existence? This is a question about an efficient cause because it seeks information about what it is, if anything, that originated and/or sustains the universe's existence. However, whereas the empirical natural sciences attempt to specify efficient causes for events and phenomena that take place *within* the universe, questions about the efficient cause of the universe itself (assuming it has one) are theological or philosophical. Things are a bit more complicated than this, however. If God sustains the universe at each moment, then presumably, he is involved in causally sustaining each particular *event* in the universe at each moment. So though an efficient cause of a certain natural event (such as a rock falling) is another natural event (such as an earthquake), God is also causing both of these events to occur by means of his being the divine efficient cause of the ongoing existence of the universe itself. Therefore, both theology and science provide explanations of events *within* nature in terms of efficient causes.

We can employ a helpful distinction made by theologians in an attempt to clarify the distinct domains of theology and science. In the example employed in the previous paragraph, God is the *primary* or *ultimate* efficient cause of the natural events in question, and the earthquake is the *secondary* or *proximate* efficient cause of the rock's falling. Theology discusses the former kind of cause, and the natural sciences investigate the latter sort of cause. Theology explains the universe itself and things that happen in the universe in terms of a supernatural cause (God), and science—according to one prevalent way of looking at it—explains only things that happen within the universe in terms of purely natural causes. This is a helpful way to distinguish theological claims about the universe from scientific ones.

However, Christians are currently divided over whether this is the right way to draw the line between these two domains of human inquiry. The view of scientific method just articulated is that of methodological naturalism. We have already encountered this thesis in chapters 10 (in connection with the intelligent design program), 14 (as applied to the science of history), and 21 (having to do with biblical criticism). Methodological naturalism is the position that the method scientists ought to employ in doing science is to explain natural events (things that happen in nature) by appealing only to other natural events. This rules out scientific theories that purport to explain regularities in nature by appealing to nonnatural causes—including God, of course. But as shown in chapter 10, Michael Behe and others have proposed scientific theories that purport to explain the alleged irreducible complexity of some biological systems by an appeal to deliberate intelligent design. Such a cause is clearly nonnatural. Consequently, the intelligent design approach in biology denies the thesis of methodological naturalism.

Proponents of methodological naturalism resist such scientific appeals to nonnatural causes for a number of reasons. First, they say that postulations of nonnatural causes to explain natural phenomena prematurely undercut the motivation to search for natural causes to account for these things. They point out that in the history of science appeals to supernatural causes to explain regularities in nature have always eventually been shown to be inadequate. An example is Newton's appeal to divine agency to explain observed anomalies in planetary orbits. Newton's theory is an example of what has become known as a "God of the gaps" account: Gaps in our understanding of how nature works are filled in by an appeal to divine agency. Though such theories seem initially apologetically advantageous because they assume that God's existence is needed to explain how nature works, their subsequent falsification not only eliminates this apologetical value but also tends to put belief in God in a bad light (because God is not necessary for the explanation after all, some conclude that God is not necessary for anything at all).

Methodological naturalists also argue that the goal of science is consensus among the members of the scientific community that certain scientific theories are true and others are false. They point out that such consensus is possible only if scientists set aside the metaphysical and theological assumptions about which they disagree. Science has the relatively limited goal of explaining how nature works. The accomplishment of this goal seems to require only the employment of empirical methods available to everyone in spite of what they may think about the ultimate origin and destiny of the universe. Moreover, some Christian methodological naturalists have suggested that our ability to explain natural phenomena within the universe in entirely natural terms is another example of the evidential ambiguity God deliberately built into the creation. They see it as another example of God's partial hiddenness, which serves to give us the freedom to interpret the world as God's creation or instead as an eternal, godless, and meaningless collection of matter and energy (see chaps. 5, 12).

Those who deny methodological naturalism reply to these arguments by insisting that (1) scientists should be open to the possibility that at a certain point an explanation that appeals to a nonnatural cause may be the best explanation available, (2) the goal of science is not so much agreement among scientists as attainment of the truth, and if God exists, the truth may be that God sometimes acts directly in the world rather than by means of natural instruments, and (3) though God may be hidden to some extent, he has also revealed himself in nature clearly enough so that we are without excuse when we deny his existence (Rom. 1:18–20). They believe that for these reasons it is legitimate for scientific theories to appeal to nonnatural causes and even to God.

Christian apologists who adopt the dual strategy of arguing against both premise 1 and premise 2 do not have to take sides in this debate. It is true that many who deny premise 2 (that Darwinism is true) believe in the doctrine of *special* creation—that God created each of the biological species (at least the human species) *directly* rather than by means of a natural process such as the process of evolution by natural selection. These people may adhere to the intelligent design approach of providing scientific explanations of at least some biological systems that appeal to God's intelligent design and agency. However, since we are not committed to denying premise 2 unless the case for premise 1 becomes overwhelming, we do not need to commit ourselves to this approach, at least at the present time.

We also need not worry that leaving open the possibility that methodological naturalism is true is a threat to the Christian worldview. Methodological naturalism does not entail *metaphysical* naturalism (the view that only nature exists). It is consistent, as should be clear from the above discussion, with monotheism. God could have created the universe in such a way that its regular operations are entirely explicable in solely natural terms. Moreover, though this would mean that the hypothesis of God's existence is not needed by science to explain regular natural events, the theistic hypothesis is still needed in philosophical accounts that purport to explain the existence and fine-tuning of the universe and, as argued in chapter 25, the existence of a universal and objective moral law.

The Challenge of Darwinism

The task in this section is to sketch the two-pronged defense of Christianity against the argument stated at the beginning of this chapter. That is, we need to suggest both reasons to cast doubt on premise 2 (Darwinism) and reasons to question premise 1 (the assumption that Darwinism is inconsistent with the Christian worldview). Creationists normally focus their efforts entirely on premise 2, and theistic evolutionists tend to think only about premise 1. We will try to maximize our chances of successfully defending the Christian worldview by exploring both. First, however, we need to clarify the nature of the evolutionary theory at issue.

Recall from chapter 10 that Darwinism is an evolutionary theory about the origin of biological species. What distinguishes it from other evolutionary biological theories is that it posits natural selection as the mechanism by which the process of biological evolution takes place (see the second section of chap. 10 for a more thorough explanation of Darwinism). The theory's appeal to this mechanism of natural selection makes possible a completely naturalistic account of the origin of biological species. Consequently, Darwin's theory conforms to the requirement of methodological naturalism to formulate scientific theories in such a way that they refer only to natural causes. It is theoretically possible for an evolutionary theory of the origin of biological species to exist that appeals also or instead to nonnatural causes (such as to God's ongoing direct intervention in the development of organisms over time). Therefore, there is nothing intrinsically naturalistic or nontheistic about an evolutionary biological theory as such.

There is agreement between Darwinists and many creationists that microevolution has occurred. The theory of microevolution holds that some small variations or changes have occurred over a relatively short period of time within certain species or genetic populations. This theory accounts, for instance, for the different varieties of birds within a given species of bird. However, creationists argue that such microevolution within a species does not entail the Darwinist view that completely new species have evolved from different, ancestor species.

The controversy over Darwin's theory of evolution typically focuses on what has become known as the macroevolutionary paradigm. This theory can be divided into two main claims. First, the thesis of *common descent* is that all living organisms are descended from a common ancestor and that the former evolved from the latter by means of a process that advanced from simpler to more complex forms. Macroevolutionists claim that the sort of evolution observed in microevolution is the same kind of evolutionary process that has occurred—over a much longer period of time—in the case of macroevolution. Darwinists claim that natural selection is the mechanism by which living organisms have evolved from their common ancestor. However, there are many scientists who affirm the thesis of common descent but deny that natural selection is the means by which biological diversity occurred. The second claim of the macroevolutionary paradigm is the thesis of the *inorganic origin of life*. According to this thesis, the initial ancestor life form from which all other living systems are descended developed from nonliving matter in such a way that its evolution can be explained entirely in physical and chemical terms (without appeal to God's special, direct creative activity).

We are not able to consider in detail either the evidence for or the case against the theses of common descent and the inorganic origin of life. In general, the best way to criticize them is to point out that the scientific evidence for them is not conclusive and that important questions need to be answered satisfactorily before the case for them can be considered adequate. Take the thesis of the inorganic origin of life, for instance, which alleges that life evolved solely by natural, chemical means. Laboratory experiments have been performed to try to substantiate this. There is no consensus in the scientific community that any of these experiments succeeded. In fact, there is currently fairly widespread acknowledgment among scientists that the thesis of the inorganic origin of life is subject to an unresolved problem that seems to show that it would not be possible in principle for life to have developed naturalistically from inorganic materials. The problem is that the origin of life requires an information replicator (such as DNA or RNA), but these information replicators require enzymes to make them, and the enzymes require the information replicators to make *them*! Some apologists argue that this problem can be solved only by means of the hypothesis that God created enzymes and information replicators together directly and supernaturally.[3] Another hypothesis is that there is fine-tuning at the biochemical level, analogous to the fine-tuning at the cosmological level discussed in chapter 10, that suffices for the development of life from inorganic origins (so that the thesis of the inorganic origin of life would be true).[4] But if this

3. See Lee Strobel, "The Evidence of Biological Information: The Challenge of DNA and the Origin of Life," chapter 9 in *The Case for a Creator: A Journalist Investigates Scientific Evidence That Points toward God* (Grand Rapids: Zondervan, 2004), in which Strobel discusses this problem with Stephen C. Meyer, who offers an intelligent design solution to it.

4. Biologist Jeff Schloss brought this hypothesis to my attention.

biochemical fine-tuning hypothesis is true, then apologists can argue, as before, that the best explanation of the fine-tuning requires an appeal to God. Either way, there is scientific evidence for theism.

As for the thesis of common descent, it is important to remember that the theory that all living systems are descended from a common ancestor from which they have evolved is separable from the claim that natural selection is the mechanism by which this diversification of species occurred. As said above, many current biologists affirm common descent but deny natural selection. Consequently, arguments against natural selection do not necessarily provide reasons to doubt the thesis of common descent. However, when addressing those who accept the macroevolutionary paradigm yet deny natural selection, apologists can ask what alternative mechanism can suffice to explain the evolution of species from a common ancestor. Moreover, apologists can challenge arguments for common descent that are not necessarily also arguments for natural selection. In addition to the evidence for microevolution, another main kind of evidence for the thesis of common descent concerns genetic similarities between certain species (such as between human beings and chimpanzees). Yet although genetic similarities between some species may be a *necessary* condition for the truth of the macroevolutionary paradigm, it is not a *sufficient* condition. The important question is whether common *descent* rather than common *design* is a better explanation of genetic similarities between different species. Though it may be, apologists can raise critical questions about whether or not it is.

Doubts about natural selection may be more valuable apologetically than concerns about the thesis of common descent. This is especially the case if natural selection is understood in such a way as to preclude the possibility of God's role in directing the evolutionary process (though natural selection does not have to be characterized in this way, as we will see). Since natural selection would involve a very long series of gradual and continuous changes in organisms, if natural selection is the mechanism of biological evolution, one would expect to see its effects in the fossil record. But important questions about the fossil record must be answered before the fossil evidence can count as adequate to confirm Darwin's thesis of natural selection. Among these questions are the following:

- What accounts for the sudden appearance in the fossil record of certain major groups of animals (the Cambrian explosion)? If they were a result of evolution by natural selection, it seems that there would be a fossil record of their evolutionary ancestors (and there is not).
- Why are there missing links in the fossil record and a scarcity of fossils for transitional species (species that clearly link evolutionary ancestors with evolutionary descendents)?
- Why doesn't the record suggest gradual evolutionary change instead of many species remaining unchanged for long periods with sudden evolutionary changes (punctuated equilibrium)?

Clearly, the absence of adequate answers to these questions would not show that the Darwinist theory of evolution is false. Moreover, a number of suggested answers have been articulated by proponents of this theory in an attempt to strengthen it. But the lack of clearly satisfactory answers to these questions does make it reasonable to conclude that the general theory of evolution by natural selection is not yet a proven fact and that it is reasonable to suspend belief about it in the meantime. This questioning approach is the sort of strategy needed to withstand the critic's argument by means of challenging premise 2.

There are, however, arguments that purport to show that Darwinism is not only doubtful but also false. We looked at one of these in chapter 10 that is based on the claim that some biological systems are irreducibly complex. As we saw, though, Michael Behe's argument—like other arguments against Darwinism—is not conclusive. Nonetheless, since the debate about whether Darwinism is true continues, it seems reasonable to doubt premise 2 at this time.[5]

Let us turn now to consider premise 1. First, it is helpful to reflect on reasons for thinking it is true. Some Christians have concluded that Darwinism is inconsistent with Christianity on the basis of the following arguments: (1) It contradicts the doctrine of special creation (that God created all biological species *directly*), and this doctrine is taught in the Bible, especially in the first two chapters of Genesis;

(2) Darwinism entails that the concept of a species is relatively indeterminate and statistical, and this is incompatible with the doctrine of the fixity or immutability of species, which is taught by the Bible in Genesis 1 and 2; (3) if the human species evolved solely by means of natural selection, then God could not have been sufficiently involved in the process to have created human beings in the image of God, a central Christian doctrine also based on Genesis 1; (4) the process of evolution by natural selection is highly wasteful and inefficient, since it proceeds in a trial and error manner that results in the extinction of many species, but God would not be wasteful and inefficient; and (5) if God created by means of the process of evolution by natural selection, then God employed a process that has death built into it (and that would involve many more deaths and extinctions than would be the case according to the doctrine of special creation), and this aggravates the problem of evil (it also means that there was death before the fall).

This is a formidable list of concerns. Can we alleviate them? The next section, which is devoted to the interpretation of the creation accounts in Genesis 1 and 2, discusses arguments 1 and 2. That leaves arguments 3 through 5.

How we respond to argument 3 depends on the view we take about the nature of human persons. Are we immaterial, nonphysical souls that have material, physical bodies (substance dualism), or are we nothing but material or physical organisms (materialism)?[6] If we are immaterial souls with material bodies, then since Darwinism applies only to material

5. For more reasons to doubt or reject Darwinism, see Strobel, *Case for a Creator*, especially chap. 2 ("Doubts about Darwinism") and chap. 8 (which features Strobel's interview of Michael Behe about irreducible complexity and intelligent design). Strobel's approach to the critic's argument is to assume that premise 1 must be true, and therefore premise 2 has to be false.

6. The next chapter looks at these two competing views of human nature in more depth.

biological organisms, it follows that, if this theory of evolution by natural selection is true, then though our bodies have evolved, our souls have not. Consequently, God could have created our souls directly and in his image even if he created bodies by means of a process of evolution by natural selection. If dualism is true, then who we are is our soul and not our body. Therefore, God's creation of human persons (souls) directly and in his image is consistent with God's creation of bodies indirectly by evolution. Of course, this leaves questions about when and how God associated human souls with human bodies, but this mystery need not undermine the plausibility of the argument just given.

Things are trickier if materialism about human persons is true. However, if it is possible for God to guide and/or constrain the process of natural selection (as opposed to just setting it in motion at the outset with no predetermination of its outcome)—just as God as primary cause continues to sustain and uphold the natural processes involving secondary causes in the universe from moment to moment—then God could bring it about that the process of evolution by natural selection results in a biological species that embodies the image of God (assuming, as the materialist does, that the properties that constitute this can be possessed by a purely material substance). Such a process would still be a natural process in spite of God's supernatural guidance of it as long as all the proximate or secondary causes involved in the process are natural.

As for argument 4, a process can be wasteful and inefficient only relative to a finite amount of resources. If it is possible to run out of needed materials, then these materials are valuable, and they in-

crease in value as they decrease in amount. Squandering such resources is wasteful, and using them inefficiently when they could be employed more efficiently is imprudent. However, God is an infinite being with an infinite supply of resources (time, space, matter, and energy) at his disposal to use in the accomplishment of his purposes. Consequently, God can expend as many of the items in his inexhaustible store as he desires without being wasteful or inefficient.

But this answer does not suffice to undermine argument 5, which charges that even if God's implementation of a process of biological evolution by natural selection to create life is neither wasteful nor inefficient, it is nonetheless *evil* because of the amount of suffering, death, and extinction it involves. As we have seen, natural selection means that only the fittest or most adaptive organisms survive. The weaker members of a species suffer as a result of their vulnerability to illness, injury, predation, and starvation. Moreover, these less capable individuals die either before reproducing or before reproducing very much. If they have offspring, they pass along their deficient genes to them so that they inherit the disadvantages and are therefore less likely to survive very long and to reproduce very much. As a consequence of this, many individual animals suffer greatly, and entire species eventually become extinct. If God created life by means of a process of evolution by natural selection, then he created by means of pain, suffering, death, and extinction. How can God be justified in employing such a method when he could have brought about much less evil by engaging in acts of special creation of species?

In reply, if we assume that *biological* death preceded the fall, then even if God created species directly rather than by means of evolution by natural selection, God created a universe in which pain, suffering, predation, and death are part of the created order. Is there a significant difference between God's creating a world that contains these things and God's creating by means of a process that involves these things? It does not seem so. Either way, God is responsible for natural evil. There does not seem to be a special or magnified problem of evil introduced by the theory of evolution by natural selection. Moreover, though the extinction of a species may be an aesthetic loss (because it involves the loss of a particular variety of animal that could have further enriched the diversity of kinds of creatures on earth), the only moral problem created by species extinction is the loss of individual members of previously existing species, and we already addressed this evil above.

But are there good reasons to think that biological death existed before sin entered the world, and is this claim consistent with what the Bible teaches? There is good geological evidence that the earth is very old, and there is good fossil evidence that human beings arrived relatively late on the scene after a number of other species of animal had already existed for quite some time (such as the dinosaurs). Moreover, the fossil record indicates that these earlier animal species were "red in tooth and claw"[7]—that predation and therefore pain, suffering, and death predated the existence and fall of human beings. But doesn't all

7. This phrase is from a line in Alfred Lord Tennyson's poem "In Memoriam A.H.H." The entire line in section 56 of the poem is "Nature, red in tooth and claw."

this contradict what the Bible teaches, especially in Genesis 1 and 2? Doesn't the Bible teach that God created the universe in only six days, and doesn't the chronology of Scripture indicate that this was only a few thousand years ago? Shouldn't we hold the young-earth creation view in order to square our beliefs with the Bible, in spite of what the scientific evidence seems to show? Doesn't the Bible teach that God created the animals on the same day in which he created human beings?

The Interpretation of Genesis 1 and 2

From the standpoint of the Christian faith, the primary question we need to ask about the first two chapters of Genesis is What does God intend to teach by means of these biblical passages? Since the Holy Spirit employed human authorship to communicate his message, this question becomes What did the author of the creation accounts in Genesis intend to convey in writing them? This is, of course, the question one should ask to understand *any* written text. To answer it adequately, one must let the text speak for itself as much as possible. This means trying to be as objective as possible by acknowledging one's own presuppositions and distinguishing them from those of the writer. This is especially important in the present context, since some conservative readers of the creation accounts assume that the creation accounts are historical, should be interpreted literally, and make true scientific claims, while some liberal readers assume that these passages are mythical, should be interpreted figuratively, and reflect an outdated prescientific worldview. Which of these assumptions are appropriate, and which are not?

To answer this question adequately, we must answer some other questions first. What was the time and place in which the author wrote the text? What was going on then and there that prompted him to write it? Who was his audience? What was his purpose in writing this work to those people in that historical and cultural setting? Moreover, what literary genre or genres did the author choose as a vehicle for accomplishing his goals? Not all of these questions are equally easy to answer with respect to Genesis 1 and 2, but we can narrow down our answers enough to make a good case for the claim that these creation accounts do not require the falsehood of Darwinism or rule out theistic evolution.

Take the questions about historical and cultural setting and audience. Biblical scholars disagree about whether the creation accounts were written fairly early in Israel's history, during their wandering in the wilderness between the exodus and the conquest of the Promised Land (the traditional view is that the author was Moses), or instead relatively late, after Judah had been exiled to Babylon (a middle view is that an exilic editor compiled materials that had been written earlier). But whichever view one takes, it is clear that the text emerged from within the community of ancient Israel and that it was written for the people of this community. Moreover, comparisons of the Genesis creation stories with the creation myths of other Near Eastern peoples with whom the Israelites had contact reveal both similarities and differences. This strongly suggests that an important part of the author's purpose was to impress upon his readers the distinctive features of Israel's understanding of God and his relationship to human beings in contrast to the religious views of Israel's neighbors. But why would the author have wanted to do this?

Whether the biblical creation narratives were written during Israel's sojourn in the wilderness, their conquest and settlement of the Promised Land, their exile in Babylon, or even afterward during the restoration, a common thread that runs through this entire history is the challenge the Israelites faced staying faithful to the one true God rather than giving in to the idolatrous and polytheistic pagan religions of their neighbors. The Bible makes this clear throughout the historical sections of the Old Testament. In light of this, it makes sense to believe that the author of the Genesis creation accounts was reminding his fellow Israelites of the superiority of their religious tradition over the others. He would do this to facilitate their continued obedience to God and their resistance to the seductive influence of the other religions.

Here are some specific highlights of themes in Genesis 1 and 2 that seem to be included to contrast Israel's worldview with the others. First, there is only one God rather than many gods. This one God created the universe deliberately and in an orderly fashion; it was not a product of chaos or chance. God made everything that exists by himself and according to his will; things did not come about as a result of sexual unions or conflicts between gods. Everything God made is good; evil is not a product of divine agency. The high point of God's creation is the creation of human beings; humans were not made by malevolent divine beings in order to be their slaves. Human beings are set apart from the rest of the creation by virtue of being made in God's image and are in charge of all the rest (Gen. 1:27–28); they are not made out of the blood of a god.[8]

Notice that these are all *theological* themes rather than *scientific* ones. That is, they tell us important truths about God and God's relationship to his creation and human beings without telling us specifically in physical, chemical, or biological terms when or how God created the universe and everything in it. This is a good thing. The Bible is God's written, special revelation to human beings in many times, places, and settings. As such, it needs to be as universally accessible as possible. In particular, it should not require any specific scientific knowledge to understand it. Most people who have read, are reading, and will read the Bible probably know either absolutely nothing or very little about contemporary scientific cosmological and biological theories. The purpose of the Bible is to provide human beings with the means to become reunited eternally with God. How would the inclusion of scientific theories or scientific language contribute to the achievement of that end? Moreover, the history of science shows that scientific theories continue to change—sometimes quite dramatically. Therefore, there is no one set of theories that it would have been appropriate for God to put in a book that he intends to stand the test of time.

Another reason to think that the Genesis creation narratives are primarily theological rather than scientific is their literary genre. A genre is a category within an art

8. See tablet VI of the ancient Mesopotamian creation epic *Enuma Elish,* which recounts Marduk's creation of human beings out of the blood of a god for the purpose of serving the gods, "that they might be at ease."

(such as literature) that is distinguished from other kinds of expression in that art by its form, style, and/or content. Examples of literary genres are poems, parables, stories, chronicles, genealogies, theological treatises, scientific explanations, and so on. General genres (e.g., fact and fiction, prose and poetry) include more specific ones (e.g., news report, novel, sermon, limerick). Though there are clear examples of genres (such as the ones just listed), it is not always easy to classify a text as one in particular (and texts often contain more than one).

What genre(s) do we find in Genesis 1 and 2? They each have some properties of narratives or stories because they each feature characters (God, Adam, and Eve) acting in a sequence of events. These narratives also have a historical-like orientation because they are written in such a way as to tell about something that happened in the past. But these stories are highly stylized in nature as well, at least in structure. For instance, Genesis 1 contains a pattern of parallelism in which the things that happen during the first three days of creation (when God creates various "spaces") correspond to the things that occur in the latter three days (when God makes things to fill up these spaces). Notice that something can be a story and yet be historical (at least in part), even if it includes such stylized elements. Tennyson's poem "The Charge of the Light Brigade" is an example of this. But this suggests that both the conservative and the liberal readers mentioned above may have some mistaken assumptions about the text. The text may have both literal and figurative elements, both historical and mythical features, and it is likely neither scientific nor prescientific in orientation (but rather not scientific at all).

One way in which the creation stories seem clearly *not* historical, however, is that the order of events described in them is arguably not chronological. This can be seen by comparing the creation story in Genesis 1 with the one in Genesis 2. In Genesis 1, God creates the plants, then the animals, and then both male and female human beings. In Genesis 2, God creates the male human being first (Adam) and then the plants, then the animals, and then the female human (Eve). There is no persuasive way to harmonize these stories to make them agree chronologically. But if we allow the text to speak for itself and to guide us in discerning the author's (or perhaps authors') intentions, we can see that the author(s) arguably did not intend to give his (their) readers a chronologically accurate account of creation. Instead, it is reasonable to think that the different order of events was chosen in each case to highlight the same general theological truth: that God made human beings to be the high point of his creation. This is emphasized in the first account by having human beings appear *last*, after a progression from lower to higher forms of life. It is underlined in the second account by

Science in general and the scientific theory of biological evolution by natural selection in particular do not provide resources adequate to show that Christianity is false.

the man being created *first* and then being in need of completion by the female after other created things are seen to be clearly inadequate for this purpose and subordinate to human beings.

We are now in a position to address the questions raised in the previous section about whether these biblical creation accounts are consistent with the cosmological theory that the earth is very old (4.55 billion years or so) and with the biological theory of macroevolution. The short answer to this question is that there is no good reason to deny that they are, since these passages were not intended to state scientific truths. They were instead written to communicate important theological truths. The Genesis creation accounts can be inconsistent with a scientific theory only if they make scientific claims that contradict the claims of the theory. But since they do not make scientific claims, they cannot be inconsistent with science.

Moreover, since they are not intended to be chronologically accurate, they are not intended to tell us, even in general terms, how or when God created the universe and human beings. But don't these accounts at least teach the doctrine of special creation (that God created all species directly rather than indirectly by means of evolution) and the doctrine of the fixity or immutability of species (that God created each species to be of a certain fixed and determinate kind rather than as types that could change and evolve over time)? Those doctrines may well be required by a completely literal reading of the accounts. However, the author's use of stylized language and his emphasis on theological themes strongly suggest that other interpretations are reasonable and that adherence to these doctrines is not required by a responsible reading of the texts. Consequently, though the creation accounts do not invite an interpretation in terms of theistic evolution, they do not exclude the truth of this theory either.

We can conclude that science in general and the scientific theory of biological evolution by natural selection in particular do not provide resources adequate to show that Christianity is false. But there is another objection to Christianity, based on a scientific claim about human nature, that purports to demonstrate the falsity of the Christian worldview. This is the claim that human beings are nothing but material organisms. The next chapter formulates this objection and suggests a variety of ways to respond to it.

Reflection and Discussion

1. How would you reply to a critic who argues that science and religion are always in conflict with each other and that, since science is superior to religion, people ought to reject religious claims?
2. Do you agree that Christian apologists ought to pursue a two-pronged strategy of defense against the anti-Christian argument based on Darwinism? Why or why not? If not, which of the other two strategies do you prefer? Why?
3. Do you agree that the biblical creation stories in Genesis 1 and 2 do not require Christians to reject Darwinism? Why or why not?

Further Reading

Pearcey, Nancy, and Charles Thaxton. *The Soul of Science: Christian Faith and Natural Philosophy*. Wheaton: Crossway, 1994.

Strobel, Lee. *The Case for a Creator: A Journalist Investigates Scientific Evidence That Points toward God*. Grand Rapids: Zondervan, 2004.

Van Inwagen, Peter. "Genesis and Evolution." In *God, Knowledge, and Mystery: Essays in Philosophical Theology*, 128–62. Ithaca, NY: Cornell University Press, 1995.

23

The Dust of the Earth

Resurrection, Minds, and Bodies

» **Outline**

- **Materialism and the Resurrection of the Dead**
  - *Materialism and Life after Death*
  - *Two Versions of Materialism*
  - *Materialism, Dualism, and Personal Identity across Time*
  - *Biblical Reasons in Favor of Materialism*
- **Problems with a Materialist Approach to the Afterlife**
  - *Biblical Reasons against Materialism*
  - *Philosophical Problems with a Materialist Account of Life after Death*
    - The Ship of Theseus Problem
    - The Body Selection Problem
    - The Shared Body Parts Problem
    - The Possible Duplicate Body Problem
- **Dualism, Human Nature, and Life after Death**
  - *Philosophical Arguments for and against Materialism*
  - *Christian Platonic (Augustinian) Dualism*
  - *Thomas Aquinas's Version of Dualism*
  - *Dualistic Options and Life after Death*

» **Summary**

Some critics argue that science shows that humans are merely material and thus incapable of life after death. Christian apologists can reply by adopting the dual strategy of arguing both against materialism and for the claim that materialism can account for life after death. A theological reason for this claim is that an omnipotent God could re-create a purely material person at the resurrection. A biblical reason is that materialism explains Scripture's emphasis on the awfulness of death and the importance of the resurrection better than dualism does. However, there are also biblical and philosophical reasons to question the prospects for a materialist account of life after death. In addition, there are serious philosophical objections to materialism itself. Christian apologists who reject materialism have at least two versions of dualism to choose from, each of which has different advantages and disadvantages.

» **Basic Terms, Concepts, and Names**

Aquinas, Thomas
Augustine
Augustinian dualism
body kind materialism
dual strategy
materialism (or physicalism)
numerical identity
personal identity across time
particular body materialism
Plato
qualitative similarity
resurrection
ship of Theseus story
Thomistic dualism

» **Reflection and Discussion**

» **Further Reading**

> I have the same hope in God as these men, that there will be a resurrection of both the righteous and the wicked.
>
> Acts 24:15

Chapter 15 looked at a historical case for the claim that Jesus was resurrected from the dead. In 1 Corinthians 15, Paul says that because of Jesus' resurrection human beings will be raised from the dead too (vv. 20–28). But some critics argue that life after death is not possible or at least unlikely to occur. Christian apologists need to respond to these allegations. Recall from the introduction that one of the statements in the Apostles' Creed is "I believe in . . . the resurrection of the body and the life everlasting." Both the truth of the Christian faith and the hope of all humanity for the fulfillment of their deepest desires are on the line.

Some critics who doubt the possibility or probability of eternal life do so on scientific grounds. They argue that science has shown that human beings are nothing but physical or material organisms. They argue further that a purely material being cannot survive its biological death. They say that we are just bodies and that when our bodies die we cease to exist—never to exist again. Because of the centrality of the doctrine of eternal life in Christianity, we can formulate this scientific argument as

a challenge to the truth of the Christian worldview itself:

1. If Christianity is true, then human beings are more than merely material organisms.
2. But human beings are nothing but material organisms.
3. Therefore, Christianity is false.

Most Christian apologists respond to this argument by arguing against premise 2. They do so because they endorse premise 1. They accept premise 1 because they believe the Bible teaches that human beings have an immaterial or nonphysical spirit or soul and that life after death (which is essential to Christianity) is possible only if this is true. The philosophical view that human beings have a material body and an immaterial soul is called dualism. Premise 2 is an affirmation of materialism (also called physicalism) and, by implication, a denial of dualism.

But some Christian apologists defend the Christian faith against this critical argument by rejecting premise 1. Some of them argue against premise 1 because they believe that materialism about human beings is true (but not of course materialism about all reality, since they believe God is an immaterial being). Others do so because they are not sure whether materialism is true, but they want to try to show that it does not matter for Christianity whether or not it is. If these latter apologists are right, then Christians do not need to enter into the philosophical and scientific debates between dualists and materialists to defend their faith. They can be freed to explore the issue with an open mind without having to worry about the outcome of their investigation. They can look at both dualism and materialism as theoretical options rather than at dualism as mandatory and materialism as necessarily false.

This chapter (like the previous chapter) engages in the dual strategy of providing arguments against both premise 1 and premise 2. As before, this approach is intended to maximize apologetical options. The first section gives some reasons to doubt premise 1. The focus is on reasons for thinking that Christianity is compatible with materialism about human beings. The case for this claim is plausible but not conclusive. Some Christians find it satisfactory, and others do not. The second section examines reasons for thinking that premise 1 is true. These include reasons to think that materialism cannot account for life after death after all. The third section provides reasons to reject premise 2. Then it sets out two versions of dualism. The first is in the tradition of Plato, Augustine, and Descartes (and others). The second was developed by Thomas Aquinas. The latter dualist view provides apologists with an attractive middle position that has the positive features of both material-

This approach is intended to maximize apologetical options.

ism and the Platonic version of dualism while avoiding many of the problems that beset these views.

Materialism and the Resurrection of the Dead

The main philosophical reason for accepting premise 1 is that life after death seems to require the existence of a nonphysical or immaterial soul. After all, the human body is a compound material organism, and as such, enough of its parts need to work together in the right way for it to function in such a way as to sustain the life of a person. When people die, their bodies cease functioning in this way. Everyone knows that a corpse is not a person. After people die, they are gone in some sense, even if their corpses are still around. Moreover, dead bodies are subject to decay, disintegration, and dispersal of their component parts, potentially in many directions far beyond their common source. If human persons are nothing but living physical organisms (i.e., if materialism is true), then it seems to follow that when these organisms are destroyed the persons that were the organisms simply cease to exist. So it seems that if materialism is true, then life after death is not possible.

But Christians affirm the reality not only of life after death but also of the resurrection of the body. If God can and will bring our mortal bodies back to life after they have died, then though these bodies are destroyed at death, they can and will be re-created at the general resurrection before the final judgment of human beings (when both the saved and the damned will be raised, according to the Bible). Therefore, even if human beings are nothing but living material organisms and so cease to exist when these organisms die, it seems that they can exist and live again when God re-creates and reanimates these organisms at the resurrection. Moreover, since God is all-powerful, and since God created material organisms in the first place (even if by means of some evolutionary process), it seems that God is capable of doing all this.

Some materialists hold that every human person is one and the same thing as a *particular* human body. According to this view, I am *this* body, and you are *that* body. If there should happen to be another body that is exactly similar to my body, in that it has exactly the same kinds of parts put together in exactly the same way, then it is *just like* me, but it is a *different person* from me. If we assume that this version of materialism is true and that God will re-create every human being at the general resurrection, then God must re-create *the very body* that is each of us. It is not enough for God to re-create a body that is exactly like ours in every respect if it is not *numerically identical to* the body that we were (and will be again).

Other materialists think that for us to be re-created at the resurrection it would suffice for God to create a body just like the one we had before we died as long as it has our mental states and psychological properties (which materialists must assume to be certain kinds of physical or material states like brain states). Though

these Christian materialists concede that it would be possible for God to create more than one material organism that is exactly the same both physically and psychologically, they hold that God in his supreme goodness simply would not do that. The one he creates is the person with whom we are identical.

Whichever of these two versions of materialism one might accept, it must accommodate what the Bible says about our future physical and psychological state or condition. What Paul says in 1 Corinthians 15 makes it clear that our bodies will be dramatically improved in some way. What he says elsewhere implies that we will be transformed psychologically and morally for the better as well. Whatever it is that makes us the individual person we are and that stays the same as long as we exist must be capable of undergoing relatively radical change. Therefore, if the materialist is right that we are just a particular body (or a certain *kind* of body), then this body (or body type) must remain unchanged in whatever way is required for our continued existence, in spite of all the ways in which we are transformed at the resurrection. It must be true to say both that some person in the afterlife is the very same person as me and that this future person (who is me) will have undergone radical change for the better as a result of God's transforming love.

One good reason for thinking that it is possible for us to continue to exist as the same person even though we undergo relatively radical physical and psychological changes is that all of us have actually already experienced this. When you look at a family photo album and see pictures of yourself as a young child, you are looking at images of *yourself* at an earlier point of time in your existence when you were dramatically different in both body and mind from how you are now. Nonetheless, this person whose picture you are looking at is, though *qualitatively* different from you in many ways, *numerically* the same person as you. Since this has already occurred in each of our personal histories, there does not seem to be a good reason for thinking that it cannot continue into the afterlife, in spite of the biological death that each of us will experience.

The dualist accounts for personal continuity in spite of these qualitative changes by means of the view that a person is, at least in part, a nonphysical, immaterial spirit or soul. Since souls are immaterial things, they can continue to exist on their own even when the material body dies, decays, and disintegrates. Moreover, the same soul can persist despite radical changes in a person's psychology, such as through the memory loss and personality alteration caused by Alzheimer's disease and other forms of dementia. The soul is like a computer disk or a CD that can store programs and data but can also be erased and have other instructions and information written on it.

Though dualism thus seems to make it easy to explain how human persons can survive both the death of their bodies and the physical and psychological changes Christians believe will occur in the afterlife, there are (perhaps surprisingly) biblical and theological reasons for thinking that the materialist approach is to be preferred over the dualist.[1] These

reasons are based on the observations that (1) the Bible treats death as a great evil (Paul says that "the last *enemy* to be destroyed is death" [1 Cor. 15:26, emphasis added]), and (2) the Bible attributes a substantial amount of significance to the resurrection of the body (see especially 1 Cor. 15:29–32).

On the assumption that dualism is true, it is hard to see why death would be such a bad thing and why the resurrection of the body would be so important. Given dualism, death is merely the separation of the body from the soul. Though the body dies, the soul continues to exist. Moreover, the souls of Christians may well go straight to be with the Lord (remember that Jesus told the repentant criminal with whom he was crucified, "Today you will be with me in paradise" [Luke 23:43]). Their disembodiment would seem to be a temporary inconvenience rather than a tragedy. Similarly, if dualism is true, then the resurrection of the body would be a good thing (because of the disadvantages of the soul's existence without one), but it would not seem to be as deeply important as Paul's defense of it in 1 Corinthians 15 suggests.[2]

On the other hand, if one of the two versions of materialism is true, then death is truly horrible and the resurrection is genuinely wonderful. If you are nothing but a living material organism (either the one reading this book right now or one just like it), then when the organism who is you dies, you cease to exist. Unlike the situation with dualism, where you would continue to exist as a disembodied spirit,

---

1. I am indebted to Trenton Merricks for these arguments. See Trenton Merricks, "The Resurrection of the Body and the Life Everlasting," in *Reason for the Hope Within*, ed. Michael J. Murray, 261–86 (Grand Rapids: Eerdmans, 1999).

2. Christian dualists reply to such Christian materialist arguments by emphasizing the importance of the resurrected body to enable the soul to *thrive* and *flourish*.

there would be nothing left of you after the death of your body (except of course for your eventually scattered physical parts, which would obviously not constitute you). In circumstances such as this, the resurrection of the body would be absolutely essential for you ever to exist again. It would be required for you to enjoy even the smallest benefit of eternal life. So from a materialist (rather than a dualist) standpoint, it may be easier to make sense of what the Bible teaches about death and resurrection.

It is time to employ the points made in this section to articulate a case against premise 1. This premise says that Christianity requires that dualism be true (to account for the possibility of life after death). But now we have two reasons to deny this, one philosophical and one biblical. The philosophical reason is that, given at least one of the versions of materialism stated, it is arguable that an omnipotent God could either somehow re-create the very same material organism that we are before death or somehow create one just like it that is the person we are. If either of these outcomes is possible, then life after death is possible from a materialist standpoint. Moreover, we have good reason to think that we can be identical with some person in the afterlife even if that person is qualitatively different from us in a number of important respects. The biblical reason is that materialism seems to fit what the Bible says about death and resurrection better than dualism does, as we have just seen.

Problems with a Materialist Approach to the Afterlife

Though these considerations may convince some people that a materialist view of persons is consistent with Christianity, others will not be persuaded. This latter group includes both non-Christian materialists and Christian dualists. They have both philosophical and biblical reasons for thinking that premise 1 is true. The philosophical reasons can be appreciated by paying attention to the two uses of the word *somehow* in the previous paragraph. Though some people have faith that an omnipotent God can re-create a person by means of re-creating a particular material organism or by means of creating a material organism exactly like that person's premortem body, others need to understand *how* these divine actions are possible. The philosophical reasons for premise 1 are reasons for thinking that even God could not pull off either of these sorts of results. We consider some of these reasons below.

The biblical reasons for premise 1 are that, in spite of the argument made in the previous section about death and resurrection, various biblical passages seem to support dualism rather than materialism. One of these is the verse already mentioned about what Jesus says to the thief on the cross next to him. Another is what Jesus tells the disciples in Matthew 10:28: "Do not be afraid of those who kill the body but cannot kill the soul. Rather, be afraid of the One who can destroy both soul and body in hell." This seems to imply that the soul and the body are two different things (and if two different things, then presumably two different *kinds* of things: immaterial and material). There are also Paul's comments in 2 Corinthians 5:6, 8 that "as long as we are at home in the body we are away from the Lord" and that he "would prefer to be away from the body and at home with the Lord."

Though these Scripture passages seem most naturally interpreted in terms of dualism, there may well be plausible materialist readings of them.[3] It is less likely that a convincing philosophical explanation can be given of how life after death is possible on materialist grounds. Whether a person rejects or endorses premise 1 in light of this depends on the amount of mystery he or she is willing to tolerate. Different explanatory problems arise for each of the two versions of materialism discussed.

In the case of the view that a person is identical to a *particular* body, we have first to figure out what it is that makes a certain body the same from one time to the next. A plausible candidate for this involves at least having exactly the same parts. If we do not require this, we face a difficulty illustrated by the ship of Theseus story: Theseus is the captain of a ship called the original ship. Over the years, pieces of the original ship are replaced by other pieces. The person responsible for these substitutions keeps all the original pieces in a pile. Eventually, every piece of the original ship is replaced by another piece. The resulting ship is the continuous ship. At this point, the shipbuilder decides to take all the pieces he has collected and put them together to make a ship. This ship is the reconstructed ship. Which of the latter two ships is identical to the original ship? They cannot both be, since they are clearly two separate ships. The continuous ship may seem to be—especially to its captain, Theseus—but in spite of its

causal continuity with the original ship, it has none of the same materials as the original ship. Only the reconstructed ship has anything material in common with the original ship (both later ships have the same *form* as the original ship, but we are talking about something that only *one* of these later ships shares with the original ship). Both the original ship and the continuous ship share the property of being commanded by Theseus. However, this property is a purely external and relative property rather than an internal and intrinsic property of the ships, and identity over time seems to require the latter rather than the former.

If we say that the same material object can persist through time even if it loses a part, then we need to say that it can persist through the loss of *all* its parts. But this would require us to say that the original ship and the continuous ship are the same ship, and this seems wrong (since it seems more plausible that the original ship is identical instead to the reconstructed ship). Therefore, it seems best to conclude that a material object can retain its identity only if it does not lose any of its parts.

It is a scientific fact that all human bodies gain and lose parts over time. Thus, given what we have just concluded, the same human person has a succession of different bodies over time. This raises some questions about the possibility of accommodating life after death given the first version of materialism. If our postmortem existence requires that God re-create our premortem body, then which of our premortem bodies should God re-create? It seems arbitrary for God to re-create one rather than another. Moreover, if God re-creates the body I had when I was

---

3. See ibid. for an attempt to show that this is the case with at least some of these verses. Merricks also lists a number of biblical passages that he argues seem more naturally understood in materialist terms.

five and also the (materially completely different) body I presently have, which of them would be me according to the materialist view? If I am identical to my body, and both are my body, then I am identical to both. But then I would be two separate things, and this is absurd. This is the ship of Theseus example applied to human bodies and persons.

To these vexing problems for a materialist view of life after death we can add one more. Suppose we attempt to avoid the foregoing problems for materialism by stipulating that God re-creates me after my death by means of reassembling all the parts of the body I possessed (or was) at the moment of my death. This would require the existence of only the *smallest* parts of my body, whatever these might be (atoms? subatomic particles?), since all the parts of my body are composed of them. Thus, we should not worry about the consequences of dismemberment or cremation.

What is problematic is the possibility that one or more of the parts of my last body could end up being a part in another person's last body. One way this could happen is through the natural processes of bodily decay, decomposition, disintegration, and dispersal. A corpse is buried in the ground. Over a long period of time, the atoms that composed it become part of the soil. Some of these atoms become part of the grass over the grave. Cows eat this grass. These cows are eventually slaughtered for the purpose of making hamburgers. Someone eats a hamburger made from one of these cows. As a result, an atom that was part of one person's last body becomes part of another person's body. If that person dies before losing that part, then this one part will

have been a part in the last bodies of *two* people. But according to the materialist view, both persons need that part to exist again. If God re-creates them both, then it seems they must share that part. But this too seems absurd. (A quicker route to the same conclusion is to imagine a case of cannibalism in which a cannibal dies right after digesting his victim. A more mundane example involves the death of an organ donation recipient right after transplant surgery.)

These sorts of considerations have led some Christian materialists to endorse the alternative version of materialism according to which God can re-create a person by means of creating a resurrection body that possesses the same physical and psychological properties as his or her premortem body. Such a body would have to have the same *type* of parts as the earlier one, but it would not have to have *exactly the same* parts. Consequently, this view avoids many of the problems of the other materialist view. However, it has a number of problems of its own. In the first place, to which of a person's premortem bodies does the resurrection body need to be exactly similar? Again, this seems to be an arbitrary matter. It does not seem satisfactory to say that it must be qualitatively identical to the body at the moment of death. The bodies of many people at death are seriously incapacitated both physically and psychologically (victims of Alzheimer's are one poignant example of this).

But even if there is a solution to this problem, this version of materialism faces other difficulties. If God can make one body qualitatively indistinguishable from one of my premortem bodies, then God can make more than one of these. If God makes one of these rather than another, then his choice cannot be based on an objective feature that one of them has and the other lacks that makes one of them my body (and so, according to the materialist, me) and the other one not. But then there is nothing objective about *either one* that makes it me, and therefore it seems that neither one could be me (how could God's arbitrary decision that one of them is me somehow make it me?).

Christians who are impressed by these difficulties with materialism often conclude that personal identity across time is possible for human beings only if at least a part of them is something that cannot gain or lose parts, that cannot be duplicated, and that possesses an objective feature that distinguishes them from other persons. Dualists are quick to point out that nonphysical souls have all these characteristics.

Dualism, Human Nature, and Life after Death

So far we have considered arguments both against and for premise 1 of the argument stated at the beginning of this chapter. As we have seen, people who are willing to accept some mystery may deny this premise on the grounds that, though we may not be able to understand how it is possible, an omnipotent God could re-create entirely material persons in the afterlife by means of the resurrection of the body. Others affirm premise 1 on the grounds that the problems discussed in the preceding section suggest that even an all-powerful God could not do this. Christians in this latter group need to provide good reasons to doubt premise

2 to defend Christianity from the critic's argument. This section considers arguments against premise 2 and then looks at a couple versions of dualism.

The first argument against premise 2 is based on conclusions drawn in the previous section about human persons and human bodies:

4. If human persons persist across time but human bodies do not (because they gain and lose parts), then human persons cannot be identical to human bodies.
5. If human persons cannot be identical to human bodies, then materialism cannot be true.
6. If materialism cannot be true, then premise 2 (which states that human beings are nothing but material organisms) cannot be true.
7. Human persons persist across time, but human bodies do not.
8. Consequently, premise 2 cannot be true.

Both Christian and non-Christian materialists take issue with premise 7 of this argument. They do this by arguing that a material organism can persist through time even if it gains or loses parts. This is precisely what the ship of Theseus example discussed in the last section calls into question. However, neither side in this debate is *obviously* correct. From the standpoint of Christian apologetics, this is okay. If the materialists are right, then we have good reason to deny premise 1. If the materialists are wrong, then we are justified in rejecting premise 2. Either way, the objection to Christianity being evaluated fails.

What reasons are there for thinking that premise 2 is *true*? The dominant argument for it is that human psychological phenomena are best explained by the materialist hypothesis. For one thing, materialism is considered by many to be the *simplest* account of human persons. Materialism says that human beings are only *one* kind of thing: a material organism. According to dualism, human beings are a composite of *two* kinds of thing: a material body and an immaterial mind, soul, or spirit. Also, many materialists are naturalists and accept materialism because it is more consistent with naturalism than dualism is (how could a metaphysical naturalist account for the existence of spiritual entities?). Also, it seems to many who accept some form of evolutionary theory of the origin of the human species (whether they are naturalists or not) that such a theory precludes the possibility that human beings have immaterial souls (how could something immaterial come about by means of a purely material evolutionary process?). Materialism also finds support in the scientific observation that all known conscious human phenomena are dependent on biological states of the human organism. An example of this is how lesions in certain parts of the brain impair memory functions. This suggests not only that the mind cannot work without the brain but also (because it is a simpler hypothesis) that the mind is *nothing but* the brain. A final contribution to the case for materialism concerns the mysteries of both the nature of immaterial souls (what can be said about them that is both informative and positive?) and the interaction of nonphysical minds or souls and physical bodies (if physical change requires a transference of physical energy, then how

can a nonphysical mind (without physical energy) produce a physical change (in a physical body)?

Though this accumulation of arguments for premise 2 is impressive, there are good reasons for thinking that it fails to provide sufficient reason to accept it. In the first place, each of these arguments is inconclusive: Even if all their premises are true, it could still be the case that human beings have immaterial minds or souls. Second, materialists have not been able adequately to account for consciousness and everything that depends on it (such as thought, sensation, and will). Moreover, it is difficult to explain how genuine (undetermined) free will is possible if human beings are merely material organisms. Finally, we can reiterate here the difficulty of showing how materialism is compatible with personal identity across time (see the above argument).

Though these points do not show that materialism is false and dualism is true, they do reveal the complicated nature of the debate about these alternative theories of human nature. There are good arguments on both sides and intelligent and reasonable contemporary defenders of both positions. This philosophical controversy is far from settled. Accordingly, it seems reasonable to conclude that an adequate case for premise 2 has not yet been made.

We have seen that good reasons exist to question both premise 1 and premise 2 of the critic's argument. Thus, the Christian faith can be defended against it. However, the discussion has left us with problems for both dualist and materialist accounts of life after death. Dualism does not seem able to account adequately for the emphasis placed by the Bible on the seriousness of death and the importance of the resurrection of the body. Materialism does not seem able to provide a basis for confidence that a person in this life can live again in the life to come. The last task in this chapter is to attempt to remove these concerns.

Plato is generally considered the founder of philosophical dualism in the Western tradition. He believed that human persons are immaterial souls that are temporarily imprisoned in a body. He also thought that human fulfillment is possible only by means of the eventual liberation of the soul from the body. He said that human happiness comes only through enlightenment and that the body's senses prevent this because of how they distort reality and that the body's appetites distract us from our pursuit of illumination. Plato, therefore, saw the soul as a good thing and the body as something bad. According to his view, souls are also naturally immortal. They cannot be destroyed because by virtue of being immaterial they do not have parts and so cannot cease to exist by means of coming apart. Platonic philosophy, like Indian philosophy, endorses reincarnation. These immaterial and immortal souls endure a series of embodiments and disembodiments until they are finally freed from bodies altogether.

The Christian Platonist Augustine adopted and adapted Plato's ideas. Obviously, he could not endorse the elements of Plato's view that are inconsistent with the Christian faith, such as the denigration of matter (which Christians believe God created good) and the affirmation of reincarnation (since Christians believe that humans are "destined to die once, and after that to face judgment" [Heb. 9:27]). He also denied Plato's thesis that souls are *naturally* immortal (are by nature indestructible), since this is inconsistent with God's sovereignty (souls are immortal only if God sustains them *super*naturally). But Augustine (and later, many other Christian dualists like Descartes) agreed with Plato that human persons are nothing but immaterial souls. As argued, this view does not seem to account for what the Bible says about death and resurrection as well as materialism does. However, as noted above, these dualists can argue that death is bad and that the resurrection is good because the soul needs a body to thrive and flourish.

The later Christian Aristotelian philosopher and theologian Thomas Aquinas developed an alternative dualist view of human nature that may avoid the problems both Platonic dualism and materialism have in accounting for the afterlife. Aquinas followed Aristotle in asserting that the human person is essentially a composite of body and soul (rather than, as Plato thought, just a soul, and as the materialists believe, just a body). Consequently, an individual human person cannot exist in his or her entirety in a disembodied state. Aquinas also agreed with Aristotle that human souls have an active part (the part that does the thinking and willing) and a passive part (the part that stores the thoughts, sensations, and feelings that enter into thinking and willing). The active part of the soul is like a computer's central processor, and the passive part is like the hard drive on which the programs and data are stored. Both Aristotle and Aquinas believed that the passive part of the soul depends for its existence on the existence of the body (it is just a certain way in which the body—we would say the brain—is structured or organized). The active part, on the other hand, is imma-terial and therefore can exist on its own even when the body dies.

Since this active part of the soul is not a person (because both the entire soul and an entire body are required for a human person to exist), its continued existence after the death of the person does not suf-fice for personal life after death. That is why Aristotle believed that death means the cessation of a person's existence for-ever. But as a Christian, Aquinas affirmed the doctrine of the resurrection of the body. When that occurs, the active part of a person's soul (the existence of which God will have upheld continuously in a kind of "soul sleep" ever since the person's death) is reunited with that person's body (including his or her passive soul). The result is the re-creation of the complete person (who ceased to exist at death).

Aquinas's theory of human nature has numerous advantages. First, it makes it clearer than Augustine's version of Plato's dualism why the material body is a good thing. It is good because it is an essential part of the nature of human beings created by God. Being human is a good thing, and one can be a human person only if one has a body, according to Aquinas's view. Second, the continued existence of the active part of a person's soul provides the continuity required for personal identity across time, which does not seem possible according to the materialist view. Third, the active part of the soul has the three features not possessed by material bodies

> **We should expect mysteries to surround any theory we adopt.**

that are needed for personal identity: (1) It is immaterial, so it does not have parts and thus cannot gain or lose parts; (2) it is a particular individual thing, so it cannot be duplicated (though it can be copied or replicated); and (3) it is objectively the active soul of one particular person rather than another.

Finally, Aquinas's theory can account for why death is so bad and the resurrec-tion of the body so good more effectively than the Christian Platonic dualists' theory can. What makes death horrible, accord-ing Aquinas's view, is that it brings about the annihilation of the person (though not, of course, of that *part* of the person called the active part of the soul). What makes the resurrection of the body such a wonderful thing, given Aquinas's posi-tion, is that it brings human persons back into existence again. Aquinas's view shares these consequences with materialism but not with Platonic dualism.

One additional point is that Aquinas's form of dualism, like the Platonic form (and unlike the first version of material-ism), does not require God to be able to re-create one of the very same bodies pos-sessed by a person in this life. As long as the body God creates is sufficiently like one of the person's earthly bodies and possesses all the contents of the passive part of that person's soul (and thus all the person's psychological properties), the complete person can be re-created at the resurrection. This still leaves a lot of mysteries unexplained (such as which premortem physical and psychological properties must be reproduced), but we should expect mysteries to surround any theory we adopt.

In sum, Aquinas's body and soul per-spective on the nature of human persons may enable us to set aside the concerns raised above about both materialist and Platonic dualist accounts of the afterlife. However, some believe that Aquinas's view inherits the problems that beset the materialist attempt to account for life after death. Though Aquinas says that the active part of a person's soul is an immaterial and thus indivisible thing, he also holds that the entire person is partly material and thus divisible into parts (because the entire person is a combination of soul and body, and the body is material and divisible). But then it seems to follow that even if the active part of a person's soul can persist into the afterlife, the entire person cannot, at least given the arguments stated above against the materialist claim that a body in this life can be numerically identical to a body in the afterlife. This criticism of Aquinas's view denies the claim made in the preceding paragraph that his theory does not require a person's resurrection body to be numerically identical with that person's premortem body (or *one* of that person's premortem bodies). This problem with Aquinas's theory suggests the need to reconsider the Christian Platonist version of dualism, even with its allegedly inferior ability to account for what the Bible teaches about death and resurrection.

In the end, all three of the views of human nature discussed in this chapter (materialism, Christian Platonist dualism, and Aquinas's version of dualism) have both philosophical and biblical advantages and disadvantages. In the absence of good reasons to prefer one of these theories over the others, we are left with a mystery concerning how to understand human nature and how God will bring about our existence in the afterlife. But we are also left with good reasons to doubt both premises of the critic's argument against Christianity with which we began this chapter. Moreover, insofar as we have good reason to believe that Jesus was raised from the dead, as argued in chapter 15, it is reasonable to believe that God will raise us from the dead as well. Our inability to understand fully *how* this will happen need not undermine our reasonable hope *that* it will occur.

Reflection and Discussion

1. Are you willing to say that a materialist view of persons is compatible with Christianity, even though it seems we cannot explain how God could re-create a material person at the resurrection? Why or why not?

2. Do you agree with a Christian materialist that Christian Platonist dualism cannot adequately account for the Bible's emphasis on the seriousness of death and the importance of the resurrection of the body? Why or why not?

3. What do you think about Thomas Aquinas's version of dualism? Do you think it is plausible and that it provides an adequate ground for the Christian hope in eternal life? Why or why not?

Further Reading

Cooper, John W. *Body, Soul, and Life Everlasting: Biblical Anthropology and the Monism-Dualism Debate*. Grand Rapids: Eerdmans, 1989.

Kreeft, Peter, ed. "Anthropology: Body and Soul." In *A Summa of the Summa: The Essential Philosophical Passages of St. Thomas Aquinas' Summa Theologica Edited and Explained for Beginners*, 241–66. San Francisco: Ignatius, 1990.

Van Inwagen, Peter. *The Possibility of Resurrection and Other Essays in Christian Apologetics*. Boulder: Westview, 1997.

24

The Death of God

Postmodern Challenges to Christianity

» Outline

- **Postmodernism, Truth, and Reality**
  - *The Metaphysical Creative Antirealism of Friedrich Nietzsche and Richard Rorty*
  - *A Postmodern Argument against Christianity Denying Objective Reality*
  - *A Christian Defense of Objective Truth and Reality*
- **Christianity and the Great Conversation**
  - *Three Postmodern Challenges to Christianity*
    - Rationality: Argumentation as Manipulation
    - Universality: No One Global Story
    - Finality: No Final Truth or Last Word about Anything
  - *Christian Replies to These Challenges*
- **Is Christianity Life Affirming or Life Denying?**
  - *The Nietzsche/Rorty Critique of Christian Values*
    - The Idea of God Ungrounded and No Longer Viable
    - Christian Morality as a Life-Denying Slave Morality
    - Life-Affirming Values Require Individual Freedom
  - *Christian Replies*
    - Creation Monotheism Is Rationally Supportable
    - Christian Morality Is the Only True Means to Affirm Life

» Summary

Postmodern philosophies share a rejection of Enlightenment assumptions. Christians can agree with some postmodern conclusions but must resist those at odds with Christianity. One radical postmodern argument against the Christian worldview is based on the denial of objective truth and reality. But Christian apologists can show that there is no adequate postmodern account of truth that can sustain this objection. Similarly, postmodern challenges to the rationality, universality, and finality of the Christian worldview arguably fail. Finally, when postmodernists insist on criticizing belief in God and Christian values, Christian apologists can show that it is reasonable to accept creation monotheism and that only Christian morality is truly liberating and life affirming.

» Basic Terms, Concepts, and Names

correspondence truth
Deism
Enlightenment, the
finality
metaphysical creative antirealism
Nietzsche, Friedrich
objective truth versus objectivity
postmodernism
pragmatism about truth
rationality
relativism about truth
Rorty, Richard
slave morality versus master morality
universality

» Reflection and Discussion

» Further Reading

> All the Athenians and the foreigners who lived there spent their time doing nothing but talking about and listening to the latest ideas.
>
> Acts 17:21

A relatively recent intellectual trend that has posed several challenges to both traditional philosophy and traditional Christianity is postmodernism. Unfortunately, the word *postmodernism* is so vague and used in so many ways that it is of questionable usefulness. Nonetheless, Christian apologists are likely to be asked how Christians can and should respond to postmodernism. Fortunately, a handful of general themes loosely characterize various contemporary thinkers and theories classified as postmodern. Consequently, it is possible to formulate a description of postmodernism to which apologists can respond.

Postmodern philosophers are united in their criticism of the central tenets of the eighteenth-century European (and to some extent American) philosophical movement known as the Enlightenment. A dominant assumption of this movement is that individual human beings are capable of knowing important universal and objective truths about the world and human nature on the basis of rational methods. Moreover, Enlightenment philosophers believe that there are universal criteria of rationality on the basis of which we can know whether we have the truth about important matters. They think that the exercise of rational methods in compliance with rational criteria enables people to grasp the true nature of reality with a high degree of objectivity (i.e., freedom from subjective factors such as bias and preconceptions).

Even though René Descartes was a seventeenth-century philosopher, he is a good example of a "modern" Enlightenment thinker (indeed, his philosophical ideas contributed significantly to the rise of the Enlightenment movement). He believed that the careful use of rational philosophical methods could lead one to attain objective certainty about the essence and existence of God, souls, and the material world. He conceived of philosophy as the foundational discipline on the basis of which natural science needed to be established. He also thought that scientific knowledge would provide human beings with a rational basis for improving life by means of the applied sciences of mechanics, medicine, and morals.

From a Christian standpoint, some of the conclusions of Enlightenment thinkers are unwelcome. For one thing, they overemphasized reason at the expense of faith. Many of them also encouraged skepticism about Christian tradition from the standpoint of autonomous individual rationality. Moreover, they tended to place more confidence in the progress of the human race by means of rational methodologies and technologies than faith in the saving work of God in history.

Many Enlightenment thinkers were Deists. Deism is the view that, though God created the universe, he does not intervene in the creation by means of providential acts, miracles, and special revelations. Deism is thought by many to be a more *rational* theological approach than traditional Christianity. Proponents of Deism believe that religion should be based only on truths and values accessible to every human being on the basis of natural human reason. In this way, people need only to employ their intellects and their consciences to know what they need to know to be rightly related to God and their fellow human beings. But Christianity is founded on particular historical truths and the need for the Holy Spirit to produce faith through God's special revelation in the Bible and in the incarnate Christ, authenticated by special acts of providence and miraculous events. Therefore, the excessive rationalism of Enlightenment Deists is inconsistent with traditional Christianity.

To the extent that postmodernists are critical of the elements of modernist Enlightenment thinking that are at odds with the Christian faith, Christian apolo-gists can view them as allies. However, many postmodernist philosophers supplement their critique of the Enlightenment with a variety of views that Christians must reject. Among these views are (1) the denial of a unified objective truth and reality, (2) the repudiation of rationality altogether on the ground that it is nothing but a tool for domination, and (3) the criticism of Christian values and virtues as oppressive and dehumanizing. This chapter suggests ways Christian apologists can defend Christianity against these postmodern claims. The next chapter takes on another hallmark of postmodernism: ethical relativism.

Postmodernism, Truth, and Reality

Friedrich Nietzsche (1844–1900) is a strong candidate for consideration as the first postmodern philosopher. He is well known for his announcement (through his fictional character Zarathustra) that "God is dead."[1] This way of putting it (rather than saying that God does not exist) was meant to convey Nietzsche's conviction that, at the time of his writing, belief in God was no longer a viable option. But belief in God is just one aspect (though the most important one) of a collection of connected beliefs about ultimate reality, such as beliefs in immaterial and immortal souls, heaven and hell, free will, moral responsibility, a fixed human nature, objective meaning, and moral values. The part of traditional philosophy that is responsible for a theory of ultimate reality that encompasses such things is called

---

1. Nietzsche's works *Thus Spoke Zarathustra* and *The Gay Science* both contain his ruminations on the death of God.

metaphysics. Nietzsche's confidence in the death of God was part of his larger assurance about the death of metaphysics.

Nietzsche held that traditional metaphysics did not provide a rational description of ultimate reality as its proponents claimed. Rather, according to Nietzsche, metaphysical theories constituted a rationalized confession of personal psychology on the part of the metaphysician. That is, whether the philosopher realized it (or would admit it) or not, metaphysical theories had more to do with what their inventor *wanted* to be true about the world than with what he *discovered* to be the case about it. Nietzsche thought that arguments provided for these theories were not good evidence for thinking they were true. Instead, they were rationalizations or justifications for accepting the theories in spite of a lack of genuinely good rational grounds. Nietzsche believed that metaphysicians projected what they wanted to be true instead of describing what they discovered to be true.

This idea that theories about the world tell us more about the theorists than about the world has become a dominant theme in postmodern philosophy. The emphasis is placed almost entirely on a theorist's *interpretation* of the facts rather than on the facts themselves. One way to put this idea is that all observation is theory-laden. That is, one never experiences anything in a fully objective and direct way. Rather, what one experiences (sees, hears, etc.) is influenced or determined by the assumptions, biases, presuppositions, and preconceived ideas one brings to one's observation.

If this viewpoint is taken to an extreme, as many postmodern thinkers do, it follows that the Enlightenment ideal of objectivity in philosophical and scientific inquiry is completely unrealizable. Instead, people are locked into their subjective points of view as they formulate beliefs about the world. Moreover, postmodernists say, since people's subjective perspectives differ from one another by virtue of their different genders, ethnic identities, cultures, historical situations, and so on, it follows that what people take to be true is an entirely relative matter.

It is important at this point to clarify a distinction between two uses of the word *objective*. One use of the word concerns our *access* to what is true and real. As mentioned in chapter 3, our access to the world is relatively objective when it is relatively free from such subjective factors as personal bias and the limitations of a particular point of view. The Enlightenment thinkers assumed that humans can enjoy a high degree of objective access to the truth about reality. Nietzsche holds instead that our access to reality is entirely subjective—completely devoid of objectivity. This first type of objectivity is *epistemological* because it has to do with factors that determine whether we can *know* the truth about reality.

Another use of the word *objective* concerns the world to which we seek access. To say that there is an objective world or objective reality is to say that there is an existing realm of objects that is not merely a subjective product of human minds. To say that there are objective truths (in this sense of the word *objective*) is to say that there are statements or propositions that correspond to or agree with the objective world (the way things really are). This second type of objectivity is *metaphysical* because it has to do with the nature of reality as it is in and of itself. Whereas epistemological objectivity comes in degrees (because we can be more or less objective in our access to the objective world), metaphysical objectivity either exists or does not exist (either there is a world that exists independently of human subjectivity, or there is not).

One conclusion that can be drawn from Nietzsche's thesis of the relativity of individual perspectives is that no one is in a position to know anything about objective reality. This was what the ancient skeptics believed. They did not, however, deny the existence of objective truth and reality (the way things are in and of themselves whether we can know this about them or not). They merely denied *knowledge* of objective truth and reality.

Many postmodern philosophers go further than this and conclude that there is no such thing as objective reality and therefore no such thing as truth in the sense of the correspondence of a thought to (or agreement of a thought with) objective reality. In the words of contemporary postmodern philosopher Richard Rorty, "Truth is made rather than found."[2] Philosophers have labeled this perspective on truth and reality metaphysical (creative) antirealism. It is the metaphysical view that there is no objective reality and that the only reality that exists is subjective, that is, created (or constructed) by human consciousness. This idea is rooted in the philosophy of the German idealist philosopher Immanuel Kant (1724–1804). He argued that the world of experience is constructed by the categories and con-

cepts of consciousness. Kant's theory is the historical, philosophical basis for the postmodern theme of the social construction of reality.

What should Christians think about these ideas, and how should they respond? It is important not to reject postmodern philosophy altogether. As mentioned earlier, to a certain extent, postmodern philosophy is compatible with and even helpful to Christianity. For one thing, Christians can agree with postmodern philosophy that humans are not capable of the degree of objectivity and certainty about what is real assumed to be humanly possible by modern Enlightenment philosophers. A less optimistic view about human reason is more compatible with the Christian emphasis on the need for faith, the virtue of humility, and how, at least in this life, we "see but a poor reflection as in a mirror" (1 Cor. 13:12). Moreover, there is a lot of wisdom in the realization that what we believe and what we value are influenced in important ways by gender, race, ethnicity, historical situation, and cultural setting. Christians can explain some of these limits to objectivity in terms of how our minds are darkened by sin (see chap. 5).

However, Christians cannot accept the postmodern adherence to metaphysical creative antirealism with its denial of objective reality and correspondence truth and its affirmation of only subjective reality constructed by human consciousness. From a Christian standpoint, there must be an objectively real world. This objectively real world contains God and the universe that God created. There was a time when God and the universe existed but human beings did not. If Christianity is true, then someone who believes that Christianity is true has a belief that corresponds to

---

2. Richard Rorty, *Contingency, Irony, and Solidarity* (Cambridge: Cambridge University Press, 1989). This quotation is a paraphrase of one of Rorty's central points in chap. 1 of this book. See especially p. 7.

reality, and someone who believes that Christianity is not true has a belief that does not agree with the way things really are. At bottom, metaphysical antirealism is a denial of the eternal reality and sovereign creativity of God. Antirealism makes all "reality" a temporary product of human creative consciousness. Because of this incompatibility between Christianity and postmodern antirealism, Christian apologists must respond to the following argument:

1. If Christianity is true, then there is objective truth and reality.
2. But there is no objective truth and reality (this is metaphysical antirealism).
3. Therefore, Christianity is false.

Since Christians must agree with premise 1, the debate centers on premise 2. But here the postmodern philosopher who denies objective truth and reality runs into a problem. Postmodernists can establish 3 on the basis of premises 1 and 2 only if they can give a good reason for thinking that premise 2 is true. But premise 2 itself denies that there is such a thing as objective truth. Could premise 2 be true in some sense even if it is not *objectively* true (i.e, made true by means of correspondence with objective reality)?

Rorty denies correspondence truth and objective reality, but he still uses the word *true* in different ways.[3] He says that the goal of inquiry is not to make our minds mirror reality but instead to achieve as much consensus among inquirers as possible. He calls a belief "true" when it is a

3. See his *Philosophy and the Mirror of Nature* (Princeton: Princeton University Press, 1979); and his *Contingency, Irony, and Solidarity.*

belief no one among one's peers objects to. He also uses the word *true* in a pragmatic sense to mean "whatever satisfies our desires." Presumably, the connection between these two uses of "true" is that beliefs that are useful in enabling us to get what we want are also beliefs that no one in our circle will criticize. This way of talking about true beliefs is satisfactory when it comes to simple observational beliefs. For instance, if I ask you whether there are any Cheerios in the cupboard and you say that you believe there are, then I won't disagree with you if I go to the cupboard and find my desire for Cheerios satisfied as a result.

However, these ways of using the word *true* are arguably unsatisfactory when it comes to controversial theoretical, philosophical claims like premise 2. For one thing, plenty of people disagree with this postmodern claim. Consequently, it is not true in Rorty's "consensus" sense of truth. To say that a consensus is required only among those in one's group and that one's group consists of those with whom one agrees about such matters is obviously to beg the question. Moreover, neither believing nor disbelieving premise 2 seems to be straightforwardly connected with whether our desires are satisfied or thwarted. It is true that believing premise 2 may satisfy some postmodern philosophers' desires not to have to deal with an objectively real God. At the same time, however, a belief in premise 2 would frustrate the desire of a Christian for such a God to exist. Since the state of affairs expressed by premise 2 would both satisfy some human desires and frustrate others, it follows that it is both true and false. But this is absurd.

In the end, it is arguable that consensus is a good thing only if what is agreed about is really true by virtue of corresponding to an independent and objective reality. Furthermore, it seems clear that many truths are incompatible with people's desires, and many falsehoods conform to what people want. Therefore, Rorty's ways of talking about truth do not help to show that premise 2 is true.

Perhaps the only way left for a proponent of premise 2 to claim that it is true is to fall back on simple relativism and just say that premise 2 is true *for that person* (even if not for others). But what could this mean other than merely that this person believes that premise 2 is true? And even if it meant something more than this, why should anyone who rejects premise 2 care that it is "true for someone else" in an unspecified sense? The bottom line is that premise 2 can be true in the sense needed for the argument to succeed only if premise 2 is *objectively* true. But it cannot be objectively true that there is no such thing as objective truth and reality.

Christianity and the Great Conversation

Even if we can set aside the radical postmodern denial of objective reality and correspondence truth, we are still faced with the skeptical postmodern rejection of any degree of objective access to objective reality. What good is objective truth if we cannot ever know what it is or even have any justified beliefs about it? A fundamental operating assumption in this book is that some claims to objective truth are more objectively reasonable than others and that we can set aside our presuppositions and biases to a great enough extent to be able to see that this is true. We have

been assuming that we are not entirely blinded by our subjective circumstances. We have taken seriously the power of good arguments and strong evidences as reliable indications of the truth.

But another postmodern theme is that all appeals to rationality and every use of argumentation and evidence are just covert employments of power for the purpose of dominating and manipulating others. To say that someone's beliefs, desires, values, or goals are irrational is to discredit them. But who's to say that the standard of rationality to which one appeals in making such claims is acceptable? If no one is in a good position to say what is objectively true, then we have no basis on which to claim that one standard of rationality is superior to another. In the end, we have only our desires to win arguments and to get other people to believe what we want them to believe and to do what we want them to do.

Postmodern philosophers are as intent on persuading others to see things their way as anyone else. But if they reject the use of rational arguments for this purpose, what, if anything, would be an acceptable replacement? Instead of employing rational arguments to support theories about what is objectively true, they can use personal narratives to recommend their subjective preferences concerning how to think and live. The intended result is an ongoing conversation in which a multiplicity of stories and viewpoints are shared.

One postmodern philosopher characterizes the central postmodern idea as the claim that "there is no totalizing metanarrative."[4] What he means is that no big

4. Jean-François Lyotard said, "I define *postmodern* as incredulity toward metanarratives"

story includes and explains all our little stories. But the Christian worldview (like all worldviews) is a totalizing metanarrative or universal story that purports to contain and explain all our individual stories. However, this postmodern thesis sounds a bit like the antirealist claim argued against in the previous section (the one objective reality denied by antirealists would be the "big story"). If we alter the claim to make it instead about *access* to reality, we have the statement that no one is in a position to think that any one universal story is more likely to be true than any other. Though this does not preclude the possibility that Christianity is objectively true, it does challenge the fundamental assumptions on which Christian apologetics is based.

Moreover, Rorty thinks of Christianity as a conversation stopper because it claims to embody the ultimate truth about what the world is like and how human beings ought to live their lives. He thinks of the Christian faith as diametrically opposed to genuinely free inquiry. Free inquiry, as far as people like Rorty are concerned, requires that we keep the conversation going, and we can keep the conversation going only as long as we avoid confident claims about ultimate truth and value. Rorty does not mind when people make claims about what is real, true, and good as long as they are willing to admit that they have no rational basis for them and that their convictions are merely a product of time and chance. Rorty thinks that people, like committed Christians, who insist on one particular view about the

(by which he meant totalizing explanations) (*The Postmodern Condition: A Report on Knowledge*, trans. Geoff Bennington and Brian Massumi [Minneapolis: University of Minnesota Press, 1984], xxiv).

way things are or the way things should be are not sufficiently open-minded to count as useful participants in the ongoing great conversation.

Let's pause to summarize the postmodern complaints about Christianity mentioned in this section. Christians are (or at least ought to be) committed to the *rationality* of Christian claims, the *universality* of the Christian worldview, and the *finality* of Christian truths. But postmodern critics say that argumentation is just manipulation, that there is no one global story but rather many local stories, and that there is no final truth about or last word on any subject—especially the nature of ultimate reality and the meaning of human life. How can Christians reply to these charges?

First, let's examine the postmodern assertion about rationality. What reasons do postmodernists have for thinking it is true? It is clear that they cannot consistently claim to have a *good reason* to endorse it (in the sense of a *rational argument* for its truth) because this is the very thing that the thesis in question says does not exist. Consequently, if they are consistent and do offer an argument for it, they have to see their use of argumentation as a power play. But if that is what they are doing, then those of us who do not agree with them have been given no good reason to change our minds, and we can simply refuse to be intimidated by them.

Suppose postmodernists respond that it is not fair of us to hold them to a rational standard of consistency, since this begs the question against them. But again, what reason can they give us for giving up on consistency as a requirement for good thinking? Moreover, if we do allow for blatant inconsistency in how we think, then we have given up any legitimate grounds for preferring one way of thinking over another. But this price is too high to pay, even for postmodernists. After all, they prefer us to think the way they do about rationality and Christianity. In the end, if they have any serious objections to Christianity, they would be better off using rational methods to formulate them, since those are the only methods that give people good reason for thinking that what the postmodernists are saying is *true* (and why should anyone care about what they are saying if it is *not* true?).

Next let's evaluate the postmodern idea that no universal narrative or story encompasses and accounts for the many stories of different individuals and diverse cultures. As said above, to distinguish this thesis from that of metaphysical antirealism (against which we argued in the previous section), we should see this as a claim about knowledge or rational belief. Given this, it boils down to the allegation that it is not possible for anyone to know or be justified in believing that one worldview is rationally superior to all the others. If this is true, then any attempt to recommend one's worldview to others on the ground that it is rationally superior to other global perspectives can seem like an arrogant imposition. If reasons are inadequate to persuade others to adopt one's worldview, then one is left with either simply telling one's story (and hoping that others will like it enough to want to make it their own) or trying to coerce others to change their minds (this is the connection between this postmodern theme and the one just discussed).

But again, what reasons can postmodernists give for this skeptical thesis? There do not seem to be any adequate general philosophical reasons for this conclusion. Rather, a satisfactory case can be made for the claim that no one can know whether any one worldview is rationally superior to its competitors only by means of a careful and detailed examination of the claims of each worldview and the arguments for and against them. This is just the sort of thing this book has tried to do. It has provided a number of arguments that contribute to a cumulative case for the claim that the Christian worldview is rationally superior to those with which it competes. It seems reasonable to believe this to be true in the absence of good reasons to think otherwise. Moreover, the claims made have been relatively modest. I have not presented my arguments as *proofs* or *demonstrations* that provide grounds for absolute certainty that Christian theism is true. Nor have I assumed that the arguments and evidences offered provide completely objective access to the truth. I have repeatedly argued instead that it is reasonable to believe that the Christian worldview is true in spite of both legitimate concerns about it and the attractive features of the alternatives. Though it would be easy for a postmodernist to argue that no one can *prove* one worldview is true, it would be much more difficult to make a case for the claim that it is not possible to show, as I have tried to do, that it is reasonable to believe that Christianity is rationally superior to its competitors.

Finally, let's look at the postmodern concern about the alleged finality of Christian truths. Recall that Rorty characterizes Christianity as a conversation stopper. Though Rorty grants that everyone has beliefs about what is real and what is good, he thinks that the contingency or accidental origin of these ideas and ideals should convince people not to take them seriously. He realizes that there is some irony involved in having convictions and commitments that one realizes are ultimately ungrounded and arbitrary. However, he thinks that only if people have such an ironic and even playful attitude about their views can they continue to carry on fruitful discussions about them with those who have different perspectives. From this point of view, committed Christians are people who are much too serious about what they believe to be true and worthwhile. They want to insist that they have good reasons for thinking that what they believe about ultimate reality is universally and objectively true. Rorty thinks Christians' insistence on having the final truth will stop a good conversation from continuing.

In reply, Christians can take issue with Rorty's assumption that their fundamental beliefs and values are purely accidental (merely a result of historical and cultural settings). If it is reasonable to believe that God exists and that Christianity is true (as argued above), then it is reasonable to think that human beings are made in God's image and that at least some of our beliefs and values are rooted in this *imago Dei*. The Bible affirms that God made what can be known about him plain to human beings (Rom. 1:19) and that the requirements of God's law are written on people's hearts and accessible to them by means of their consciences (Rom. 2:15). If all this is true, then there is nothing accidental about people's beliefs in God and universal moral standards. To deny this without argument is to beg the question against theists in general and Christians in particular.

Rorty claims that traditional beliefs in objective reality, correspondence truth, God, and absolute morality should be discarded because they are no longer useful. However, we have already seen the problem with replacing "true" with "useful." Also, whether these beliefs are useful or not depends on who we are and what our purposes are. We have already seen the difficulty of getting by without assuming the existence of objective reality and truths that correspond to it. Those of us who have the goal of finding out as much as we can about what is objectively real and what is truly valuable will arguably find a belief in God and absolute morality useful. From a Christian standpoint, nothing could be more useful than adopting the Christian worldview and living one's life on the basis of it. Nothing less than one's eternal destiny is at stake. If all this is right, then there is also no more worthwhile topic of conversation than the claims of the Christian faith. If Christianity is guilty of stopping a conversation, then perhaps that conversation was not worth continuing. Moreover, Rorty's rejection of the traditional views about truth and rationality and his repudiation of God and absolute morality seem like arbitrary restrictions on a conversation that has been going on for a long time. If anyone is likely to be guilty of stopping a good conversation, it is someone who adopts Rorty's postmodern assumptions.

This ends the defense of the Christian commitment to rationality, universality, and finality against postmodern criticisms of them. However, I do not want to give the impression that there is nothing worthwhile in the postmodern approach to these things. Postmodernists are right to caution us against the use of argument for the exploitation and abuse of others. They are also correct in their warning against an ethnocentric narrowness that precludes attempts to understand and appreciate alternative narratives and stories. Finally, their aversion to dogmatism and close-mindedness as obstacles to fruitful discussions is appropriate. Christians should be equally opposed to exploitation, ethnocentrism, and dogmatism. But Christians, unlike radical postmodernists, can give a rational justification for this by an appeal to God and absolute morality.

> **Christians should be equally opposed to exploitation, ethnocentrism, and dogmatism. But Christians, unlike radical postmodernists, can give a rational justification for this by an appeal to God and absolute morality.**

Is Christianity Life Affirming or Life Denying?

Jesus calls himself the Good Shepherd and contrasts himself to the thief, who "comes only to steal and kill and destroy" (John 10:10). He says he has come so that his followers "may have life, and have it to the full" (John 10:10). Indeed, everyone familiar with John 3:16 knows that "whoever believes in him [Jesus] shall not perish but have *eternal* life" (emphasis added). It would seem, then, that Christianity offers both the highest *quality* of life and the maximal *quantity* of life possible. What could be more life affirming than that?

Nietzsche, however, thought of Christianity as life *denying*. He went so far as to label the Judeo-Christian value system that had come to dominate Western civilization a slave morality. He claimed that shortly after the arrival of Christianity onto the stage of history this slave morality subverted the earlier Greco-Roman master morality. The value system of the Greeks and the Romans had idealized the aristocrat and the warrior. It had heralded the virtues of courage, physical strength, and military skill. It had placed the noble, well-born, powerful, and wealthy masters at the top of the social hierarchy and the common, weak, and poor slaves at the bottom. Nietzsche considered this master morality life affirming in that it celebrated and reinforced natural human impulses and abilities.

But then the Christians came along and turned all this upside down. The people to admire from a Christian standpoint are those who are humble, compassionate, and meek. They are the ones who love their enemies, turn the other cheek, and forgive whoever offends them "seventy times seven times" (Matt. 18:22). They are the ones who deny themselves and take up their crosses to follow Jesus. When they follow Jesus, they are ideally willing to follow him in spite of suffering, persecution, and even a martyr's death. After all, this was the path that Jesus himself trod. Nietzsche saw all this renunciation and self-sacrifice as life denying.

To Nietzsche, Zarathustra's prophecy that "God is dead" was good news. He was exhilarated by it. If there is no God, then there is no basis for Judeo-Christian morality, and those who realize this are free to engage in a revaluation of values. They are liberated—even redeemed—from the oppressiveness of living under the life-denying commandments of the Jews and the Christians, with all the suppression of desire and appetite that goes along with trying to obey these rules and all the guilt feelings that afflict people when they fail to do so. Once free from the restraints and constrictions of slave morality, people can become like little children: innocent and creative. They can become innocent because there is no longer any basis on which to condemn them. Their creativity can be exercised in their fashioning for themselves a new, life-affirming value system on the basis of which they can construct themselves and shape their lives. This is a kind of absolute freedom: freedom from all external moral standards and freedom to adopt whatever internal moral standards one chooses.

If we add Nietzsche's critique of Christian morality to Rorty's complaints about Christian inquiry, we can see that, from the perspective of these postmodern philosophers, Christians are not only conversation stoppers but also party poopers. This concern about Christianity should be familiar to Christian apologists and their conversation partners. How many people have hesitated to commit themselves fully to Christ because of the sacrifice required by the submission of their wills and lives entirely to the will of God? From an outsider's perspective, the prospect of living the Christian life can seem depressing and even frightening. Paul says that Christians are "slaves to God" (Rom. 6:22). This can raise troubling questions in the minds of many non-Christians. What if this enslavement should result in my never being able

to have fun again? If I surrender the control of my will and the satisfaction of my desires to God, then won't I have to give up everything in which I find pleasure and enjoyment? Augustine struggled with a divided will before he finally gave it entirely to Christ in a garden in Milan. Before that conversion experience he reports in his *Confessions* that he prayed, "Grant me chastity and continence, but not yet!"[5] Many postmodern thinkers see all these struggles to repent of sin as needless and dehumanizing.

Rorty follows Nietzsche in his critique of Christian morality but thinks that Nietzsche went too far when he threw out liberal democratic values along with it. Nietzsche viewed egalitarianism as an offshoot of the Judeo-Christian ideas that all humans are created in God's image and equally valued and loved by God. He believed this to be a denial of the truth about human beings, because he considered some people to be better than others in important ways. He thought that an emphasis on universal human equality would result in a "leveling down" that would give the advantage to the lowest common denominator among people to the detriment of those who are truly great. However, Rorty is concerned that Nietzsche's aristocratic and privatized individual moralities could provide an excuse for cruelty, which Rorty thinks of as "the worst thing we can do."[6] So Rorty modifies Nietzsche's approach to morality by recommending that people be allowed to live their *private* lives as they please while conducting their *public* lives in such a way as to respect the rights of others not to be harmed. Of course, in light of

5. St. Augustine, *Confessions*, 8.7.17.
6. Rorty, *Contingency, Irony, and Solidarity*, 74.

Rorty's rejection of correspondence truth and rational argumentation, he cannot (and does not try to) provide a reason for the truth of such a liberal democratic way of organizing individual lives and the societies in which they are lived. He just says that he prefers it and hopes you will too. Rorty's liberalized version of Nietzsche's critique of Christian morality seems likely to be characteristic of most secular critics of the Christian faith today.

In sum, the Nietzsche/Rorty postmodern perspective entails two claims, one negative and one positive, to which Christian apologists must respond:

1. Christian values are life denying and so should be rejected.
2. People should be free to live however they want as long as they do not violate anyone's rights.

According to claim 1, since God is dead, there is no good reason to tolerate oppressive and dehumanizing Christian morality. According to claim 2, everyone should do his or her own thing but in such a way as to live and let live. This postmodern worldview is pervasive today. How can Christians reply to it?

One way to block Nietzsche's attack on Christian values is to deny his claim that God is dead and to back this up by appealing to the case for God's existence laid out in part 2 of this book. Then one could support Christian theism by employing the evidence discussed in part 3. One could then argue that since God exists and became incarnate in Christ, we should live by Christian values because it is God's will for us and because the only way to follow Jesus is to do so. This should be an important part of the Christian reply

to Nietzsche, especially since he does not offer any arguments for the nonexistence of God. However, this rejoinder would not get entirely to the heart of Nietzsche's concern with the Christian ideal, which has to do with the *content* of Christian morality as much as with its *ground*. He complains that the Christian way of life extinguishes everything that makes life worth living.

The first thing Christians should point out here is that Christianity does require self-denial, self-sacrifice, renunciation, suffering, and service to others. This much should be beyond dispute. The real question is whether the ultimate consequences of these attitudes and behaviors are generally good or generally bad. Clearly, Nietzsche believes that the results of Christian living are bad. On the face of it, this may seem to be the case. However, as it says in the book of Proverbs, "There is a way that seems right to a man, but in the end it leads to death" (14:12).

The most natural way of thinking about the good life for human beings is that it consists in the experience of pleasure and the avoidance of pain and suffering. The ancient Epicureans believed this to be the case, and they developed a hedonistic philosophy of life around this conviction that has been very influential over the centuries. Pleasure is a result of the satisfaction of appetites and desires—a consequence of getting what we want. We desire food, drink, sex, comfort, security, power, prestige, money, health, and friendship, among many other things. What could be more natural—and more right—than to fulfill our desires for these things? When our desires are unsatisfied, we experience frustration, suffering, and pain. Much of our lives are spent trying to avoid these negative experiences. What could be wrong with this?

Even the Epicureans realized that not all desire satisfaction is ultimately a good thing. Though some of our desires are natural (inborn), others are unnatural and vain. An example of the latter is the desire for rich foods that are not necessary to sustain life. Indulging in a desire for them tends to undermine good health and deplete one's financial resources. The wise person learns that one must forego some short-term pleasures for the sake of long-term happiness. To achieve my ideal body weight, I may need to cut down on the amount of ice cream I eat. This is a step in the direction of Christian morality, because it acknowledges the need to deprive oneself in some circumstances for a greater good. However, the ultimate goal of Epicureanism is egoistic (one's own good) rather than altruistic (the good of others). Moreover, it has exclusively to do with satisfaction in this life rather than including fulfillment in the life to come.

What both Nietzsche and the Epicureans fail to see is that human beings cannot be their own masters. We cannot become happy simply by means of taking charge of the standards of our own desire satisfaction and their implementation in our lives. What Paul told the Romans (in Rom. 6) is true. No matter how we live, we will be slaves—either slaves to our own sinful

> **What both Nietzsche and the Epicureans fail to see is that human beings cannot be their own masters.**

desires or slaves to the will of God. There is no third alternative. The best argument for this claim is empirical. Both one's own experiences and what one learns about the experiences of others bear it out. The more we try to live our lives as we please, the more we become captive to our sin and miserable as a result. The more we try to live our lives as God pleases—with the help of the Holy Spirit—the more we experience the freedom and joy of life in Christ that Paul recommends to the Galatians (see Gal. 5). Paradoxically, the life that seems right to fallen human beings—a life of pleasing oneself—is a life that leads to slavery, misery, and death. The life that seems wrong to Nietzsche—a life of pleasing God and serving others—is a life that leads to freedom, joy, and life. Apologists can make the best case for the Christian way of life by modeling it in their lives and urging others to give it a try.

In replying to claim 2, we see that Rorty does not provide a reason for thinking it is true. Instead, he affirms his own preference for the liberal democratic ideal it expresses and hopes he can make it appealing to others through rhetorical means rather than philosophical argumentation (such as by means of literature and film). He admits that in denying the possibility of providing a rational justification of democratic values by an appeal to the nature of objective reality he has no principled way to show that they are any better than totalitarian values, such as those of Nazism. He also acknowledges that this makes his moral perspective ethnocentric and relative. But he does not think of this as a bad thing.

A response to this is twofold. First, it is reasonable to believe that the Christian worldview is true. Consequently, it is reasonable to believe that there is an objective basis on which to show that democratic values are superior to totalitarian ones. Rorty's protestations to the contrary are ineffective without reasons to back them up. Second, the next chapter argues that postmodern ethical relativism of the sort embraced by Rorty is objectionable, unfounded, and arguably false.

Reflection and Discussion

1. What are the advantages and disadvantages of postmodern philosophy from a Christian standpoint? What would you say to a Christian who completely rejects postmodernism? How would you respond to a Christian who embraces postmodernism in its entirety?
2. How would you explain to someone what many postmodern philosophers say about reality and truth and how it differs from what they say about knowledge and reason? Is this distinction important? Why or why not?
3. How would you elaborate on the reply in this chapter to Nietzsche's condemnation of Christian values and ethics as life denying? Would your response to Nietzsche be equally effective whether or not God exists? Explain.

Further Reading

Benson, Bruce Ellis. *Nietzsche, Derrida, and Marion on Modern Idolatry.* Downers Grove, IL: InterVarsity, 2002.

Greer, Robert C. *Mapping Postmodernism: A Survey of Christian Options.* Downers Grove, IL: InterVarsity, 2003.

Philips, Timothy R., and Dennis L. Okholm, eds. *Christian Apologetics in the Postmodern World.* Downers Grove, IL: InterVarsity, 1995.

25

It's All Relative

Cultural Differences and Moral Universalism

» **Outline**

- **The Problem with Ethical Relativism**
  - *Three Objections to Societal Ethical Relativism*
  - *Three Objections to Individual Ethical Relativism*
  - *Problems with Arguments for Ethical Relativism*
    - The Argument from Cultural Relativism
    - The Argument from Tolerance
    - The Argument from Exceptions to Moral Rules
- **The Moral Argument for God's Existence**
  - *The Argument Stated*
  - *Why Theism Best Explains Universal and Objective Morality*
    - Theism Is Superior to Nontheistic Platonism
    - Theism Is Superior to an Explanation Based on Natural Selection
- **Some Additional Apologetical Consequences of Universal Morality**
  - *The Euthyphro Dilemma for Theism*
  - *Problems Facing Ethical Relativists Who Employ the Argument from Evil*
  - *The Apologetic Value of Christians Living Moral Lives*

» **Summary**

Ethical relativism (ER) is deeply inconsistent with core Christian claims. Thus, critics can argue against Christianity from the standpoint of ER. However, there are a number of serious objections to both societal and individual versions of ER, and the principal arguments for ER fail to establish their conclusions. The alternative to ER is ethical universalism, and the moral argument for God's existence is based on this view. According to this argument, theism provides a better explanation of an objective and universal moral standard than do all nontheistic alternatives. Critics argue on the basis of the Euthyphro Dilemma that there is no acceptable way to explain the relationship between God and morality. However, apologists have at least three explanations available, each of which is rationally superior to the nontheistic alternatives. Moreover, critics committed to ER cannot consistently employ the argument from evil for atheism. Finally, Christian apologists have good apologetical reasons to commit themselves to living moral lives (with the help of the Holy Spirit).

» **Basic Terms, Concepts, and Names**

altruism
cultural relativism
Darwinistic explanation of morality
divine command theory of morality
ethical relativism (ER)
ethical universalism
Euthyphyro Dilemma, the
individual ER
Lewis, C. S.
moral argument for God's existence
Mother Teresa
Murdoch, Iris
Plato's forms
Protagoras
societal ER

» **Reflection and Discussion**

» **Further Reading**

> In those days Israel had no king; everyone did as he saw fit.
>
> Judges 21:25

One of the hallmarks of contemporary postmodernism is the view that there are no universal and objective moral norms. Stated more positively, it is the idea that morality is relative. This is actually an old thesis. It goes back at least as far as the ancient Greek sophist Protagoras, whose book *On Truth* contained the statement "Man is the measure of all things, of the things that are, that they are, and of the things that are not, that they are not."[1] This is typically interpreted as a commitment to relativism in general and ethical relativism in particular. The more recent manifestation of this view is a result of both the postmodern denial of objective truth and reality and observations of cultural moral relativism in contemporary cultural anthropology (i.e., observations of differences in moral beliefs and practices from one culture to another).

Postmodern ethical relativism poses a serious threat to Christian belief. The Christian worldview entails the existence of a universal and objective moral standard. Consequently, if there are no ethical universals, then Christianity is false. According to ethical relativism, ethical principles, rules, and norms are relative to human cultures, societies, groups, or individuals. According to this view, there is no such thing as right and wrong beyond what one's group accepts as right and wrong (or, in the case of individual ethical relativism, beyond the content of one's own moral beliefs). Since human beings disagree with one another about many moral matters, it follows that there is more than one standard of right and wrong. This flies in the face of the Christian position that there is only one moral standard and that this ethical criterion is the content of God's will rather than a matter of human opinion or preference.

Ethical relativism strikes at the heart of the Christian faith. According to Christian theism, God is supremely morally good, and the complete nature of God's goodness is beyond human knowledge. This makes sense only if there is only one standard of moral goodness that transcends what humans think or want to be the case about

---

1. Author's translation. Another English translation can be found in John Mansley Robinson, *An Introduction to Early Greek Philosophy* (New York: Houghton Mifflin, 1968), 245.

right and wrong. The Bible expresses this truth about God in terms of God's perfect righteousness and holiness. Moreover, the biblical doctrine of human disobedience, unrighteous, fallenness, and sin presupposes the existence of a universal divine moral standard. To sin is to fall short of God's one standard of moral perfection. Furthermore, the doctrine of sin is the basis of the doctrines of salvation and judgment. According to Christianity, the fundamental human problem is separation from communion with God because of sin and the misery and death that result from sin. This is the problem that God graciously acted in history to solve by means of the incarnation, atonement, and resurrection. This plight of humanity is what makes the gospel of Christ good news. Those who refuse God's loving offer of salvation from sin in Christ are subject to judgment and eternal damnation in hell as the penalty for their wrongdoing. But people are responsible for how they choose to live only if they have freely diverged from a standard of morality rooted in more than merely human authority. If ethical relativism is true and there is no such standard, then the thread that ties together the doctrines of God, sin, salvation, and judgment is removed, and the fabric of the Christian faith falls apart.

This gives the critic an opportunity to argue as follows:

1. Ethical relativism is true.
2. If 1, then the Christian faith is false.
3. Therefore, the Christian faith is false.

The considerations just mentioned support premise 2. The task in the first

> **If ethical relativism is true, then the thread that ties together the doctrines of God, sin, salvation, and judgment is removed, and the fabric of the Christian faith falls apart.**

section of this chapter is to make a case against premise 1 and for the existence of universal morality. The second section argues that the best explanation of the existence of a universal moral standard is that God exists. Finally, the third section discusses an apologetical problem that concerns the precise relationship between God and morality, a dilemma that faces critics who employ the argument from evil, and some practical consequences of the reflections on God and morality for Christian apologists.

The Problem with Ethical Relativism

Ethical relativism (ER) is both subject to serious objections and based on faulty arguments.[2] ER comes in two main forms: societal ER and individual ER. According to the former, what is right and wrong for a person[3] is whatever is considered right

2. This section draws on Frances Howard-Snyder, "Christianity and Ethics," in *Reason for the Hope Within*, ed. Michael J. Murray, 375–98 (Grand Rapids: Eerdmans, 1999).

3. The expression "right for a person" (and "wrong for a person") is ambiguous. It can mean either "right when performed by that person," as in "driving a car is right (permissible) for adults but wrong for children," or "right according to that per-

and wrong by the majority of people in that person's society. According to the latter, right and wrong is determined for each person by whatever that person believes to be right and wrong.

The first serious problem with societal ER is that it cannot account for societal moral progress. Moral progress occurs in a society when a mistaken moral belief is replaced by a true moral belief or when an immoral practice is supplanted by a moral one. An example of moral progress in the United States and Europe is the abolition of slavery (mentioned in chap. 21 as among the positive contributions of the Christian church to society). Though everyone agrees that this is a case of societal moral improvement (however much our society may also have deteriorated morally in other respects at the same time), it is impossible for societal ER to accommodate this. According to societal ER, whatever a society accepts as right and wrong at a given time is what is right and wrong at that time. Thus, since slavery was accepted by U.S. society in the 1700s, according to societal ER, slavery was morally right for citizens of the United States at that time. Since slavery is no longer accepted in the United States, it is now morally wrong, according to societal ER. However, moral progress or improvement entails that a morally unacceptable practice that

son," as in "the Holocaust was right for Hitler." With the former interpretation, the expression is used to make a claim about what *really is* right for a person, and with the latter interpretation, the expression is employed only to make a claim about what that person *believes* to be right (whether it really is right or not). Throughout this chapter, expressions of this form should be interpreted in the former sense rather than in the latter sense. My thanks to Frances Howard-Snyder for pointing out this ambiguity and for suggesting a way to clarify it.

was considered acceptable at one time is discovered at a later time to be (and to have been) unacceptable. But this is what cannot be the case if societal ER is true. This view has no way of accounting for moral practices to be considered acceptable by a society and yet actually morally unacceptable.

The second serious problem with societal ER is that many people (and in some sense all people) belong to more than one group or society, and the majority in each of these groups can have incompatible moral views. For instance, Frances Howard-Snyder asks us to consider the case of an American feminist named Susan who lives in Saudi Arabia.[4] She is a member of both American and Saudi Arabian societies. The majority of people in the former society thinks it is morally permissible for a woman to drive a car, and the majority of people in the latter society believes this is not morally right. Societal ER entails that since Susan is a member of both societies her operation of an automobile is both morally right and morally wrong. But this is absurd. Either she is wrong to drive, or she is right; she cannot be both right and wrong (and even if she could be, she would have no way to decide what she ought to do). Therefore, societal ER is unacceptable.

A third and final serious problem with societal ER is that it allows for majorities to be extremely intolerant of those with whom they disagree about moral matters. For instance, the majority of people in some Muslim countries believe that it is morally wrong for a Christian to preach the gospel to a Muslim in that country. If societal ER is correct that this majority

4. Howard-Snyder, "Christianity and Ethics," 377.

agreement makes those Muslims right and these Christians wrong, then societal ER can be used to sanction intolerant treatment of the Christian minority. But this intolerance seems to be immoral. Therefore, societal ER is objectionable (the same reasoning applies, of course, in a case of a Christian majority oppressing a Muslim minority).

Individual ER does not fare any better. Though it avoids the problem of multiple group membership and the intolerant treatment of one societal group by another in the same society, it is subject to the problem of not being able to account for moral improvement. It is clear that individuals experience moral improvement. But if whatever an individual believes to be right and wrong at a given time is what is right and wrong for that person, then it is never possible for him or her to develop morally by means of coming to see that a certain behavior he or she considered moral was and is really immoral.

Another problem with individual ER is that it precludes the possibility of genuine moral disagreements (which seem possible and often actually occur). If Mary believes that abortion is sometimes a morally acceptable practice, then according to individual ER, abortion is sometimes right for Mary. If Sally believes that abortion is always an immoral practice, then individual ER entails that abortion is always wrong for Sally. But if this is the only way to interpret the beliefs of Mary and Sally about the morality of abortion, then it is not possible for them to have a genuine disagreement about the moral status of abortion. They could have a genuine disagreement of this sort only if what one believes (e.g., that abortion is right) contradicts what the other one believes (e.g., that abortion is wrong). But there is no contradiction in saying that abortion is sometimes right for Mary but always wrong for Sally.

The most serious difficulty with individual ER is that it sanctions any behavior as long as the person engaging in the behavior sincerely believes it is morally permissible. Consequently, according to individual ER, what the terrorists responsible for the 9/11 tragedy did was morally permissible for them to do simply because they believed it to be. But this is clearly wrong. So individual ER is mistaken.

With all these problems that beset both versions of ER, we may wonder why anyone would believe either of them to be true. What follows discusses the three best arguments for ER in general. In each case, it will be clear that these arguments fail to establish their conclusions.

The first argument is based on the observations of cultural anthropologists that certain practices are accepted as morally okay by some cultures that are prohibited as morally forbidden by others. Examples of such practices include polygamy, infanticide, and cannibalism. The anthropological view that this is the case is often called cultural relativism. It is the thesis that *beliefs* about right and wrong (as well as what values are accepted and what practices are approved) vary from culture to culture. Supporters of ethical relativism argue that cultural relativism entails ethical relativism, which, as we have seen, is the position that what *is* right and wrong varies from society to society (or individual to individual). Here is the argument:

4. Beliefs about right and wrong vary from one culture or society to another (this is *cultural* relativism).
5. If 4 is true, then what *is* right and wrong varies from one culture or society to another (that is, cultural relativism entails ethical relativism).
6. Therefore, right and wrong is relative to cultures or societies (this is *ethical* relativism).

One problem with premise 4 is that it leaves unspecified the extent to which cultures vary in their moral beliefs. It is unreasonable to think that there is no moral agreement at all among cultures (as a matter of fact, cultural anthropologists generally agree that in every culture incest is considered immoral). If there is any moral agreement among cultures, then the possibility is left open that some moral universals exist in spite of intercultural disagreements about other matters. If there are at least some moral universals, then ethical relativism (which states that *all* moral standards are relative to societies or individuals) is wrong.

Moreover, premise 5 is arguably false. If we assume that different cultures have different beliefs about right and wrong and so disagree among them about morality, it does not follow that what *is* right and wrong is simply a function of what the majority of people in each culture or society believes to be right and wrong. This would follow only if it were *generally* true that disagreements about the truth concerning something mean that there is no objective truth about that thing. For instance, it does not follow from the fact that people disagree about whether a certain scientific claim is true that the claim is not objectively true or false but instead

true for the person who believes it is true and false for the person who believes it is false. There was a time when some people believed that the sun revolves around the earth, and some believed that the sun does not. But from this disagreement, it does not follow that the sun both does and does not revolve around the earth. Instead, the former group of people was simply mistaken. Disagreement about what is true does not entail that the truth is relative.

But this leads to the second argument for ER. The previous paragraph implied that a given society can be mistaken about whether something is morally acceptable or not. But isn't it arrogant, intolerant, and ethnocentric to conclude that a society is mistaken in some of its moral beliefs? Isn't this just what ethical universalists (people who think that there is only one standard of morality) would think about societies other than their own (since such people are likely to think of their own moral standard as being the right one)? The second argument for ER arises out of these concerns:

7. The true moral theory must not sanction arrogance, intolerance, and ethnocentrism.
8. But ethical universalism does sanction these negative attitudes.
9. So ethical universalism cannot be true.
10. If ethical universalism is false, then ethical relativism is true.
11. Therefore, ER is true.

There are problems with both premise 7 and premise 8 of this argument. Let's start with premise 8. A proponent of ethical universalism can reasonably insist that this view does not sanction these objectionable attitudes at all. If there are universal and objective truths about what is right and wrong, and if there are various things that can prevent human beings from having complete and infallible moral knowledge (as from a Christian standpoint there are likely to be at least because of the distorting effects of sin), then we should expect that every society will have only partial and at some points faulty views about what is right and wrong. There is nothing arrogant, intolerant, or ethnocentric about moral universalism combined with an acknowledgment of such human limitations. What is arrogant, intolerant, and ethnocentric is to assume without sufficient warrant that one's own moral beliefs are all true and that all beliefs incompatible with them are false. But this additional assumption is not entailed by ethical universalism.

The problem with premise 7 is not that it is false (it is clearly true) but rather that an ethical relativist cannot consistently endorse it. To say that the true moral theory should not sanction arrogance, intolerance, or ethnocentrism is to imply that it would be absolutely and universally morally wrong for someone to adopt these attitudes. But a relativist says that nothing is *absolutely* and *universally* morally wrong. Therefore, a relativist cannot consistently employ premise 7 in an argument for ER.

The last argument considered here for ER is that the true moral theory must allow for exceptions to moral rules and that this is something ER does that ethical universalism does not do. For instance, it seems there are circumstances in which it would not be wrong to lie, such as when one is trying to protect innocent human lives from criminals intent on harming

them. In reply, though some versions of ethical universalism may treat every moral rule as absolutely exceptionless, this is not the case with sophisticated brands of universalism. All that is required for ethical universalism to be true and ER to be false is that *some* types of actions be always absolutely wrong regardless of the circumstances or consequences. A good example of such a type of action is torturing human infants just for the fun of it. This type of behavior seems clearly to be absolutely and universally morally wrong. It seems clearly not to be possibly right relative to some people, consequences, or circumstances. If so, then ethical universalism is true, and ethical relativism is false.

The Moral Argument for God's Existence

If there is a universal moral standard, as we just argued there is, then what explains its existence? According to the moral argument for theism, there can be a universal moral standard only if God exists:

1. There is a universal moral standard.
2. If 1 is true, then God exists.
3. Therefore, God exists.

One way for nontheists to resist accepting the conclusion of this argument is to find reasons to deny premise 1. But it was the burden of the previous section to defend premise 1 against such arguments. Moreover, as C. S. Lewis points out in *Mere Christianity,* people who deny premise 1 belie their alleged relativistic orientation by how they act when they are wronged.[5] Nothing brings out the moral absolutist in an avowed moral relativist like an occasion for moral indignation prompted by a perceived injustice. This observation does not prove that moral universalism is true, but it does support the position that everyone *believes* it is true, regardless of what people might say to the contrary. If there are good reasons to reject ethical relativism, and no one really believes it is true anyway, then the dispute is narrowed to premise 2.

Theists have a good explanation for the existence of a universal moral standard. They can say that moral principles, laws, or rules exist that apply to all human beings in all places and at all times because God is the source of morality and created human beings with the rationality and freedom required for his moral law to apply to them. They can say that if God did not exist, then everything would be permissible.[6] They can say that the existence of a moral *law* can be explained by the existence of a divine moral *lawgiver.* If there is something I ought to do, then I have an obligation to do it. If I have an obligation or duty to do something, then I am bound by the requirement that creates this duty. But how can I be bound to behave in a certain way unless the requirement that I do so comes from a source that has the requisite authority to hold me accountable for my actions? And how can there be such an authority unless it resides in a personal being? The idea of an impersonal authority does not seem

to make sense. All these considerations contribute to the support of premise 2.

But this theistic explanation of the existence of a universal moral standard can be a good one without being the *best* one. If there is another explanation that is better, then premise 2 is doubtful. Some people have affirmed the existence of a universal moral standard but denied the existence of God. Among these are the eighteenth-century atheistic French philosophers such as Denis Diderot. The British Platonist philosopher and novelist Iris Murdoch is another example of a person who held this combination of views.[7]

But it is one thing to affirm the existence of universal morality in a godless world and another thing altogether to explain how this could be possible. Murdoch appealed to Plato's transcendent world of impersonal and eternal forms or ideals for this purpose. However, though this is an *explanation* (which is what we need), it is arguably not a *good* explanation. If it is, it is reasonable to think that the theistic explanation is *better.*

Recently, many nontheistic philosophers have appealed to Darwinism to explain the existence of a universal morality. The idea is that certain moral convictions and sentiments have taken root in the human psyche because they have survival value. Why do people the world over subscribe to the Golden Rule ("Do to others what you would have them do to you" [Matt. 7:12])? The reason given by these theorists is that this conviction (and a desire to abide by it) leads to cooperative

5. C. S. Lewis, *Mere Christianity* (New York: Macmillan, 1943), 19–20.

6. Something about which both the Christian Fyodor Dostoyevsky and the atheist Jean-Paul Sartre agreed.

7. See Iris Murdoch, *The Sovereignty of Good* (London: Routledge, 1970); and idem, *Metaphysics as a Guide to Morals* (London: Chatto & Windus, 1992).

behavior, and cooperative behavior tends to promote the survival of the human species. This explanation competes with the theistic one in accounting for the existence of common moral beliefs and practices among humans. It seems to be a better explanation than the Platonic one mentioned above. Is it a better explanation than the one that appeals to God? Even if we cannot show that it is, if there are no positive reasons to discount it, then its existence puts the theistic explanation in doubt.

But there are good reasons to doubt the evolutionary account of the existence of a universal moral standard. In the first place, the claim that there is a universal moral standard is not merely the claim that all human beings share a common core of moral beliefs. It is the position that one set of moral norms is *binding* on all human beings. But an evolutionary theory of the biological origin of moral beliefs (and the behavior resulting from them) cannot possibly account for this. At best, such a theory can explain why people *believe* that they are morally required to behave in certain ways. It cannot explain why people *actually are* subject to these requirements. But this is something that Christian theism can explain.

Second, an evolutionary account of morality that appeals to natural selection and survival value cannot explain the existence of genuinely *altruistic* ideals and behaviors. Such ideals require self-sacrifice in certain circumstances, and genuinely self-sacrificial behavior does not have survival value—at least not for the individuals who place their well-being and survival in jeopardy for the sake of others. Can this behavior be explained as being conducive to the survival of the *species*

of which these self-sacrificing individuals are members? Though it would seem so, what an evolutionary account cannot explain is why people like Jesus, Gandhi, and Mother Teresa are nearly universally admired as ideal models for personal emulation. What makes these altruistic people exemplary in people's minds is not that they were willing to sacrifice themselves for the good of the human species (as a kind of abstract entity) but that they cared about human beings *as individuals* enough to sacrifice their own well-being and even survival for them. Moreover, Jesus and Mother Teresa spent most of their time with down-and-out people like lepers, whose survival does little to contribute to the reproductive fitness of the species. From the standpoint of Darwinism, such an altruistic ideal and the behavior that is based on it are both irrational and excessive. But they make perfect sense from the standpoint of Christian theism, according to which the very heart of God as revealed in Christ is a giving and self-sacrificial love that God not only lavishes upon us but also calls us to imitate in our relationships with others.

If we assume that the evolutionary theory of universal morality is the only viable alternative to the theistic account, then it seems safe to conclude at this point that the latter is the best explanation available. If so, then there is good reason to accept premise 2 and therefore also, given the case for premise 1, the hypothesis that God exists. As a result, we can add this argument to the cumulative case for theism. Moreover, because it is a *moral* argument, it highlights God's goodness in a way that the cosmological and teleological arguments do not. In addition, as we have seen, the *Christian* version of theism provides the resources to explain the existence of the moral ideal of altruism. To the extent that this is more true of Christianity than of either Judaism or Islam (and the centrality of Christ's sacrifice in the former suggests that it is), we have also acquired additional support for the Christian worldview.

Some Additional Apologetical Consequences of Universal Morality

So far this chapter has shown how Christian apologists can defend both universal morality and the central doctrines of the Christian faith against the threat of ethical relativism. It has also shown how the affirmation of universal morality can serve as the basis for another argument for God's existence. The final section discusses a handful of apologetical consequences of these conclusions.

In the first place, we must pause to consider an additional challenge to Christian theism posed by the commitment to both universal morality and the existence of God. This problem begins with a question: What is the relationship between God and morality? Is morally right behavior right simply because God wills it? Or is it rather the case that God wills or commands certain behaviors because they are made right by some universal standard of morality independent of God? If we choose the first alternative, morality would seem to be a purely arbitrary matter. For instance, according to that view, it is right for us to abide by the Ten Commandments merely because God wills us to. But suppose God were to will instead that we act in ways contrary to the Ten Commandments. If the only thing that made moral behavior moral

was God's will, then actions such as adultery and dishonesty would become moral according to that supposition. But then it looks as if morality is not based on God's rational choice of what he recognizes as independently moral but instead is a function of God's arbitrary will. If to avoid this unwelcome consequence we opt for the second alternative, then there is a universal standard of morality independent of God, and God is therefore not the absolutely sovereign Creator and Lord of everything other than God. We are faced, then, with a dilemma. Given the two options, it follows that either morality is arbitrary or God is not absolutely sovereign. Neither of these results seems satisfactory from a Christian perspective.

This dilemma, called the Euthyphro Dilemma (since it was first stated in Plato's dialogue *Euthyphro* in a conversation between Socrates and his friend Euthyphro) has been much discussed by philosophers and theologians through the centuries. Christians are not in agreement about how to solve it. Some endorse the divine command theory of morality (which affirms the first option above) and try to show that it does not make morality arbitrary. Others defend the reality of an independent moral standard and argue that it does not lead to an objectionable diminishment of God's majesty. Still others attempt to formulate a middle view, according to which God's unchanging loving nature is the ground or standard on the basis of which God issues the commands that determine what is right and wrong. This third option is thought by many to provide a way to show that morality is not arbitrary (since it is rooted in God's loving nature) and that the standard of morality does not compromise

God's sovereignty (since it does not exist separately from God).

Unfortunately, we do not have the space to pursue this debate here. For our purposes, it will suffice to argue that all three of the theistic views mentioned above are rationally preferable to any nontheistic attempt to account for the existence of universal morality. This is especially the case with the first and third alternatives, which clearly make morality dependent on God. As for the second position, though it entails that the moral standard is in some sense independent of God (and so stands in some tension with the moral argument for God's existence discussed above), God's existence and creative activity are still required to account for the fact that human beings are by nature capable of understanding, affirming, and acting on the basis of the moral law. Moreover, God's providential purposes provide a meaningful context within which it makes sense for us to live morally. Without this big theistic picture, it would not be clear why we should care about right and wrong.

A second consideration suggested by this conversation about universal morality and God has to do with the argument from evil against God's existence. This argument, which we discussed in chapter 11, concludes that God does not exist on the ground that evil exists and that God does not have a reason that would justify him in allowing evil to exist. Let us reflect briefly on what it means to say that evil exists. To say that there is evil in the world is to say, at least in part, that the world is not as it *should* be. But to say this is to imply that there is a standard of goodness relative to which the existing state of affairs falls short. Moreover, it is to imply that there is a universal *and objective* standard of goodness relative to which the world does not measure up. If the standard of goodness in question were merely relative and subjective, then the argument from evil would not get off the ground. The existence of an all-good and all-powerful God would not be jeopardized by there being no reason to justify the existence of a state of affairs that is bad only relative to some societies or individuals (but not to other societies or individuals).

But if the atheistic argument from evil presupposes the existence of a universal moral standard, and if the existence of a universal moral standard cannot be adequately explained unless God exists (as argued above), then the critics who employ the argument from evil are in a tough spot. If such critics deny that universal morality exists, then they cannot employ the argument from evil. If they affirm the existence of universal morality, they must find a rational way to resist the moral argument for God's existence. So they are either deprived of the strongest argument against theism, or they are faced with having to refute a strong argument

> **If the atheistic argument from evil presupposes the existence of a universal moral standard, and if the existence of a universal moral standard cannot be adequately explained unless God exists, then the critics who employ the argument from evil are in a tough spot.**

for theism. This is a hard dilemma from which to escape.

The third and final observation about God, morality, and Christian apologetics is a practical one. Chapter 1 pointed out that Christian apologists who manifest the work of the Holy Spirit in their lives through their gentleness and humility will increase the effectiveness of their apologetical efforts and also help to confirm the Christian worldview, since it predicts the moral transformation of those who are committed to Christ. Christian apologists can direct the attention of critics, seekers, and doubters to the reality of a universal moral standard and to the God who commands our obedience to it not only by means of the arguments in the first two sections of this chapter but also through striving to live in conformity to it with God's help. Just as it is inconsistent for critics to insist that morality is relative and yet to live as if it were universal, so it is inconsistent for Christians to affirm that there is a universal morality to which God holds us accountable and yet to live as if everything were relative or even as if it did not matter how one chose to behave. Christians who preach universal morality should care about both individual righteousness and social justice. It is apologetically important to practice what we preach.

If Christians make an effort to live righteously (by means of the power of the Holy Spirit), they can become living reminders of the difference made by the reality of a universal moral standard enforced by the authority of God. This difference is manifested in a variety of ways.[8]

8. I am grateful to my colleague Robert Wennberg for some of these ideas.

In the first place, if some things are universally right and wrong and there is a God who cares about how we choose to live, then how we live really matters. Universal morality in a world created by God introduces a certain seriousness to life that would be lacking if ethical relativism (and so atheism) were true. Moreover, given the doctrines of heaven and hell, how we exercise our free will and how we choose to treat one another take on eternal significance. Our choices determine the kinds of people we become, and the characters we acquire determine our ultimate destinies.

This seriousness and significance of life in a moral order governed by God also provide human beings with an opportunity to cultivate a strong resolve to become people who are capable of fulfilling the righteous requirement of God's law by being able to fulfill the two Great Commandments: to love God with all our heart, soul, mind, and strength and to love our neighbor as ourselves. The Christian worldview provides a context in which one has reason to be motivated to be a good person and to live well. As said in the previous section, it is a picture of reality into which the moral ideal of altruism easily fits. In a godless and ethically relativistic world, there would be no basis on which it would be reasonable to strive to live a self-denying and self-sacrificial life out of love for other people, especially one's enemies (this is a consequence of atheism that Nietzsche saw clearly [see chap. 24]). But in the world created by God in which love is the sum of the universal moral law and in which God himself provided the supreme example of love in the death of Christ, it makes sense for people to strive to live lives of sacrifice and service for the sake of others.

An additional reason it would make sense for people to suffer and even to die for others in a moral world created by a loving God is that such people can look forward to God's righteous judgment and reward of their selfless faithfulness. What the Bible says about God's judgment of the world means that Christians who know that what they do really matters and who consequently resolve to live exemplary lives can be confident that God will forgive them for their failures and reward them for their efforts.

In sum, Christians who commit themselves to practicing righteousness and justice and who are enabled by God's Spirit to succeed in their endeavors can bear witness to the importance of this life and can inspire others both by their resolve to improve morally and by their hope of reward for doing so. Christians who do these things can contribute to the attractiveness and plausibility of the Christian worldview. Philosophical arguments against ethical relativism (and for ethical universalism) and personal examples of commitment to God and universal morality can combine to show that the Christian faith is both more likely to be true and more worthy of allegiance than any postmodern relativistic account of morality and reality.

Reflection and Discussion

1. How would you explain to a critic of moral universalism that the view that there is only one moral standard that applies to everyone at all times and in all places does not imply that anyone can be absolutely sure about the correct answers to all questions about what is right and wrong?
2. Do you agree that an appeal to God provides the best explanation of the existence of a universal moral standard? Why or why not?
3. What do you think is the best solution to the Euthyphro Dilemma? Explain.

Further Reading

Beaty, Michael D., ed. *Christian Theism and the Problems of Philosophy.* Notre Dame: University of Notre Dame Press, 1990. See especially the essays in part 3: "Moral Theory and Theism," 289–377.

Hare, John. *The Moral Gap: Kantian Ethics, Human Limits, and God's Assistance.* New York: Oxford University Press, 1997.

Kreeft, Peter. *A Refutation of Moral Relativism: Interviews with an Absolutist.* San Francisco: Ignatius, 1999.

Conclusion

Cultivating Christian Commitment

> What, after all, is Apollos? And what is Paul? Only servants, through whom you came to believe—as the Lord has assigned to each his task. I planted the seed, Apollos watered it, but God made it grow. So neither he who plants nor he who waters is anything, but only God, who makes things grow. The man who plants and the man who waters have one purpose, and each will be rewarded according to his own labor. For we are God's fellow workers; you are God's field, God's building.
>
> 1 Corinthians 3:5–9

These words of Paul to the Corinthians provide a good basis for a closing brief meditation on Christian apologetics. Paul's remarks can help us to remember the purpose of Christian apologetics, the tasks of a Christian apologist, the significance of an apologist's work, and the rewards of faithful apologetical labor.

Purpose. Though Paul does not say in this passage what the "one purpose" is of the person who plants and the person who waters, it is clear from the Pauline corpus as a whole that this single goal is to cultivate Christian commitment. As we have seen, Christian commitment involves a surrender of one's entire self—heart, soul, mind, and body—to God as he is revealed in Jesus Christ. Though the *proximate* goal of a Christian apologist is to provide reasons, grounds, evidences, and arguments for the claim that the Christian worldview is at least as rational as all the worldviews with which it competes, the *ultimate* goal is to enable people to thrive in God's garden as fully mature "plants" that give glory to God by flowering in the way that God intended. Christian apologists should be ever mindful of this ideal outcome of their efforts.

Tasks. According to Paul, the Lord assigned him the task of planting and Apollos the task of watering. He says that the Corinthians are "God's field." This should remind us that Christian apologists are God's servants and fellow workers whose job it is to water and to weed in order to contribute to the growth of people's faith in the Christian gospel. Moreover, just as diverse sorts of plants need different kinds of care (and the same varieties of vegetation require some things at one time and other things at another), so also people with different attitudes and in alternative circumstances—believers, doubters, seekers, and critics—have needs that correspond to their situations. Christian apologists should follow Paul in attempting to be "all things to all people so that by all possible means [they] . . . might save some." Paul says, "I do all this for the sake of the gospel, that I may share in its blessings" (1 Cor. 9:22–23 TNIV).

Significance. Paul reminds us that what human beings do in their apologetical gardening work is completely insignificant apart from "God, who makes things grow" (1 Cor. 3:7). Christian apologists are God's partners in the cooperative work of foster-ing faith. However, we are the servants, and he is the Master. Moreover, as stressed throughout this book, the work of apologetics is not always necessary and never sufficient for the cultivation of Christian commitment. Apologists should take these limitations to heart so as to have a properly humble sense of their role in God's work. Christian apologists can sometimes have a tendency to develop a sense of personal superiority as they attempt to show the rational superiority of the Christian faith. It is important for them, therefore, to remember Paul's observation that "knowl-edge puffs up, but love builds up" (1 Cor. 8:1). The work of apologetics should be the work of humble and loving servants adding what they can to the work of the master gardener.

Rewards. Finally, Paul says that "each will be rewarded according to his own labor" (1 Cor. 3:8). Christian apologetics is an activity—it is a *work.* Furthermore, this labor of love for God and others can be performed in better and worse ways. It is my hope and prayer that this book will supply some of the resources you need to be competent and faithful in your pursuit of this holy endeavor. May you "always be prepared to give an answer to everyone who asks you to give the reason for the hope that you have" (1 Pet. 3:15). And may God reward you richly for your efforts.

Other Books on Christian Apologetics

Allen, Diogenes. *Christian Belief in a Postmodern World: The Full Wealth of Conviction.* Louisville: Westminster John Knox, 1989.

Evans, C. Stephen. *Why Believe? Reason and Mystery as Pointers to God.* Grand Rapids: Eerdmans, 1996.

Kreeft, Peter, and Ronald K. Tacelli. *Handbook of Christian Apologetics: Hundreds of Answers to Crucial Questions.* Downers Grove, IL: InterVarsity, 1994.

Moreland, J. P. *Scaling the Secular City: A Defense of Christianity.* Grand Rapids: Baker, 1987.

Murray, Michael J., ed. *Reason for the Hope Within.* Grand Rapids: Eerdmans, 1999.

Purtill, Richard L. *Reason to Believe.* Grand Rapids: Eerdmans, 1974.

Sire, James W. *Why Should Anyone Believe Anything at All?* Downers Grove, IL: InterVarsity, 1994.

Strobel, Lee. *The Case for Christ: A Journalist's Personal Investigation of the Evidence for Jesus.* Grand Rapids: Zondervan, 1998.

———. *The Case for Faith: A Journalist Investigates the Toughest Objections to Christianity.* Grand Rapids: Zondervan, 2000.

Index

abortion 351
Abraham 247, 249, 252
absolute inerrancy 276
absolute morality 340–41
Adam and Eve 314
Adams, Robert 46, 49
Advaita Vedanta 96n13, 257, 263
agnosticism 8, 71, 287
alternative worldview 25–26
altruism 355–56
ambiguity 25
ambitious apologetics 24
analogy 129–31
anatta 260, 261, 262
angels 102
annihilationism 233–34
Anselm 12, 34, 107, 110, 232
anthropomorphic polytheism 101–2
antirealism. *See* metaphysical
    antirealism
anti-Semitism 249, 295
Apocrypha 279n4
apologetics. *See* Christian
    apologetics
apologia 18
apology 18
Apostles' Creed 6, 7, 318
apparent polytheism 100
approximation argument 46–48
Aquinas, Thomas 41, 58–59, 107,
    129, 147, 302, 319, 327–29
argument from amount 155, 157
argument from evil 144–47, 148,
    152, 157, 159, 357
arguments for God's existence. *See*
    theistic proofs
Aristotle 55, 59, 107, 115, 216, 302,
    303, 327–28
arrogance 24, 69, 352–53
assurance 272
atheism 8, 71, 139–40, 159–62, 287
Atman 257
atonement 173, 227, 229–33, 238,
    243, 263–64

Augustine 12, 34, 52, 55, 67–68, 69,
    107, 110, 129, 145, 164, 202, 302,
    319, 327, 342
autonomy 32

Behe, Michael J. 127, 133–35, 304,
    309
belief 13, 31
Bible
    authority 7
    on God's nature and character
        107–8
    inerrancy 276–77
    inspiration 274
    interpretation 288–89
    and philosophy 107–8
    and science 303, 313–15
biblical criticism 287–92
    higher criticism 22, 174n2
    textual criticism 174n2
biblical methodologism 283, 288–89
biblical naturalism 289–92
big bang theory 92n9, 118
Bodhisattva 260, 262
body kind materialism 320–24
body-soul dualism. *See* Christian
    Platonic dualism
Book of Mormon 275
Brahman 96n13, 257–58
Brown, Dan 175n3, 292–93
Buddha 256
Buddhism 243, 246, 255–57, 259–62,
    263–64
building metaphor 21
Bultmann, Rudolph 200–201, 289

Calvin, John 229n2, 232, 274
canon 173n1, 279–81, 292–94
capable nonbelief 161, 163–64
Chalcedon, Council of 215
Chesterton, G. K. 183n9
Christian apologetics
    as harmful 45–49
    as impossible 40–45
    limits of 24–27
    nature of 19–21

as necessary 32–34
    purpose of 21–24
    relevance of 60
    as unnecessary 30–32
Christian dualism. *See* Christian
    Platonic dualism
Christianity
    as conversation stopper 339–40
    as cosmically competitive 23–24
    as life denying 341–43
    reasonableness of 22–24
Christian Platonic dualism 202,
    321–22, 325, 326–29, 332
Christian worldview 20, 348, 361
    and evidences 42
    as metanarrative 338
    as universally and objectively true
        44–45
church 278–81
    failures of 292, 294–96
    successes of 295–96
circular arguments 20, 274
claims 77
close-mindedness 341
Coady, C. A. J. 193n3
Collins, Robin 137n12
commitment 13, 19, 31, 83, 359,
    361–62
common descent (Darwinism) 307–8
common grace 40–41, 237
community 278
comparative rationality 23–24
compassion, in Buddhism 260–61,
    262
Confucianism 257
consciousness 92, 96–97
consensus sense of truth 336
consistency 338
consumerism 22
contingency cosmological argument
    120–25, 131
contingency monotheism 105, 106,
    118, 124, 243, 258
contingent existence 105–7, 111, 122
contingent truths 46–47
conversion 68

Copernican view 302
correspondence truth 335–37, 340, 343
cosmological argument 113–25, 128, 140
cosmological dualism. *See* dualistic monotheism
creation 305. *See also* nature
creation account (Genesis), 311–14
creationists 306
creation monotheism 105–7, 118, 124, 172–73, 188, 191, 193, 245, 246, 251
creation myths, in ancient Near East 312–13
creation polytheism 105–7
creeds 7
cremation 324
critics 76–78, 81, 83
crucifixion 204
Crusades 252, 295
culpable nonbelief 161, 163–64
cultural anthropology 348, 351–52
cultural relativism 351–52

damnation 173
Darwin, Charles 131, 134
Darwinism. *See* evolution
Da Vinci Code, The (novel) 175n3, 292–93
Davis, Stephen T. 183n8, 234n8
death 152, 210, 286, 310–11, 321, 322, 327, 328, 343
Deism 333
Democritus 91, 95
demons 102
denominations 7
depravity 42–43
Descartes, René 107, 110, 319, 327, 332
design argument. *See* teleological argument
desire 261
determinism 91
Deuterocanonicals 279n4
dictation theory of inspiration 275
Diderot, Denis 354
disembodiment 321, 327
divine command theory of morality 356
divine hiddenness 159–66, 209
dogmatism 341
Dostoyevsky, Fyodor 354n6
doubt 9–10, 11, 48, 33–34, 76, 82–83, 278
doubters 76–77, 80–82, 83, 279
dualism. *See* Christian Platonic dualism

dualistic monotheism 105–7, 118, 124, 243
dual strategy (evolution) 300–301, 305, 319

Eastern Orthodox Church 7, 223n3, 279n4
efficient cause 115–17, 303–4
egalitarianism 342
eightfold path 259, 260, 261
emotions 56, 78
empty tomb 205–6
Enlightenment 332–33, 334, 335
enlightenment (Buddhism) 256, 259–62
enlightenment (Hinduism) 256, 257–58
Enuma Elish 313n8
Epicureans 33, 343–44
Epicurus 91
epistemological objectivity 334–35
epistemology 215
eternal life 58–59, 210, 243, 318, 341
eternal necessary relations 223
eternal punishment 233–34, 243
ethical relativism 347–59
ethical universalism 349, 352–53, 358–59
Ethiopian Eunuch 78–80
ethnic cleansing 296
ethnocentrism 341, 352–53
Euthyphro Dilemma 356
evangelism 10, 33–34, 43
Evans, C. Stephen 46n1, 49, 193n3
evidence 9, 11, 31, 33, 42, 81–82. *See also* testimonial evidence
evidentialism 9, 10, 12, 34–37, 47, 193n3, 288
evil 22, 140, 141–52, 209
  amount of 155, 156–58, 166
  as illusion 97
evolution 22, 94, 93, 131–36, 299–301, 306–11, 326, 354–55
exclusivism (salvation) 242–47, 264
existentialism 52–53, 200–201
ex nihilo creation 105, 106, 118, 145
experience 35–36
  of salvation 273–74
exploitation 341
extinction 310–11
eyewitnesses 177–80, 196, 205, 206

faith
  birth of 79
  and reason 11–12, 19, 21, 30–32
  strengthening of 34
"faith seeking understanding" 12, 34
fellowship 10, 83

fideism 12, 31
final causes 303
finality of Christian truths 338, 339–40
fine-tuning argument 136–40, 300, 307–8
foreknowledge 238
forgiveness 57–59
fossil record 308, 311
foundational belief 116
foundationalism 37n3
four noble truths 259, 261
freedom 32, 165, 193, 326, 342–43, 344
free will theodicy 149–51, 152, 156
Freud, Sigmund 286
fruit of the Spirit 26–27
fulfillment 94, 96
fully human 219
fundamental beliefs 19
Funk, Robert 176

Galileo 108, 301, 302
Gandhi 355
gardening metaphor 13, 21, 26, 176, 362
general revelation 39, 40–41, 237, 275
genetic fallacy 287
gentleness 25, 27
Gnosticism 202, 293
God
  attributes 111, 131
  and evil 311, 357
  goodness 193
  hiddenness 159–66
  as infinite 103
  love 160, 235–36, 239
  and morality 354, 356
  as mysterious 39, 40
  outside time and space 111, 119
  in pantheism 96–97
  as personal 55, 119–20, 124, 261
  and universe 105–7, 109–10
"God is dead" 341, 343
"God of the gaps" 305
Golden Rule 354
Gospel of Thomas 173n1, 176
Gospels 173–81
grace 80
greater evil 147
greater good 146–47, 150
great-making properties 110
Greek pantheon 101–2
guilt 51, 56–57, 58

happiness 58–59, 67
Harvey, Van A. 189n2, 193n3

heart 64–65, 67–72, 83, 125
Hegel, G. W. F. 95, 98
Heidegger, Martin 53, 201
hell 233–34, 236
Heraclitus 95
heresy 7, 279
Hesiod 102
Hinayana 260
Hinduism 8, 95, 96n13, 97n16, 100,
   243, 246, 255–59, 263–64
historical criticism 284, 287–92
historical Jesus 175
historical reliability 174–75, 206
history 190–91, 292–97
Hitler, A. 156
Holocaust 296
Holy Spirit 11, 32, 34, 36, 43, 67,
   236, 242
   and Christian belief 270–73
   and the church 278–79
   and experience 284
   and faith 79
   and human reasoning 26
   witness of 177
Homer 102
Howard-Snyder, Daniel 159n2,
   166n5, 183n8
Howard-Snyder, Frances 350
human nature 32, 92–94
   and incarnation 218–19
Hume, David 34, 116–17, 131n3,
   145, 185, 187–89
humility 24, 26, 27, 69

ideal polytheism 102–3, 104
idolatry 22, 33, 251
image of God 32, 109, 194, 309–10,
   313, 340, 342
immateriality 111
immortality 58–59, 60
immutability 111
impersonal reality 96–97, 263–64
incarnation 173, 213, 217–20, 243
independent existence 106–7, 111,
   120–24, 131, 260
individual ethical relativism 349, 351
infinite punishment 234–35
infinite regress 118–19, 123
injustice 142
inorganic origin of life 307
Inquisition 295, 302
insincere questions 77–78
instrumental good 82, 146
intellect, and will 67–68
intelligent design 131–36, 137–38,
   261, 300, 304–5, 309
interpretation 334
intolerance 350–51, 352–53

intrinsic goods 82
irenic apologetics 24–25
irreducible complexity 113–35, 304,
   309
Islam 105, 118, 243, 246, 249–52,
   263, 264

Jesus
   death 6, 229, 248, 272
   deity 21, 177–83, 214
   and Islam 249–52
   and Judaism 247–49
   miracles 185–96
   person and work 6, 8, 264–65
   resurrection 6, 188, 199–211, 229,
      248, 272
Jesus as example (atonement) 230
Jesus as victor (atonement) 230
Jesus Seminar 175–76
Jews 8
John, Gospel of 64, 177, 179, 181
Joseph of Arimathaea 205
joy 344
Judaism 105, 118, 243, 246, 247–49,
   263, 264
Judeo-Christian worldview 237
justifying reason, for evil 157–59

Kalam cosmological argument
   117–20
Kant, Immanuel 335
karma 256, 261
Kierkegaard, Søren 39, 46–49, 52n1,
   78
kingdom of God 194
knowledge 59–60

language, of apologetics 21–22
law of nature 187–89
Leibniz, G. W. 107, 114n1
Leslie, John 137n11
lesser gods 104
Lewis, C. S. 7, 21n2, 135, 195n5, 353
liar, lunatic, or Lord argument
   181–84, 208
liberal Christians 230
liberal democratic values 342–45
liberation (Hinduism) 258
life 344
literary genres 313
Locke, John 34
logical contradiction 214–15, 223
love 68, 94, 150
   for God 358
   for neighbor 358
Luke, Gospel of 178–79
Lyotard, Jean-François 337n4

macroevolution 307–8, 314
Madhva 106, 243, 259, 263, 264
Mahayana Buddhism 260, 262, 263
Manicheanism 106, 145
Mark, Gospel of 178
Marxism 88
mass hallucination theory 208
master morality 341–42
materialism 22, 91–93, 96, 310,
   317–29
Matthew, Gospel of 179
meaning 51, 52–55, 56, 60, 94
mechanistic explanation 303–4,
   306, 308
Melchert, Norman 58n6
"mere Christianity" 7, 229
merely human 219
Merrick, Trenton 321n1, 323n3
Messiah 248–49
metanarrative 337–38
metaphysical antirealism 335–36,
   339
metaphysical naturalism 90, 118,
   188, 243, 306
metaphysical objectivity 334–35
metaphysics 90n2
methodological naturalism 90n2,
   190–91, 289, 292, 304–6
Meyer, Stephen C. 307n3
microevolution 306–7, 308
middle knowledge 238–39
mind 326
miracles 64, 185–96
misery 78
missing links, in fossil record 308
Mitchell, Basil 20n1
modalism 222
modest apologetics 24
monism 263–64
monotheism 89, 98, 99–111, 263–64
moral argument for God's existence
   140, 353–56, 357
moral evil 143–44, 148, 149–50
morality 140
   Nietzsche on 341–43
moral law 354
morally significant free will 149–51
moral universalism. See ethical
   universalism
Mormons 275
Morris, Leon 81
Morris, Thomas V. 109n10
Mother Teresa 355
Muhammad 249, 252
multiple attestation 207
Murdoch, Iris 354
Murray, Michael J. 23n4
Muslims 8, 275

mutation. *See* random mutation
mystery 40
myth 175, 189–90, 193

narrower teleology 136
natural consequences theodicy
150–51, 152, 156
natural evil 143–44, 146, 148, 150–52, 310–11
naturalism 22, 95–96, 100, 102, 283, 284, 326. *See also* biblical naturalism; metaphysical naturalism
natural law theodicy 151–52, 156
natural selection 93, 131–36, 299–301, 306–11
nature 90–91, 95–96, 303–4
necessary existence 105–7, 111, 114–15, 122
necessary truths 46
negative apologetics. *See* weeding
neutral stance 19
New Age spiritualities 95, 265
Newton, Isaac 305
Nicene Creed 7
Nietzsche, Friedrich 53, 333–35, 341–45, 358
Nightingale, Florence 295
nihilism 22
Niles, D. T. 25
nirvana 260, 261, 262
non-Christian theists 8
noncomparative rationality 23–24
nonculpable nonbelief 161, 163–64
nontheists 8, 9
numerical identity 217, 221, 261, 320–21, 329
numinous 271

obedience 13
objective meaning 54
objective reasoning 46
objective truth 44, 334–35, 340, 348, 353
objective uncertainty 48–49
objectivity 290–91, 334
offensive strategy 21
old earth theory 314
omnibenevolence 103, 111, 145, 220
omnipotence 103, 111, 145, 146, 220
omnipresence 220
omniscience 103, 145, 220
opinions 44
oral tradition 180
order 128
originating efficient cause 115–16
orthodoxy 7
Otto, Rudolph 271

pain 22, 142, 144, 148, 152, 156, 209–11, 310–11, 343
panentheism 97n16, 100, 105, 118, 145, 243, 258, 263
pantheism 22, 89, 94–98, 100, 105, 106, 118, 243, 257, 258, 263
Papias 178
Parmenides 95
particular body materialism 320–24
Pascal, Blaise 53–54, 55, 68–72, 77–78, 107, 165, 271
Pascal's wager 70–72, 77–78
passion argument 48–49
Passion of the Christ (film) 204, 249
Paul
on apologetics 361–62
on death and resurrection of Christ 204–5
on general revelation 41
on intellect 68
on polytheism 101
on reason 32, 33, 69
on resurrected bodies 320, 321
on sin 42, 64–67
on the Spirit 270–71, 272
penal substitution 229–32
"people of the book" 250
perfect being theology 107–10
perfections 110–11, 131
personal identity across time 325, 326, 328
personality 102–3
Peter, on Spirit 271–72
philosophy 32, 173, 332
physicalism 91, 318
physical resurrection 203, 206
Pilate 77–78
Plantinga, Alvin 10, 35–37
Plato 18, 293, 319, 327, 354, 356
Platonic dualism 202, 319, 327–29
pleasure 343
Plotinus 95
pluralism. *See* religious pluralism
polemics 20–21
Pol Pot 156, 296
polytheism 22, 33, 89, 98, 99–105, 243, 251
Porter, Steven 231–32
positive apologetics. *See* watering
postmodernism 22, 25, 331–45, 348
and relevance 52
postmodern worldview 20
postmortem salvation 238–39
postponement argument 48
power 294
practical problem of evil 143
practical purpose 302–3

practical reason 68, 70–72
pragmatism, on truth 336, 340
preaching 272
predication 221
preferences 44
presupposing Christian truth claims 20
pride 69
primary cause 304, 310
principle of universal explanation 113–24
probable arguments 131
problem of evil 22, 140, 141–52, 209, 233
process theology 97–98, 145
proofs. *See* theistic proofs
proportionalism 34, 47
Protagoras 348
Protestants 7
psychology 285–87
of unbelief 66
punishment 231–35
punishment theodicy 148–49, 151

quest for the historical Jesus 175
Qur'an 249, 250–51, 275

Ramanuja 95, 97n16, 243, 258–59, 263, 264
Ramm, Bernard 274n3
random mutation 93, 132, 139
rationalism 12, 31, 34, 37
rationality 19, 23, 286
of Christian claims 338, 340
postmodernism on 338–39
rationally resistible 23
reached but unsaved 235–36
real polytheism 100
reason 10–11, 12, 21, 30–32, 68–70, 92, 108
reasonable belief 160–61
reconciliation 57–59, 264
Red Cross 295
redemption 228
reincarnation 261, 327
relationships 55
relative truth 44–45
relativism 22, 243–44. *See also* ethical relativism
relevance 52
religious diversity 210, 247
religious pluralism 22, 88, 241–45
repentance 70
restlessness 78
resurrection 173, 317–29
in Islam 250, 251
resuscitation model 201

rhetoric 32, 34
risk 49
Roman Catholic Church 7, 279n4,
    302
Rorty, Richard 335–37, 338, 339–40,
    342–45
Rowe, William 157

sacrifice model (atonement) 229–32
Sagan, Carl 90
salvation 173
    in Hinduism or Buddhism 256
samsara 261
sanctification 281
Sanhedrin 205
Sankara 95, 96n13, 243, 257–58,
    259, 263, 264
Sartre, Jean-Paul 53, 354n6
satisfaction (atonement) 229–30, 232
scandal of particularity 243
Schellenberg, J. L. 159
schism 279
science 22, 135, 301, 302–6, 332–33
    and miracles 190
scientific objectivity 290–91
secondary causes 304, 310
secular humanism 88, 91
secular state 296
seekers 76–77, 78–80, 83, 162
self-defeating thesis 37
self-evident claims 35, 37, 116
Semmelweiss, Ignaz 146
senses 35–36, 37
September 11, 2001 attacks 156
service 10, 13
ship of Theseus story 323, 325
Siddhartha Gautama 256
sin 22, 65–67, 70, 71, 142, 144, 173,
    193, 209, 263–64, 271, 349
    in church history 295–97
    and disordered love life 164
    and human intellect 42–43
sincere questions 77–78
skepticism 22, 25, 81, 201, 243–44,
    339
slave morality 341–43
slavery 295, 350
    to sin 67, 344
Smith, Quentin 91n8
social science 101
social trinitarianism 223
societal ethical relativism 349–51

Socrates 18, 356
Son of God 180, 182, 193–95
soul 310, 319, 321, 322, 325, 326,
    327–28
soul sleep 328
special creation 309
special revelation 275, 277
species, fixity of 308, 309
Spinoza, B. 95, 107, 115n2
spiritual bodies 203
spiritual immortality 202
spirituality 265
sports metaphor 21
Stackhouse, John G., Jr. 27n7, 89n1
Stalin, J. 156, 296
Star Wars (films) 106
Stoics 33, 95
stolen body theory 205, 207
stories 338, 339
    of salvation 273–74
Strobel, Lee 307n3, 309n5
subjective meaning 53
subjective truth 44, 45
substance, in Godhead 216
suffering 22, 142, 144, 148, 152, 156,
    209–11, 310–11, 343, 359
    in Buddhism 259–62
    as redemptive 262
supernaturalism 89, 99, 100, 201
sustaining efficient cause 115–16
Swinburne, Richard 20n1, 105n4
swoon theory 204

Taoism 257
teleological argument 114, 127–40,
    261, 300
teleology 303
telos 128
Ten Commandments 356
Tennant, F. R. 136
Tennyson, Alfred Lord 311n7, 313
Tertullian 40
testimonial evidence 81, 192–93, 196
theater metaphor 21
theism 8, 89, 139–40
theistic evolution 309–11, 315
theistic proofs 9, 11, 41–42, 131
theodicy 148–52, 157
theoretical problem of evil 143
theoretical purpose 303
theoretical reasoning 68, 70–72
Theravada Buddhism 260, 262, 263

Thomas 80–82, 83, 203
totalitarianism 296
transcendence 55–59, 60
transformation 57–59
Trinity 6, 83, 103, 108–9, 173, 213,
    215–17, 220–24, 243
tritheism 222
trust 13, 31, 49
truth 336. See also objective truth;
    subjective truth
    suppression of 66–67
two-minds model (incarnation) 220

uncertainty 25, 48–49
understanding 43, 52, 59–60
universalism 233–34
universality, of Christian worldview
    338, 340
universal morality. See ethical
    universalism
universal narrative 339
universal truth 45
universe 90–91
    as eternal and cyclical 256
    existence and order of 114
    and God 109–10
unreached 235–36, 242

van Inwagen, Peter 90n4
Vedas, the 256, 257, 259
Vendata 96n13

war 149
watering 14, 17, 21, 24, 83, 176
weeding 14, 17, 21, 24, 83, 176
Wesley, Charles 209
Whitehead, Alfred North 98
wickedness 144
wider teleology 136
will, and intellect 67–68, 71
Wilson, Jonathan S. 229n1
witch hunts and trials 295
worldview 87–98
worship 10, 12–13, 264
wretchedness 70, 78
wrong tomb theory 205

Xenophanes 101–2

young-earth creation 311

Zoroastrianism 106